CONTEMPORARY
SOVIET POLITICS

Fourth Edition

CONTEMPORARY SOVIET POLITICS
An Introduction

Donald D. Barry
Lehigh University

Carol Barner-Barry
University of Maryland, Baltimore County

Prentice Hall, Englewood Cliffs, New Jersey 07632

Library of Congress Cataloging-in-Publication Data

Barry, Donald D.
    Contemporary Soviet politics : an introduction / Donald D. Barry,
Carol Barner-Barry.—4th ed.
        p.   cm.
    Includes bibliographical references and index.
    ISBN 0-13-170424-9
    1. Soviet Union—Politics and government—1985– 2. Soviet Union—
Economic conditions—1985– 3. Soviet Union—Social
conditions—1970– I. Barner-Barry, Carol II. Title.
JN6531.B35 1991
320.947′09′048—dc20   90-41331
                                                                                              CIP

This book is dedicated to
Brian, Colleen, Daniel, and Andrew
for whom
a very different world
is in the process of being created.

Editorial/production supervision: Cyndy Lyle Rymer
Prepress buyer: Debbie Kesar
Manufacturing buyer: Mary Ann Gloriande

©1991, 1987, 1982, 1978 by Prentice-Hall, Inc.
A Division of Simon & Schuster
Englewood Cliffs, New Jersey 07632

Printed in the United States of America
10 9 8 7 6 5 4 3 2 1

ISBN 0-13-170424-9

Prentice-Hall International (UK) Limited, *London*
Prentice-Hall of Australia Pty. Limited, *Sydney*
Prentice-Hall Canada Inc., *Toronto*
Prentice-Hall Hispanoamericana, S.A., *Mexico*
Prentice-Hall of India Private Limited, *New Delhi*
Prentice-Hall of Japan, Inc., *Tokyo*
Simon & Schuster Asia Pte. Ltd., *Singapore*
Editora Prentice-Hall do Brasil, Ltda., *Rio de Janeiro*

CONTENTS

CHAPTER FOUR
Political Culture and Socialization: The Era of Glasnost   *40*

PART II   STRUCTURE AND PROCESS

CHAPTER FIVE
The Constitution: Adding Substance to Form   *69*

CHAPTER SIX
The Government: The Politics of Empowerment   *87*

CHAPTER SEVEN
The Communist Party: The Loss of Monopoly Power   *115*

CHAPTER EIGHT
The Legal System: The Attempt to Create a Socialist Law-Governed State   *148*

PART III   ECONOMIC POLITICS

PART IV   PROBLEMS AND POLICIES

CHAPTER FOURTEEN

PART V   CONCLUSION

CHAPTER FIFTEEN

APPENDIX A

APPENDIX B

APPENDIX C

Preface

The USSR has been in a transitional stage since early in the Gorbachev era. The magnitude of changes during this time have been truly breathtaking, a fact most keenly brought home to the authors during the process of writing this fourth edition of a book first published in the late 1970s. Over the past couple of years we have rewritten, in some cases several times over, the seemingly sound revisions that we had initially made to the previous (1987) edition of this book. At this point we are reasonably confident of two things: that we have been able to provide a fairly accurate analysis of Soviet politics at the point it reached in the early months of 1990; and that further momentous changes are in store that can only be hinted at and dimly perceived at this point.

This, then, is a book for a transitional period. It provides an analysis of the opening up of Soviet society from the late 1980s on, of the momentous developments that led to the demise of the one-party system, and of the economic and political mechanisms devised by Gorbachev and others to cope with the multiple crises facing the country. Whether such developments provide a basis for successfully coping with these crises is an open question, and one that cannot yet be addressed.

Many people have aided us in preparing this edition. In particular we would like to name the following colleagues and associates: Joan Costello,

Domokos Hajdo, Richard Matthews, Richard Mills, Richard Newell, Mark M. Peters, Barbara Phillips-Seitz, Elaine Rusinko, Oles Smolansky, Iris Wingert, Steve Young, and the reviewers, Charles B. McLane of Dartmouth College and Edward Taborsky of the University of Texas at Austin. The staffs of the Fairchild-Martindale Library of Lehigh University and the Albert E. Kuhn Library, University of Maryland, Baltimore County, provided assistance of various kinds. At the latter institution Sally E. Hearn and Joyce Tenny deserve special mention. The Government Department of Lehigh University and the Political Science Department of the University of Maryland, Baltimore County, supported the authors through the period of the revision. Particularly helpful with word processing and other secretarial services were Dorothy Windish, Matilda DiDonato, and Helen Pasquale. Finally, we would like to thank our associates at Prentice Hall, who have worked with us in bringing this effort to completion. Particular mention should go to Karen Horton, Senior Editor, Political Science, as well as to Dolores Mars and Cyndy Rymer.

Donald D. Barry

Carol Barner-Barry

Major Administrative Divisions of the USSR

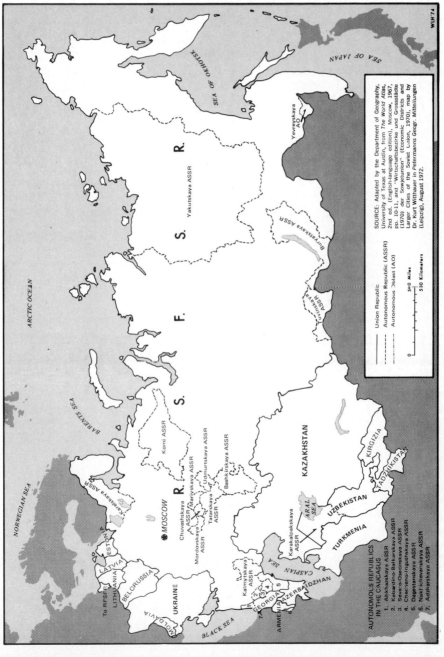

SOURCE: Adapted by the Department of Geography, University of Texas at Austin, from *The World Atlas*, 2nd ed. (English-language edition), Moscow, 1967, pp. 10-11, and "Wirtschaftsbezirke und Grossstädte (1970) der Sowjetunion" (Economic Districts and Larger Cities of the Soviet Union, 1970), map by Dr. Kurt Witthauer in *Petermanns Geogr. Mitteilungen* (Leipzig), August 1972.

Union Republic
Autonomous Republic (ASSR)
Autonomous Oblast (AO)

0   540 Miles
0   530 Kilometers

AUTONOMOLS REPUBLICS
IN THE CAUCASUS

1. Abkhazskaya ASSR
2. Kabardino-Balkarskaya ASSR
3. Severo-Osetinskaya ASSR
4. Chechno-Ingushskaya ASSR
5. Dagestanskaya ASSR
6. Nakhichevanskaya ASSR
7. Adzharskaya ASSR

ARCTIC OCEAN
BARENTS SEA
NORWEGIAN SEA
SEA OF OKHOTSK
SEA OF JAPAN
CASPIAN SEA
BLACK SEA
ARAL SEA

R.   S.   F.   S.   R.

MOSCOW

Yakutskaya ASSR
Buryatskaya ASSR
Tuvinskaya ASSR
Komi ASSR
Karelskaya ASSR
Chuvashskaya ASSR
Mariyskaya ASSR
Mordovskaya ASSR
Udmurtskaya ASSR
Tatarskaya ASSR
Bashkirskaya ASSR
Kalmytskaya ASSR
Karakalpakskaya ASSR
Yevreyskaya AO

KAZAKHSTAN
KIRGIZIA
TADZHIKISTAN
UZBEKISTAN
TURKMENIA

ESTONIA
LATVIA
LITHUANIA
BELORUSSIA
UKRAINE
MOLDAVIA
To RFSFR
GEORGIA
ARMENIA
AZERBAIDZHAN

WLH 74

From *Problems of Communism*, XXIII, No. 3 (May-June 1974), 3, U.S. Information Agency.

xi

CONTEMPORARY
SOVIET POLITICS

ONE
SOVIET POLITICAL STYLE:
The Ghosts of Lenin and Stalin

Soviet political life is dominated by the benign image of Lenin and the brooding shadow of Stalin. When Lenin died in 1924, he left the fledgling Soviet state a mixed legacy (Tucker, 1987). During the period of War Communism, when the Bolshevik revolutionaries were still struggling to consolidate their victory against a variety of opposing forces, Lenin pursued the sort of harsh policies that are characteristic of civil war periods. These included a disregard for human life and the use of a ruthless police power—both justified in the name of winning the postrevolutionary civil war. On the other hand, during the period of the New Economic Policy (NEP) from 1921 to his death, Lenin encouraged a level of individual initiative and entrepreneurship that has been unequaled until the Gorbachev reform.

When Stalin succeeded Lenin as leader of the Soviet Union, he drew on the first legacy and set about destroying the second. Because his tenure in office covered the major formative, or institution-building, years of the Soviet state, he was able to shape it according to his own design. What emerged was a highly centralized polity and economy, run by a massive bureaucracy. The people were treated as cogs in the wheel of progress, and those who did not "fit in" faced the prospect of harsh repression and, perhaps, even death. Coupled with this was a glorification of Stalin which placed him on the level of a secular god: all that was good flowed from his benevolent rule, and all that was evil was caused by "enemies of the people" and "wreckers" who had to be rooted out and destroyed.

For a while, this Stalinist polity seemed to work well. Under it, the Soviet Union emerged from its peasant and largely preindustrial past to become part of the industrialized world. As it moved past the initial stages of industrialization and began trying to catch up with an increasingly sophisticated technological world, the old Stalinist system became more and more dysfunctional. In addition, the system of collectivized farming that had been brutally imposed on the peasantry repeatedly failed to furnish the Soviet people with adequate nutrition—either quantitatively or qualitatively. By the time of Stalin's death, it was clear to many of his heirs that reform was in order. Because of the governmentally orchestrated deification of the man himself, however, the process of reform could not be separated from the need to modify the ideas which the Soviet people had about the man who was largely responsible for creating their political system.

Since 1953 when Stalin died, there have been two major reform periods. Each has been associated with a Soviet leader, the first with Khrushchev and the second with Gorbachev. In both cases, efforts to introduce reforms into the Soviet political and economic systems were accompanied by an attempt to remove Stalin from the status of demigod. In the case of Khrushchev (who was closer in time and in thinking to the Stalinist period), this took the form of trying to turn Stalin into an unperson, of erasing him from Soviet history. In the case of Gorbachev (whose early life was spent under Stalin, but who was far less influenced by him), it has taken the form of acknowledging Stalin's place in Soviet history, but gradually allowing him to be reduced to the fallible, sometimes vicious, human being that he was.

Between these two reform periods, there was an era of retrenchment under Brezhnev. There were some attempts to rehabilitate Stalin, but the major thrust was to perpetuate the Stalinist system and to exploit its potential for enriching the lives of those in control. This led to what is now being called the "period of stagnation," during which some of the more dysfunctional aspects of the Stalinist system pushed the Soviet Union to the brink of economic collapse. It also turned the faith of the Soviet people in a better future under socialism (and eventually communism) into a bitter cynicism.

Soviet politics has always focused on the image of a strong and benevolent leader. First it was Lenin, the "Father of the Revolution." He was followed by Stalin, who became the center of what was later called a "cult of the personality." Khrushchev presided over a cultural "thaw" which permitted some reinvigoration of Soviet artistic life and the rehabilitation or posthumous rehabilitation of thousands who had languished or died in Stalinist imprisonment. Yet at the same time, in the economic sphere many of his reforms failed and caused him to be regarded by many as "hare-brained" or overly impetuous in his efforts to improve the lot of the Soviet people. His successor, Brezh-

TABLE 1.1   Top Soviet Political Leaders and Their Posts

Leader	Years in Power[1]	Principal Post	Other post
V.I. Lenin	1917–1924	premier[2]	—
J.V. Stalin	1926/7–1953	general secretary of Communist Party, 1922–1952; first secretary,[3] 1952–1953	premier, 1941–1953
N.S. Khrushchev	1954–1964	first secretary, 1953–1964	premier 1958–1964
L.I. Brezhnev	1964–1982	first secretary, 1964–1966 general secretary, 1966–1982	president,[4] 1977–1982
Iu.V. Andropov	1982–1984	general secretary, 1982–1984	president, 1983–1984
K.U. Chernenko	1984–1985	general secretary, 1984–1985	president, 1984–1985
M.S. Gorbachev	1985–	general secretary, 1985–	president, 1988–

[1]Indicates the years in which the person was generally recognized as the single top leader.

[2]Official title: Chairman, Council of People's Commissars, 1917–1946; Chairman, Council of Ministers, 1946 and after.

[3]The title of General Secretary was replaced by First Secretary between 1952 and 1966.

[4]Official title: Chairman of the Presidium of the Supreme Soviet (1938–1989); Chairman of the Supreme Soviet, 1989–1990; USSR President, 1990–   .

nev, presided over a process of cultural and economic retrenchment. The legacy of Khrushchev surfaced, however, in the rise and persistence of an internally diverse, but profoundly committed, dissident movement. Finally, beginning with Andropov and continuing through the brief rule of Chernenko, a new period of reform took hold, reaching its current proportions under the leadership of Gorbachev.

It is an exciting time in the Soviet Union. Things are happening (or have even become routine) that could never have happened even a few short years ago. The result is that Soviet political life is changing in ways that are revolutionary, given the perspective of Soviet history. It is within this framework that we consider Soviet political style, the basic ground rules and the atmosphere in which Soviet politics takes place. Prior to the Gorbachev era, it could be said that the Soviet political system possessed three basic and interrelated characteristics: (1) politics were "closed politics" rather than "open politics"; (2) policy making was marked by tension between those who would preserve the status quo with only marginal changes and those who advocated more basic reform, especially in the economic sphere; and (3) a political culture organized around the symbolism of Lenin. Let us look at these three basic characteristics in greater detail, considering how the Gorbachev reform has affected each in turn.

The term "political ground rules" was just used. Some might object that the Soviet system is one without ground rules. This has never been true, and it is less true now than before. Every political system that persists has to develop a set of basic understandings regarding how the "game" of politics is to be played. The alternative is anarchy (Brickman, 1974). Although these rules may change over time and although they may differ significantly from those of the Western democracies with which we are most familiar, it is always safe to assume that rules exist in some form.

After Stalin consolidated his power in the late 1920s, Soviet politics operated under a primary ground rule: Soviet politics was closed politics.[1] What this meant was that important political decisions ("who gets what, when, and how") were made behind the scenes with little or no advance public discussion or opportunity for direct public influence on the policy-making process. There were often widespread discussions of policy proposals. These discussions, however, were more ritualistic than substantive and few, if any, significant changes resulted. The goal of the public participation encouraged by the leadership seemed to be mainly a psychological one. It was intended to mobilize support for the new policy and to give the illusion of public participation.

From this closed political style many of the other characteristics of Soviet politics flowed: the structure and operations of the Party and the government, the uses to which the mass media were put, the nature of the electoral and judicial systems, and the extent to which individuals and organizations could participate in governing. All of these were crafted to preserve the prerogatives of the top leadership based on the principle of closed politics. And since closed politics could be better maintained by a few people than by many, this meant that the top leadership had to be kept small and, by definition, very elite.

The Soviet system has not always been closed to the same degree. Movement toward a more open discussion of political issues and some rather frank criticisms of shortcomings in the system were aired during the Khrushchev "thaw" period (especially 1956 to 1957 and 1961 to 1962). This thaw, however, was relatively short and was followed by retrenchment. But even at the peak of the Khrushchev reform there was no basic change in ground rule number one: Final decisions are made behind closed doors.

The Gorbachev era has been characterized by a gradual movement toward opening up the political system. Relatively uncontrolled public voicing of dissatisfaction and discussion of policy alternatives have become common. Investigative journalism is flourishing. An increasing number of contested elections are being held, not only to fill economic positions (like factory man-

---

[1]Closed politics could be traced to an earlier point in Russian and Soviet history, but space does not permit this to be done here.

ager), but even to fill the ranks of the newly reformed Soviet legislature. And perhaps most surprisingly, there has been a decisive movement toward the creation of a multiparty system. True, this has mostly been a reform "from above." It has, however, the potential for creating a Soviet political system that is a relatively open one. The Soviet people are being given the opportunity to take a more active role in their own political and economic destiny. How far this will go or how it will ultimately stabilize will, to a large extent, affect every other aspect of Soviet life.

The second basic ground rule has been that policy making is marked by a tension between those who would preserve the status quo with only marginal changes and those who advocate sweeping, even revolutionary, reform. A bit of historical background is needed to clarify the evolution of the profound wariness of change to be found among the Soviet people, both inside and outside the leadership. Policy battles—often bloody ones—between conservatives and reformers were a feature of the Russian political scene long before the Soviet period. Perhaps the most obvious pre-Soviet case in point is the history of the reign of Peter the Great, who tried to open Russia to the West. Thus, the conservative-versus-reformist tensions we see in the Soviet Union today have deep roots in Russian history.

When considering the Soviet period, it is necessary to begin with Lenin's death. Because he did not designate a clear successor, there was a struggle for power waged according to the rules of closed politics. Stalin eventually won. The defeated politicians, rather than retiring, perhaps to try again later, were victimized. This victimization took various forms and went through several stages. For the most serious contenders (e.g., Trotsky, Zinoviev, Kamenev, Bukharin) it almost invariably resulted in death by unnatural means and condemnation as "traitors," "wreckers," and "enemies of the people." They were blamed for the shortcomings of the Soviet system and, by extension, for the sorry lot of the average Soviet citizen. Victimization cum obliteration was a common fate of opponents or supposed opponents during much of the Stalin period and for a time after his death.

This was, to some degree, a simple reflection of the paranoid aspects of Stalin's personality. But there were also situational factors. Stalin was implementing policies, such as the collectivization of agriculture, that were radical departures from the past. Opponents of the new policies could easily be perceived as posing a threat to the success of changes which Stalin saw as imperative. Why not get rid of them once and for all? This process of scapegoating acquired a momentum of its own and, in a sense, became an accepted method for dealing with political rivals in the Soviet system.

These events are close enough in time to be very real to the contemporary Soviet political elite. The perception of radical reform as diffusely threatening may lurk in the minds of many contemporary Soviet leaders, although no such dramatic scapegoating has taken place since the middle 1950s. Defeated or out-of-favor politicians have been allowed to remain alive after their fall from power, but have lived in obscurity. The loss of the status and power that comes with positions at the top, however, has no doubt been difficult for these former leaders, even though they have been allowed to live reasonably comfortable lives (Voslensky, 1984, p. 35).

Currently, scapegoating has primarily involved the dead, most notably Brezhnev. He has been sharply criticized for creating the situation that made an economic reform imperative, and his honors and memorials have gradually disappeared. For example, the city of Brezhnev has had its former name restored and the plaque on his home in Moscow has been removed. Also, many former Brezhnev associates, most notably his son-in-law, are in jail. This hardly amounts to scapegoating, however, since they were clearly guilty of the corrupt practices which were pervasive during the Brezhnev era. And, of course, the damning revelations about the Stalin years also serve to fix the blame for conditions that the current regime is trying to remedy. Thus, it might be argued that this relatively mild (by comparison) scapegoating is largely placing blame where it is deserved.

There is, however, a tendency toward self-protectionism and conservatism which is not limited to the top leadership; inertia permeates Soviet society and creates one of the most formidable barriers to the Gorbachev reform. This clinging to the status quo is strongly reinforced by a number of factors (Cohen, 1984). One is the bureaucratic and conservative tradition inherited from tsarist Russia and elaborated under Soviet rule. It has spawned a class of Soviet citizens with both the desire and the means to defend their positions and privileges or even (in the case of many ordinary people) small gains. Their imperative to do so is constantly fed by the persistence of the scarcity of goods and services. The deprivation which they desire to avoid is real and visible. Also, there is a history in Russia and the USSR of man-made and natural disasters which creates a situation of chronic anxiety on the part of much of the population and which leads people to place a high value on security. The purges of the 1930s and the devastation of World War II, for instance, linger in the memories of significant numbers of Soviet citizens. Known evils have the virtue of having been around long enough that most people have developed a strategy for coping. Thus, the Soviet system is, at present, a highly immobile one in which new ideas find it difficult to gain a foothold. These factors have led to a certain sense of hopelessness in the Soviet populace in the face of strong indicators that major reforms are necessary and despite the exhortations of their new leadership.

It is clear that Gorbachev and the other members of the Soviet political elite recognize that some kind of reform, particularly in the economic sector, is of crucial importance. It is equally clear that there are differences within the top leadership regarding the extent and pace of such reform. A compromise currently seems to be in place. Experts are allowed considerable freedom to debate the merits of various reforms, from the marginal to the truly radical. Actual reform implementation, however, is usually (but not invariably) approached in a cautious way. The problems faced by the current Soviet government are not the sort that can be dealt with quickly or easily.

The final ground rule has to do with the political culture of the Soviet Union. From very early in the Soviet period, it was organized around the memory of Lenin. The Soviet Union was, until recently, militantly atheistic and had a history of creating difficulties for those who choose to practice religion.[2] There was, however, an official faith of sorts, pervading both political and social life. It was secular and tied to the past. What was that faith? It was a faith in Marxism-Leninism symbolized by the image of Lenin. During the Gorbachev years, the public adulation of the current leadership has been kept to a minimum. This leaves only Lenin.

Never mind that he was another "ends-over-means" politician (although the best the Russians have produced), that he sanctioned the purging of his enemies, and that he instituted the concept of equating opposition with disloyalty, paving the way for the kind of regime Stalin built. Until recently, he was portrayed as larger than life and virtually without human fault.[3] It was part of Soviet mythology, propagated by the ideological network, to believe that, in a truly religious sense, Lenin lives on. Posters with a likeness of Lenin carried such slogans as "Lenin Lived, Lenin Lives, Lenin Will Live," "Lenin—More Alive than All of the Living," and "Lenin Is with Us."

And then, of course, there is the Lenin Mausoleum itself. This shrine has been the symbolic heart of the country (in Red Square beside the Kremlin Wall). Thousands of fervent worshipers come to view the Founding Father's embalmed body—literally hundreds every day the mausoleum is open.[4] Then there is the polished honor guard and, in the tomb, the reverent silence (except for the muffled shuffling of feet). Lenin himself—his apparently well-preserved body encased in glass—is a spectacle worthy of any religion. What need for religious experience and emotional unity has the embalmed body of the spiritual leader of communism tapped among the communist faithful in this atheistic state? It is not coincidental, probably, that the religious tradition of the Russian Orthodox Church provided for the embalming and public viewing of saints and other leaders of the Church.

And if all of this were not enough to convince one of the deification of Lenin, there was more. In somewhat the same way that the pantheist sees God in the trees and the birds and the very air, Lenin in the Soviet Union was also ubiquitous, albeit in more concrete forms. To illustrate this, let us trace the

---

[2]With a dramatic visit to the Vatican in 1989, Gorbachev officially cast off this heritage of religious persecution and sanctioned a movement toward greater religious toleration and freedom, which will be discussed in Chapter 12.

[3]Recently, the official Soviet press (most notably *Pravda*) has published writings that suggest Lenin might have laid some of the groundwork for the current problems besetting the country. Such suggestions, however, have been few and relatively mild. But this seems to presage a movement toward treating Lenin as less of a god and more of a human historical figure (see, for example, *The Washington Post*, December 30, 1989, p. A12).

[4]Whether this practice should continue has also been debated.

trip from the suburban campus of Moscow University to the downtown campus—a trip we made hundreds of times when we were living at the University. First, we would leave our dormitory, situated in a part of Moscow called Lenin Hills, and choose between taking a bus via Lenin Prospect or riding the subway named in honor of Lenin. If we were in a hurry we would opt for the subway, which was quicker. After the University Station, the first stop was the Lenin Hills Station, located on a bridge high over the Moscow River offering through huge windows a panoramic view of Lenin Stadium. Since we frequently had research to do, we would get off at the Lenin Library Station and enter Lenin Library, the Soviet equivalent to the U.S. Library of Congress. We could go on in this vein, but the picture is clear.

This sense of the eternal and ever-present Lenin was not accidental, of course, but was based on a long-term and highly orchestrated effort. Shortly after his death an "Immortalization Commission" was created to handle the embalming and to regulate development of the Lenin myth.[5] And, even though under Stalin the Lenin cult "grew cold and lifeless" as the glorification of Stalin grew, it was easy and natural for Khrushchev to renew the myth and inaugurate "the slick and cloying cult of Lenin" (Tumarkin, 1983, p. 206).

Is it possible that the deified Lenin, like the deified Stalin, is falling victim to the new honesty which glasnost (openness or candor) has brought to the Soviet political scene? To some extent, perhaps. Articles and fiction that are, to some degree, critical of Lenin have been appearing in progressive journals, such as *Novyi Mir* and *Oktiabr',* as well as in the Communist Party newspaper, *Pravda.* At least in the short run, however, there seems to be an official limit. In spite of glasnost, the regime seems hesitant to leave the topic of Lenin's role in Soviet history open to unfettered debate.

Never, in either Russian or Soviet history, has the image of the state been separated from its personification in its ruler—be he Tsar or leader (General Secretary) of the Communist Party. In other words, the notion that loyalty to the nation can comfortably and naturally coexist with opposition to a particular regime has not been part of Soviet political culture (Tucker, 1987, p. 202). In his effort to reform the Soviet political and economic system, Gorbachev has tried to modify this orthodoxy, particularly with regard to glorifying himself. At the same time, he has tried to perserve a picture of Lenin that legitimizes the reform and brings it within acceptable symbolic boundaries. Thus, we see him invoking the NEP Lenin, and downplaying the Lenin of War Communism.

Both Russia and the Soviet Union have been, in essence, nations of believers—what Robert Tucker (1987, p. 207) calls "a belief culture." Something important was lost when Khrushchev shattered belief in the deified Stalin

---

[5]For example, the Immortalization Commission in 1924 prohibited the display of Lenin's likeness on candy wrappers and other labels. This was done after complaints about a cigarette package carrying Lenin's portrait, which, when dropped on the pavement resulted in pedestrians "unwittingly stepping on Lenin's face" (Tumarkin, 1983, p. 237).

and the unquestionable righteousness of all Soviet governments. The corruption and stagnation of the Brezhnev years further corroded this belief and, with it, the willingness of the people to hope and to strive. Perhaps the greatest task before the reformers is the revival of that belief on a new basis. In order to have any hope of accomplishing this, it would seem that there is a limit to the extent to which they can permit the demythologizing of the one heroic figure left to revere—Lenin. But . . . can they control the momentum for truth which they, themselves, have unleashed?

REFERENCES

BRICKMAN, P. (1974). *Social conflict: Readings in rule structures and conflict relationships.* Lexington, MA: D.C. Heath.

COHEN, S.F. (1984). The friends and foes of change: Reformism and conservatism in the Soviet Union. In E.F. Hoffman & R.F. Laird, eds., *The Soviet polity in the modern era,* pp. 85–104. New York: Aldine.

TUCKER, R. (1987). *Political culture and leadership in Soviet Russia: From Lenin to Gorbachev.* New York: W.W. Norton.

TUMARKIN, N. (1983). *Lenin lives! The Lenin cult in Soviet Russia.* Cambridge, MA: Harvard University Press.

VOSLENSKY, M. (1984). *Nomenklatura: The Soviet ruling class.* New York: Doubleday.

TWO
HISTORICAL FACTORS:
The Soviet Political Heritage

The Soviet system was not a complete break with the past, even though its originators claimed that it was. They themselves were products of the Russian political tradition and were influenced by it. And much of contemporary Soviet politics has some relationship to the nature of Russian politics as it developed in the centuries before the October Revolution of 1917.

To note this relationship is not an argument in favor of historical determinism. That is to say, it should not be asserted that the Soviet Union was somehow "destined" to evolve as it has because of inevitable historical forces pushing it in a certain direction. The historian's understanding of history is not complete enough to allow the explanation of historical developments with that degree of precision. Willful human behavior *can* affect social and historical developments; we are not merely prisoners of our past or of inevitable historical forces. Nor are we saying that the present Soviet Union is merely prerevolutionary Russia in contemporary guise. The French have a saying, *Plus ça change, plus c'est la même chose* (the more things change, the more they stay the same). Popularizers of history use this idea as the starting point for theories about historical developments, and the concept has been widely applied to Russia and the Soviet Union.

What we are saying is that there are certain factors in Russia's past that have predisposed it to develop in the way it has rather than in a way more typical of most of modern Western Europe. This is not the place to attempt a comprehensive analysis of Russian history. Instead, what we will do is to sketch the broad outlines of the historical factors that are particularly relevant to the way Soviet politics has developed.

Recorded history in the territory of Russia dates from the ninth century. Kievan Rus, as the state was known, was a feudal state in every way. Its main outside contacts were not with feudal Europe, however, but with the Byzantine Empire in what is now Turkey. Byzantine influence on Russia was pervasive and strong. Its legacy included the Cyrillic alphabet (rather than the Latin alphabet used in Western Europe), the imperial title of "tsar" (a corruption of "Caesar"), Orthodox Christianity, and the concept of the god-emperor, who combined in his person the authority of the pope and the emperor. After the seat of the Byzantine Empire, Constantinople, fell to the Turks in the fifteenth century, the grand dukes of Moscow proclaimed their city the "Third Rome," asserted leadership of the Orthodox Church, and adopted the Byzantine double-headed eagle, which became the symbol of Russia's tsars.

In the meantime, the state of Kievan Rus had been destroyed in the thirteenth century by the Mongol invaders, who maintained their control for the next two centuries. Under this particularly cruel despotism, the Moscow princes emerged as the tribute collectors for the Mongol-Tatar overlords. The Moscow princes treated their subjects, and the other princes of Russia over whom they gained influence, with the same barbarism they had come to expect in dealing with the Mongol-Tatar khans.

Ivan III finally overthrew the khans in 1480 and established Moscow's control over wide areas of what is now Russian territory. His rule was marked by a strong centralization of control and the use of force against any challengers to his authority. These characteristics were, to a greater or lesser extent, typical of the reigns of all of his successors.

Russia thus emerged from two hundred years of Mongol domination with a strong inclination toward centralization and autocracy. It had been cut off for centuries from contact with western Europe, missing in particular the liberating effects of the Renaissance and the Reformation. The latter was particularly important in that it might have stimulated the questioning of authority as an outgrowth of the conflict between church and state. Such questioning led western Europe down a path basically different from that of Russia, where authoritarian absolutism supported by a state-dominated church existed right up until the time of the 1917 Revolution.

The centralized autocracy of the tsars was not accompanied by notable predictability in succession to the throne, even after the establishment of the Romanov dynasty in 1613. Heirs were often eliminated as more powerful contenders seized power. To take the eighteenth century as an example, the century began during the reign of Peter the Great, who ruled from 1682 to 1725. It ended with the reigns of Catherine the Great (1762 to 1796) and her son Paul (1796 to 1801). Between these two periods, as Sidney Harcave has put it, there were "six rulers, three female and three male. Of the women, the first was amiable but incapable, the second neither amiable nor capable, and the third reasonably acceptable. Of the males, the first was a child, the second an infant, and the third an adult with the personality of a child" (Harcave, 1953, p. 88).

What is equally interesting to note is the means of accession and the fates of these rulers. Like Ivan the Terrible, Peter the Great had slain his son, so there was no clear heir to the throne. Peter's second wife, Catherine, who had been a peasant girl from Livonia on the Baltic Sea, seized power by force and held it until she died in 1727. She was succeeded by Peter's grandson, twelve-year-old Peter II, who died of smallpox three years later. Then came Peter's niece Anna, who died in 1740, to be succeeded by her six-week-old grand-nephew, Ivan VI. The latter was dethroned and later murdered by Peter's daughter Elizabeth, who was succeeded in 1762 by her nephew, a German prince crowned as Peter III. He was dethroned six months later by his wife (who became Catherine the Great) and murdered in prison by her friends. The century was ended under the reign of Catherine's incompetent son Paul, who was strangled by officials of his own court in 1801.

The nineteenth century saw greater regularity in succession to the throne. But this century of revolutions was not a calm one, nor one in which political stability was achieved. There were only five more tsars. None of them could be called enlightened, with the possible exception of Alexander II, the "reforming tsar," who emancipated the serfs and made other reforms early in his reign. Subsequently, he pursued reactionary policies until he was assassinated by a terrorist bomb in 1881.

This instability of succession hardly permitted the kind of continuity and calm necessary for the gradual development of constitutional traditions or democratic institutions. And indeed, no effective opposition to the monarchy developed during the eighteenth century. As early as 1550 Ivan the Terrible had established the *Zemsky Sobor* (Assembly of the Land), an assembly of lesser nobility, clergy, and urban bourgeoisie. Although it possessed only meager powers, it did succeed in limiting the authority of the boyars, powerful nobles who were contending with the tsars for ascendancy. It also was instrumental in electing Michael, the first of the Romanovs, as tsar in 1613. Thereafter its power declined, and it was eventually abolished by Peter the Great.

Peter, in his effort to westernize and modernize the autocracy, created a bureaucratic system founded on merit and established an Imperial Governing Senate, an institution that was designed to serve as an executive cabinet. But none of Peter's reforms pointed in the direction of popular government. Elective city councils (*dumas*) were established in 1785 under Catherine the Great. The conditions for representation and voting were severely restricted to the more affluent classes, however, so the *dumas* constituted no important reform.

Shortly after the emancipation of the serfs in 1861, Alexander II signed a law establishing *zemstvos,* assemblies for rural self-government. They provided for indirect and unequal suffrage and were deliberately weighted to allow the nobility to dominate. But in spite of their shortcomings, the *zemstvos* provided popular initiative for change. Their accomplishments in such areas as primary education, health, and the application of progressive agricultural techniques were impressive. In later years, however, the powers of the *zemstvos* were reduced, and the proportion of noble representation was increased. *Zemstvo* meetings held in secret were broken up by the police, with repressive action taken against *zemstvo* leaders. This promising reform was thus gradually neutralized by the reactionary forces in power.

What we have described so far is a picture of Russian political development extending well into the nineteenth century. Two basic characteristics are paramount. First, it established a repressive autocratic tradition founded on despotic political rule with roots traceable not to western Europe but to the Byzantine Empire and two centuries of Mongol hegemony in Russia. Second, and growing out of this tradition, it created an uncongenial atmosphere for the development of self-government at a time when movement in this direction had become well established in the West.

A small number of foreign observers wrote about life in Russia during this period, and some of them commented on these two characteristics. Perhaps the best known is the Marquis de Custine, a French nobleman who traveled through Russia in 1839 (Custine, 1951). Custine's sketch of Russia (first published in 1843) parallels the work of his countryman Alexis de Tocqueville on the United States a few years earlier.[1] Custine related that he "went to Russia in search of arguments against representative government," but "returned from Russia a partisan of constitutions." He admired the picturesque sights of Moscow, Petersburg, and Nizhni Novgorod, commented favorably on the beauty of Russian churches (particularly St. Basil's in Moscow), characterized Russians as a "naturally engaging people," and praised their intelligence, adroitness, and ingenuity.

But on matters political his comments were almost unrelievedly negative, often relating to the particular implications for everyday life of the despotism and lack of self-government then prevailing. He returned again and again to themes such as Russia's insulation from the outside world and its suspicion of foreigners, coupled with attempts to show outsiders a false picture of conditions. He noted an absence of personal liberty and the repression of all opposition (by, among other means, declaring dissidents to be insane and incarcerating them). There were the familiar police officials, government informers, and pervasive secrecy, all of which prevented official discussion of accidents and disasters and discouraged Russians from talking with strangers. Finally, Custine commented on the necessity of people to lie, feign, and dissimulate in the course of their everyday lives and the attempt of the government to dominate

---

[1] *Democracy in America,* which was first published in 1835. Tocqueville's analysis, however, is much more flattering to its subject.

everything (Custine, 1951, pp. 57–68, 97, 151–152, 265, 332–3, 339–40, 352–353 and 372). A good case can be made, then, that a significant part of Soviet political culture can be traced to the political situation in mid-nineteenth-century Russia and earlier.

Integrally connected with the characteristics of despotism and an absence of representative institutions is a third great theme of Russian history, which manifested itself conspicuously in the nineteenth and early twentieth centuries: the development of a revolutionary tradition growing out of frustration with the apparent impossibility of change by peaceful means. The Decembrist Revolt in 1825 is an early milestone. This attempt to replace Nicholas I by his brother Constantine, accompanied by the demand for a constitution, was put down by force. The prominent leaders of the revolt were hanged. More relevant, perhaps, is the anarchism that developed in the middle years of the nineteenth century. The strands of intellectual movements in Russia during this period are many and complex, but among them were elements of populism (*narodnichestvo*), some adherents of which became committed to insurrectionary means in desperation when other methods failed. A terrorist organization known as People's Will (*Narodnaia Volia*) emerged in the 1870s with the aim of assassinating government officials. Its successes included the killing or wounding of a number of important persons, among them Tsar Alexander II who was assassinated in 1881. The members of the movement genuinely believed that the "revolution of the deed" would lead to popular uprisings that would, in turn, overthrow the old regime. Instead, their efforts brought even more severe repression from the government, and the resistance movements were driven underground.

A major instrument in effecting this repression was the political police. Though theoretically a part of the bureaucracy, this "eyes and ears of the emperor" operated largely independently and without check. A strong political police force dates from 1826, when Nicholas I created the notorious "Third Section" (of the tsar's Imperial Chancellery) in reaction to the Decembrist Revolt of 1825. Its agents were everywhere, watching other government officials, regular citizens, and foreigners. It attempted to infiltrate dissident organizations and supervised political prisons and places of exile. Later placed in the ministry of interior and called the *Okhrana,* the autonomous political police became an important instrument of all succeeding tsars. Reliance on secret police, then, was learned by the Bolsheviks in their experiences with the tsarist *Okhrana*. Its carryover into the postrevolutionary period under various titles[2] was a logical consequence of the political battles the Bolsheviks fought to gain power.

A notable event in the late-nineteenth-century struggle between the tsarist

[2]The Soviet secret police have gone under the following names: Cheka (1917–1922), GPU (1922–1923), OGPU (1923–1934), NKVD (1934–1938), NKVD/MKGB (1938–1945), MVD/MGB (1945–1954) and KGB (1954 and after).

regime and its opponents was the execution in 1887 of a member of the People's Will, Alexander Ulyanov. His younger brother, who later took the name Lenin, became the founding father of the Soviet Union. Lenin is said to have understood from his brother's fate that the terrorist approach was doomed to failure. Out of this came his more systematic efforts to create change based on the writings of Marx and Engels.

The works of Marx began to be translated into Russian shortly before Lenin's birth in 1870. The first Russian Marxist organization was founded in 1883 by Georgy Plekhanov, a former populist, and others. Lenin became a Marxist during the following decade and visited Plekhanov in exile in Geneva in 1895. Later that year, after his return to Russia, Lenin was arrested for subversive activities and spent the next four and one half years in prison and Siberian exile. Incarceration and exile was a common fate of Russian revolutionaries. Infiltration of revolutionary movements by police agents and informers—leading to the arrest of movement leaders—was frequent. Lenin's desire to minimize the chances of infiltration no doubt reinforced his determination to establish a movement based on a small group of professional revolutionaries working in secret.

Originally considered a follower of Plekhanov, Lenin later broke with him over several important matters of doctrinal interpretation and Party organization. On the latter, Lenin advocated, not a mass parliamentary party, but an elite core of revolutionaries who could seize power. They would then organize a "dictatorship of the proletariat" on behalf of the workers. His famous and oft-quoted passages in the 1902 pamphlet "What Is To Be Done?" contain the essence of Lenin's views. He said that "no revolutionary movement can endure without a stable organization of leaders maintaining continuity," and that because of the need to combat the government and the political police, "such an organization must consist chiefly of people professionally engaged in revolutionary activity" and "must perforce be not very extensive and must be as secret as possible." Lenin returned again and again to the ingredients of small size and secrecy, holding that the latter element could never be achieved by a mass organization. In another passage, he proposed "to concentrate all secret functions in the hands of as small a number of professional revolutionaries as possible" (Lenin, 1961, pp. 452–453 and 464). Finally, Lenin felt that the party must act with unity, not divisively. For this purpose, he formalized the concept of "democratic centralism," which prohibited dissent from established party policy. Thus, the main elements were an elite party of professional revolutionaries whose policies were adopted in secret behind a facade of complete unity.

Revolutionary agitation continued after the turn of the century, culminating in the revolution of 1905. Although it was not successful, the revolution, combined with the Russian defeat in the war with Japan, led a frightened tsar to issue the October Manifesto (1905). This document promised the establishment of a popular assembly, or *Duma,* a constitution, and free rights of political participation. To balance the *Duma,* a Council of State was created as an upper house, half of whose members were appointed by the tsar. No proposal of the *Duma* could become law without the approval of both the Council of State and the tsar. The tsar's ministers in the Council of State were responsible only to him. Although the beginnings of constitutional government had been created, the balance of power still lay strongly on the side of the monarch.

When the first *Duma,* elected in 1906, clashed with the tsar's ministers and outspokenly advocated further reforms, the tsar dissolved it. The second *Duma,* convened the next year, met the same fate. Before elections for the third *Duma* were held, the tsar unilaterally changed the electoral law to reduce the electorate and further favor the propertied classes over other voters. This *Duma* (1908 to 1912) and its successor (1912 to 1917) were much more conservative in composition, but the efforts of minor parties, particularly the Constitutional Democrats or Cadets, to criticize the government and fight inefficiency led to hope in some circles that a genuine constitutional monarch might yet evolve.

A severe blow to this hope was the First World War, which proved to be a military disaster for Russia. The fourth *Duma* looked into the incompetent way in which the government waged the war, but its proposals for wide-ranging reforms were ignored. Exhausted by the war, with widespread food shortages, transportation difficulties, and other disruptions at home, the country drifted toward anarchy. Great crowds of striking workers filled the streets of Petrograd (formerly St. Petersburg, later to be Leningrad) in early and mid-March of 1917. When troops employed to disperse the crowds decided to join the demonstrators, a critical point was reached. The *Duma* had again been ordered dissolved by the tsar, but it elected a temporary committee to aid in the restoration of order. This temporary committee secured the abdication of the tsar and formed the Provisional Government, which attempted to assert its authority in the country. However, later that year it was overthrown by the Bolsheviks, the wing of the Russian Social Democratic Labor Party led by Lenin. It should be emphasized that neither the March Revolution nor the abdication of the tsar had been engineered by the Bolsheviks. Their leaders, including Lenin himself, were in exile or prison at the time.

During the early days of the March Revolution, local revolutionary councils (soviets) were established across Russia. The most important of these was in Petrograd. The soviets included representation from various sectors of the populace and were very different in character from the middle-class Provisional Government that they opposed almost from the start. Alexander Kerensky, the vice-chairman of the Petrograd Soviet and a member of the Social Revolutionary party, joined the Provisional Government to handle liaison with the Petrograd Soviet. He was the Provisional Government's only socialist and was to become its last leader. The Provisional Government chose to continue Russia's participation in World War I, which was a very unpopular decision. This, combined with its ineffectiveness in coping with urgent economic problems and demands for reform, helped spell its end. The Bolshevik strategy was to gain control of the soviets and thereby oust the Provisional Government.

In August, General Kornilov, the army commander, attempted to overthrow the government, abolish the soviets, and establish a right-wing government. The attempt was repulsed, but only with the help of revolutionary troops and a union of the various parties in the Petrograd Soviet. This further divided those who had supported the Provisional Government. When the Bolsheviks moved to take power by force in November,[3] the Provisional Government was too weak to resist successfully. Power came to the Bolsheviks not so much because they had widespread popular support but because the majority had lost confidence in the Provisional Government.

After gaining power, the Bolsheviks still had to face several years of bitter civil war against a combination of forces bent on their overthrow.[4] And because after the March 1917 Revolution they had clamored so vociferously for a constituent assembly, they felt compelled to hold elections shortly after the seizure of power. The Bolsheviks gained only 25 percent of the vote in the election. After one day, when they were unable to compel the constituent assembly to do their bidding, armed guards under their control closed the session. Thus ended the first genuinely elected legislative body during the period of Soviet rule.

Clearly, then, the Bolshevik leaders took power by force and were determined to maintain it that way. Little in the background of Lenin or his comrades—or, for that matter, in the prevailing currents of Russian history—inclined them to try to establish a liberal democracy. Lenin purported to believe in mass participation; he once remarked that "every cook must learn to administer the state." However, this would clearly be controlled participation under the leadership of the elite band of Bolsheviks. This sort of mass participation has been a characteristic of the Soviet system, but it has little in common with democracy as the term is generally understood.

So the Bolsheviks brought with them in their accession to power the practices learned from their long years of conspiratorial struggle against the tsarist regime. In the absence of an alternative tradition of open, pluralistic politics, this mode of operation has dominated the political scene throughout Soviet history. The scholar-diplomat George Kennan brilliantly analyzed the importance of this heritage for this system. Noting the lack of accountability or of formal procedures for establishing authority, Kennan observed that these faults were compounded by the absence of "a clear code of personal and col-

---

[3]By the old Russian calendar the Revolution occurred in October. The Bolsheviks soon adopted the Gregorian Calendar used in the West, which moved the date to November 7. In the Soviet Union, however, it is still referred to as the October Revolution.

[4]This was the period of War Communism mentioned in Chapter 1.

legial ethics" to which the leaders might have referred in solving the problems that faced them in administering the state. The "traditional rules of revolutionary ethics," he stated, were not well suited to running a government. Thus, after destroying the edifice of the tsarist state and all opposing political forces,[5] the Bolshevik leaders turned to victimizing each other. The code of ethics of the revolutionary period, which had implied fair treatment of other revolutionaries of the left since they were fighting a common enemy, was first narrowed to the Bolsheviks alone. But it did not stop there: "If the Socialist-Revolutionary deserved death, what did the Bolshevik deserve who leaned to Socialist-Revolutionary or Menshevik, or other unacceptable views?" (Kennan, 1966, pp. xiv-xvi). This question was not answered in Lenin's lifetime, though he expressed forebodings in his famous "Testament," written in late 1922 and early 1923, in which he recommended that Stalin be removed from the post of general secretary of the Party because he had accumulated immense power and because of his rudeness toward comrades. The matter of whether it is permissible to apply the death penalty to Party comrades was settled at the end of 1934 when Stalin arranged the murder of Kirov and set off the period of the great purges (Kennan, 1966, pp. xiv–xvii).

The period of political murder ended soon after Stalin's death, and discredited leaders began to be treated in a milder fashion. A debate has gone on for years about whether Stalinism was a logical outgrowth of the system Lenin had created or some terrible aberration. In defending the latter point, for instance, the dissident Soviet historian Roy Medvedev, a Leninist, has written that "it was an historical accident that Stalin, the embodiment of all the worst elements in the Russian revolutionary movement, came to power after Lenin, the embodiment of all that was best" (Medvedev, 1971, p. 362). Certainly nothing dictated that a person of Stalin's paranoid mentality had to succeed Lenin.

But as Western biographers of Lenin have shown, he did not eschew terror and the murder of opponents of the Bolsheviks (Fischer, 1964, pp. 20–21, 247–248, 278, 375; Shub, 1948, pp. 303–311; Conquest, 1972, pp. 98–102). And to maintain Bolshevik control in a country facing increasing unrest due to economic difficulties, he engineered changes in intra-Party practices that effectively eliminated opposition voices in the name of Party unity and paved the way for the victimization of opponents. Resolutions drafted by Lenin and adopted by the Tenth Party Congress in 1921 effectively forbade the existence of factions within the Party and seriously limited freedom of criticism. There is evidence that secret-police methods began to be used against intra-Party opposition almost immediately thereafter (Schapiro, 1960, pp. 322–323, 334–336, 358–360). In other words, Lenin laid the basis for the end of intra-Party democracy. It was only a short step from the tactics Lenin condoned to the practices Stalin employed after Lenin's departure from the scene.

[5]To some extent this struggle continued until the end of the civil war in 1921.

Leaders since Stalin have avoided his excesses in the treatment of opponents. Particularly under Khrushchev and Gorbachev, thousands of victims of the Stalin period have been rehabilitated, their honor—if not their lives—restored. But Stalin's successors have as yet been unwilling to examine very closely Lenin's role or to question the extent to which he paved the way for Stalinist rule.

REFERENCES

CONQUEST, R. (1972). *V.I. Lenin*. New York: Viking Penguin.

CUSTINE, MARQUIS DE. (1951). *Journey for our time: The Russian journals of Marquis De Custine*. trans. and ed. Phyllis Penn Kohler. Chicago: Regnery Gateway.

Fischer, L. (1964). *The life of Lenin*. New York: Harper & Row.

HARCAVE, S. (1953). *Russia: A history*. Philadelphia: Lippincott.

KENNAN, G. (1966). Introduction. In Boris I. Nicolaevsky, *Power and the Soviet elite*. New York: Holt, Rinehart & Winston.

LENIN, V.I. (1961). *Collected works*. Moscow: Foreign Languages.

MEDVEDEV, R. (1971). *Let history judge: The origins and consequences of Stalinism*. New York: Alfred A. Knopf.

SCHAPIRO, L. 1960. *The origins of communist autocracy*. Cambridge: Harvard University Press.

SHUB, D. (1948). *Lenin*. New York: Doubleday.

THREE
IDEOLOGY:
Does It Make a Difference?

The main issue to be raised in this chapter is simple to state: What role does ideology play in contemporary Soviet politics? The answer is not nearly as easy to supply. In fact, it can be argued that it is impossible to supply because it is impossible to read the minds of the Soviet leadership or survey any reasonable sample of the Soviet populace. We can look at what the leaders say, compare it to what they do, and try to come to some conclusions about the extent to which their actions were influenced by the ideological precepts that they continually enunciate. But reasonable persons can, and do, differ in their conclusions on this point. Correspondingly, we can talk to those Soviet citizens who are accessible to us, but we cannot know whether what they say is typical or even if they are being honest with us. Thus, of all the aspects of Soviet politics that attract the attention of Western writers, none has been less satisfactorily treated than ideology—in spite of the fact that the amount of scholarly and journalistic writing on the subject is enormous.

Why, you may ask, should I care about the relationship of ideology to politics? If you examine political behavior with sufficient care, you ought to find out a good deal about how the Soviet political system operates. True enough. And such an approach is sufficient—if one is not tempted to ask "why?" as well as "how?" But to limit attention to the "how?" is more of a problem in the study of the Soviet Union than it would be in a study of many other countries. This is because the Soviet Union has always had an official ideology, an authoritatively approved set of political ideas to which all Soviet citizens were supposed to subscribe.

This set of ideas not only provided the framework for political behavior, but the Soviet leadership historically maintained that it contained within it the key to understanding the future development of societies. In other words, it was supposed to have predictive value. An authoritative Soviet source described these two features succinctly:

> The Marxist science of the laws of social development enables us not only to chart a correct path through the labyrinth of social contradictions, but to predict the course events will take, the direction of historical progress and the next stage of social advance. (Dutt, 1961, p. 17)

The same author added elsewhere that "Marxism Leninist theory is not a dogma but a guide to action" (p. 19). One can see, then, the much greater importance which was ascribed to ideology in Soviet politics than has been common in Western politics.

Not everyone agrees that political ideas in the Soviet Union have been all that important. In fact, most non-Marxist Western scholars are dubious about the predictive value of Marxist ideas, and even Soviet leaders now acknowledge that citizen behavior has seldom measured up to ideological expectations. But even the current leadership finds it necessary to deal with the importance of ideology. This makes it important to examine the ideology in light of elite and mass beliefs and behaviors, as well as current policy initiatives, and to determine what functions it has traditionally served in the Soviet system.

THE OFFICIAL NATURE OF SOVIET IDEOLOGY

Much scholarly effort has been expended on defining and discussing the concept of ideology, and a great deal of disagreement surrounds its use (Sargent, 1987, pp. 5–7; Christenson and others, 1971, pp. 1–35; Ingersoll and Matthews, 1986, pp. 6–11). This vagueness and lack of a generally accepted definition of the term has led some writers to discard it entirely in favor of other expressions such as "belief system" or "value system." We have not chosen this alternative, both because ideology is the term that Soviet writers themselves use and because it is so pervasive in the writings of Western analysts of Soviet politics.

We referred previously to a political ideology as a "set of political ideas." A more elaborate definition would be "a belief system that explains and justifies a preferred political order for society, either existing or proposed, and offers a strategy (processes, institutional arrangements, programs) for its attainment" (Christenson and others, 1971, p. 5). This definition is somewhat open-ended, in that it could refer to a personal belief system ("my ideology," "X's ideology") or the prevailing belief system of a whole class, race, or nation. Although the second connotation is the more common one (at least with reference to the Soviet Union), the word is employed in both ways in the West.

The American political scientist Robert Lane, for instance, in his book *Political Ideology,* "undertook to discover the latent political ideology of the American urban common man" through in-depth interviews with fifteen American males. He describes ideologies as "group beliefs that individuals borrow" (Lane, 1962, pp. 3, 15). The emigré sociologist Vladimir Shlapentokh, who left the Soviet Union in the 1970s, posits a somewhat different distinction between these two levels of ideology: (1) "pragmatic," which has to do with the real conditions of Soviet life; and (2) "mythological," which amounts to a "secondary reality" that the leadership attempts to impose on the populace (Shlapentokh, 1986; Shlapentokh, 1988).

The official Soviet conception of ideology, by contrast, has historically allowed for no such variations. The authoritative *Political Dictionary* defines ideology as "the totality of political, legal, moral, religious, artistic, and philosophical views which express the interests of one or another class." Ideology arises, the *Political Dictionary* continues, "as a reflection of the conditions of the material life of the society and of the interests of certain classes. . . . The ideology of the working class and its party is Marxism-Leninism—the revolutionary weapon in the struggle for the overthrow of the exploitative system and the building of communism" (Ponomarev, 1958, pp. 199–200).

Thus, Marxism-Leninism has been the "official" ideology of the Communist Party of the Soviet Union, which until recently has been the lone repository of permissible political thought in the orthodox Soviet belief system. All political systems to some extent possess an official ideology of this kind. The difference is a matter of degree. In Western countries, we like to think that the political ideas which individuals espouse are freely chosen. Although research in political psychology might cast doubt on this belief,[1] at least we can say that Western governments make considerably less effort to inculcate a single approved set of political ideas than the Soviet government has in the past. The official Soviet ideology is an imposed ideology which used to be impressed upon the citizenry with a thoroughness that had no parallel in the West.

Has this imposition been successful? To answer this question we would have to determine what the aims of ideological imposition have been, that is, the functions the ideology is designed to perform. This is a matter to which we will return at the end of the chapter. But for the present we can say that many citizens appear to accept Marxism-Leninism as the basis for their political judgments. Yet it is becoming increasingly clear that a considerable number

---

[1]Particularly research having to do with socialization and reference group influences.

do not. This could be seen during the Brezhnev years in some of the statements made by members of the dissident movement. More recently, glasnost-inspired questioning and criticism of many aspects of the Soviet system indicate that such skepticism went well beyond the ranks of the dissident movement. Thus, while ideological indoctrination may have had considerable influence in the past, it never eliminated competing ideas.

How does one acquire an ideology? The briefest answer is through socialization—through one's life experiences, those events by which one comes to understand one's place and role in society. Along with such understanding comes a set of attitudes toward life, society, and politics. Some of this socialization takes place informally, perhaps even unconsciously, "through the skin." For example, a person builds up attitudes toward authority on the basis of treatment by parents and other authoritative figures. Much socialization is more formal, however, influencing people through such channels as formal education, the media, and religious instruction. It is primarily within these more formal avenues of socialization that organized attempts to affect people's political belief systems (that is, their ideologies) take place. The official Soviet ideology was historically propagated mainly through official and consciously manipulated socialization channels.

THE SOURCES OF SOVIET IDEOLOGY

As the previous quotations from the *Political Dictionary* show, Marxism-Leninism has traditionally been considered the ideology of the Soviet state. Marxism, as a social theory, is designed to provide a framework for the understanding of human history, as well as present and future social developments. It also sets forth the image of a better society to be achieved at some unspecified point in the future. The key element is the relationship between labor and the instruments of production.

History, in Marx's view, proceeds according to a dialectical process.[2] Marx borrowed the concept of dialectics from the philosopher Hegel, who believed that history had to be understood as an ongoing process in which humanity was achieving ever new levels of freedom and rationality. Marx's adaption of Hegel's concept of the dialectical movement of society was his positing of the economic factor as the key ingredient in the dialectical process of historical development. Thus the terms *dialectical materialism* and *historical materialism*.

Marx offered an economic interpretation of history based on the class struggle. As he put it, "the history of all hitherto existing societies is the his-

---

[2]Laird and Laird (1988, p. 55) define dialectics as "a method of logic used by Hegel and based on contradiction of opposites (thesis and antithesis) and their continual resolution (synthesis). Marx adapted this to historical materialism."

tory of class struggle.'' Nevertheless, it would be a mistake to think of Marx's theory as either unicausal or solely concerned with economic matters. Marx's collaborator, Friedrich Engels, helps explain why their writings were sometimes too narrowly understood:

> Marx and I are ourselves partly to blame for the fact that the younger people sometimes lay more stress on the economic side than is due it. We had to emphasize the main principles vis-à-vis our adversaries, who denied it, and we had not always the time, the place or the opportunity to allow the other elements involved in the interaction to come into their rights. (Tucker, 1978, p. 762)

According to the laws of historical development, societies move through successive stages from primitive communalism to slave-based society to feudalism to capitalism to socialism. The culmination of the process is the building of an ideal communist society in which the means of production belong to all and the laborer works both for himself or herself and for society as a whole. Each of the stages prior to communism carries within itself as part of the dialectical process the seeds of its own destruction—its own inherent contradictions that will eventually destroy it. With the rise of capitalism, the main antagonistic classes were the proletariat (urban workers) and the bourgeoisie (owners of the means of production). In the capitalist stage the exploitation of the workers by the bourgeoisie was the key dialectical element that would eventually lead to socialism, under which exploitation would cease.

Socialism, however, is but a stage in the development toward communism. Although there are no hostile social groupings under socialism, certain contradictions and survivals of the past in the minds of citizens must be eliminated. Communism implies the overcoming of these problems, the institution of complete public control of the economic system and self-government, and the achievement of a sufficient economic and technological level of development to guarantee abundance. Justice is embodied in Marx's principle, ''From each according to his ability to each according to his needs.''

Lenin's most important contribution to Marxism was his application of the theory to the conditions existing in Russia early in the twentieth century. Marx had treated the collapse of capitalism as inevitable. Although he aspired to participation in movements for political change—he once wrote that ''the philosophers have *interpreted* the world in various ways; the point however is to *change* it''—his contributions were largely in setting down the basic theoretical framework. Lenin, by contrast, both conceived the organizational basis and strategy for revolution and led the successful struggle to establish a regime based on Marxist ideas. His most important theoretical contributions were his ideas on party organization and his theory of revolution.

Lenin favored a small group of disciplined professional revolutionaries operating in secret rather than the mass organization advocated by some of his fellow Russian socialists. He also argued with them about the possibility of revolution in Russia at that time. Marxian precepts seemed to require a mature capitalism before a socialist revolution could take place, and Russia was only at a primitive stage of capitalist development. Lenin argued, however, that on the organizational base that he devised, it was not necessary to await the full maturation of capitalism in Russia before taking power. The party could act for the proletariat and thus speed up the inevitable process. Lenin's practical genius, along with his ability in persuading his comrades that it was possible to telescope the stages leading to revolution, helped to bring the Bolsheviks to power in 1917.

These ideas of Marx and Lenin are among their most important theoretical contributions. But they concentrate largely on the historical processes and tactics leading to the creation of the socialist state, rather than on guidelines for running that state. The writings of Marx, in particular, were very sketchy on practices to be used after the seizure of power. As Louis Fischer put it, for the Bolsheviks trying to maintain their positions after November 1917, "Marx was no Baedeker" (Fischer, 1964, p. 254).

In order to construct an ideology suitable for running a modern state, Soviet leaders have had to go beyond Marx and Lenin to embrace other ideas. How can the characteristics of Soviet Marxism-Leninism be reasonably defined? A brief but acceptable cataloging of the elements of Soviet ideology is that of the American political scientist Alfred G. Meyer:

[The] doctrine consists of the following parts:

1. a philosophy called Dialectical Materialism;
2. generalizations about man and society, past and present, called Historical Materialism;
3. an economic doctrine called Political Economy, which seeks to explain the economics of capitalism and imperialism on the one hand, and of socialist construction on the other;
4. a body of political thought, or guidelines, now called Scientific Communism, which deals, first, with the strategy and tactics of communist revolutions, and, second, the political problems of socialist states; and
5. the official history of the CPSU (Communist Party of the Soviet Union). To this one might add the shorter-range pronouncements made by the Party interpreting current affairs and determining goals and priorities. (Meyer, 1966, p. 273)

If these are the main elements of Soviet political ideology, where is one to find the details, the specific ideas and values? The amount of such material is extremely large, and this is where the problem of the content of Soviet ideology begins to get difficult. There are, as mentioned, the works of the fathers of Soviet ideological thought such as Marx, Engels (Marx's collaborator in much of his work), and Lenin, as well the writings of numerous less important political thinkers and actors who were their followers. The latest official edition of the collected works of Lenin consists of 55 volumes. The second edition of the works of Marx and Engels in Russian totaled 50 volumes plus several volumes of indexes. Then there are the Soviet leaders after Lenin. To take only recognized top leaders: Stalin's collected works filled 13 volumes; Khrushchev's amounted to 8 volumes; 9 volumes of Brezhnev's collected works were published as well as a number of other individual and multivolume works; several books of the writings and speeches of Andropov and Chernenko appeared during their short tenures, and the same has been true of Gorbachev in his years as top leader. Also important is Gorbachev's 1987 book *Perestroika,* a volume translated into several languages and intended to introduce his ideas to people in the West.

The quotation from Meyer mentioned the official history of the CPSU; but it is relevant to ask, Which history? The history written during Stalin's time and attributed to him (*The Short Course*) was the authoritative pronouncement on the subject for a long time. But it was repudiated and withdrawn several years after his death. Since then, official party histories have been rewritten frequently in an attempt to accommodate what the current leadership is willing to have historians tell about the Soviet past (Mcneill, 1977). The impetus for exploring the "blank spots" in Soviet history quickened dramatically under Gorbachev. In fact, it got to the point where history examinations for secondary school pupils were canceled in 1988 so that textbooks could be brought into line with the wealth of new information being made public (*The New York Times,* May 31, 1988, p. A1). The next official Party history will undoubtedly provide a much fuller and more honest look at the Soviet past than any former version.

The Meyer passage also mentions "scientific communism." This is a relatively new concept, introduced officially with great fanfare as an independent part of Marxism-Leninism only in 1962. Since then, many books on the subject have been written, including the textbook, *Scientific Communism,* the seventh edition of which was published in 1985 with a first printing of one-half million (*Nauchnyi Kommunizm,* 1985). This treats philosophy as a science, asserting that "for the first time in the history of mankind's spiritual development, Marx and Engels turned philosophy into a science, into a highly effective method of the revolutionary transformation of the world in general and the society in particular" (Krapivin, 1985, p. 10).

In a slightly different category was the 1961 Party Program, described as "a program for the building of communist society." This document (the size of a 150-page book) purported to define "the main tasks and principal stages of communist construction." It was, in other words, no less than a blueprint for introducing communism into all important aspects of Soviet life. But many of the specific provisions of the Party Program were so closely associated with Khrushchev that they were disowned by his successors. In 1981 Brezhnev announced that it was time the Party updated its program. Subsequently, a commission was formed to write a new version, which was adopted at the Twenty-seventh Party Congress in 1986. The new program was much less utopian in tone. It abandoned predictions in the earlier version about soon overtaking the West and about a quick transition from socialism to communism (Evans, 1987).

Finally, there is the last sentence of the quotation from Professor Meyer concerning the "shorter-range pronouncements made by the Party interpreting current affairs and determining goals and priorities." Such pronouncements might include any of a number of statements made at plenary meetings of the Party Central Committee. Recent examples are the encouragement of cooperative economic undertakings by citizens as an alternative to state-controlled economic activities, or the "new thinking" in foreign policy, which purports to provide the basis for a more accommodating view of the USSR's place in the world. These pronouncements really amount to concrete interpretations of the basic ideology, rather than constituting additions to the central core. Also, the movement toward a multiparty electoral system is considerably diluting their impact.

This quick review of the sources of Soviet political ideology and its main categories should make two things clear. First, the volume of ideological materials is enormous. Second, it is not always certain what is currently accepted and approved. In addition, this uncertainty has grown with the progress of the reform. Thus, this mass of ideological materials can be viewed as an archive of potentially useful materials that can be drawn on as the need arises. It has been said of the Bible that some passage can always be found as justification for almost any religious point of view. Or, more poetically,

> One day at least in every week
>   the sects of every kind
> Their doctrines here are sure to seek
>   And just as sure to find. (DeMorgan, 1947, p. 159)

If this is true of the Bible, it is also true of the classics of Marxism-Leninism in the sense that their volume is so great and that the writing is frequently vague and ambiguous. Even where the meaning of a passage is reasonably clear, Soviet leaders have not been above distorting it to serve their own ends. Soviet history is replete with such instances. One of the best known and most important is the identification of Lenin with Khrushchev's campaign for "peaceful coexistence," which became known as "the Lenin principle of peaceful coexistence." Even the Chinese Communists claimed that Khrushchev distorted Lenin's intention in using the term, and some Western analysts think this point is sound (Leonhard, 1974, pp. 64–66).

As mentioned before, a considerable amount of the material in this ideological archive has fallen into disuse, often because certain concepts have become embarrassing or no longer useful. Also, they may have been associated with leaders now discredited. But the Soviet approach to these matters is extremely flexible. Concepts and ideals can always be revived again, as is occasionally done with long-forgotten statements by Lenin. In fact, "new" ideas of Lenin that were not known previously but that support current Soviet policies, have sometimes been published. The ideas of discredited leaders may be revived with a leader's rehabilitation, or they may be used when necessary without identifying them with that leader. Whatever practice is used, great effort is normally made to emphasize that new developments are consistent with the basic doctrine and amount, at most, to "creative adaptations" of it. The current version is that previous versions were "distortions" and oversimplifications and that the reform leadership is returning to a more accurate reading of the works of Marx and Lenin.

If this is the totality of the Soviet ideological repository, so to speak, what parts of it can be anticipated to be of real importance in the 1990s and how may they affect the way Soviet leaders will behave?

THE DOCTRINAL NUCLEUS

The casual reader of Soviet writings might conclude that Soviet politicians are fond of quoting Marx and Lenin. Over the years the habit of quoting the founding fathers of Soviet ideology has become expected behavior. Nor does this practice extend only to politicians. Journalists, lawyers, historians, economists, in fact all people writing in what may be broadly defined as the humanities and social sciences (and, in Stalin's day, many of those in the natural sciences as well), traditionally had to establish their orthodoxy by citation. Especially in a book or scholarly article, appropriate references were considered *de rigueur*. Failure to include them would be seen as an important omission. For both politicians and nonpoliticians, such citations afforded protection by reminding all who cared that the writer was devoted to ideological orthodoxy (however that may have currently been interpreted).

In many cases the bows to the fathers of communism seemed perfunctory: a quote or two and nothing more for the rest of the book or article. When carried to extremes, such citationism led to sterile discourse, a fact about which even Soviet authorities often complained. In the current reform period this practice has been considerably moderated, and this may lend credibility, since the citations that do appear may be perceived as more carefully chosen and appropriate.

If Soviet writers and speakers, especially politicians, have traditionally been expected to quote Marx and Lenin, what can one say about the sincerity with which they have done so and the degree to which ideological principles have influenced the content of the ideas which they have attempted to translate into behavior? These matters have perennially been at the heart of the controversy about Soviet ideology among Western scholars, whose views diverge widely. And, increasingly, Soviet commentators have begun to agonize over the proper place of ideology in public discourse. What follows, therefore, is our view, accompanied by references to the opinions of other scholars.

The British economist Peter Wiles has written that "Communists are governed by their sacred texts" and that it "is more than seeking doctrinal justification for what they want or are forced to do." For example, according to Wiles, tasks like the collectivization of the peasantry are inherently both difficult and disagreeable. He goes on to point out that "no one is forced to perform them; no one in his right mind would want to perform them. Yet they have been achieved. . . . The reason is of course that the Communist leaders are not in their right mind; they are in Marx's mind" (Wiles, 1964, p. 356). In short, they are seeing the world through a set of perceptual screens that have been constructed on the basis of Marx's ideas about how the world works. This leads to a tendency to see what confirms these Marxist ideas and to miss seeing what does not.

At the other end of the scale is the view of the historian Robert Daniels. In his numerous writings on the subject, Daniels has taken a rather cynical view about the sincerity with which ideological beliefs are held. He has written, for instance, that ideology "is an instrument for rationalizing after the fact" (Bell, 1965, p. 601). Similarly, France's Emmanuel Todd has written: "We must not think . . . that the Russian Communists are 'ideologically motivated.' Rather, we should see them as perfect cynics" (Todd, 1979, p. 132). And the Soviet Academician Andrei Sakharov has remarked that the Soviet regime is characterized by "ideological indifference and the pragmatic use of ideology as a convenient 'facade'" (Sakharov, 1977, p. 294).

Most Western writers reject extremes. Our own position is that since the leaders of the Soviet state have spent their adult lives living within the system and have received most of their education under it, it seems likely that, to varying degrees, they accept the basic principles of the doctrine and have a view of the world that is shaped, or at least heavily influenced, by Marxism-Leninism; and this includes, by the way, leaders like Gorbachev. Just by its influence on the thought processes of Soviet leaders, in other words, the ideology has an impact on their behavior. This idea has been captured best by Paul F. Cook, a U.S. State Department official:

> If one looks upon ideology, however, not as the operational code of the international communist conspiracy, not as a blueprint for the attainment of world communism, but rather as a system of thought in a more restrictive sense, as *Weltanschauung,* especially one increasingly imbued—or contaminated if you will—by traditional Russian values, then it retains its relevance as a determinant of Soviet policy. (Cook, 1974, p. 4)

This view of ideology does not suggest a very rigidly held faith. One of the characteristics of recent Soviet leaders has been their flexibility with regard to doctrine. A difficulty in sorting out the impact of ideology on action stems from the Marxist-Leninist penchant for fusing the two, for discussing "the unity of theory and practice." As Khrushchev once put it, "Marxism-Leninism teaches that theory divorced from practice is dead, and practice which is not enlightened by theory is blind.'' So doctrinal changes are evident from time to time in spite of efforts by Soviet authorities to affirm the consistency of the doctrine.

Undoubtedly the most significant challenge to the constancy of Soviet ideology has come from the Gorbachev reform. As Gorbachev and his supporters have examined the many aspects of Soviet life embraced by the concept of perestroika, a number of the shibboleths of the past have been challenged— to the point where the question of whether the Soviet Union can genuinely be called a socialist society has been raised. Gorbachev himself has reacted defensively to such charges, insisting that he remains loyal to the basic ideological precepts:

> We see that confusion has arisen in some people's minds: aren't we retreating from the positions of socialism, especially when we introduce new and unaccustomed forms of economic management and public life, and aren't we subjecting the Marxist-Leninist teaching itself to revision? . . . No, we are not retreating a single step from socialism, from Marxism-Leninism. . . . But we resolutely reject the dogmatic, bureaucratic and voluntaristic legacy, since it has nothing in common either with Marxism-Leninism or with genuine socialism. . . . Questions of theory cannot and must not be resolved by any sort of decrees. A free competition of minds is necessary. (*CDSP, 40,* no. 7, 1988, pp. 3-4)

As shifts in ideological interpretation and variations in the application of certain principles take place, however, it is necessary to ask what have been the most basic precepts governing the Soviet system up to the current reform period and how have they been modified by the reform. There is some controversy as to which precepts belong in this group; we offer the following as ones that the leadership has made a conscientious effort to implement throughout the Soviet period: the sanctity of the Communist Party; socialist ownership of the means of production; collectivism; atheism; and antagonism toward other social systems.

The Sanctity of the Communist Party

The sanctity of the Party was always the supreme article of faith. The Party has been above criticism, as have its top leaders—except when a campaign is orchestrated against one or a small group of them. Then they have been distinguished from the Party and designated as an ''anti-Party group'' or castigated for ''harm to our Party.'' Until recently, the Party's monopoly on major policy making in the Soviet Union has confirmed the place of the Party in the belief system, as did the confirmation of the dominance of the Party in such documents as the USSR Constitution. Also, the concept of ''democratic centralism,'' which was the cornerstone of Party and state operations in the country, sought to insure the control over the country of the Party leadership in Moscow. As Daniel Bell put it, "the doctrinal core . . . is not any specific theoretical formulation, but the basic demand for belief in the Party itself" (Bell, 1965, p. 602).

As the Gorbachev era progressed, more and more people began to advocate a multiparty system and some union republics even passed laws permitting more than one party. Also, alternate centers of political activity, such as popular fronts and parliamentary coalitions, began to play a significant role in Soviet political life (Mann, 1990). In the past these movements would have been ruthlessly crushed. The new reform leadership at first intrepidly maintained that the maintenance of the monopoly of the Party's political power was non-negotiable. As events in Eastern Europe led to the abolishment of Communist Party–dominated systems and the establishment of multiparty rule and as some of the union republics began moving in the same direction, the resolve of the leadership in Moscow began to weaken.

At first, Gorbachev was willing to do business with the leaders of other politically active noncommunist groups, but not to relinquish the leading role of the Communist Party. Subsequently, popular pressures forced reconsideration of even this basic tenet (*The Washington Post,* February 5, 1990, p. A1) and on February 7, 1990, the CPSU Central Committee voted to give up the Party's constitutionally guaranteed monopoly on power (*The Washington Post,* February 8, 1990, p. A1). Subsequently, the Congress of People's Deputies modified the constitution accordingly.

As the Soviet Union moves into the 1990s, then, it is clear that "sanctity" is no longer the best word to use in describing the position of the Communist Party in the Soviet Union. What its role and power position will be by the year 2000 remains to be seen—and is virtually impossible to predict.

Socialist Ownership of the Means of Production

What this principle has meant historically is state ownership and control of virtually all economic activity, centralized planning of the economy, and a prohibition of "private property," meaning property that could be used for "speculation" or illegal economic gain.[3] To stimulate lagging economic performance, the Gorbachev regime has made several changes aimed at stimulating greater individual initiative in the economy, including the adoption of laws on individual and cooperative economic activity. Also, it was authoritatively stated that "the principal basis for the formation of the new look of socialism is the radical restructuring of the whole system of property relations" (*Pravda,* July 16, 1989, p. 3). In the Spring of 1990, the legislature set about doing just that (*Vedomosti*

[3]"Personal" (*lichnaia*) property has been distinguished from "private" (*chastnaia*) property in Soviet law and has always been permitted. Personal property includes things used for individual consumption or enjoyment (for example, clothing, books, an automobile, a house) that are not used for the economic exploitation of other persons. For more details see Feldbrugge and others, 1985, p. 585.

S'ezda Narodykh Deputatov SSSR i Verkhovnogo Soveta SSSR, no. 11, 1990, pp. 197–210).

Developments of this kind have contributed to charges (such as those rejected by Gorbachev in the quotation included previously) that the USSR is departing from its socialist precepts. In fact, Ed Hewett, an American specialist on the Soviet economy, predicts that the major issue for the Soviet leadership in the 1990s will be: "What is socialism and what is property under socialism?" (*The Washington Post,* January 26, 1989, p. A21) Soviet leaders, however, still insist that the *basic* character of the economic system remains socialist, and this undoubtedly is true, even if the definition of key terms, such as "property," is in the process of mutation (*The New York Times,* October 1, 1989, p. 15).

Collectivism

If the hallmark of Western liberal thought is individualism, it is collectivism that has always reigned in Soviet theory. Some writers suggest that collectivism found a congenial setting in Russia because *sobornost'* (a sense of community or togetherness) was widely held to be a positive virtue in the Russian past (Berman, 1963, p. 221). Whether or not this link is an accurate one, the collective idea is firmly imbedded in Soviet theory and practice. A whole battery of related Russian words is used to describe the phenomenon: *kollektivizm* (collectivism), *kollektivnost'* (collectivity), and, most important, *kollektiv* (the collective).

Broadly speaking, the term *kollektiv* refers to the peer group of the individual—but a peer group that operates in a way with which most Westerners will not be familiar. One writer who has understood its role is Allen Kassof:

> The peer group—or, to use the Soviet term, the collective—is the setting for group pressure. The Large Soviet Encyclopedia defines the collective as "a joining of people who are linked together by common work, general interest, and goals. (A collective of workers in a factory, a collective of employees of an institute, a collective of scientific workers at a higher educational institution, a collective of the students of a school)." The task of the collective is to instill in Soviet citizens habits of collectivism—that is, to discourage "egoistic striving" and to foster an acceptance of group control over values, attitudes, and behavior, not only during the formative years but throughout adult life as well. (Kassof, 1965, p. 42)

The doctrinal tenet of collectivism has extremely wide implications. It means no less than the superiority of the peer group's norms over the values and preferences of the individual.

The peer group's norms, in turn, may well be inspired from higher up in the political system or may amount simply to the personal interpretation of the responsible Party representative in the group. Such norms involve matters such as the work collective's censure of a person who habitually reports late for work or the student collective's cleanliness inspections of dormitory rooms. In anticipating the future of collectivism in the Soviet Union, one runs up against the fact that it has, to date, been tightly controlled by the CPSU. Therefore, the question for the future is whether it will stand or fall with the fortunes of the CPSU or whether the principal of collectivism will transfer to the many new groups forming outside the confines of the CPSU.

Atheism

A long-standing tenet that is traceable to Marx, atheism has always been favored by the Soviet leadership. The degree of toleration or harassment of believers and religious organizations has varied over time, but the basic opposition remained firm until quite recently. The about-face came in 1989. Under the pressure of popular discontent and nationalism, the reform leadership made the decision to accept fully the right of all Soviet believers to practice their religions and to legitimize this policy by enacting it in the form of a law guaranteeing religious freedom.

This was announced in connection with a visit by Gorbachev to the Pope in Rome, during which the two leaders announced a corresponding decision to establish diplomatic relations between the Soviet Union and the Vatican, a historic departure from the Soviet past. At the same time the Ukrainian Catholic Church was legalized, ending a ban on what had been the largest forbidden religious organization in the world (*The Washington Post,* December 2, 1989, p. A1). Thus, although the CPSU still maintains an official preference for atheism, the impact of this ideological position has been considerably diluted in practice.

Antagonism toward Other Social Systems

Khrushchev's endorsement of the idea of peaceful coexistence between antagonistic socioeconomic systems marked a significant change in Soviet doctrine. For although Khrushchev traced the idea of peaceful coexistence to Lenin, his interpretation of the concept amounted to a revision of the Leninist thesis concerning the inevitability of wars under imperialism. This did not imply complete relaxation of tensions between capitalism and socialism, because economic competition between the two camps was to continue in order to demonstrate which system was superior. It did, however, shift the emphasis from the military sphere to the economic sphere as an arena for the antagonism to be expressed, a point regarded with considerable skepticism by most Western governmental leaders. On the other hand, Soviet leaders never asserted that peaceful coexistence extended to the ideological sphere. As Khrushchev put it, "ideological differences are unbridgeable, and they will continue to exist" (*Pravda,* November 7, 1957, p. 2).

Gorbachev's statements on "new thinking" in foreign policy have softened the hard edges of Khrushchev's rhetoric, but they have also acknowledged the differences to which Khrushchev alluded. In his book *Perestroika,* Gorbachev speaks of a "contradictory but interconnected, interdependent, and essentially integrated world." He advocates "peaceful competition between different social systems . . . to encourage mutually advantageous cooperation rather than confrontation and an arms race" (Gorbachev, 1987, pp. 139–254). This position was put to a test in late 1989 when Poland, East Germany, and Czechoslovakia abruptly dispensed with authoritarian communist rule and moved rapidly toward multiparty democracy. Soviet commentators on these developments repeatedly invoked the image of a "common European home" in which all countries would be free to choose their own form of political system.

The decision by the Soviet leadership to permit this to happen without interference—and even encourage it in some ways—marked a new era in world politics. Antagonism toward other social systems as a policy supported by the use of military force in Eastern Europe came to an end, and the Soviet leadership officially supported the right of other nations to self-determination—going so far as to acknowledge that previous actions, such as the crushing of the "Prague Spring" by Soviet troops, were wrong. As the era of perestroika proceeds, the possibility of further accommodation between the Soviet Union and other social systems may indicate that this aspect of the doctrinal nucleus, like some of the others, has diminished in importance, or at least been relegated to the distant future when the Soviet Union will be able to compete economically on the world stage with some hope of success.

This list of elements for a doctrinal nucleus is short when one considers the volume of doctrinal writing. Perhaps the most obvious omissions involve the doctrines of historical and dialectical materialism and associated concepts such as the class struggle. But these promise to be of little relevance during the 1990s. As the foundation of the whole edifice of Marxist-Leninist doctrine, they undoubtedly affect the way Soviet leaders look at the world and act as the prism through which they see and understand social phenomena. But such concepts appear to have little obvious influence on the way they react to events or on the policies they adopt. According to Richard Lowenthal, "there are vast parts of Communist ideological structure, such as the scholastic refinements of dialectical materialism or the labor theory of value which in their nature are so remote from the practical matters to be decided that their interpretation cannot possibly affect policy decisions" (Lowenthal, 1960, p. 59).

This point appears to apply to Soviet leaders and followers alike. As Boris Shragin, a philosopher and emigrant from the Soviet Union, has put it: "Practically no one in the Soviet Union takes Marxism seriously. Its basic theses, let us say the 'dictatorship of the proletariat,' have absolutely nothing in common with contemporary Soviet political reality" (Shragin, 1974, p. 4). The dissident emigré Vladimir Bukovsky put it more bluntly: "From top to bottom, no one believes in Marxist dogma anymore, even though they continue to measure their actions by it, refer to it, and use it as a stick to beat one another with: it is both a proof of loyalty and a meal ticket" (Bukovsky, 1978, p. 73).

Although this may be extreme for reasons discussed previously, there is an element of truth. The basically instrumental way in which the Soviet leadership has tended to approach ideology may be why the doctrinal nucleus seems to be crumbling so decisively under the onslaught of current political imperatives, both within and outside of the Soviet Union. The fact that there has always been an intensely practical quality to the way in which the Soviet leadership have used Marxism-Leninism may make it easier for them to back off from its historical implications without being forced to abandon it completely. On the other hand, what seems most likely at the moment is that Marxism-Leninism will become increasingly identified with the Communist Party (rather than with the Soviet government) in a political atmosphere in which competing ideologies, as well as competing groups, will continue to arise and become significant forces in the political arena.

THE FUNCTIONS OF IDEOLOGY

This is a period of instability within the Soviet political system, because the basic nature of the way in which the political game is played is rapidly changing. In the past, the ideology has performed some valuable functions which have constituted the glue holding the system together. How these functions will be handled in the future remains uncertain. With this in mind, it is important to take a close look at what the important functions were and how Marxism-Leninism played a role in maintaining political stability.

The Control Function

During the period in which the Communist Party was above criticism, it was subject to no challenges in running the country. There were no economic aggregations powerful enough to compete with the state. Collectivism, controlled by the state, facilitated "correct" political ideas and behavior among the populace, and antagonism toward other social systems justified the exclusion of "harmful" and "alien" ideas from outside. Finally, atheism served to discourage people from the attraction of competing faiths or loyalties. Obviously, then, political control was one of the major functions of the ideology. In fact, we would maintain that it was the most important. All other functions enhanced the control aspect and none contravened it.

In this period of political uncertainty and change, two issues arise. First, to what extent will the control function continue to be primary? This involves the historical Russian fear of anarchy and the corresponding need for a strong ruling figure (backed by an oligarchical elite) at the helm (Kennan, 1986). Second, if this control function can no longer be performed in the future as it was in the past, what will replace it? The recently instituted strong Presidency? People in Western democracies are used to a reasonable amount of superficial disorder in their political systems. The Soviets are not. Whether they can easily come to terms with the rough and tumble atmosphere of a democratic country and a free press or whether nostalgia for the relative calm and stability of an authoritarian system will prevail remains to be seen.

The Communications Function

Soviet leaders have always spoken in the language of Soviet ideology, using its categories and key terms as a framework for discourse. It is probably no exaggeration to say that one would have been denied a political role in Soviet society if one had not been able or willing to manipulate the language of ideology. Even ordinary Soviet citizens on occasion seemed to think in terms of this language, as in the following conversation between a Moscow taxi driver and an American:

> "Communism isn't a fairy tale, like God. For centuries people talked about such a thing as God; no one has a scrap of proof. But you can see Communism being built. It isn't a matter of faith or fairy tales, but of work. Look at our university. Look at Moscow, building itself up. Look at our steel mills."
>
> [The American replies:] "Look at our steel mills."
>
> "Ah son, that's just the point. It's the system that counts. Can't you see that? You have capitalism there, so that your steel mills, even if they are ahead of ours, mean profits and greed. It's the law of capitalism, the rule of whoever can grab most. But the law of socialism is sharing; our building means progress for everyone and for civilization. It's not just the factories that count, but who owns them and what is done with them and how people feel about them. Our factories are ours, so we are building Communism, not selfishness." (Observer, 1969, pp. 188–189)

It was through the ideological code of communication that political differences of opinion were expressed, and one had to be aware of the subtle distinctions and nuances of that code to catch the differences. In addition, the need to pay homage by citing ideological sources like Marx and Lenin, coupled with this tendency to use the approved formulations, placed significant restraints on discussion.

Now the outside observer, reading the Soviet press or watching televised sessions of the reformed Supreme Soviet, is struck by the extent to which the old elements of discourse have been reduced in importance. They are still there, but not to the extent that they were in the past. Beside them there has arisen a more robust and combative discourse in which people seem to feel more free to say what they mean in a direct and precise way. The number of topics it is possible to discuss openly has also grown enormously under glasnost. In fact, to an American, it is both fascinating and amusing to observe Gorbachev expressing some of the resentment and impatience toward the press that is almost routinely expressed by American presidents and other political leaders.

The Legitimizing Function

Taken as a whole, the ideology always served to legitimize current political and economic arrangements in the Soviet Union. If the Soviet people had to work hard, as is suggested by the taxi driver's remarks, their work was in service of a higher goal. The means used to arrive at that goal had less importance than the goal itself. The Party, as the speaker for the proletariat, claimed that its rightful role was running the system, that is, determining the best means to achieve the goals set by the ideology. As the sole interpreter of historical truth (that is, where both the world and the Soviet Union had been and were going), it could assure that its primacy was maintained.

Social integration involves the shared internalization of values by a group of people. This sharing helps to enhances group loyalty and cohesiveness. As Brzezinski and Huntington have put it:

> For citizens to share in certain beliefs they must make almost automatic responses to certain key notions, symbols, or aspirations. Such responses create social cohesion and make the functioning of the system possible. Political indoctrination of the citizen, by making him nationally conscious, integrates him socially and politically, and this inevitably makes for the further spreading of the elite's ideology or political beliefs. (Brzezinski and Huntington, 1964, p. 47)

It is clear that the Party and the ideology can no longer play this role for many Soviet citizens. This is a very serious problem, because "Russia has always been, in various ways, a society of believers, its culture a belief culture" (Tucker, 1987, p. 207). Marxism-Leninism, as a belief system, has lost vitality and is being challenged in a multitude of ways. For the ordinary Soviet citizen (and much of the elite) this is profoundly unsettling, because it challenges the values and priorities of a lifetime. If the reform is successful, it must include a belief system that will make the Soviet people comfortable with "a mixed economy, a non-repressive polity, . . . an unregimented cultural life," a tolerance for diversity, and a cooperative stance toward the rest of the world (Tucker, 1987, pp. 208–209). This would be a profound departure from the past, but it could also create a Soviet Union that would be more worth believing in.

The Unifying Function

Soviet ideology has been unifying in its attempt to rise above and gloss over religious, nationality, and other differences. This has had both international and domestic relevance. It supplied doctrinal cohesion with foreign communist parties and socialist movements. Also, it justified the maintenance of the international socialist system against threats to any of its members (the rationale for the now repudiated 1968 invasion of Czechoslovakia). The emphasis on a classless society attempted to dignify manual labor and mitigated the divisive problem of class distinctions. Being antinationalist, Marxism-Leninism could justify the repression of "bourgeois nationalism" on the part of nationality groups within the country in favor of rule by the party that represents all workers of all nationalities (Wesson, 1972, pp. 142–145).

Unfortunately for both the reform leadership and the Soviet Union itself, this unifying function was not very effective in erasing differences, but only in hiding them behind a facade of unity. With glasnost and democratization, divisive forces have burst to the surface and threaten the future of the reform effort, domestic peace and security, and even the territorial integrity of the Soviet Union as a nation. It is clear that the ideology failed decisively to unify the country in any valid way. Given both the level of diversity and the lack of toleration for diversity that currently exists among the various Soviet peoples, it is difficult to see what will serve to unify the Soviet Union in the future. In some ways, the need to find a way of performing the unifying function may be one of the most difficult problems facing the current Soviet leadership.

REFERENCES

BELL, D. (1965). Ideology and Soviet politics. *Slavic Review, 24,* 601.

BERMAN, H.J. (1963). *Justice in the USSR.* New York: Vintage.

BRZEZINSKI, Z. and Huntington, S. (1964). *Political power: USA/USSR.* New York: John Wiley.

BUKOVSKY, V. (1978). *To build a castle: My life as a dissenter.* New York: Viking.

CHRISTENSON, R. and others. (1971). *Ideologies and modern politics.* New York: Dodd, Mead.

COOK, P.F. (1974). The Soviet Union in the year 2000. Seminar notes from a talk delivered at the Russian Research Center of Harvard University, December 19, 1974.

DeMORGAN, A. (1947). Matter to spirit: Preface. In Burton Stevenson, ed., *The home book of quotations.* New York: Dodd, Mead.

DUTT, CLEMENS. (1961). *Fundamentals of Marxism-Leninism.* Moscow: Foreign Languages Publishing House.

EVANS, A. (1987). The new program of the CPSU: Changes in Soviet ideology. *Soviet Union, 14,* 1, 1–18.

FELDBRUGGE, F. and others. eds. (1985). *Encyclopedia of Soviet law.* Dordrecht, The Netherlands: Martinus Nijhoff.

FISCHER, L. (1964). *The life of Lenin.* New York: Harper and Row.

GORBACHEV, M. (1987). *Perestroika: New thinking for our country and the world.* New York: Harper and Row.

INGERSOLL, D.E. and MATTHEWS, R.K. (1986). *The philosophic roots of modern ideology.* Englewood Cliffs, NJ: Prentice-Hall.

KASSOF, A. (1965). *The Soviet youth program.* Cambridge: Harvard University Press.

KENNAN, E.L. (1986). Muscovite political folkways. *The Russian Review, 45,* 115-181.
KRAPIVIN, V. (1985). *What is dialectical materialism?* Moscow: Progress Publishers.
LAIRD, R. and LAIRD, B. (1988). *A Soviet lexicon.* Lexington, MA: Lexington.
LANE, R. (1962). *Political ideology.* New York: Free Press.
LEONHARD, W. (1974). *Three faces of Marxism.* New York: Holt, Rinehart and Winston.
LOWENTHAL, R. (1960). The logic of one-party rule. In A. Dallin, ed., *Soviet conduct in world affairs.* New York: Columbia University Press.
MANN, D. (1990). An argument for legalizing opposition to the CPSU. *Report on the USSR, 2,* 11, 11-12.
MCNEILL, T. (1977). Historiography belies history: The CPSU remakes the past. *Radio Liberty Research,* no. 127/77.
MEYER, A.G. (1966). The functions of ideology in the Soviet political system. *Soviet Studies,* 17, 273-285.
Nauchnyi kommunizm. (1985). Moscow: Publishing House for Political Literature.
Observer (1969). *Message from Moscow.* New York: Alfred A. Knopf.
PONOMAREV, B.N., ed. (1958). *Politicheskii slovar'.* Moscow: Publishing House for Political Literature.
SAKHAROV, A. (1977). On Aleksandr Solzhenitsyn's letter to the Soviet leaders. In M. Meerson-Aksenov and B. Shragin, eds., *The political, social and religious thought of Russian "samizdat"—an anthology.* Belmont, MA: Nordland.
SARGENT, L.T. (1987). *Contemporary political ideologies.* Chicago: Dorsey.
SHLAPENTOKH, V. (1986). *Soviet public opinion and ideology.* New York: Praeger.
SHLAPENTOKH, V. (1988). The XXVII Congress—A case study of the shaping of a new Party ideology. *Soviet Studies,* 40, 1-20.
SHRAGIN, B. (1974). The International Conference of Slavists at Banff, Canada. *Radio Liberty Research,* no. 330.
TODD, E. (1979). *The final fall.* New York: Karz.
TUCKER, R., ed. (1978). *The Marx-Engels reader.* Second edition. New York: W.W. Norton.
TUCKER, R. (1978). *Political culture and leadership in Soviet Russia.* New York: W.W. Norton.
WESSON, R.G. (1972). *The Soviet Russian state.* New York: John Wiley.
WILES, P. (1964). *The political economy of communism.* Cambridge, MA: Harvard University Press.

FOUR
POLITICAL CULTURE AND SOCIALIZATION:
The Era of Glasnost

In our eyes, the meaningful formation of a new Soviet culture has begun. And, together with it, a political person who is participant in the public process—with his own opinions and positions, with his own preferences and activities. (Fedor Burlatskii, *Pravda,* July 18, 1987, p. 3)

It seems to me that the process of democratization and perestroika is having a pernicious effect on some people. It is as if they had been waiting to irresponsibly criticize and blacken everything on earth, without asking the question: Is this in the interests of socialism, for the good of the Soviet Motherland? (N. Pavlov, letter to *Pravda,* September 14, 1987, p. 3)

A political culture is a set of beliefs about politics and government that is widely shared by a group of people, usually the citizens of some political unit, such as a nation. These beliefs tend to be so basic that the people who hold them are largely unconscious of them; they simply take them for granted. To the extent that they think about them at all, everyone in a political culture *assumes* that most or all others share their beliefs. Often "it is literally impossible for them to conceive how it could be different" (Elkins and Simeon, 1979, p. 137). A person is most likely to become consciously aware of his or her political culture when it is being challenged, during times of radical change.

In the Soviet Union, until recently, the control of the Communist Party was so pervasive that, for most people, the Party leadership could decisively influence the content of political culture.[1] It was aided in this by the beliefs and attitudes its people inherited from hundreds of years of autocratic rule in Russia and in most of the other lands which now make up the Soviet Union. Since the Revolution in 1917, there had been little in the social sphere that had not been touched by official Communist imperatives. Even the conduct of private life was heavily influenced by political considerations. As Burlatskii implies in the previous quotation, the private citizen was essentially passive. Politics was the active concern of a relatively small number of people, primarily the leadership and Party activists. With the advent of political reform, the situation began to change. If the current governmental and electoral reforms persist, the potential role of the individual in the political process will be far greater than in the past. At the same time, much of the economic reform will reduce direct Party control over the economy and, as a result, shrink the scope of what is considered overtly "political."

In this chapter, we will be considering the way in which Soviet citizens acquire the beliefs and attitudes of their political culture—their political socialization. In this, the era of glasnost, analyzing the process is no easy matter. Many of the most important rules of the game seem to be constantly changing. And as can be seen in Pavlov's letter (quoted previously), not everyone is comfortable with these changes. Despite such objections, it is probably safe to say that the Soviet Union will never be quite the same again. In short, Soviet political culture is in a state of flux, and it is impossible to know when and how it will stabilize and what it will be like when it does.

At present, the regime is attempting to socialize people to accept and support radical changes in their political culture. This is inherently a problem. Radical change introduces so much uncertainty in people's lives that there seems to be an instinctive tendency on the part of most people to resist. Change appeals most to risk takers and to those who think they have nothing to lose. Most Soviet citizens do not fall into either category. The problem is aggravated by the fact that there is disagreement within the political elite over the methods, pace, and ultimate goals of reform. Political socialization in the Soviet Union today, then, is aimed at a moving target. This causes considerable confusion and uncertainty both inside and outside that country.

There are two basic perspectives that can be used in thinking about political socialization (Barner-Barry and Rosenwein, 1985, pp. 80–81). First, there is the perspective of the individual. From this point of view, socialization is the process through which a person acquires political attitudes, beliefs, and patterns of behavior. Second—and emphasized in this chapter—there is the group or institutional perspective. From this point of view, socialization is the process by which persons or groups attempt to influence the development and evolution of political beliefs, attitudes, and behavior in others. Usually, this is

---

[1]There are clear exceptions to this generalization. In this connection, see Chapter 11.

a status quo–oriented process. The current political regime, aided by other segments of the society, such as the schools or patriotic organizations, attempts to mold and maintain "good citizens."

It need not, however, be status quo oriented. For example, some families or groups may consciously attempt to produce nonconformists or to convert individuals into "rebels" or "reformers." The latter is precisely what the Gorbachev regime is currently trying to do. This process is made more difficult by the inescapable fact of selective perception and retention, which leads people to see the present largely in terms of their past experiences. Also, there is the natural diversity of human beings, which leads them to process incoming information in varying ways. Therefore, each individual takes the political information supplied and creates his or her own personal ideas about "political reality."

Because of the Soviet leadership's heavy use of mass communication, it is fairly easy to identify the nature and direction of its conscious efforts to socialize its people. In its attempt to foster "proper" beliefs and behaviors in the population, the political elite has historically used a wide range of resources. These have included a rigidly state-controlled press and educational system. Now, in the era of glasnost, the job has become more complicated and both the people and their leaders are struggling with the problem of where to draw the line regarding freedom of political expression, be it verbal or behavioral. In many ways, the "human factor" is the most unpredictable and troublesome factor in the entire reform effort (Gorbachev, 1987).

What is glasnost? The word, glasnost, is usually translated "openness" or "publicity," but can be translated "candor." It is not a new idea in Russian or Soviet political culture. In the 1850s and 1860s it was a slogan of the reformists and was used by Lenin early in the Soviet period. It was a motto of the 1960s and 1970s among dissidents advocating greater freedom of expression. And Andropov invoked glasnost to point to the need to make the Party more responsive to the people in combating corruption and mismanagement (Tucker, 1987, p. 145; Kirk, 1975, pp. ix, 112). It is fair to say, however, that Mikhail Gorbachev has given glasnost new significance, as well as making it one of the few Russian words most well informed, non-Russian-speaking people know. In the years since 1985, when Gorbachev became General Secretary of the CPSU, glasnost has become the label for a gradually increasing willingness to be more honest about the problems, as well as the successes, of the Soviet past and present.

At the moment, it is probably fair to say that glasnost is the success story of the reform—albeit a mixed blessing from the point of view of the often embattled leadership. While it has proved hard for the regime to produce quick and easy gains in the economic sphere, it has been easier to create much more freedom of expression. Glasnost, however, is not without its opponents. In fact, one of the major tasks of the reform is defining the scope and limits of glasnost. Even those who support reform are frequently uneasy with the embarrassing revelations that have been made in the name of glasnost, especially about the evils of the Stalin era and the failures of the recent past. From Gorbachev on down, they see some of the uses of glasnost as encouraging discord within Soviet society. On the other hand, there are those who are constantly calling for more revelations in increasingly sensitive areas. The greater freedom experienced by Soviet citizens has not only led to more freedom of speech. It has also taken the form of actions which range from peaceful demonstrations to political violence.

Thus, for the leadership, there is the constant problem of how to balance demands for more glasnost against the fear of anarchy. Since periodic outbursts of political violence were a hallmark of Russian history long before the Soviet period, these concerns have some rational basis. In general, however, Gorbachev has leaned in the more liberal direction on glasnost. This may be because it is a much easier area in which to bring about rapid, significant change for the better. Also, after unleashing the dissatisfaction of the Soviet people with the previous state of their economy and political life, he can try to use this dissatisfaction to gain their active support for major economic and political reform.

Glasnost has greatly affected the entire political socialization process in the USSR. In this chapter, we will be looking at those customs and institutions which are the vehicles by which Soviet political culture has been passed on from one generation to another. Because the situation is currently in a state of rapid change, we will confine ourselves largely to describing—as accurately as possible in a period of uncertainty—what is happening. At this point in time it is only possible to make informed guesses about where all of this is leading and about what the long term impact will be.

More specifically, we will focus on the symbols and formal institutions the Soviet leadership has traditionally used to influence the development of its citizens' political attitudes, beliefs, and behavior. We will look first at the characteristics and aims of the socializing process. Next, we will consider the institutions through which the process is carried out. Throughout the discussion, we will try to indicate the ways in which they seem to be changing.

THE MAIN CHARACTERISTICS
OF THE SOCIALIZATION PROCESS

Certain approaches to political socialization have traditionally been so pervasive in Soviet life that they could fairly be characterized as major aspects of Soviet political culture. Some of them seem to have been more affected by the reform than others. The ones we think are most important are (1) the large-scale use of political symbols and messages; (2) the manipulation of information to achieve political goals; (3) the expectation that citizens "voluntarily" participate in political activity; (4) the responsibility of individuals for each other's behavior; and (5) the use of rewards and punishments to achieve politically desirable behavior. Because of the state of flux in Soviet political culture, we will confine our discussion of these to the situation as it was in the recent past and the way in which it seems to be changing. After this, we will move to a more concrete consideration of the institutions that have a socializing impact (at least theoretically) on Soviet citizens at various points in their lives.

The Pervasiveness of Political Symbols and Messages

November seventh, it is clear
Is the reddest day in all the year.
Through the window look ahead,
Everything outside is red!

(Soviet child's nursery school
rhyme; Bukovsky, 1979, p. 60)

In terms of the visual dimension alone, the ubiquity of politics has traditionally been staggering. Particularly during national holidays, Soviet cities and villages have taken on a highly political aspect. To a lesser extent this has been true throughout the year. The color red has appeared everywhere. There have been banners lauding the glory of the Communist Party and the Soviet People and exhorting everyone to work harder for the greater glory of the Soviet Union. There have been pictures and statues of the great heroes of communism, Marx, Engels, and Lenin, as well as the leaders of the current regime. There have also been pictures, albeit much smaller of ordinary people—that is, people who are ordinary in most respects, but who may have distinguished themselves in service to the Soviet Union by manufacturing more screwdriver handles than anyone else in the factory or by performing an equivalent feat in other walks of life. There have often been pictures of dead or living foreign heroes together with expressions of solidarity with their struggle against the oppressors of their people.

These political symbols could be found everywhere—in subways, in schoolrooms, in ships, in offices, on billboards, on sides of buildings, on book covers, and in store windows. In short, it has always been difficult to go about daily life without seeing a political message frequently. If you add to this the same sort of message in the audio dimension—from radio and television—the effect was overwhelming. And, we suspect, the average Soviet citizen probably tuned it out most of the time. To the extent they did not, it seems to have fostered a cynical attitude toward everything and everybody portrayed in this propaganda barrage.

This situation has presented the reformers with both a problem and an opportunity. To the extent that they are trying to mobilize the active support of the public, they are hampered by the fact that many have become numb and cynical. The messages of the reformers about the benefits of change, thus, tend to be ignored or regarded as just more empty promises. To the extent, however, that the reformers are willing to make obvious changes, they immediately capture the attention of the public by jarring them out of their accustomed apathy. This is one of the reasons why glasnost has been relatively effective. For example, television was previously so boring that anything smacking of investigative—or even entertaining—journalism attracts a large audience. Live broadcasts of the new Supreme Soviet are watched, unlike live coverage of the U.S. Congress, which evokes almost universal indifference. One reason why economic reform is much harder to bring about is the lack of any equally concrete means of overcoming public apathy and cynicism.

The current leadership has shown its sensitivity to this problem by beginning to soft-pedal this aspect of the propaganda system. The two times of the year at which it has peaked have been the two major political holidays, November 7 (the anniversary of the Bolshevik Revolution) and May 1 (International Workers' Day). Recent celebrations have shown a new restraint in the use of political symbols and messages. Everything is still decked with red banners and patriotic symbols. But portraits of Soviet leaders—with the exception of Lenin—have been conspicuously absent. Political slogans, although still used, are not as numerous and are more restrained in content. Thus, the new leadership seems to be more sensitive to the problems associated with propaganda overkill.

The Manipulation of Information

The way people view life and their role in it is greatly influenced by information about their surroundings and the wider world. Until recently, Soviet citizens have had a very limited perspective. What they learned about their country and the rest of the world was what the Party leadership decided they should know. There was little of the clamor of competing and often contradictory information that constantly assaults us. Certainly the more thoughtful people, like some of the Moscow University students and faculty among whom we have lived, knew that important information was being withheld. They realized the implications of the periodically occurring changes in what was "true." It would have been misleading, however, to generalize from these few elite and intellectually gifted members of the society to the entire population. The average Soviet citizen probably still does not think much about whether he has an accurate picture of the world.

This situation also poses both a problem and an opportunity for the reformers. For Soviet intellectuals, glasnost has brought a rapid increase in more accurate information, which has been highly significant and energizing. This is critical from the point of view of the reformers, because the active support of these intellectuals is needed to plan and implement the reform. The increase in reliable information has, however, barely caused a ripple in the daily life of the average Soviet citizen. For them, the burning issue is not having a more accurate and complete picture of the world. Rather, it is how well the stores are stocked and the quality of the lifestyle available to them. In fact, if anything, the barrage of information about societal problems glasnost has unleashed calls their attention to all the problems inherent in getting those stores better stocked and in achieving that lifestyle. This can, and does, foster discontent with the current leadership.

In a technologically advanced country like the Soviet Union, the educational system is the chief source of information about the world, and the Soviet educational system has been tightly and centrally controlled. Only books and teaching which would inculcate the "correct" attitudes and information were allowed. Moreover, rote learning was emphasized. Questioning and innovative thinking were discouraged. When he was *New York Times* correspondent in Moscow during the Brezhnev era, David Shipler came to the following conclusion:

> Nowhere in the younger years are the style of education and the matrix of expectation more clearly visible than in the approach to art. The stress is on drawing, painting, or modelling realistically, often according to a rigid prescription. In one class, youngsters made clay roosters all looking the same. The teacher was quite proud. . . . Teachers display considerable uneasiness about artwork that is out of the well-defined groove. An American friend, watching a class of eight-year-olds in Moscow copy a drawing of a snowman with such precision that their work might have been paper tracings, noticed one boy coloring his snowman yellow. The youngster received a stern reprimand. (Shipler, 1983, pp. 60–61)

The teacher who encouraged students to question and probe was not likely to last long—at least outside of the most advanced and elite scientific institutions.

This did not mean that Soviet students were taught only lies and distortions. There were disciplines, like physics, mathematics, and geology, in which the curriculum differed little from the norm in other parts of the world. This was also true of substantial subfields within disciplines, such as those areas of law that were not politically sensitive. In other fields, however, like Soviet history, teaching was expected to reflect the Party line of the moment. Attempts to achieve a balanced and factually based presentation of significant historical events was condemned as "bourgeois objectivism."

This approach to education has also affected the course of economic reform. To move the economy in a more entrepreneurial direction and to make Soviet products competitive in the world market, a much more innovative spirit is necessary. This is difficult to achieve when the people who must make this happen have been taught to define the "right" answer to a problem as the answer that is pleasing to the teacher or that follows the Party line most closely. In this sense, the traditional Soviet educational system has probably made a large proportion of the Soviet population unable to take the kind of individual initiative that is now being urged upon them by the reformers.

Also, although the vast Soviet propaganda machine is encouraging them to participate in the reform, many Soviet citizens see this as just another campaign to make them work harder and take unwelcome risks. These problems were acknowledged by the Party Central Committee in 1987 when it announced a new plan for the continuing political and economic education of workers (*Pravda,* April 15, 1987, pp. 1–2). Stating that the existing system had failed to convey an adequate understanding of the reform, the leadership mandated the use of discussion of differences of opinion in political and economic education classes designed for workers.

What was true of the education system was true of the media. Newspapers, television, radio, books, periodicals, and other forms of mass communication were strictly and centrally controlled. Their role was bringing the Party's policy to the people. One of the main areas in which glasnost has had a substantial impact is in the stance of the media. Although it cannot be said that Soviet journalists are as free as most Western journalists, they are no longer obliged to parrot the Party line. As a result, there has been a flowering of investigative journalism.

Different newspapers and periodicals have taken on dramatically different political colorations, and issues are being debated in a way that was unimaginable just a few years ago. Television has also begun to do its share. In the process, it has become much more responsive to the needs and preferences of its viewers and, not incidentally, considerably more interesting. In short, what seems to be happening is a kind of "normalization" of the Soviet media making it more comparable to the media in the Western world.

Finally, information was controlled by strict limitations which the government put on contact with persons and ideas from outside the Soviet Union. There was a virtually constant campaign to discourage informal contacts between Soviet citizens and foreigners, and the campaign became more or less strident as the situation demanded. Now we see Western politicians being interviewed by Soviet journalists, as well as Soviet leaders being interviewed by Western journalists—and both of these being made available to the Soviet public. More Soviet citizens than ever are visiting the West, frequently even staying in private homes. And, perhaps most surprisingly, Soviet and American military experts are being given tours of each other's previously top secret military facilities. Finally, all jamming of foreign broadcasts into the Soviet Union ended in 1988.

Most of this is being both covered and commented on by the Soviet media. As a Soviet friend remarked to one of the authors, "There is so much in the press nowadays that I can't find time to read all of it." In fact, some journals and newspapers have become so popular that the publishers periodically have problems meeting the demand for subscriptions and newsstand copies. Again, however, it is probable that this change is more significant to some parts of the Soviet populace than to others.

"Voluntary" Participation

Experimental and other research by Western psychologists in the area of role playing is suggestive with regard to Soviet political socialization. According to Daryl Bem, "it would seem very difficult to play a particular role all of one's life without 'internalizing' part of it, that is, without beginning to believe part of it" (Bem, 1970, p. 66). This effect can be seen in the following anecdote by a former Soviet citizen:

> I knew, for instance, a student who was Russian. Very bright. I remember his reading Solzhenitsyn during our second year. I knew about it: we sort of trusted each other. But then he joined the Party, and is making a big career. But at the same time, in the depths of his heart he disliked the regime very much. But you can't live with a split personality. It's very difficult. You have to justify what you are doing. You can't be disgusted with yourself. *You have to readjust your philosophy to your way of life.* (Swafford, 1979, p. 32)

This adds considerable significance to the fact that one of the hallmarks of Soviet society is the pressure for Soviet citizens to participate in a great number and variety of politically significant activities. They are not paid to participate; they may choose not to. But the subtle pressure of expectation is everywhere and it falls disproportionately on the young, on Party members, and on non-Party members occupying key positions. One learns at a very young age that to "get ahead" one has to do some things "voluntarily."

From cradle to grave, regime-sanctioned political activity, whether motivated by sincere belief or sheer opportunism, seems to be important if you are ambitious. It can result in leadership positions in school, coveted educational opportunities, the best jobs, good housing, and so forth. These rewards, however, are not direct and immediate. Rather, they seem to come when they come, but it has been a good calculated risk that they will—sooner or later. The Soviet citizen who volunteers more or less opportunistically, then, may hope that the rewards will come; but there is no guarantee.

If Bem and his fellow psychologists are right, a person in this position will be more likely to change attitudes than one who can count on a direct and immediate reward. In addition, there is a wealth of social-psychological evidence suggesting that actively playing a role is more likely to socialize a person to a given set of beliefs than if that person is merely the passive receiver of someone else's indoctrination efforts. Seldom is the Communist Youth

League (*Komsomol*)[2] member paid off directly and immediately for volunteering to give political lectures at a factory. This person is most likely, however, to be pushed unconsciously a little further in the direction of believing the political message which these lectures contain. At the very least, the Soviet system of "volunteer politics" replaces unstructured free time with structured efforts at building political support for the system and current regime.

What are some of the most common jobs for which "volunteers" are expected? A Communist Youth League member might be put in charge of the program for a group of Young Pioneers.[3] Members might volunteer at their school or university to clean lab equipment or paint walls, or to do needed farm work during holidays. Perhaps the classic type of "volunteer" labor is the *subbotnik* (from the Russian word for Saturday, *subbota*). As the name implies, it involves voluntary unpaid work on Saturdays and began in 1919 (Luke, 1985, p. 130).

Currently, a *subbotnik* is celebrated with great fanfare on the Saturday nearest the birthday of Lenin (April 22), though they may also take place at other times of the year. All workers are expected to do an extra day of work; the money earned or saved is collected and spent on some socially beneficial project, such as a research center. There is a tremendous media "hype," and some celebrities contribute labors that are symbolic and inspirational. For example, during a 1980 *subbotnik* the Soviet cosmonauts orbiting the earth symbolically vacuum cleaned their spaceship. The average Soviet citizen, however, does nothing more glamorous or exciting than work an extra day for no pay. For example, after the 1988 April *subbotnik* the Soviet evening news (*Vremia,* April 18, 1988) announced that 156 million workers had participated at their place of work contributing one billion 380 million rubles worth of labor. In 1987, glasnost-inspired letters began to arrive in the offices of some newspapers complaining about the fact that the *subbotnik* often amounted simply to unpaid labor forced on workers. For example, one writer said that his local officials resorted to the *subbotnik* when leaves fell or when there were snow storms, rather than properly mobilizing municipal services (*CDSP, 39,* no. 49, 1987, p. 19).

In general, there has been a dilution of this Party-based volunteer labor system during the reform period. This has not, however, necessarily meant that less volunteer work was being performed (although it might). What has been most notable is the extent to which politically active Soviet citizens have been turning their energies toward volunteer activities outside Party auspices. This has caused the growth of many new organizations, some—but not all—devoted to political goals. Whether these activities will help them "get ahead,"

[2]The Communist Youth League is an organization for people from fifteen to twenty-seven years of age.

[3]An organization for children age ten to fifteen.

as Party-related work has in the past, remains to be seen. To some extent it is dependent on the degree to which political pluralism takes hold and flourishes in the Soviet political context.

Collective Responsibility

Every Soviet citizen has definitely been his brother's or sister's keeper. Your behavior used to be and still is everybody's business. One of the authors can recall the following experience:

> I was sitting in a trolley car, nose buried in a book, when I heard an imperious "DEVUSHKA!" ("YOUNG WOMAN!") It soon became clear that it was directed at me, so I looked up—into the face of a righteously indignant middle-aged Soviet woman. Having finally gotten my attention, the woman began abusing me for my lack of courtesy. When I protested innocence (after all, I was quietly sitting and reading and bothering no one), I found that my sin was one of omission. Unnoticed by me, an elderly woman had gotten onto the trolley and, in the opinion of the indignant woman at least (and no one contradicted her), I should have made it my business to notice this fact and leap up offering my seat. The fact that I had not seen the old woman was irrelevant. Sheepishly, I got up and offered my seat; there was little else to do, since ignorance was obviously no defense and it was equally obvious that the old woman did need to sit more than I did. I soon came to dread the sound of the imperious "DEVUSHKA!" It invariably meant an embarrassing incident during which I would be hard put to defend myself, but it did make me much more guarded in my behavior than I had ever been in the United States.

More recently, a visiting journalist observed that "complete strangers will come up and tell you that you must tie your shoelaces, that you mustn't swim in the river after a picnic, that your car is dirty and you should clean it" (*The Washington Post,* August 19, 1982, p. A1).

This phenomenon, which might be regarded as an officially sanctioned busybodyism, is one of the most difficult things for Westerners to adjust to in Soviet life. Whereas we are taught to mind our own business, Soviet children are taught responsibility for their playmates' behavior. This lesson is begun in the early school years when classroom teachers are supposed to encourage competition between rows of children to see which row can achieve the highest standards of behavior and performance. Large charts are posted in the school giving the standings of the rows, both for single activities and overall. Later the children "graduate" from membership in rows to membership in Young Pioneer and *Komsomol* groups. This system covers a wide range of activities. For example, a superior student may be assigned to help an inferior one. This type of peer group supervision does not end with childhood. When we lived in the dormitory at Moscow University, we were subject to periodic unannounced cleanliness inspections by our *Komsomol* floor committee. The results of these inspections were posted in the lobby for all to read.[4] The special impact of such experiences on young people grows out of the vulnerability of children and teenagers to peer influences. Being reminded of your shortcomings can be doubly painful if it is in the presence of your peers.

This form of socialization continues throughout life when the school collective is replaced by a housing collective or a work collective. These groups, unknown in the United States, are very powerful in the Soviet Union. They have the capacity to supervise almost all facets of a member's life, be it relations with his or her spouse, the discipline of children, or the diligence with which a job is done. The central role of the collective in Soviet life can be seen in the following quotation from a Soviet book on social psychology:

> The moral foundation of the personality is laid in the family, but the full flowering and formation of the personality of human beings can be achieved only in the working collective. That is, in the working collective, where common labor is carried out on the principle of comradely cooperation and mutual aid and where the unity of state, social and individual interests is assured, a person can completely realize himself and have the sensation of being a participant in a common cause—the building of communism. (Semenova, 1984, p. 84)

This emphasis on the centrality of the work collective to the organization of Soviet life has recently received attention in Soviet law. A law "On Work Collectives and Increasing Their Role in the Management of Enterprises, Institutions and Organizations," was adopted in 1983 (*Izvestiia,* June 18, 1983, pp. 2–5; *Izvestiia,* June 19, 1983, pp. 1–2). Its thrust was toward consultation with workers in periodic mass meetings. Actual worker participation in management did not seem to be intended (Teague, 1984). For many workers, however, increased participation has come about with the electoral reforms, which permit them to vote for their top management, as well as with the tendency of strike committees to remain active in monitoring their supervisors and local political leaders.

All this emphasis on collectivism may seem alien to those who place a high value on individualism. But there is a positive side: collectivism's contribution to preserving public order. Jane Jacobs in her landmark book, *The Death and Life of Great American Cities,* makes the point that the safety of city streets is directly related to the extent to which there are "eyes upon the street, eyes belonging to those we might call the natural proprietors of the street" (Jacobs, 1961, p. 35). A neighborhood in which there is a sense of community responsibility for what happens on the streets and in the corridors of buildings will be much safer than one in which there is none. Though this

[4]One wonders about the extent to which the declining popularity of the *Komsomol* might be associated with such activities—now that it is more possible to express and act on previously suppressed resentment.

is not the whole story, the positive features of collective responsibility should not be overshadowed by its all-too-obvious potential for abuse.

The Carrot and the Stick

In Western commentaries more emphasis has been placed on the punishments which have threatened Soviet citizens than on the rewards which have lured them. Thus, Westerners who have regularly read or seen media reports on the Soviet Union tend to be quite well informed on the mistreatment of those Soviet citizens who have not conformed to the wishes of the leadership. They are much less aware of the benefits to be derived from going along with the system. In part, this has been a result of the choices made by Western reporters and editors; we too are prone to have our opinions molded by the information that is fed us by the mass media. The saving grace is that this selection is not controlled from the center as the Soviet version has been.

Our bias is much more related to the fact that the experiences of opposition leaders and colorful figures make better stories. But it also stems from the relative ease with which North Americans and Western Europeans understand the punishments. The attractiveness to Soviet citizens of many of the rewards is difficult to comprehend because the conditions of Soviet life are so different. For example, it would seldom be effective to bribe an American to compromise his beliefs by promising him the opportunity to rent a desirable apartment. In the Soviet Union, however, most people live in housing that would be considered substandard by Americans. Even some of the newest and "nicest" apartment complexes resemble nothing so much as crudely built public housing in the United States. These, though, are an improvement over a single room or a shared single-family size apartment. Coupled with this is the fact that rents in the Soviet Union are so low that almost anyone can afford a desirable apartment—the trick is to find one. This is where having good connections with powerful officials becomes valuable.

The system of rewards tends to be an interlocking affair in which the acquisition of some of the rewards significantly increases a person's chances for further rewards. First, and perhaps most crucial, is educational opportunity. In the Soviet Union to a much greater extent than in the West, higher education or advanced training has been the key to upward mobility and financial success.[5] To realize your ambitions, you must first be admitted to one of the top universities, institutes, or training schools. Known "troublemakers" have found the path strewn with obstacles, as have the children of known "troublemakers." Now, with the definition of "troublemaker" blurring, the efficacy of this as a punishment may diminish significantly in the future.

The good "connections" that lead to a good education have also tended

---

[5]This may gradually change if and when entrepreneurial opportunities increase significantly.

to lead to a good job in a desirable location (preferably Moscow or Leningrad). Good jobs pay well. And if the job is prestigious enough, it may also carry with it better than average housing accommodations, a second home in the country, household help, an automobile, and numerous other luxuries. To date, the reformers have cut back on these privileges to only a limited extent. The effort is to gradually tie these rewards to the possession and productive use of special skills or education, as well as entrepreneurial ability. Other rewards, which have been accessible to even the humblest factory or collective-farm worker, have included awards for unusually successful groups of workers, medals for outstanding individual workers, and official titles (like "Heroine Mother" for bearing and raising ten or more children). Increasingly these are being converted into monetary rewards more geared to productivity in world terms.

If this describes a sampling of the rewards, what of the punishments? The punishments have often been the opposite of the rewards. You might be denied admission to a university, institute, or trade school. If graduated, you could be assigned to an inappropriate or low-status job in some undesirable and remote place. This could, in turn, bring low pay or good pay in a situation where there is little to spend it on. Also, your lack of priority would probably result in inferior housing conditions. Although these were some of the milder punishments, they were not to be scoffed at, since they could greatly affect your daily life.

More ominous were the punishments reserved for the "difficult" cases. Although the use of these has greatly diminished since Gorbachev took office, they still occur from time to time. First, and perhaps mildest, is the constant harassment experienced by nonconforming Soviet citizens and, on occasion, their families or friends. Measures in this category include dismissal from one's job or the voiding of one's residence permit to live in a desirable location. More extreme is incarceration in a prison, which now seems to be used only in extreme cases and for relatively short periods of time. One of the most extreme current measures is simply getting the person out of the Soviet Union permanently. Trotsky was exiled in this way in 1929, but the measure was not used again until 1974, when the Nobel Laureate Solzhenitsyn was arrested, questioned, and summarily flown out of the Soviet Union. In the Gorbachev era, it was used to exile a leader of the movement to get Nagorno-Karabakh annexed to Soviet Armenia. On the whole, however, people whom the regime might consider troublemakers are usually willing to leave the country if they are given permission. Increasingly, the Soviet government has been willing to give that permission.

The punishment-reward approach is probably the least effective approach to political socialization. Why? A person clearly threatened with punishment or enticed with rewards is more likely to be openly defiant or to go along with what is expected without altering basic attitudes and values. If successful political socialization is to be defined as something more than eliciting external compliance (and we think it should be), conformity without conviction is not the most desirable outcome of the process. As indicated previously, however, there is evidence that if a person plays a role for a long enough period of time, there is a good chance attitudes will change to become more in tune with the role.

MAJOR SOCIALIZING INSTITUTIONS

Now that we know some of the more important ways in which the message can be conveyed, it is time to look at the medium. In a sense, it is virtually impossible to single out a small group of institutions that can be said to do the job of political socialization in any country. This is even more true in the Soviet Union, where virtually every facet of life brings a person into contact with political messages. The only reasonable thing to do is to concentrate on those institutions that bear the brunt of the socializing task. This will be done here on an institution-by-institution basis in the approximate order the average Soviet citizen might come into closest contact with them during his or her journey from cradle to grave.

The Family

The first and most obvious institution in a person's life is the family. In the Soviet Union, families come in a variety of compositions and sizes, ranging from the extended family of Central Asia to the two-person families of many unwed mothers. The most common type is the urban nuclear family composed of mother, father, and one or two children. There was a time when there was considerable conflict over child-rearing methods and values between the young Soviet regime and the traditional families of the various Soviet nationalities. This friction has gradually declined over the years, since Soviet parents are now persons born and raised well after the Revolution and since the policies of the government have changed. For example, religious training was once a major source of tension between families and the government. Now, although there are clearly many exceptions, a large number of Soviet parents have no strong religious beliefs. Also, the government has recently become significantly more tolerant of religious practice and education.

Attachment to old customs of child raising is also fading—rapidly in the cities and slowly in rural areas and ethnic strongholds such as Central Asia. The evidence is strong that a majority of Soviet parents are, for many reasons (including expediency, ideological agreement, and job pressures), more than willing to shift significant responsibility to the state. That is, they view political socialization as the job of the educational system and of youth groups. The family's role is seen as supportive, rather than central. The most common form of parental participation in political socialization is the discussion of domestic and foreign current events, as well as of the ideological and political content of art and literature. According to a recent report (Semenova, 1984, pp. 45–46), more than 40 percent of older schoolchildren regularly discuss political news with their fathers. Another 31 percent hold such discussions periodically. These discussions are based mainly on newspaper, radio, and television news reports.

The Educational System and Youth Organizations

We must have *a contemporary concept of the democratic management of public education,* a necessary shift from conservative methods of management to democratic ones. . . . I am speaking, first of all, about the widest possible development of self-government in institutions of basic and higher education. (E.K. Ligachev, *Pravda,* February 18, 1988, p. 3. Emphasis in the original)

The Soviet educational process has traditionally been centrally controlled by the various all-union (national) and union republic educational bureaucracies. Currently, as the preceding quotation indicates, there is a movement toward giving more autonomy to both schools and teachers. One of the first steps in this direction was the abolishment in 1988 of the USSR Ministry of Education, the USSR Ministry of Higher and Secondary Specialized Education, and the State Committee for Vocational and Technical Education. These three were replaced by a new State Committee for Public Education. This was significant because it allowed the reformers to get rid of many entrenched bureaucrats, whom they blamed for the failure of previous school reforms and for the generally unsatisfactory state of Soviet education (see, for example, *Pravda,* December 21, 1988 p. 3).

The Soviet educational establishment is a large one. As of 1987, approximately 110 million people were enrolled in a variety of types of educational programs (*Pravda,* January 24, 1988, p. 3). Preschool institutions are not, technically speaking, part of the Soviet educational system. However, they give about 17 million children (58 percent of the preschool population) their first educational experiences outside the family. Since about half of the Soviet work force is composed of women, the need for child care is substantial. Soviet parents usually solve child-care problems in one of two basic ways. One solution is the *babushka* (grandmother), who lives with the family and takes over the main burdens of housekeeping and child care. This situation was very widespread in the past, but is disappearing as professional and skilled mothers increasingly become professional and skilled grandmothers (see, for example, Pond, 1988, p. 33). The second solution, day-care centers, are destined to increase in importance in the future. There are two basic types: (1) the infant and toddler centers (*iasli*), which accept children up to the age of four, and (2) the nursery school–kindergartens (*detskie sady*), which accept four-to-six-year-olds.

Up to five years of age the educational emphasis is on health-promoting activities and the learning of basic skills, such as feeding and dressing oneself. At five, however, the process of instilling patriotic feelings in the children begins. There are simple lessons on their local community, the Soviet Army, and Lenin. Later, these are supplemented by lessons on the international situation and on other nationalities. Respect for Soviet national symbols, such as the flag, is also taught.

At age six the child enters the first grade and can expect to continue in school for the following eleven or twelve years. At this point begins a much more pronounced emphasis on the collective. The Soviet child immediately finds himself or herself a member of many groups that are in a constant state of competition. Rows in a classroom compete, classrooms in a school compete, and schools in a region compete. In this context it is not hard to understand why the notion of competition between social systems and competition between nations comes easily to a Soviet citizen. For them it is part of the natural order of things.

In short, competition is certainly not discouraged in the USSR. If anything, it receives more official emphasis in Soviet schools than in American schools. But there is one key difference: competition is between groups, not individuals. Among individuals in a group, cooperation and mutual aid are encouraged. "Individualism" is still frowned upon in the Soviet Union (*Pravda,* February 18, 1988, p. 4). And the mix of competition and cooperation becomes even more complex when competing groups at one level (e.g., the rows in a classroom) become part of a cooperating collective at another level (e.g., the classrooms in a school building).

Superimposed on this structure and further increasing its complexity is the competitive relationship between the "links," which are the smallest units of Soviet youth groups. The earliest youth group that a child may join (and virtually all do) is the Young Octobrists. This organization accepts children from seven to ten years old. At ten, the children may become Pioneers and, again, membership is almost universal. From the Pioneers the next step is the Young Communist League (*Komsomol*). Here universality of membership ceases. A degree of selectivity is introduced that is similar to, though less stringent than, the admission process necessary for Communist Party membership. At this level, persons are only admitted on an individual basis, not by whole classrooms, as is sometimes the case with Pioneers. Young people from ages fifteen to twenty-seven are eligible to become *Komsomol* members, but aspiring members must be sponsored either by a *Komsomol* member of two-years standing or by a Communist Party member. They must also give evidence of desirable character traits.

Together with the regular school courses in social studies, the members of these youth organizations get additional citizenship training during activities outside school. Let us use the Pioneers as an example, since their activities are probably formative for the largest number of Soviet adults. They have Pioneer Palaces and Houses, Young Technicians' stations, Young Naturalists' stations,

Young Tourists' stations, libraries, sports teams, art and music groups, and summer camps. Within this framework the members both learn and teach younger Pioneers.

The political and patriotic orientation of the Pioneers is clear in the ceremony for admission to membership. In the presence of older Pioneers, *Komsomols,* teachers, leaders, and parents, the new members take the following pledge:

> I (family name, first name), entering into the ranks of the All-union Lenin Pioneer Organization, in the presence of my comrades, do solemnly promise:
> —to fervently love my Motherland;
> —to live study and strive as Lenin willed and as the Communist Party teaches;
> —to always obey the rules of the Pioneers of the Soviet Union. (Kabush, 1985, p. 53)

Three of the rules which the Pioneer has promised to obey are:

> The Pioneer is committed to the Motherland, to the Party, and to communism.
> The Pioneer honors the memory of those who have died for their country and prepares to be a defender of the Motherland.
> The Pioneer is a friend to all Pioneers and to the children of the workers of all countries. (Kazanskaia, 1976, pp. 52–53)

The political content of the Pioneer program is also clear from such activities as participation in the November 7 and May Day parades, as well as ritual visits to lay flowers at monuments to Lenin. Indeed, the combination of attractive facilities and programs with a strong collectivist and patriotic message makes these youth groups potentially powerful agents of political socialization.

In 1984 the Supreme Soviet approved a school reform plan that was a product of the Brezhnev-Chernenko era (*Izvestiia,* April 13, 1984, pp. 1,4). The goal of this reform was to change the school from a primarily educational institution into a place where children would get much more training in citizenship and where they could be prepared for productive work by age sixteen (*Izvestiia,* May 4, 1984, pp. 1,3). These goals were to be realized by the early 1990s. Innovations were to include new textbooks and courses, such as a new social studies course designed to inculcate communist ideals, socialist internationalism, and pride in the USSR. Also, there was to be a new group of elective courses on ideology. Starting in the second grade, vocational training was to occupy an ever larger proportion of the school week, with many more children channeled into vocational-technical schools upon completing the ninth grade. This aspect of the reform seemed aimed at enlarging the size of the skilled labor pool and decreasing the number of students aspiring to higher education. It also seemed to be designed to improve the productivity of Soviet workers.

By 1987 the progress of this reform was so unsatisfactory that a plenum of the CPSU Central Committee was devoted to educational problems. In particular, there seemed to be a lack of success in the area of vocational instruction and a feeling that the only outcome had been a lowering of standards in basic education. Thus, the leadership decided to abandon many of the goals of the 1984 reform and to institute their own "restructuring" of the educational system (*Pravda,* August 27, 1987, p. 2; *Pravda,* February 18, 1988, pp. 1–4).

The cornerstone of the current educational reform seems to be a more rigorous general educational system, designed to prepare students for specialized work in industry and in the professions. There is an emphasis on training the students to handle the technological innovations of the future. As was mentioned previously, more discretion is being given to the schools to encourage creative methods of teaching and increase the number of advanced classes in all subjects. The general-education schools are no longer to be given primary responsibility for vocational education. Now they only prepare students to enter vocational-technical schools. There is an increased emphasis on the role of industry in training the skilled workers it will need in the future.

The training given in both the vocational-technical schools and by industrial enterprises is seen as being built on the strong educational base that students acquire in the general education schools. In particular, computer education is emphasized, as is the provision of other types of equipment for everything from physical education to laboratories. To mobilize public support for this effort, elected councils have been established to oversee the management of both general education schools and vocational-technical schools (*Pravda,* July 2, 1988, p. 9).

Largely unresolved was the question of what to do about the ideological and patriotic goals of the 1984 reform. At first the leadership reaffirmed the importance of teaching all subjects within a Marxist-Leninist framework. At the same time, however, surveys showed that large numbers of students were not interested in Marxism-Leninism and that many thought that the social sciences are not important (see, for example, *Radio Liberty Research,* 382/87, p. l). Ultimately, this resulted in the removal of required ideology courses from the curriculum of institutions of higher education. Abolished were courses on dialectical and historical materialism, the history of the CPSU, and "scientific communism." These were replaced by courses on the social and political history of the twentieth century, contemporary socialism, and general philosophy. Also, teachers and students were given more control over course content (*Report on the USSR,* October 20, 1989, p. 28).

A balanced, honest teaching of history is a matter of particular concern, since the reassessment of Soviet history has been a primary thrust of glasnost:

Nowadays, much is said about historical truth. And, however bitter it may be, we must talk about it and write about it in order to benefit from its lessons for the present and for the future. It is important to transmit the full, unedited truth to the next generation without slander and without embellishment. We have experienced everything from the joy of victory to the bitterness of failure, the heroic and the tragic. But the most important thing is that we have behind us the glorious history of a great people. (*Pravda,* February 18, 1988, p. 3)

Also, there is to be more emphasis on economic training, aesthetic education, and the development of national-language–Russian bilingualism. In short, we see the Soviet leadership attempting to tailor education to meet the current and projected needs of the reform and to deal with some of the more pressing political problems of the present and immediate future.

To be part of the 17 to 20 percent of high school graduates admitted to an institution of higher education, students must have graduated from a general-education school or the equivalent. They must also pass a set of examinations. Prior to 1986 there were four entrance exams. In that year a guideline was issued that reduced the number to three. The fourth was replaced by an interview process which was geared toward assessing the appropriateness of the prospective student's vocational goals.

In 1988 new regulations were published that gave institutions of higher education more leeway to fit the examination process to their own needs. There may be from three to five exams. One must be in Russian language and literature or the language and literature of one of the major Soviet ethnic minorities. In addition, at the discretion of the school, exams in areas other than the applicant's proposed field of specialization may be given on a pass-fail basis. The exams can be given in Russian or in the language of the republic in which they are being given. Veterans, orphans, and applicants with certain outstanding qualifications may be given preferential treatment (*Pravda,* March 17, 1988, p. 6).

While the 1984 educational reform was a product of the Brezhnev-Chernenko regime, the higher education reform that began in 1987 was clearly a product of the Gorbachev regime (*Pravda,* March 21, 1987, pp. 1–3; also see *Pravda,* March 25–28, 1987). It seemed to be a response to the fact that institutions of higher education were turning out graduates who were poorly prepared to participate in the reform. There were too many specialists in some fields and not enough in others. Graduates often were not well enough trained in their field of specialization. Finally, and perhaps most important, they were products of a system which did not train them to show initiative or exercise leadership. On the basis of a survey of high school students, a teacher made the following observation:

> We were alarmed by the fact that the graduating students gave correct, but slogan-like, rote answers to the questions: What does it mean to be a fighter for restructuring? How do you see your role in the restructuring of the educational system? From their answers, it was apparent that these youngsters had not formed an active, civic position, a desire for independence and positive, practical activity. (*Pravda,* July 1, 1988, p. 2)

Consequently, the goals of these changes in the education system seem to be to gear students' majors more closely to societal needs, to make the process of instruction more participatory, and to encourage greater student self-government. Also, instruction for many seniors is being combined with appropriate paid work, students are being allowed to do more independent work, and the number of compulsory courses is being reduced.

In adulthood the collectivist influence of the school and youth groups is continued. Reminiscing about his young adult years, Sergei Zamascikov, a former Soviet citizen, has observed:

> The net of primary Komsomol organizations and committees that exists in every factory, institution and educational establishment places the young Soviet person in a situation where on every important issue in his life—from acquiring an obligatory recommendation for university admission to obtaining a ticket to the local disco—he has to deal with the Komsomol, and, in one way or another, to conform with its ideology. (*The Washington Post,* September 11, 1983, p. C2)

Despite this, however, membership in the *Komsomol* is decreasing. The head of the *Komsomol* reported in October 1989 that *Komsomol* membership had declined by 4 million during the previous twelve months and that during the last five years it had dropped by 10 million members (*Report on the USSR,* February 23, 1990, p. 49). Even more dramatic was the decision of the Estonian *Komsomol* to abolish itself in 1990. This decline in membership is a matter of concern for the CPSU, since it appears that many of the young people who might have joined the *Komsomol* in the past are joining unofficial youth groups over which the Party has far less control.[6] Thus, the *Komsomol* is currently engaged in an effort to restructure itself to make it more attractive to Soviet youth, and this includes distancing itself somewhat from the CPSU (*Izvestiia,* July 31, 1989, p. 1).

Supplementing the influence of the *Komsomol* is the influence of the collective. All students become members of collectives at their universities or institutes. For those who enter the work force directly from general education or vocational-technical schools, the collectives are at their place of work and their place of residence. In either case, their lives are heavily influenced by the cooperative efforts of their collectives and local *Komsomol* organization.

For those who are *Komsomol* members or who become Party members, the role of political socialization activities in their life looms even larger. They are expected to engage in constant political work among their non-Party colleagues and neighbors, both to inculcate and to enforce the values currently associated with being a good Soviet citizen. They are also expected to lead exemplary lives in order to demonstrate to others how a good citizen conducts his or her affairs. Finally, Party members are supposed to work constantly to

---

[6]For a discussion of unofficial youth groups see Chapters 11 and 14.

upgrade their own ideological level, not only by keeping up with Party and government activities in the mass media, but also by participating in agitation and propaganda activities and by attending political schools.

The Media

Glasnost is intended to strengthen socialism and the spirit of our people, to strengthen morality and the moral climate of society. In addition, glasnost means criticism of shortcomings. It does not, however, mean undermining socialism and socialist values. (Mikhail Gorbachev, *Izvestiia,* July 16, 1987, p. 2)

Until the advent of glasnost, all types of media defined news to be what the Party told them it was, directly or indirectly. As a practical matter, this meant mostly stories highlighting current Party policy or Soviet economic advances. Ultimate control over content rested with higher Party officials. Day-to-day decision making on all but the most sensitive issues was usually done by lower-level bureaucrats. In cases involving highly trusted journalists, this amounted to self-censorship. For example, in an interview in the United States a senior political commentator on Soviet television described his work in the following way:

Of course we have to express views which are official in our country. It's quite a responsibility, because no one (no censor) reads what we are saying before we go on the air. There's no revision. Our second bulletin comes on at 11 p.m. and there's no one around to ask or to check. . . . So we have full responsibility for what we say. (*The Baltimore Sun,* January 31, 1984, p. B1)

Notable here is, first, his apparent acceptance of censorship as the norm, and second, his seeming lack of ambivalence about functioning as a spokesperson for the government.

Glasnost has changed all this and, with it, the very nature of the Soviet media and journalism. First, and most obviously, Soviet media has become much more interesting. Instead of endless, monotonous stories about happy workers, there are stories about what life is really like. Second, instead of merely turning government and CPSU policies and documents into "news stories," more and more Soviet journalists are going out and doing true investigative journalism. Third, instead of confining themselves to extolling the virtues of the Soviet government and CPSU, the media is increasingly adopting the stance of critic and forum for the discussion of alternative policies. Of course, the extent to which these changes have taken hold varies across media forms and across sources within each type of media. On the whole, however, there is much more real content, and the Soviet people are responding by taking a greater interest:

Never before has the word of the journalist enjoyed such attention as it does today. "But, did you read?" "Did you watch?" "Did you listen?" These questions can be heard everywhere. People are thinking, arguing, being indignant, and rejoicing. And, it is natural during the last three years that the number of issues of periodicals has grown rapidly and that there are incomparably more television viewers and radio listeners. The press is rightly called the tribune of democracy and glasnost, the bright, active means of perestroika. (*Pravda,* April, 14, 1988, p. 1)

It is important to note three things, however. First, this enthusiasm is not universal. Many in the journalistic community have had trouble adjusting to the new work style and responsibilities thrust upon them. In some cases, they control newspapers or magazines and have kept them more or less the way they were before glasnost. In other cases, they have left their jobs and, often, their profession as well. Second, with time, the people's enthusiasm for and fascination with a more honest and informative press is bound to wane; there are already signs that the novelty is wearing off (Tolz, 1989, pp. 12–13). Third, the Soviet people have not been universally enthusiastic about these changes (see, for example, *Pravda,* September 14, 1987, p. 3).

Glasnost's main supporters have been the educated urban elite. Among many less educated persons in the countryside, all this information about the flaws in their system has caused uneasiness, as well as increased indignation about the hardships in their own lives. What glasnost has done is to increase the flow of bad news and to reduce the flow of good news. Without the faith that this is only a first step toward changing the bad news to good news, people may see life as more difficult and hopeless. Many ordinary people think that significant, positive change in their lives is unlikely. They have been disappointed too often in the past.

The proper balance between good and bad news, therefore, is a matter of controversy within the political elite, expressed in arguments about how far glasnost should be permitted to go. This is not a good-guys-versus-bad-guys issue. Even Gorbachev himself has shown considerable impatience with some of the stories appearing in the media and has attempted to exert control over content which he sees as potentially harmful to the reform, labeling it as "populist demagoguery, nationalistic or chauvinistic currents, or unruly group interests" (*Report on the USSR,* December 8, 1989, p. 22). The reform leadership, as well as their conservative critics, came to power in a political system where open, freewheeling criticism of political leaders was unimaginable. Their theoretical enthusiasm for a free press is being tempered by the realities of what this can mean for their ability to achieve their objectives. This should not be surprising, given the perennial tensions between American political leaders and the press. In fact in 1989 a top official of the Bush administration expressed sympathy with the frustration Gorbachev was experiencing in his relations with the Soviet press (*The Washington Post,* October 20, 1989, p. A36).

Since the leadership still controls the media, this means that there is much more ambiguity, as well as ambivalence, in the instructions issued to journalists. Clearly there are still limits, but they are harder to pinpoint. Consider the following instructions to journalists contained in an editorial in *Pravda* (April 14, 1988, p. 1), the official newspaper of the CPSU:

> During the new stage of perestroika, the primary tasks of journalists are definitely the following: To aid the further democratization of our life and the mastering of economical methods of management. To seek and support everything new and progressive. To be on the side of those who are moving perestroika and our society along the way of renewal.

Obviously, this set of instructions leaves much room for interpretation. It makes the journalist a propagandist for leadership policies in a situation where there are far more open policy differences among the leadership than ever before and where journalists have been given much more responsibility for the selection and content of their stories. This can be challenging or threatening, depending on the position of the particular journalist involved. At best, it carries risks.

Since the reform has been aimed at an incredibly complex set of problems in the Soviet system, much of the reporting mandated by the foregoing instruction would seem to involve specific shortcomings, and this is currently the way those in the forefront of investigative journalism are proceeding. But how do you know when you have gone too far? Returning to the *Pravda* editorial we see another set of ambiguous instructions:

> Glasnost makes increased demands on journalists. Professional competence, an honest, even scrupulous, handling of the facts is not a virtue, but a duty of the journalist. His every word must be trustworthy. Some authors, however, who do not possess the necessary knowledge are doing a superficial analysis of present and past events, tolerating mistakes and inaccuracies, limiting themselves to half-truths. The readers are unanimous: In the service of candidness and criticism, it is not necessary to create opposing groups or indulge in outspoken speculations in order to achieve transitory popularity.

In short, avoid sensationalism. This would be fine if there were general agreement as to what is sensational. Unfortunately, there is not. So, Soviet journalists know that they can go only so far—but the limit is a hazy one.

Initially, the process of introducing glasnost was a very tentative one. The first main thrust drew on a time-honored custom among Soviet newspapers: printing letters containing complaints from their readers. During 1985 and 1986 it became apparent that these letters were taking on an increasingly frank tone about some of the economic and other deprivations of Soviet life. At the same time, there appeared scattered reports about crimes, accidents, and natural disasters, none of which had been reported in the past except under unusual circumstances, such as the death or injury of foreigners. After the Twenty-Seventh Party Congress in early 1986, there was an increase in reporting about societal problems, such as drug abuse, poor health-care delivery, and official corruption (particularly with reference to the Brezhnev era).

The nuclear accident at Chernobyl marked a significant turning point. In the hours and days following the accident, the Soviet media was silent. Finally, when Scandinavian authorities began reporting unusual levels of radioactivity and piecing together the story, the Soviet media reluctantly began reporting the incident. The initial attempt to keep the nuclear disaster a secret was sharply criticized all over the world and seemed to trigger a new policy. Subsequently, immediate reports about major accidents and natural disasters began to appear in the Soviet media. This was related to a more general policy shift in the direction of an open society. At the end of 1986, dissident physicist and Nobel Peace Prize winner Sakharov was released from internal exile in Gorkii and immediately interviewed by NBC and CBS—in a studio made available by the USSR Television and Radio Committee.

During 1987 and 1988 the press had to decide how to cover the first large-scale internal violence since the advent of glasnost, a confrontation between Armenians and Azerbaidzhanis over the disputed territory of Nagorno-Karabakh. A massive earthquake in Armenia complicated the situation. Compared with the past, there was a surprising amount of coverage, but the reporting was far from complete by Western standards. For example, the press attempted to downplay the extent to which ethnic animosities were continuing— even in the midst of unbelievable earthquake devastation. This seemed to reflect a fear on the part of at least some of the leadership that publicity might aggravate the situation. Also, there seemed to be the fear that too much information would encourage comparable ethnic clashes in other areas of the USSR where there is also serious friction between ethnic groups (Sheehy, 1988).

Subsequently, however, emboldened members of the press criticized this decision on the ground that inadequate reporting had created more problems than it had solved: "We left the field open for rumor and provocation, and that was a good deal of what led to the (violence) in Sumgait" (*The Washington Post,* April 27, 1988, p. A26). This and other criticisms of the way in which the leadership had responded to the open hostility in Armenia and Azerbaidzhan were broadcast in a prime time 90-minute television documentary on the events in Transcaucasia. The influence of this policy decision seemed to carry over to late 1989, when Soviet television gave surprisingly complete coverage to the crumbling of communism in country after country in Eastern Europe. This was particularly significant since, unlike the Soviet reform from the top, these East European revolutions were from below and took place during a period when there was considerable dissatisfaction among the Soviet people with the progress of the reform.

Just as notable during 1987 and 1988 was the increasing willingness of the media to address openly the evils of the Stalin years. An early breakthrough was the broadcast of a two-hour documentary on May 16, 1988. It included information and historical footage on the purges and show trials of the 1930s, as well as information on the negative aspects of Stalin's forced collectivization, industrialization, and World War II decision making. Together with concurrent and subsequent revelations in the print media, movies, literature and the arts, it served to bring the Soviet people face-to-face with events in their past that had previously been kept secret or only presented in favorable terms.

Another milestone occurred at the time of the Nineteenth Party Conference during the summer of 1988. The conference itself was notable because of the frank and emotional nature of the speeches made and the topics covered. Even more remarkable was the extensive news coverage, which was followed avidly by the Soviet people: "People are chained to the television and the radio. The interest is enormous and passionate." An elderly woman was quoted as saying: "I sat in front of my television and I cried. My brother disappeared under Stalin. . . . And to think that now people can talk so freely. It is a miracle." (*The New York Times,* July 2, 1988, p. 7).

At the same time, the scope of glasnost in the media was expanding in other ways. For example, there were reports on the previously denied existence of such things as strikes by workers, neo-Nazi groups in the USSR, anti-Semitism, and the more sordid aspects of the fighting in Afghanistan. In this situation of rapid change, it was hard to discern what the limits of glasnost were or should be—a matter that certainly concerned Gorbachev and his associates. Realizing that the new openness would permit the airing of antireform as well as proreform sentiments, a number of Soviet officials, including Gorbachev, made it known to key members of the media that the reform process should be given unequivocal support. To reinforce this there were repeated reminders that ultimate control over the media still rested with the CPSU and that the current freedom exercised by the media should not, therefore, be abused.

Beginning in the late 1980s the media became the vehicle for repeated attempts by Gorbachev to mobilize the masses. Although glasnost had built him a relatively solid power base among the educated urban elite, there were signs that the reforms were not gaining much support among the vast majority of Soviet citizens. Their attitude toward the reform hinged more on its impact on the day-to-day realities of their lives, and economic reform was proving much more difficult than the leadership had anticipated. In fact, there were signs that economic conditions were actually getting worse instead of better (a situation common during reform periods).

The beginning of this effort to appeal to the people took place in September 1988, during a trip to Siberia. For days Soviet television showed pictures of Gorbachev touring factories, visiting grocery stores, and listening patiently to people's complaints about their living conditions. He was clearly trying to project the image of a leader who cares about his people and who is trying to respond to their needs. The latter became apparent when he returned to Moscow and, almost immediately, unleashed a major shake-up in the leadership. He also began putting more emphasis on shifting power from the CPSU to governmental bodies—from local soviets to the legislature of the USSR— which would be soon be chosen in contested elections by the very people whose complaints he had been hearing. This use of the media to mobilize the masses behind the reform continued into the 1990s with extensive coverage of additional reforms from the top and of the electioneering of candidates for governmental offices under the new system of contested elections, followed by live coverage of the proceedings of the newly elected Congress of People's Deputies and the revamped Supreme Soviet.

This increased freedom of the press has been coupled with a loosening of other publication restraints.[7] Perhaps most important in this respect has been the growing willingness and ability of editors to publish literary works previously suppressed by the censors. This includes major poets and authors from the past, such as Anna Akhmatova, Nikolai Gumiliov, and Boris Pasternak. It also includes more contemporary authors such as Anatoly Rybakov, whose *Children of the Arbat* is an exposé of the Stalin era. Even the political writings of such purge-era "enemies of the people" as Bukharin are no longer beyond the pale.

Liberalization has not been limited to Soviet authors. Such previously forbidden works as George Orwell's novels, *1984* and *Animal Farm,* have also been published. Furthermore, it was announced in 1988 that 3,500 books that had not been available in Soviet libraries had been put back on the open shelves and that more would follow. A commission set up by *Glavlit* (The Main Administration for Safeguarding State Secrets) in 1987 was responsible and was continuing to review restricted titles with the goal of returning all but the most objectionable to the open shelves of libraries. In late 1988 there was an exhibition of long-suppressed books at Lenin Library in Moscow. Not only did it include books by purge victims like Bukharin and Kamenev, it also contained the memoirs of Aleksandr Kerensky, the head of the Provisional Government that was overthrown by the Bolsheviks in 1917.

Although there has been a virtual revolution in the official press and literature, Soviet authorities are still struggling with what to do about unofficial publishing efforts. Many unofficial or *samizdat* publications are now permitted. They do, however, still have problems with gaining access to photocopying and printing facilities and supplies. Also, there have been reports that unofficial publishers have been persecuted (Tolz, 1989, p. 13). There have also been efforts to restrict the distribution of the more radical magazines and newspapers. Thus, Soviet publishing has grown much more interesting because its mandate has been changing with the advent and development of glasnost.

---

[7]*Glavlit* (The Main Administration for Safeguarding State Secrets) still exists, but the scope of its ability to block publication has been greatly reduced. Local censors, however, sometimes make decisions that are more restrictive than those being made at the national level (Wishnevsky, 1988).

Also, the journalists and writers have become much more enterprising in pushing the limits of what is permitted. This, in turn, has caused some nervousness on the part of a political leadership used to a tame and malleable media. Where all this will lead is not yet clear. What is clear, however, is that it would be very difficult for any future conservative leadership to put the genie back in the bottle.

THE FUTURE

The Soviet leadership may be entering a phase in which it will become harder and harder to maintain control over the process of political socialization. This implies the gradual development of a Soviet political culture that is significantly different from the Soviet political culture of the past. At present, however, there is no indication of a wish to turn back—at least from those who are currently in power. In fact, the government is routinely making decisions which will make central control over ideas even weaker in the future. For example, the U.S. Xerox Corporation and the Soviet government have agreed to a joint venture under which public photocopying centers are being set up in the Soviet Union.

It is undeniable that glasnost has made a tremendous difference in the amount and type of information available to the Soviet public. Overall, the Soviet Union has become a much less propagandized society. This has the potential for a profound effect on the socialization of a whole new generation. And since socialization continues throughout the life cycle, its effect is not limited to the younger generation. Soviet citizens still do not have freedom of expression and freedom of the press as they are understood in the United States. But it is undeniable that glasnost has moved the Soviet Union in that direction.

If this is true, it can be argued that there has been a basic change in Soviet political culture. And, in fact, there is evidence that the attitudes and beliefs that many Soviet people hold about their political system are changing. Political arguments and criticisms of the leadership can be heard on the streets, not just in people's homes. Ordinary citizens are more willing to question their leaders, including Gorbachev himself—even when the exchange is being recorded by television cameras. And these exchanges are being broadcast throughout the country, thus creating models for more of this sort of behavior.

To a great extent the future of this trend hinges on whether contested elections continue to be held and the degree to which they involve true competition—not just between individuals but also between points of view and policy alternatives. It also hinges on the extent to which the officials and governmental bodies that emerge from these elections are given real power. Gorbachev talks about wanting the Soviet people to take direct control of their own destiny; more and more of them are acting as if they think that it is possible to do so. This is not only a change from the Soviet past, it is a change from the entire past of the Russian people.

REFERENCES

BARNER-BARRY, C., and ROSENWEIN, R. (1985). *Psychological perspectives on politics.* Englewood Cliffs, NJ: Prentice-Hall.

BEM, D. (1970). *Beliefs, attitudes, and human affairs.* Belmont, CA: Wadsworth, Brooks/Cole.

BUKOVSKY, V. (1979). *To build a castle: My life as a dissenter.* New York: Viking.

ELKINS, D.J. and SIMEON, R.E.B. (1979). A cause in search of its effect, or what does political culture explain? *Comparative Politics, 11,* 127–145.

GORBACHEV, M. (1987). *Perestroika: New thinking for our country and the world.* New York: Harper & Row.

JACOBS, J. (1961). *The death and life of great American cities.* New York: Random House.

KABUSH, V.T. (1985). *Pionerskie, simvoly, ritualy, traditsii.* Minsk: "Narodnaia asveta."

KAZANSKAIA, G.S. (1976). *Uchitel' i pionerskii otriad.* Moscow: "Prosveshchenie."

KIRK, I. (1975). *Profiles in Russian resistance.* New York: New York Times.

LUKE, T.W. (1985). *Ideology and Soviet industrialization.* Westport, CO: Greenwood.

POND, E. (1988). *From the Yaroslavsky Station,* 3rd ed. New York: Universe.

SEMENOVA V.E., ed. (1984). *Sotsial'no-psikhologicheskie problemy nravstvennogo vospitaniia lichnosti.* Leningrad: Izdatel'stvo Leningradskogo Universiteta.

SHEEHY, A. (1988). Soviet media coverage of recent events in Armenia and Azerbaijan. *Radio Liberty Research,* no. 109/88.

SHIPLER, D. (1983). *Russia: Broken idols, solemn dreams.* New York: New York Times.

SWAFFORD, M. (1979). *Political attitudes and behavior among Soviet university students.* Washington, DC: Office of Research, U.S. International Communication Agency.

TEAGUE, E. (1984). The USSR Law on Work Collectives: Workers' control or workers controlled? *Radio Liberty Research,* no. 184/84.

TOLZ, V. (1989). The Soviet press. *Report on the USSR, 1,* 52, 12–14.

TUCKER, R. (1987). *Political culture and leadership in Soviet Russia.* New York: W.W. Norton.

WISHNEVSKY, J. (1988). Censorship in these days of *glasnost'. Radio Liberty Research,* no. 495/88.

FIVE
THE CONSTITUTION:
Adding Substance to Form

In the American political system, the U.S. Constitution is a document of great importance. Semester-long or year-long courses devoted to the interpretation and development of the Constitution are given in both universities and law schools. And the U.S. Supreme Court, the conclusive interpreter of constitutional provisions, is an organ of great power and prestige in the American system.

The USSR Constitution has held no such place in the Soviet system, and has rightfully been given little attention by most analysts of Soviet politics. Of late, however, there have been indications that constitutional provisions, including the governmental structures that they create, will play a more significant role in the way the Soviet system operates. Thus, some attention needs to be given to the constitution. This chapter will cover the following subjects: (1) a brief history of Soviet constitutions; (2) the place of the constitution in the Soviet system; (3) the question of whether the Gorbachev-era amendments signal new importance for the constitution; and (4) constitutional change and the political process.

SOVIET CONSTITUTIONAL HISTORY IN BRIEF

The first constitution of the Russian Soviet Federated Socialist Republic (RSFSR), was adopted in July 1918 and served as a model for the documents adopted in the areas of the former Russian empire, such as Byelorussia, the Ukraine, Azerbaidzhan, Armenia, and Georgia, as they were gradually taken over by the Bolsheviks in the years after the Revolution. Formal federation among the states associated with the RSFSR was achieved late in 1922 with the creation of the Union of Soviet Socialist Republics (USSR). Its constitution went into effect in January 1924.

The details of these first two documents need not detain us here. They did not differ greatly from each other, and except in detail and terminology they set up systems of government that were essentially similar to those that followed. The third constitution, dating from 1936, was in force for over forty years. In October 1977 it was replaced by a new constitution,[1] a much longer document but one with many similarities to the 1936 charter. The adoption of this new constitution was preceded by a much publicized period of discussion of a draft version, as the 1936 constitution had been. Regarding the 1977 process, it was reported that over 140 million Soviet citizens took part in the discussion, 1.5 million meetings were devoted to it, and about 400,000 proposals for changes in the draft were received. In the end, however, the changes in the final version of the document resulting from the discussion were not very important.

Soviet authorities claimed at the time that this discussion was testimony to "the genuinely democratic character of the Soviet system." Closer to the mark, however, would seem to be the conclusion of a Western analyst that what took place was "a public debate of gigantic proportions and minimal depth" (Feldbrugge, 1979, p. xi). In 1988, 1989, and 1990, a number of significant amendments to the 1977 Constitution were made, and further amendments have been promised by the Gorbachev regime. These amendments were also preceded by a broad discussion of the proposed changes, but this time a more far-reaching and genuine exchange of views took place. Both the changes and the process of their adoption will be discussed presently.

The 1936 Constitution was adopted in the midst of the "great terror" that existed from 1936 to 1938, the greatest political purge in Soviet history. Some analysts have suggested that the introduction of a new constitutional document at this time was an attempt on the part of Stalin and his cohorts to convince the world that the Soviet Union was, after all, a state run according to law. But it was not only a matter of the purges giving the Soviet Union a bad name that influenced the adoption of a new constitution. There was also the growing fascist threat, which the Soviet Union was attempting to combat. Stalin needed the cooperation of communist parties of foreign countries with other parties of the Left in "united fronts" against the fascists. To have the Soviet Union, then the only communist state, appear to be more democratic than had heretofore been thought would not hurt. The introduction of a more

---

[1]For the reader's convenience the text of the 1977 constitution, as amended through March, 1990, is included as Appendix A.

democratic constitutional document, moreover, was welcome at home. The Soviet Union was a country to which Western ideas were not completely alien. Marxism, after all, was a Western import. Many Soviet intellectuals, in particular, were strongly attracted to the West. Thus, the introduction of "progressive" ideas from the West, such as a set of democratic constitutional provisions, would help in gaining legitimacy for the regime both at home and abroad.

Whatever the actual importance of these considerations, the adoption of the constitution was justified primarily on other grounds. Socialism, it was said, had been achieved in the USSR, and this was the "constitution of victorious socialism." Since antagonistic classes had been eliminated, leaving only workers, peasants, and intellectuals as different varieties of "toilers," and since, with the abolition of private employment, a socialistic economic system had been established, new state arrangements consonant with these achievements could be made. It was also the "Stalin Constitution," so named supposedly because Stalin was the titular chairman of the document's drafting commission, but really so designated to provide another jewel for the leader's crown. This designation ceased to be used when Stalin's star went into decline.

Stalin called the constitution "the only thoroughly democratic Constitution in the world." This is absurd, of course. But many of the provisions of the 1936 Constitution were impressive and represented considerable improvement over previous Soviet documents. Universal suffrage by secret ballot replaced a system of limited suffrage, which excluded priests and other former members of the bourgeoisie. The representatives of the new bicameral Supreme Soviet were directly elected, whereas the old Congress of Soviets had been indirectly elected. The 1936 Constitution was also slightly more realistic than its predecessors in that it mentioned, although only briefly, the important place of the Communist Party in the Soviet system. Finally, a detailed and extensive listing of "Basic Rights and Duties of Citizens" was included for the first time in a federal constitution.

Among the rights were several that would have been novel for Western constitution writers of the time, including the "right to work," meaning "guaranteed employment," as well as rights to rest and leisure, education, and maintenance in old age. In addition, more familiar provisions were included that guaranteed freedom of expression, separation of church and state, the inviolability of the person and the home, and equality of nationalities, races, and the sexes. The duties were closely tied to the socialist nature of the system. Citizens were expected to abide by the constitution and the laws, to maintain labor discipline, to perform public duties honestly and "to respect the rules of socialist community." They were charged with safeguarding public property "as the sacred and inviolable foundation of the Soviet system." They were pledged to defend the motherland. These passages stressed the citizen's obligation toward the state and the community and effectively reversed the emphasis found in many Western constitutional documents on the rights of the individual against the state.

The 1977 Constitution bore many similarities to its 1936 counterpart. True, it was considerably longer (174 articles and some 13,000 words, as against 146 articles and 8,000 words); but in large part the additions and changes were cosmetic. A long prologue, missing in the 1936 document, contains some keys to the theoretical underpinnings of the new constitution. Why a prologue of this sort is necessary requires some background explanation. In the Marxist-socialist world constitutions have served as sorts of signposts, indicating where a country has been and where it is going. They have represented the fulfillment of past objectives and the promise of future achievements. Marxian thought dictates looking at the world in terms of stages of development. This is a "given" of historical analysis. It applies, of course, to the history of the Soviet Union as well. Thus, it has been seen as fitting that new constitutions be adopted to regulate affairs in the successive important stages of Soviet history. There is abundant evidence that, at least until recently, Soviet constitutional experts held to this point of view. For example, an authoritative compilation of Soviet constitutional documents from the 1950s states that each constitution "represents a stage in the continuing historical path" of the Soviet state and is "the legislative basis of the subsequent development of the life of the state" (*Istoriia Sovetskoi Konstitutsii,* 1957, p. 3).

In line with this reasoning, the prologue to the 1977 Constitution speaks of the Soviet Union as a "developed socialist society" that is "an objectively necessary stage on the road to communism" and a higher stage than the socialism proclaimed in the 1936 Constitution.[2] Accordingly, it was said that the tasks of the dictatorship of the proletariat had been fulfilled and that a new kind of state, "the state of the whole people," had been created. With this "socio-political and ideological unity" achieved, the superior position accorded to workers could be abandoned; thus the elective representative bodies were now called "soviets of people's deputies" rather than "soviets of workers' deputies."

In the articles of the 1977 Constitution itself, perhaps the most important change involved the more prominent position accorded to the Communist Party. In the 1936 document it was mentioned twice, briefly. These references were basically repeated in 1977, but Article 6 of the 1977 Constitution went much further, calling the Party "the leading and guiding force of Soviet society and the nucleus of its political system, of all state and public organizations." The party was charged with determining "the general perspective of society's development and the line of domestic and foreign policy of the USSR." As will be indicated below, article 6 was revised in 1990 to eliminate the Communist Party's monopoly on political power.

---

[2]The concept of developed socialism was abandoned during the Gorbachev period.

THE PLACE OF THE CONSTITUTION
IN THE SOVIET SYSTEM

It is important to analyze the place that the constitution holds in the Soviet system. A political system may be described as constitutional, or as having constitutionalism, when the exercise of political and governmental power therein is *defined* and *limited* (Friedrich, 1968, pp. 24–26; McIlwain, 1947, pp. 21–22). It is precisely this lack of definition of, and limitation on, political powers that has characterized the Soviet constitutions. As Carl Friedrich has put it, "as a political process, the constitution can be described as analogous to the rules of the game insuring fair play" (Friedrich, 1968, p. 123). But as pointed out in Chapter 1, it is a lack of recognized rules that has traditionally characterized the way Soviet politics is played. Nor were such rules needed, given the basic assumptions about the way the Soviet system was supposed to work. What the Bolshevik leaders imported from the West was constitutional form, not substance. A constitution defines the power and duties of governmental organs because some contention, some conflict in the way the country is to be governed, is expected. So the rules of conflict management are set out from the start. But the stated Soviet assumption about the way the governing process works has been one of consensus. Since the contradictions inherent in previous societies have been eliminated under Soviet socialism (so the reasoning goes), the bodies mentioned in successive Soviet constitutions were expected to operate in an essentially conflict-free way.

Thus, successive Soviet constitutions have described the formal organs of government and lists their powers. But the organ that has traditionally been the focus of power in the Soviet system is the Communist Party. And even in the 1977 Constitution, in which the Party was mentioned more prominently than in previous constitutions, no attempt was made to define its formal powers.

What about the matter of limiting power? It stands to reason that since the formal governmental organs have had little power, there would be little that could really be limited by the constitution. But since Party policies were often channeled *through* the governmental apparatus, the constitution might have served as a limitation on the formal implementation of Party policy. There are a number of constitutional provisions that might limit state power. To take one of the most obvious examples, Article 50 of the constitution guarantees citizens "freedom of speech, of the press, and of assembly, meetings, street processions and demonstrations." Several factors detract from or condition this guarantee, however. First, the rights mentioned in Article 50 are prefaced by the phrase (also present in the 1936 Constitution) "in accordance with the interests of the people and in order to strengthen and develop the socialist system." This might be interpreted to limit the objectives for which the rights might be used. Another potential restriction is the provision in Article 39 that the "enjoyment of citizens of their rights and freedoms must not be to the detriment of the interests of society or the state or infringe the rights of other citizens," a formulation that could be used to justify repression of dissident activities. As the reform era that began in the late 1980s continued, these and other restrictions on the right to expression began to be examined more seriously.

Glasnost unleashed the suppressed desire of many citizens to air their views and grievances. Some of them began to take Article 50 seriously and to take to the streets, and this quickly led the authorities to further define the provisions of Article 50. For instance, in the area of demonstrations, a series of laws has been adopted regulating public gatherings and requiring advance permission from the local authorities; giving the police new powers in controlling demonstrations; and meting out stiff penalties for violation of these laws. Moreover, local authorities are allowed to adopt further regulations restricting demonstrations. For instance, Moscow has barred all demonstrations in the central squares of the city.[3] These laws have not been met with quiet acquiescence, however. The desire to expand the boundaries of permitted expression is great, and is being voiced by a variety of diverse sources. Advocates of reform, members of the legal profession, and the authorities are participants in a continuing effort to find a point of equilibrium on these issues.

Thus, the conflict-free days of earlier Soviet constitutionalism have passed from the scene. New attitudes toward constitutions, and new constitutional provisions themselves, are needed for the era of glasnost and perestroika. There is a consensus that a new document, completely replacing the 1977 Constitution, is needed. But with the rapid political changes that commenced at the end of the 1980s, it was not possible to wait for the drafting, discussion, and adoption of a completely new document. Constitutional change has come in installments.

THE LATE 1980s: START OF A NEW DIRECTION

Since, under the old constitutional reasoning, conflict among governmental bodies was not contemplated, Soviet spokesmen have traditionally rejected the principle of separation of powers. It is a mark of the radical nature of changes under Gorbachev that Soviet theorists seem to be reassessing this matter.[4] The need to provide genuinely independent authority for certain governmental organs, so that they can serve as counterweights against the power of other bod-

---

[3]These measures were adopted in 1987 and 1988. Their texts or analyses of them may be found in the following sources: *Ved. SSSR*, 1988, no. 31, item 504; *Ved. SSSR*, 1988, no. 31, item 505; *Ved. RSFSR*, 1988, no. 31, item 1005; *The New York Times*, September 2, 1987, p. A3.

[4]While the term separation of powers (*razdelenie vlastei*) has not come into general use, it is mentioned on occasion by lawyers and others advocating reform.

ies, has become a given in the debates about political reform. Constitutional revision under Gorbachev has proceeded in several stages. First, a set of important amendments to the 1977 Constitution was adopted in December 1988. When several of these amendments were strenuously opposed by a coalition of Moscow reformers and deputies from some of the union republics, further amendments were made in 1989. A commission was established in 1989 to adopt a completely new constitutional document. And further important changes were made in 1990, most notably the elimination of the provisions on the Communist Party's leading role and the creation of a new office of President of the USSR. These changes, taken together, are by far the most significant constitutional developments since Stalin introduced the general governmental arrangements that existed since the Constitution of 1936. Although they will be discussed in more complete historical context in Chapters 6 (on governmental operations) and 8 (on the legal system), the basic features of the changes will be examined here.

In his speech at the time of the adoption of the 1988 amendments, Gorbachev acknowledged that "much in the Constitution of 1977 is already in need of replacement." But he indicated that for the present, changes should be made only regarding matters previously decided upon (i.e., those questions initiated earlier by the Party authorities for which draft proposals had been prepared and subjected to public discussion; *Izvestiia,* November 30, 1988, p. 2). The changes made affected the wording of almost one-third of the articles in the Constitution (55 out of 174), but substantive amendments were considerably more limited. They can be summarized under the following ten points:

1. A new "highest organ of state power," the Congress of People's Deputies, was created (Article 108). This body, in effect, took the place of the USSR Supreme Soviet, although the latter was not abolished but was given a somewhat altered role.

The Congress of People's Deputies is a representative body made up of 2,250 popularly elected deputies (the old Supreme Soviet had 1,500) chosen on three bases: 750 from territorial units based on population size; 750 on nationality-territorial units; and 750 from social organizations such as the Communist Party, the trade unions, and others. As well be discussed presently, this last form of representation has been opposed by numerous reformers.

This large body is given an impressive list of functions (see Article 108), but it meets in regular session only once a year, for a few days. Among the Congress's duties are naming the USSR Supreme Soviet and the Chairman of the USSR Supreme Soviet, which are to have much enhanced authority in comparison with their earlier functions.

2. The redesigned Supreme Soviet is designated (Article 111) as "the continuously functioning legislative, management and control organ of USSR state power." It consists of two bodies, the Council of the Union and the Council of Nationalities, both chosen by the Congress of People's Deputies

from its membership. The Supreme Soviet has 542 members, and one-fifth of its membership will be changed each year by the Congress. The Supreme Soviet meets in regular spring and autumn sessions each year, each session intended to last 3 to 4 months (Article 112). It is also given an impressive list of functions, including naming the Council of Ministers, the Defense Council, the Supreme Court, the Procurator General, and other top posts and organizations (Article 113). The Supreme Soviet has the power to adopt laws (*zakony*), which is also given to the Congress of People's Deputies. This is just one area of apparent overlapping and duplication between the two bodies that some Soviet commentators have raised questions about.

3. With the enhanced importance and lengthened sessions of the Supreme Soviet, the authority of the Presidium of the Supreme Soviet has been diminished. But the Presidium continues to exist as a body "set up to organize the work of the USSR Supreme Soviet" (Article 118). And it is authorized to perform a number of other functions, including coordinating the activities of the standing committees and commissions of the Supreme Soviet.

4. The top official of this redesigned legislative hierarchy is designated by the Russian word *predsedatel'*. This is usually translated as "chairman," and the somewhat analogous post under the old arrangements was commonly referred to as "Chairman of *the Presidium of* the Supreme Soviet.[5] The new position is *predsedatel'* of the Supreme Soviet (not of its Presidium), and until 1990 even some Soviet sources translated the word in this context as "president." But with the creation of a real presidency in 1990, the term "Chairman of the Supreme Soviet" is now normally used. Under the 1988 amendments, the position was clearly the most important one in the new governmental structures. But when the presidency was created in 1990, the Chairman of the Supreme Soviet became a much less significant post. Its functions now are largely limited to coordinating the activities of the Supreme Soviet Presidium and chairing the sessions of the Congress of People's Deputies.

5. Parallel structures were originally established for the lower levels of state power, the union republics, autonomous republics, and local soviets. But a broad array of opposition to these provisions developed, both in Moscow and in some of the union republics, and in late 1989 the constitution was amended further to accommodate this resistance (*Izvestiia*, December 23, 1989, p. 1). As amended, it is up to the union and autonomous republics to decide whether they should have a two-tier or a one-tier legislature; the republics also have the right to decide whether the chairman of the supreme soviet should be popularly elected or chosen by the republic legislature; the principle of deputies being chosen by public organizations was eliminated for the national Congress of People's Deputies, and on the union republic and autono-

---

[5]Western journalists and others sometimes referred loosely to this post as that of "President."

mous republic levels, the question of such representation is to be given to the union republics to decide. On all of these matters a number of union republics have chosen to depart from the practice used at the USSR level. And it seems certain that this will increase the pressure at the national level to reconsider these matters as well. The substance of the arguments that led to these 1989 changes is described in the section on constitutional change and the political process.

6. A person cannot serve on more than two levels of soviets (Article 96). That is, one could be elected to the national and the union republic congress of people's deputies, but then not also to a local representative body. The previous constitutional provision said this limitation should apply "as a rule," but often the rule was ignored. And an amendment (also Article 96) prohibits certain administrative officials, such as members of the council of ministers, from being elected as deputies to the soviet at the corresponding level of government. This provision is sometimes cited as an example of separation of powers in the Soviet system (*Izvestiia,* November 9, 1988, p. 2). But the provision contains numerous exceptions, which allow chairmen of councils of ministers, other leading administrative officials, judges and arbitrators to be deputies. So the separation is only partial.

7. The term of office of all representative bodies is five years (Article 90). Previously it was five years at the USSR, union republic, and autonomous republic levels, and two and one-half years for local soviets. The officials appointed by these representative bodies are permitted to serve no more than two terms (ten years) in a row (Article 91).

8. One of the most discussed aspects of the Gorbachev era is the idea of contested elections, i.e., abandoning the long Soviet practice of allowing only one candidate for each legislative seat. Part of the 1988 amendments amounted to a rewriting of Chapter 13 of the Constitution, on the electoral system, to provide the basis for this kind of election. In addition, a law adopted by the Supreme Soviet on the same day as the constitutional amendments sets forth more detailed rules for conducting elections at the USSR level (*Izvestiia,* December 4, 1988, p. 1). The key constitutional provision designed to permit contested elections is the following: "The number of candidates for people's deputies is not limited" (Article 100). But there is a large number of other provisions, in the amendments and in the 1988 electoral law, that bear on this brief assertion. These details, as well as the realities of electoral procedures, will be examined in Chapter 6.

9. A new 23 member USSR Committee on Constitutional Oversight was created (Article 124). The Committee is responsible for reviewing laws of the USSR, as well as acts of subordinate bodies, to assure their correspondence with the USSR Constitution.

10. Several important changes regarding the judicial system were made:

a. Previously judges in people's courts, the lowest rung on the judicial ladder, were popularly elected in the typical one-candidate elections mentioned previously. Now people's court judges are chosen by the local soviet one level higher. Presumably this is to prevent undue local influence on the functioning of these courts. Higher level judges are, as before, chosen by the soviet at the same level (the members of the USSR Supreme Court by the USSR Supreme Soviet, the union republic supreme court by that union republic's supreme soviet, and so forth). The terms of office of all judges is ten years (it was five years before); and the term of office of lay people's assessors is five years (it was two and one-half years for assessors at the people's court level before; Article 152).

b. A further attempt was made to guarantee the independence of judges and assessors from outside influence, and sanctions were laid down in the constitution for those who attempt such influence (Article 155).

As was indicated previously, these changes were described as the first stage in a series of political and constitutional reforms. In its first session in June 1989 the Congress of People's Deputies created a 107-member commission, headed by Gorbachev, to draft a new constitution (*Izvestiia,* June 10, 1989, p. 3). Work on the draft was expected to take up to two years (S. S. Alkeseev in *Nedelya,* 1989, no. 32, pp. 2–3).

These changes were extremely important in their own right. Taken together, they amounted to an empowering of governmental, particularly legislative, bodies in a way that had never existed before in the history of Soviet power. Watching these events in process, one could not but conclude that they constituted a serious challenge to traditional Communist Party supremacy. But even these developments did not completely prepare the observer for the 1990 amendments.

As the new legislative bodies became accustomed to their increased power, and as organized groups multiplied and gained in membership, the push to eliminate the Communist Party's favored position grew in strength. Led by the late Andrei Sakharov and others, reform legislators sought to place the question of revising article 6 of the Constitution on the legislative agenda in 1989. Although they were defeated in this effort, they made it plain that the issue would not go away. This was at the time, it will be recalled, when communist regimes were being ousted in several countries in Eastern Europe, with tacit Soviet acquiescence.

Gorbachev and his Party allies decided to acknowledge what seemed to be inevitable in early 1990. At a Party Central Committee meeting in February, the elimination of the Party's power monopoly was proposed and adopted. This created a kind of power vacuum, however (particularly for Gorbachev himself), and so the further need was seen for creating a strong position in the state structure to be occupied by a single leader. Therefore, accompanying the elimination of the Party's monopoly position was the creation of the post of president (*prezident* in Russian) of the USSR.

Gorbachev came to see the need for the presidency only reluctantly. Less than six months earlier he had insisted that he did not endorse the creation of such a post or even the word *prezident* (*Izvestiia,* August 20, 1989, p. 2). But along with the demise of the Party came a set of internal problems, most notably violent ethnic unrest in various parts of the country, the increasingly separatist sentiment of leaders and movements in several union republics, and a series of debilitating strikes, particularly by coal miners, in mid-1989. A strong political force, particularly one that could deal with crisis situations, came to be seen as a compelling need, not only to Gorbachev but also to a broad segment of the Soviet population.

The two most important changes in the 1990 amendments, then, had to do with the elimination of the Communist Party's monopoly and the creation of the post of president. Among other amendments, one symbolizing the changed attitudes toward property and ownership was also included. It will be discussed below.

The constitutional adjustments regarding the Communist Party's position required relatively little change. The words in the document's Preamble referring to the "leading role of the Communist Party—the vanguard of the people," were eliminated. The key provisions in Article 6 had described the Party as "the leading and guiding force of Soviet society and the nucleus of its political system, of all state organizations and public organizations" and had assigned it the function of determining the general lines of domestic and foreign policy development. These were replaced with a statement to the effect that the Communist Party, "other political parties," and other organizations may participate in the operation of the political system. Further changes were made to other articles to indicate that political parties and other organizations could now be established (Article 51), as long as they operated within the framework of Soviet law and did not advocate forcible change of the Soviet system or engender social unrest in other ways (Article 7).

Further changes were made in several articles (6,7,10,11,12, and 13) in order to allow for more flexible concepts of property and ownership in the USSR. Whereas "private property" had been forbidden under previous Soviet law, it was now to be permitted, at least in limited form, under the name "citizen property." On the basis of this constitutional change, new laws on land and property were adopted by the legislature spelling out the details of the new property arrangements.

Much more comprehensive, however, were the new constitutional provisions on the president. They involve the creation of a completely new institution, and a consequent rearrangement of power and authority with regard to other governmental institutions. A new chapter, 15(1), was added to the Constitution, containing one extensive article (Article 127) with numerous provisions. A brief description of the powers and functions of the president will be given here. The reader should consult the Constitution (Appendix A), particularly article 127, for further details.

The presidency is to be a popularly elected post for which any citizen between the ages of 35 and 65 can run. Regarding the first incumbent for the office, however, an exception was made to the popular election provision, allowing the president to be chosen by the Congress of People's Deputies. Gorbachev was chosen in this way in March 1990. A person may serve as president for no more than two five-year terms. As a partial move in the direction of separation of powers, the president cannot be a deputy to any legislative body.

The president is provided both broad authority and a number of specific powers by the Constitution. The president is designated as "the guarantor of Soviet citizens' rights and freedoms and of the USSR Constitution and laws." He is empowered to take measures necessary to protect the sovereignty and security of the USSR. He represents the USSR both within the country and in international relations. In terms of the president's more specific powers, the following are among the most important: nominating a number of officials, including the chairman of the USSR Council of Ministers, chairman of the USSR People's Control Committee, chairman of the USSR Supreme Court, USSR prosecutor general, and USSR chief state arbiter, whose names are submitted to the Congress of People's Deputies for confirmation; raising the question with the Supreme Soviet or the Congress of the removal of these officials, with the exception of the USSR Supreme Court chairman; participating in the nomination and release of ministers and other members of the government; signing laws adopted by parliament, with a veto power, which can be overridden by a two-thirds majority in both houses of the Supreme Soviet; suspending acts of the USSR Council of Ministers; coordinating the military and defense efforts of the country, as supreme commander in chief of the armed forces; acting in a variety of foreign policy capacities, including negotiating and signing international treaties, accepting foreign diplomatic representatives and appointing USSR diplomats for work abroad; deciding questions of USSR citizenship; declaring war, a partial or general mobilization, martial law, a state of emergency, and temporary presidential rule (several of these functions to be performed in consultation with other state bodies); submitting to the Congress of People's Deputies the question of replacing the membership of the Supreme Soviet, if the two houses of that body become deadlocked; issuing binding edicts based on USSR laws and the Constitution.

This list of duties and functions of the president is certainly impressive. It will require some period of actual operation of the office to determine how much of a shift in the balance of political power has been effected by these changes. What can be said, however, is that not all of the powers that Gorbachev wanted were granted to him in the constitutional changes. The proposed changes were presented initially in draft form, first in the Supreme Soviet and then in the Congress of People's Deputies (only the Congress can amend the Constitution). Media coverage indicates that there was considerable controversy over some parts of the proposal, and on a number of issues Gorbachev had to back down. He pushed for quick passage of the draft, but the deputies insisted that some meaningful discussion take place. On several points the adopted version reduced the power of the president. Thus, for instance, although the president can propose the appointment and call for the removal of a number of officials (Article 127 (3)(6)), his ability to seek the removal of the USSR Supreme Court chairman was eliminated, a move designed to protect judicial independence. Likewise, the original draft gave the president the power to propose members of the Constitutional Oversight Committee, a function now given to the Congress of People's Deputies, based on nominations by the Chairman of the USSR Supreme Soviet. And in the original draft the president's veto power included the right, if the Supreme Soviet overrode his veto by the required two-thirds vote, to refer the matter to the Congress of People's Deputies. In the final version, if the veto is overridden the president must sign the law.

In spite of these modifications, the president's power is formidable, and Gorbachev got most of what he wanted in the constitutional changes. And on the matter of avoiding popular election for the first five-year term, he also carried the day, against strong support for popular election from many deputies and from large segments of the public. In analyses of the presidency made after the office was established, some commentators maintained that no significant shift in the constitutional balance had taken place.[6] But this is clearly not the case. The presidency replaces the Party General Secretary as the single most significant position in the USSR. Whether the presidency, which seemed so necessary to create in the difficult days of 1990, can be integrated into the constitutional framework previously established is an open question. Achieving that integration will require not only effective counterbalancing mechanisms in the other governmental bodies (the Congress of People's Deputies, the Supreme Soviet, the Constitutional Oversight Committee), but also persons occupying the position of president who are willing to act responsibly and not seek to create a dictatorial regime. Given the Soviet experience with the accumulation of personal political power, this is asking a great deal from the fledgling institutions recently created.

CONSTITUTIONAL CHANGE AND THE POLITICAL PROCESS

Since Soviet constitutions, until recently, have not defined or limited political power, it might be thought that Soviet politicians would be indifferent to them.

---

[6]Supreme Soviet Chairman Lukyanov, for instance, said that the changes did not diminish the power of the legislative bodies "to any significant extent." *Pravda,* April 2, 1990, p. 3.

This has not been entirely the case. The symbolic and potential importance of constitutional provisions has led to some contention, often behind the scenes, about what is referred to as the "basic law." Several Soviet leaders appear, in fact, to have had difficulty getting their colleagues to go along with constitutional changes they proposed. As early as 1959, Nikita Khrushchev promised that basic revision of the constitution was being drafted. Khrushchev was named Chairman of the Constitutional Drafting Commission in 1962, a position that Brezhnev took over after replacing Khrushchev in 1964. Like Khrushchev, Brezhnev seemed committed to the adoption of a new constitution yet incapable of bringing the project to fruition. In 1966 he promised that the document would be completed by the fiftieth anniversary of Bolshevik rule in November 1967. In 1972 he promised that a text of the constitution would be released by the Twenty-Fifth Party Congress in 1976. Both of these dates came and went without a new constitution, and it was clear that sufficient opposition existed to block the project.

During all of these years, Brezhnev had been gaining strength relative to his Politburo colleagues, however, and by 1977 the time was ripe for the issue to be resolved. At a Party Central Committee meeting in May, two important developments took place: A draft of the new constitution was approved, and Nikolai V. Podgornyi, chairman of the Presidium of the Supreme Soviet, was dropped from the ruling Party Politburo. As subsequent events were to show, these developments were clearly connected. The next month Brezhnev took over Podgornyi's post of chairman of the Supreme Soviet Presidium, a position then equated with being the ceremonial president of the country. Some analysts have suggested that Podgornyi opposed the new constitution because of disagreement with certain of its provisions. Whether this is so is not clear. It does seem likely, in any case, that he resisted being replaced in the Presidium chairmanship by Brezhnev and so was removed from both the Politburo and the Presidium in what amounted to a forced retirement. Subsequent leaders followed the Brezhnev example. Shortly after having become general secretary of the Party both Andropov and Chernenko also assumed the Presidium chairmanship. Gorbachev waited more than three years before taking over the Presidium chairmanship, perhaps because his position was not yet secure enough to bid for the post. But in 1988 he became Presidium Chairman as a prelude to assuming the new and more powerful position of President of the USSR.

Political interest in constitutional change is not limited to the realm of high Party politics, however. As was mentioned, public discussion preceded the adoption of recent constitutions. And other occurrences suggest the considerable symbolic significance of constitutions for some people. During the process of adopting union republic constitutions in 1978 (following the adoption of the USSR Constitution the previous year), an issue involving national language in the three Transcaucasian republics of Armenia, Georgia, and Azerbaidzhan arose. These three were the only of the fifteen union republics with provisions in their previous constitutions designating the language of the major ethnic group in each republic as the state language of that republic. When these provisions were dropped from the drafts of the 1978 constitutions, protest demonstrations were reported to have taken place. The central authorities quietly backed down on this issue, and in the final versions of the constitutions for these three republics, the language provisions were restored (*The New York Times,* April 19, 1978, p. A5; *Radio Liberty Research,* no. 82/78, April 18, 1978; Feldbrugge, 1979, p. 288).

Further ethnic unrest accompanied the adoption of the 1988 constitutional amendments. These amendments were proposed in mid–1988, a time of considerable ethnic ferment, particularly in the Baltic republics of Estonia, Latvia, and Lithuania and in the Transcaucasian republics. Several of the proposals were seen by some opponents as enhancing the central control of the national government at the expense of the republican governments. The Estonian Supreme Soviet went so far as to declare its right to veto all-union legislation that infringed upon its autonomy and to declare the land and other resources within its boundaries the sole property of the Estonian Republic. Although Latvia and Lithuania did not, at that time, adopt such radical measures, they expressed similar concerns about the proposed constitutional amendments. The central Soviet government, through the Presidium of the USSR Supreme Soviet, found the Estonian actions to be at odds with the USSR Constitution and declared them null and void (*Izvestiia,* November 28, 1988, p. 1). At the same time the central authorities made some concessions to the concerns expressed. Gorbachev acknowledged that some of the proposed amendments had been adopted hastily and perhaps without sufficient consultation with the union republics. He promised that the next stage of political reform would consider the expansion of republican rights. And several of the provisions of concern to the ethnic protesters in the draft version of the amendments were modified in the final version (Sheehy, 1988). The problem did not end there, however. Several republics, most notably Lithuania in 1990, have pushed for further autonomy, and have adopted legislation that Moscow considers to be in violation of the USSR Constitution. This issue, which is certain to continue for years if force is not used to suppress it, goes to the very heart of the central authorities' conception of the meaning of Soviet federalism. Moreover, the issue of language policy has also taken on important constitutional significance. As was indicated previously, in the 1970s only three republics pushed to have the indigenous language declared the state language of their republic. By the end of the 1980s virtually every Soviet republic had considered or adopted such legislation (Dailey, 1989, p. 31).

But the critics of the 1988 amendments were not just concerned about ethnic issues. As was indicated earlier, a broad discussion (of both the constitutional amendments and the law on elections) took place, with hundreds of thousands of comments and suggestions reportedly submitted by specialists and members of the general public. The tone of the comments on this occasion was more genuine, searching, and critical than before. Some people wanted to know why the period of discussion lasted only one month. Others sought to discuss revising aspects of the political system not taken up in the draft laws, which the authorities would not permit. This public involvement in constitutional change has continued since the new tone was set in 1988.

In a sense, the starting point for the measures adopted in December 1988 was the 19th Party Conference held five months earlier. The conference had adopted a series of resolutions for reforming aspects of the political system, and some critics charged that the provisions in the draft laws were contrary to promises made in these resolutions. The most notable of these was the conference resolution statement that people's court judges were to be elected by the local soviet body *one level above* the level at which they would serve. But when the draft of the amendments appeared in late October 1988, it provided for those judges to be chosen by the soviets on the same level (*Izvestiia,* October 22, 1988, p. 2). As was indicated previously, there has long been concern about improper influence by local authorities on judges, and the public criticism of this provision of the draft was substantial. In the version finally adopted, this provision was changed back to conform with the Party Conference recommendation. But some critics wondered why the draft version had departed from the conference recommendation, one offering the view that it was "the result of the command-bureaucratic system which is mortally afraid of economic and governmental organisms that are independent" (Feofanov, 1988).

Relatively speaking, however, the provision on judges was a minor point in the amendments, and much of the public discussion was aimed at the changes in the structure of the high organs of state. These were the matters addressed in part by the 1989 amendments. Most prominent was the creation of the Congress of People's Deputies. Many commentators wanted to know why both a Congress and a Supreme Soviet were needed, since their functions were in part duplicative. Others were bothered by various aspects of the new electoral system, particularly the provision that accorded 750 seats in the Congress (one-third of the total) to public organizations like the Communist Party. This scheme seemed unwieldy, particularly if and when the number of public organizations eligible for representation grew. The feature of only having the Congress popularly elected, with the Supreme Soviet and the chairman of the Supreme Soviet indirectly elected (by the Congress), seemed to many commentators to go against the democratic principles being professed by the leadership. Some wanted to know who in the Congress, a body likely to be docile and easily manipulated, would control the selection of the Supreme Soviet and its chairman. The late Andrei Sakharov, for instance, who supported many of Gorbachev's initiatives, expressed disquiet about the potential for abuse in these arrangements (*The New York Times,* November 2, 1988, p. A1; November 12,1988, p. 6).

But while concessions were made on a number of other points (Gorbachev reported that 26 of the 55 articles in the constitutional amendments and 32 of the 62 articles in the law on elections were modified on the basis of the public discussion; *Izvestiia,* November 30, 1988, p. 2), the leadership originally gave no ground on these issues. The fact that it eventually went along with changes on these matters indicates something important about the degree of control the leadership (and particularly the central Party authorities) has been able to maintain over the process.

It is clear that the Party initiated the process of political reform and, for a time, was able to guide its course of development. On the basis of the 19th Party Conference in June–July 1988 a Central Committee plenary meeting in July appointed a commission headed by Gorbachev to prepare recommendations for carrying out the political reforms outlined by the conference. Drafts of the constitutional amendments and the electoral law were prepared and reviewed by this Party commission and then published for public discussion (*Izvestiia,* October 19, 1988, p. 1). At the end of the public discussion the Party Central Committee met again to approve the modified drafts of the reforms, and only then was the matter turned over to the Supreme Soviet for formal discussion and adoption (*Izvestiia,* November 29, 1988, p. 1). Ultimate control, in other words, was maintained by the Party.

But as was indicated, the public discussion aired serious disagreements with the Party-engineered changes. And when it came time to adopt parallel amendments at the union republic level, things had changed: The Party itself was no longer the monolithic, disciplined body that it had long been; and other interests, primarily but not exclusively those on the union republic level, had developed and were pushing their own reform agendas. Even by the late 1980s, then, the central leadership had to some extent lost control of the process. And when, in 1990, the further constitutional amendments were adopted, the weakened position of the Communist Party became evident to all. The constitutional underpinning of the Party's dominance was eliminated, and the design for further transfer of real political power to the state was effected by the creation of the presidency. The import of these developments goes well beyond the matter of constitution-writing in the Soviet Union. It is of basic significance to the future of the whole Soviet system, since it involves the place of the Party in guiding the USSR. This is a topic addressed more appropriately in Chapter 7.

REFERENCES

DAILEY, ERIKA. (1989). Update on alphabet legislation, *Radio Liberty Report on the USSR, 1,* 32, 29.

FELDBRUGGE, F.J.M., ed. (1979). *The constitutions of the USSR and the union republics: Analysis, texts, reports.* Alphen aan den Rijn, The Netherlands: Sijthoff & Noordhoff.

FEOFANOV, Y. (1988). "Who done it?" *Moscow News,* no. 50, 3.

FRIEDRICH, C. (1968). *Constitutional government and democracy.* Fourth edition. Waltham, Mass.: Blaisdell.

Istoriia Sovetskoi Konstitutsii (v Dokumentakh, 1917–1956). (1957). Moscow: Gosu-darstvennoe Izdatel'stvo Iuridicheskoi Literatury.

MCILWAIN, C. (1947). *Constitutionalism ancient and modern.* Revised edition. Ithaca, N.Y.: Cornell University Press.

SHEEHY, A. (1988). "The first stage of Gorbachev's reform of the political system and the nonRussian republics." *Radio Liberty Research,* no. 520/88.

SIX
THE GOVERNMENT:
The Politics of Empowerment

The constitutional changes of the late 1980s and 1990 described in the last chapter created the potential for the most profound shift in political power in Soviet history. Most directly affected by these changes are the government (the subject of this chapter) and the Communist Party (the subject of Chapter 7). To facilitate the reader's understanding of these important developments, the procedure used in this chapter will be to examine several aspects of governmental structure and operation, looking first at how these institutions formerly functioned and then at the new arrangements.

Governmental structures in Western polities are typically of two general types: representative institutions, usually popularly elected, and bureaucratic or administrative bodies, whose members are chosen by a variety of means. This division of functions has operated in the Soviet Union as well, but with certain differences. Since the Communist Party has traditionally been the focus of power, governmental institutions have been relatively insignificant. This has applied in particular to representative bodies, whose members were chosen in sham elections and whose functions largely involved the formal legitimization of policy decisions made elsewhere. The governmental bureaucracy, though not as powerless as the representative bodies, was basically responsible for carrying out administrative functions based on the Party's dictates. We will look first at the representative bodies and then examine the bureaucratic apparatus.

ELECTIONS

To those familiar with parliamentary or presidential elections in the West, Soviet elections before 1989 appeared to be a rather pointless exercise. On the
one hand there was the constitutional guarantee of "universal, equal and direct suffrage by secret ballot" (Article 95). On the other hand there was the
whole of Soviet electoral practice since elections began to be held under this
provision in 1938. The basic features of Soviet elections will be familiar to
those having even a passing acquaintance with the Soviet past: one person
running for each seat in an uncontested election and over 99 percent of the
electorate participating, with virtually all of them voting for the unopposed
candidate (rather than voting against by crossing out the name, the only other
act envisaged in Soviet electoral practices). In this most *pro forma* of arrangements, only a minuscule number of candidates did not receive the required 50
percent of the votes cast, and this virtually never happened in the national or
republic-level elections, only at the local levels (Gilison, 1968; Van den Berg,
1978). Even where such a defeat took place there was no possibility of simultaneously electing another person by means of the write-in vote, because a write-
in was considered to invalidate the ballot. Election, therefore, depended on
nomination, and this process was also suitably controlled to allow only "desirable" candidates to be put forward. Six kinds of bodies were allowed to nominate candidates. Since all of these bodies—Communist Party organizations,
trade unions, the Komsomol, cooperatives and other public organizations,
work collectives, and meetings of servicemen in their military units—were
sanctioned by the regime, they provided an initial screening process. Although
it was possible for more than one candidate to be nominated for a single seat—
indeed, such a practice would seem to be implied in allowing a number of
kinds of organizations to make nominations—it always worked out that only
one candidate ran for each legislative seat. Obviously, by some informal,
behind-the-scenes process a single candidate was chosen.

The actual casting of ballots was a similarly orchestrated arrangement.
After obtaining a ballot paper at the local voting place by presenting identification, the voter cast a valid ballot simply by placing the paper in the ballot box
(*urna*), which was usually suitably located under a giant portrait of Lenin. In
other words, no marks needed to be affixed by the voter. It was a simple act
of transference from election officials to ballot box, with the voter as medium.
And the typical individual's participation in the whole Soviet political process
was summed up in the hollowness of this act.

In spite of the seeming emptiness of process, the Soviet authorities expended considerable effort and money on the electoral process. A vast network of election commissions existed to handle all phases of the elections. In
addition to the nominating process, a campaign of sorts was run in which the
nominee's name was made known to the people of his or her constituency.
The candidate even made a preelection speech to a meeting of voters.

Why did they go to all this trouble? Probably for several reasons. First, the elections were seen as a legitimizing device for the people in power. No matter how meaningless they may have appeared, they could be said to provide some basis for the claim that the people were behind the leaders. Moreover, the results could offer no encouragement to would-be opponents of the regime, since they indicated how completely the leadership was in control. Further, there was some ideological justification, no matter how dubious, for such elections. It was said that since Soviet society did not contain the inherent contradictions of capitalist society (classes, the profit motive, and so on), there was no need to have contested elections. Finally, comparisons were often made between Soviet and Western elections. Strongly criticized was the role of money in the latter, particularly in the United States. Whatever else could be said about Soviet elections, it was certainly true that individual candidates did not need to raise great amounts of money for their campaigns. So the former Soviet voting practices were justified by a combination of pointing out the negative aspects of Western electoral politics and showing how the Soviet mode of election fit in so well with the classless, nonantagonistic nature of Soviet society.

In actual fact, it is clear that Soviet voting was not the monolithic demonstration of support for the regime that the leadership insisted on proclaiming. Evidence shows that voter support was at times well below the 99-plus-percent level always reported (Zaslavsky and Brym, 1978, p. 366; Karklins, 1986; Roeder, 1989). And at times, even in the 1960s and 1970s, would-be reformers were bold enough to recommend that genuinely contested elections be introduced (see, for example, *The New York Times,* March 22, 1966, p. 2; *CDSP, 17,* no. 14 (1965), p. 5; Van den Berg, 1978, p. 358). When the reformist atmosphere of the Gorbachev era began in earnest, many of the electoral practices of the past were quickly abandoned. We will turn now to the changes in Soviet elections that were introduced at the end of the 1980s.

The move to change the electoral system just described developed gradually, as the era of glasnost permitted the airing of diverse views across a range of subjects. Electoral reform was part of a more general reform of the political system that received strong impetus from the nineteenth Party Conference in 1988 (see Chapter 7). The Conference decisions led to the 1988 constitutional amendments described in Chapter 5. On the same day that these constitutional amendments were adopted, a new electoral law, which served as the basis for the new electoral format, was passed by the national legislature (*Pravda,* December 4, 1988, p. 1).

It is clear that the Party hoped, through these new electoral arrangements, to maintain considerable control over legislative elections and thus over the legislative process. But a number of developments have, over time, diluted Party control. The following discussion will concentrate on the USSR-level elections of 1989, with only brief reference to republic-level and local elections.

As indicated in Chapter 5, the new supreme legislative organ is the Congress of People's Deputies. This 2,250-member body was designed to meet for one or more rather short sessions each year. It appoints a 542-member standing legislature, the Supreme Soviet, from the membership of the Congress. The Supreme Soviet normally meets twice a year for longer periods. Since the Supreme Soviet is an appointed rather than an elected body, it will be discussed later.

The Congress of People's Deputies was originally composed of deputies chosen in three ways: 750 from territorial electoral districts based on numbers of voters; 750 deputies from national-territorial districts based on the federal structure of the country: 32 deputies from each union republic, 11 from each autonomous republic, 5 from each autonomous oblast (province), and 1 from each autonomous okrug (region); and 750 from all-union social organizations, including 100 from the Communist Party, 100 from the trade unions, 100 from cooperative organizations, smaller numbers from such bodies as women's councils (75 deputies) and scientific organizations (75 deputies), and even lower representation for organizations like the Soviet Children's Fund (5 deputies) and the All-Union Voluntary Temperance Society (1 deputy). As was indicated in Chapter 5, great popular dissatisfaction was expressed with the third mode of allocating seats, and at the end of 1989 the constitution was again changed to eliminate representation for social organizations in the USSR Congress of People's Deputies and to allow the union republics to decide upon such representation at the lower levels. But the deputies chosen to the national Congress in 1989 were permitted to serve out their five-year terms.

One of the major objections to allocating seats to social organizations (aside from the general view that it was undemocratic) was the fear that the Party leadership could ensure the selection of a large bloc of deputies who could be counted on to help control the Congress's actions. This fear seemed to be realized in part almost immediately, when the leadership of several social organizations, most notably the Communist Party, engineered the nomination of only as many candidates as there were seats to be filled, thus obviating the possibility of democratic choice within these organizations. A particularly egregious example of rigged elections was in the USSR Academy of Sciences, to which 20 seats were allocated. Andrei Sakharov was nominated by more than 60 academic institutes, but the Academy's election screening committee eliminated him and other popular reformers from the recommended list of candidates. According to the procedures established, however, this list had to be approved by a general meeting of Academy of Sciences delegates. But liberal supporters of Sakharov within the Academy were able to thwart the academy leadership's effort by refusing to support the approved list (only eight candidates received the required 50 percent of the delegate votes). Rebuffed, the Academy leadership backed down, and Sakharov and several other liberal reformers were chosen to seats in the Congress (*Moscow News,* 1989, no. 7, p. 14).

The basis for choosing the other 1,500 deputies to the Congress of People's Deputies was potentially more democratic. The electoral law provides for single-member districts, "universal, equal and direct suffrage by secret ballot," campaign expenses covered from state funds, and the nomination of an unrestricted number of candidates for each seat (Articles 1, 12, and 37 of the Electoral Law). However, electoral practices left some room for diluting the good intentions of these provisions.

Nominations for people's deputies could come from labor collectives, social organizations, meetings of servicemen in military units, and meetings of voters in places of residence. Electoral commissions, chosen by the local soviets, were set up in neighborhoods and electoral districts to administer the elections. Higher electoral commissions, headed by a 35-member Central Electoral Commission, were also established. But particularly in the first election, in 1989, when there was little experience with genuine electoral practices, the spirit of the electoral reform was not always followed. Considerable discretion was exercised by the electoral commissions, and if they were controlled by antireform forces, campaign irregularities of various kinds could occur. For instance, one of the ways to nominate candidates was at meetings of voters at places of residence. At least 500 voters were needed for a quorum at such meetings. Numerous examples were reported of local authorities "packing" a meeting place with their supporters so that voters sympathetic to other candidates could not attend. And although campaign funding was supposed to come from the state, some candidates connected with wealthy organizations received large supplemental financing from their supporters ("Money for Democracy," *Moscow News,* 1989, no. 20, p. 9). Although the new arrangements suggested that contested elections should be the norm, the electoral law did not prevent one-person races. And numerous local Party bosses and their supporters, accustomed to the electoral practices of the past, arranged for candidates to run unopposed. As one observer complained in summing up his views on the nomination process: "Each of us must clearly realize that the games the apparatus is playing will not vanish of their own accord" (*CDSP, 41,* 1989, no. 4, p. 7).

But by 1989 the authorities could no longer act with complete impunity toward the voters. The press had been awakened, and some publications in particular were prepared to report violations of the letter and the spirit of the new provisions. And new political forces, in the form of popular fronts, political clubs, and nationality movements, had been formed and saw the importance of participating in the formation of the Congress of People's Deputies. In addition, individual citizens manifested considerable interest in the elections, as shown by, among other things, great numbers of letters to the media.

Thus, although the nomination process was not completely democratic, neither was it anything like the highly orchestrated charades of the past. According to official figures, 2,895 candidates were registered for the 1,500 seats, an average of over 1.9 per seat. In terms of contests, there was one candidate in 384 districts, two in 953, three in 109, four in 27, and five or more in 27 (*CDSP, 41,* 1989, no. 10, p. 17).

Before discussing the electoral results themselves, several details of the electoral rules should be explained. First, to be elected requires that the winner receive over 50 percent of the total vote.[1] This aspect of the Soviet system is similar in many respects to the "single member district majority" system used at present in France, but unlike the plurality system used in legislative elections in Great Britain and the United States. If no candidate receives an absolute majority, a second election must be held. If three or more candidates ran on the first ballot and there was no winner, then the top two compete in a runoff election (Article 60 of the Electoral Law). If two or fewer candidates were on the first ballot and none was elected, there must be a completely new election, including a repetition of the nominating process (Article 61 of the Electoral Law). One might wonder how a second election could be needed in a contest involving two or fewer candidates. This has to do with a further peculiarity of the Soviet electoral system. One casts a ballot in favor of a candidate by crossing out the names of all other candidates. If all names are crossed out (even in a one-person race), then no one gets that vote. Thus, even a candidate running unopposed could fail to win a seat by having his name crossed out on more than half of the ballots. As the 1989 election neared, it became clear that there was considerable public awareness of the potential for using this aspect of the rules. Many voters questioned the authorities on what might be called "crossing-out practices."[2] And a campaign of sorts developed to cross out on principle the names of candidates running unopposed.[3] The use of these aspects of the rules contributed to some surprises in the 1989 election.

Election Results

Over 172 million people participated in the 1989 election, almost 90 percent of registered voters. Although not as impressive a figure as reported in the sham elections of the past, this turnout indicated a high level of genuine public interest. Just as significant were some of the results. In Moscow the maverick politician and former high Party official Boris Yeltsin won 89 percent of the vote in defeating the candidate of the local Party machine, the director of a Moscow limousine factory. Numerous other liberals were chosen over more conservative opponents. And recently awakened nationality interests scored well in their areas. For instance, the Lithuanian movement Sajudis won

[1]This is termed an "absolute majority." Some countries such as Great Britain only require the winner to receive more votes than any other candidate. This is a "plurality."

[2]See the answers of the secretary of the Central Election Commission to a series of readers' questions on this subject in *Izvestiia,* March 23, 1989, p. 1.

[3]See, for example, the picture of the placard held up at a Leningrad election rally proclaiming "Cross Out the Name of the Single Candidate" in *Moscow News,* 1989, no. 14, p. 9.

almost 90 percent of the seats allotted to the republic (Girnius, 1989a, p. 29; Girnius 1989b, p. 24).

Just as important were some of the defeats. Numerous local Party officials did not win (about 20 percent according to one government figure; *Report on the USSR, 1,* no. 14, 1989, p. 34). Certainly the most spectacular loss was that of Leningrad Party chief and candidate Politburo member Yuri Solovyev, who was running unopposed (Solovyev's political career ended shortly thereafter when he was removed from his Leningrad and Politburo positions as a result of the electoral defeat).

In all, runoff elections were required in 76 districts where there was no winner in races involving three or more persons; and new elections were needed in 199 districts where one or two candidates had run unsuccessfully the first time.[4] These elections were held in the weeks after the original elections, and the composition of the Congress of People's Deputies was finally achieved shortly before the body's first meeting in May 1989.

THE SOVIET LEGISLATIVE PROCESS

The Composition of the Legislature

As was indicated previously, the noncontested elections in the old Supreme Soviet meant, in effect, that the members of the Supreme Soviet were appointed. As a result, representation of various categories of the population was handled according to what amounted to quotas. Thus, for instance, Communist Party members numbered about 70 percent of the Supreme Soviet, and women about one-third of the parliament. Workers and collective farmers were said to comprise half of the body, about the same percentage as members with partial or complete higher education. Deputies below the age of thirty numbered about 20 percent of the Supreme Soviet. These figures were quite consistent throughout the 1970s and 1980s (Barry and Barner-Barry, 1987, p. 84). Since the Supreme Soviet was an essentially powerless body, the authorities could afford to practice a kind of tokenism and populate it with representatives of groups that were not found in large numbers in more important bodies.[5] Thus, although the 30 to 33 percent figure for women was well under their 53.3 percent of the total Soviet population, it was well above their per-

[4]In addition, new elections were held in three districts in Armenia where there was less than 50 percent voter turnout, the threshold required by the electoral law, on the first vote. And a new election was required in one district in Kazakhstan where the person elected had died (Mann, 1989a, p. 3).

[5]In the union republic and lower soviets this tokenism was even more pronounced. Thus, for instance, the "quota" for women in local soviets was about 50 percent; that for workers and collective farmers approached 70 percent; and that for deputies below age 30 was about one-third. Data from Barry and Barner-Barry, 1987, p. 84.

centage in the Communist Party (about 27 percent). And in higher Party bodies, of course, women have always been much more underrepresented. One of the by-products of the empowerment of the new legislative structures in the USSR has been the sharp drop in the representation of women (see the following discussion).

Orchestrating the composition of the legislature in the ways just described became impossible when the Congress of People's Deputies was created. The old quotas disappeared, and a more diverse legislature was chosen. The groups whose numbers were artificially inflated by the quotas suffered, as the following figure shows:[6]

	1984 Supreme Soviet	1989 Congress of People's Deputies
% women	32.8	14
% workers and collective farmers	51.3	43
% deputies under age 30	22	8

At the same time, representation increased for other groups such as highly trained professionals (scientists, professors, journalists, and so forth), whose percentage went from 6 in 1984 to almost 10 in 1989. Several clergymen were elected to the Congress, a profession that had never been represented in a Soviet legislature before (*Izvestiia,* May 6, 1989, p. 3). The group whose numbers grew the most in the new legislature was the Communist Party, but this apparent rise in the Party's influence requires some explanation. Party representation went from 71 percent in 1984 to 87 percent in 1989. In some ways this was to be expected, since the Party leadership initiated the changes in legislative structure and, as the only organized political party, it was poised to launch a serious election campaign. In numerous contests Party members ran against each other, and so it was inevitable that a Party member would win. But what is most notable about the results is the *kind* of Party members elected in 1989. The data show that the top of the Party, in other words, high-level professional politicians, were less well represented in the 1989 Congress (both in percentage and in absolute numbers) than in the 1984 Supreme Soviet (*CDSP, 41,* no. 18, 1989, p. 5). Many of the Party members in the Congress were not professional politicians, and they could not be counted on by the leadership to provide monolithic support. As a result, proceedings of the Con-

[6]Sources for these figures: Barry and Barner-Barry, 1987, p. 84; Mann, 1989, p. 5.

gress were much less predictable than the high level of Party membership might have suggested.

Legislative Sessions

The presiding officer at a joint session of the two houses of the Soviet national legislature, the Supreme Soviet, asked members of each house to vote on a law in question. To each house he said: "Those who are for adoption of this law please raise their hands. Please lower them. Who is opposed? None opposed. Who abstains? No abstainers. The law has been adopted" (*Zasedaniia,* 1983, p. 139). This quotation is from the proceedings of a 1983 session of the Soviet legislature. It typifies legislative practice from early in the Soviet period until the late 1980s and is consistent with the mythology erected by Soviet ideologues to justify such procedures.

According to this mythology, the Soviet Union is a state that has long since reached socialism and eliminated antagonistic classes. Therefore, one would not expect differences to be manifested in legislative voting. As we saw previously, this is the same kind of rationale that justified the absence of contested elections. Without contending interests, Soviet legislative bodies could be incredibly efficient at processing large amounts of business in short periods of time. In exercising the substantial formal authority granted it by the constitution, the USSR Supreme Soviet, the highest legislative body from 1938 to 1989, completed its business in sessions that averaged less than a week per year. Although unanimous voting helped in achieving this efficiency, it was not the only device enlisted to this end. Essentially, Supreme Soviet meetings amounted to the ceremonial completion or ratification of the policy-making process, on which all of the essential work had been done elsewhere. The main purpose of collecting 1,500 Supreme Soviet deputies in Moscow for a few days each year was not to sound them out on popular views in their constituencies. If anything, the objective was to have the deputies carry the word outward from the center. If some "localism" did creep into Supreme Soviet proceedings at times, it amounted to a very primitive form of constituency representation and typically had little effect on policy-making.

The old Supreme Soviet was a bicameral legislature made up of the Soviet of the Union (750 members elected every five years from electoral districts based on population size) and the Soviet of Nationalities (750 members elected every five years as representatives for the various national territorial units). Since the Supreme Soviet met only for a few days each year, there were no full-time legislators. Supreme Soviet deputies had other full-time jobs, which served as the basis for their election to the Supreme Soviet. In some respects, election was a reflection of the position one had achieved in Soviet society. All of the most important Party and governmental officials and a number of top scientists and intellectuals (such as the president of the USSR Academy of Sciences) were always members. For these persons membership amounted to yet another affirmation of their status. Being chosen to serve in the Supreme Soviet could also provide a reward for good work, an honor bestowed on less exalted Soviet citizens who distinguished themselves in their fields of endeavor. A local factory would give great attention to one of "its" workers elected as a deputy, and considerable local prestige was attached to the honor. Almost invariably the worker chosen had an excellent work record, was active in Party or Komsomol affairs, and was attempting to improve himself or herself through further training or education. He or she was also typically depicted as a "good comrade." To the extent that Supreme Soviet deputies could serve as the "media for the message" from Moscow, of course, it was important that such persons command the respect of their coworkers.

In addition to the prestige and the chance for political advancement that such election afforded, other nonmaterial incentives were also important: the feeling of being in the "in group," of mixing with the "real" leaders, and of spending a few days a year in Moscow at government expense. For the lathe operator from far-off Sakhalin Island, in the Pacific Ocean, this last may have been a particular incentive.

Legislative sessions under the new structures are very different. First of all, there are two legislatures, the Congress of People's Deputies and the Supreme Soviet. Both possess the power to make laws, but the Congress has certain exclusive powers, including adopting and amending the constitution; ratifying the appointment of certain high officials who are named by the Supreme Soviet (the chairman of the Council of Ministers, the procurator general, the chairman of the USSR Supreme Court, the chairman of the USSR People's Control Committee, and the USSR chief state arbiter); and appointing members of the USSR Supreme Soviet and its chairman.

The constitution provides for at least one regular session of the Congress per year, as well as extraordinary sessions convened when needed. Two sessions were held during the Congress's first year, each lasting about 12 to 13 days each. The Supreme Soviet, "the permanently-operating legislative and monitoring organ of USSR state power" (Article 111 of the Constitution), meets twice annually in longer sessions ("each lasting 3–4 months as a rule," according to Article 112 of the Constitution).

The Supreme Soviet is composed of two houses of equal size, the Soviet of the Union and the Soviet of Nationalities. Up to one-fifth of the membership of each house is renewed each year.[7] In addition to its legislative functions, the Supreme Soviet appoints the Chairman of the Council of Ministers (this choice is ratified by the Congress of People's Deputies), ratifies the composition of the Council of Ministers, as recommended by the Chairman of the Council, and exercises a number of other powers, such as interpreting USSR

[7]In the original constitutional amendment on this matter, adopted in December 1988, the renewal was for one-fifth of the members of both houses. This was changed to "up to one-fifth" by the Congress, by constitutional amendment, in December 1989 (*Izvestiia*, December 29, 1989, p. 1).

laws and ratifying or denouncing international treaties (Article 113 of the constitution).

The operation of the new legislative structures generated enormous public interest when they were first convened in 1989. The sessions of the Congress were televised live, and full stenographic records of the proceedings were published in some newspapers. So great was the public attention focused on the Congress that a 20 percent falloff in industrial production was reported:[8] Workers were watching the live television coverage of the Congress rather than tending to their jobs. When the first session of the new Supreme Soviet was convened, the decision was made to abandon live coverage of the proceedings, and subsequently the same was done with sessions of the Congress.

The Congress sessions themselves proved to be lively but somewhat chaotic. As in many legislatures, time constraints limit the number of deputies who get to speak, and, perhaps because of the television coverage, some deputies have tended toward grandstanding when they finally achieve the podium. The chairmen of the sessions sometimes act arbitrarily in running legislative proceedings (Gorbachev once simply turned off Andrei Sakharov's microphone in order to end his remarks), and various forms of audience harassment (hissing, clapping, attempting to shout down) of speakers voicing controversial views have been common. On numerous occasions complaints have been made about deputies milling about the hall and thereby disrupting proceedings, particularly while votes are being taken. Difficulties with a new electronic voting system were experienced at first, and after it was running there were charges that some deputies voted both with their own cards and with those of absent deputies (see, for example, *Izvestiia,* December 20, 1989, p. 1; December 21, 1989, p. 3). Early sessions were characterized by a lack of appreciation of the importance of procedures, which resulted in a good deal of confusion.[9] Critics saw an absence of what was often called "parliamentary culture."

All of this is understandable in a political system with little tradition of either democracy or genuine legislative activity. As the sessions proceeded, signs of progress in addressing some of these problems could be seen. Permanent Standing Orders (a document called a *reglament* in Russian) covering the proceedings and activities of the Congress of People's Deputies, the Supreme Soviet, and their subordinate organs was adopted in December 1989 (*Izvestiia,* December 28, 1989, p. 1).[10] It provides a set of rules regarding parliamentary

[8]Demographic researchers reported a high in live coverage of 200 million viewers over the 12 Soviet time zones, 25 percent greater than any previous audience (*The New York Times,* May 31, 1989, p. A4).

[9]Numerous Soviet observers understood the importance of procedure in regularizing legislative activity, however. As the deputy editor of the *Moscow News* put it in 1989: "Procedural questions are of secondary importance in an established parliament. But in a new parliament, they are sometimes even more important than the most acute political issues" (Vitaly Tretyakov, "Whose Hopes Will It Justify?" *Moscow News,* 1989, no. 24, p. 7).

[10]For a discussion of the process of discussion and adoption of the Standing Orders, see Mann, 1990.

activities and the relationship of legislative bodies to other governmental organs, and should be of considerable help in bringing order to parliamentary proceedings. Deputies and observers alike quickly saw the necessity for more legally trained personnel connected with the Congress. Only 35 lawyers had been elected as deputies, about 1.5 percent of the body ("Narodnye deputaty SSSR—Iuristy," 1989, p. 56). The need was seen, therefore, for staff lawyers to aid in law drafting, but such specialists were in short supply, and in the beginning, no funds had been set aside to pay them (*Izvestiia,* November 9, 1989, p. 1).[11] Legislators also require office space, secretarial help, and all manner of other support, and some efforts were made to address these needs. A 26-floor office building on Kalinin Prospect in Moscow was vacated in 1989 for use by deputies and legislative committees (*Moscow News,* 1989, no. 40, p. 14). Expense money for legislators was set at 200 rubles per month for deputies (the same pay received by members of the old Supreme Soviet), and a salary of 500 rubles a month was provided for Supreme Soviet members, supplemented by a daily allowance of 15 rubles and certain transportation and vacation benefits (*Moscow News,* 1989, no. 42, p. 13).[12] Since Supreme Soviet membership was to become more like a full-time occupation than in the past, salary levels of this kind were needed. In spite of the chaos of some of the sessions, the Congress has also been characterized by a large amount of interesting, spontaneous activity. A former weightlifting champion and new legislator, Yuri Vlasov, broke one of the strongest taboos of Soviet society early in the first session of the Congress by attacking the KGB as a "threat to democracy" (*The New York Times,* June 1, 1989, p. A1). Another deputy sarcastically criticized Politburo member Yegor Ligachev, the Politburo official in charge of agriculture, "who understands nothing about it [agriculture] and who made a mess of things in ideology" (*CDSP, 41,* no. 27, 1989, p. 12).

Nor was the Congress merely a forum for bold statements. It initiated several actions during its first session aimed at asserting greater authority for the legislative branch and enhancing its role as a policymaker. For instance, in a move to protect freedom of expression, it repealed a provision in a recently adopted edict that made punishable the "discrediting" of public bodies or officials (*Izvestiia,* June 11, 1989, p. 8). It established several important commissions, including one to investigate apparently unjustified attacks on demonstrators in Tbilisi, the Georgian capital, by the military. And it succeeded in slowing down some action that was highly unpopular in certain circles, such as the creation of the Committee on Constitutional Supervision.

When the Congress returned for its second session in December, 1989, it

[11]*Izvestiia* offered the following comparison in 1989: The number of staff persons working for the U.S. Congress was approximately 34,000, while the size of the apparatus serving the Supreme Soviet was 600 (*Izvestiia,* October 15, 1989, p. 2).

[12]Maintenance expenses for deputies were estimated to be 40 million rubles per year in 1989, compared with seven million for the old Supreme Soviet (*Moscow News,* 1989, no. 42, p. 13).

adopted several important pieces of legislation and, after long and difficult debate, promulgated important constitutional amendments. By the time of the second session of the Congress, however, a considerable amount of disillusionment with the body seemed to have set in. In spite of its feistiness, it largely followed the dictates of Gorbachev and his lieutenants. Moreover, it was increasingly seen as a large and cumbersome body, ponderous in taking action. It suffered by comparison with the Supreme Soviet and the legislative committees and commissions, which were seen as relatively more efficient. And with the country's great need to solve severe problems, the wisdom of maintaining a two-tier national legislature was being increasingly called into question, especially after the 1989 constitutional changes that allowed the union republics to dispense with the two-tier scheme.

Thus, after the first flush of enthusiasm with regard to the Congress, the Soviet leadership and the public seemed to look increasingly to the Supreme Soviet to address the country's challenges. The Supreme Soviet is, of course, marked by some of the same problems that characterize the Congress. A new body unaccustomed to the give-and-take of genuine legislative politics, it has also lacked "parliamentary culture."[13] But its smaller size and longer sessions give it the potential to accomplish more.

Among the earliest acts of the Congress of People's Deputies when it is first convened after an election is to name the Supreme Soviet and its top officers. In 1989 Gorbachev was easily elected Chairman of the Supreme Soviet on the first day,[14] and Lukyanov was chosen first deputy chairman several days later, after an extensive grilling on the floor of the Congress. The Supreme Soviet was also quickly chosen, on the second day, before potential opposition to some of those elected could be organized. As a result, a number of well-known liberals were left off the list, and the body that was elected was seen by some as unlikely to challenge the Gorbachev leadership significantly.[15]

As it turned out, however, the Supreme Soviet would be a more autonomous, responsible body than early predictions suggested. Notably excluded from selection to the Supreme Soviet was Boris Yeltsin. However, in an extraordinary parliamentary move, one of those who was chosen to the Supreme Soviet proposed on the floor of the Congress to resign in favor of Yeltsin, and thus the latter was able to secure a seat.

Like the Congress, the Supreme Soviet had a rather low percentage of women (17 percent) and a high proportion of Communist Party members (86

[13]Gorbachev used the term in a speech at the end of the Supreme Soviet's first session (*Izvestiia,* August 5, 1989, p. 1).

[14]One deputy, A. M. Obolensky, nominated himself to run against Gorbachev but did not receive enough votes to be placed on the ballot. Boris Yeltsin was nominated but withdrew. Gorbachev was elected by a vote of 2,123 to 87 (*CDSP, 41,* no. 21, pp. 17–19).

[15]Yuri Afanasyev, a deputy and rector of the Moscow State Historical Archives, called those chosen an "aggressive-obedient majority," a "Stalinist-Brezhnevist Supreme Soviet" (*CDSP, 41,* no. 23, p. 2).

percent). But also like the Congress, the percentage of high Party officials among this number was far below that of previous Supreme Soviets (Mann, Monyak, and Teague, 1989, pp. 30–31). The relatively independent stance taken by many of these lower-level Party members contributed to some of the surprising results of the session.

Probably the most important function performed by the Supreme Soviet in its first session was the confirmation of members of the Council of Ministers. In the past they would have been confirmed as a group and without discussion. But under the new arrangements, ministerial candidates were considered individually, were required to answer questions before the assembled deputies, and were sometimes subjected to searching criticism. A number of candidates were actually rejected by the Supreme Soviet. During the course of the confirmation process, a change in voting rules in the Supreme Soviet was adopted in order to make confirmation easier: Rather than a majority of all 542 members of the Supreme Soviet, only a majority of deputies attending a session was thereafter required. On the same day that this change was made, minister of defense and candidate Politburo member Dmitrii Yazov was confirmed as minister of defense after an acrimonious debate. Had the rules not been changed earlier that day, Yazov would not have been confirmed, as the vote he received fell short of a majority of the whole Supreme Soviet (Foye, 1989, p. 11).

The Supreme Soviet also made substantive progress on an ambitious legislative agenda and responded responsibly to some of the developments of the day, at times going against Gorbachev's wishes. For instance, it defeated Gorbachev's proposed ban on strikes, at a time when work interruptions by miners posed a serious economic problem (Mann, 1989b, p. 2) And certain of its members defended an editor who had incurred Gorbachev's ire, apparently preventing the editor's removal.

An issue that Gorbachev tried hard to prevent the Supreme Soviet (and the Congress) from considering was the repeal of Article 6 of the Constitution, on the Communist Party's monopoly on power. As indicated in Chapter 5, he and his colleagues succeeded in keeping it off the legislative agenda during the early sessions of both the Supreme Soviet and the Congress. But in the 1990s, under mounting pressure from various sources, they finally relented. By action of the Congress of People's Deputies, Article 6 was revised to eliminate the Communist Party's dominant position.

One of the aspects of legislative operation that eroded the Party's former position was the relative openness of parliamentary proceedings. In addition to television coverage and verbatim reports in the press, reporters, both Soviet and foreign, have had much greater access to legislative leaders and deputies. A *Washington Post* correspondent described this "access-heaven" as follows:

> During the sessions of the new legislature, reporters can "work" the Kremlin the way they might the corridors of the U.S. Congress, collaring the head of the

KGB, the leading generals, poets, former political prisoners, Mikhail and Raisa Gorbachev. (David Remnick in the *Manchester Guardian Weekly,* August 20, 1989, p. 19)

In other ways as well, parallels to Western parliamentary practices seem to be emerging in the new Soviet operations. Particularly in discussions about curbing elite privileges, deputies often cite foreign experience, such as the operation of ethics committees in the U.S. Congress (see, for example, "Soviets Appreciate U.S. Congress' Ethics," 1989; also *Izvestiia,* July 1, 1989, p. 2). Bills introduced in parliament go through "first reading" (*pervoe chtenie*) and "second reading" (*vtoroe chtenie*), common parlance in the West, before being adopted.[16] And the question of voting no confidence in the government, one of the central elements in Western parliamentary operations, has even been introduced. No provision on nonconfidence votes was included in the 1988 amendments to the USSR Constitution. But a number of Soviet deputies advocated its adoption as a necessary element of parliamentary government. It was not a complete surprise, therefore, when a provision for voting no confidence was included in the 1989 constitutional amendments. Part 4 of Article 130 now reads: "The USSR Supreme Soviet can express no confidence in the USSR Government. A resolution on this question is adopted, on a vote, by not less than two-thirds of the total number of members of the USSR Supreme Soviet." Article 173 of the Standing Orders of the Congress and the Supreme Soviet expanded upon this statement, providing: "In a case where the activity of the USSR Council of Ministers is considered unsatisfactory, the USSR Supreme Soviet may raise the question of changing the composition of the Government of the USSR and also may express non-confidence in the USSR Government as a whole. Decrees on this questions are adopted by a majority of votes of not less than two-thirds of the total number of members of the USSR Supreme Soviet" (*Reglament,* 1989). Note that these provisions mention only the Supreme Soviet. Before they were adopted, a no confidence motion was proposed during the second session of the Congress of People's Deputies in December 1989. It was easily turned back,[17] but the fact that it was permitted to be considered suggests that nonconfidence motions may be entertained in the Congress as well. Another Western parliamentary device adopted by the

---

[16]The terms "first reading" and "second reading" were defined in the "Temporary Rules" of the proceedings of the Congress of People's Deputies and the Supreme Soviet, *Vedomosti S'ezda Narodnykh Deputatov SSSR i Verkhovnogo Soveta SSSR,* 1989, no. 7, item 17. They are spelled out in more detail in the permanent Standing Orders of these bodies (*Reglament,* 1989, Articles 129–147).

[17]During the December 19, 1989 discussion of the government's proposals for economic reform, deputy Iu. E. Andreev moved that the Congress express nonconfidence in the government (*nedoverie pravitel'stvu; Izvestiia,* December 20, 1989, p. 6). The motion was accepted by the chair and eventually voted on. It was reported as defeated (*Izvestiia,* December 21, 1989, p. 2). No vote count was reported in the stenographic record published in *Izvestiia.* But Francis X. Clines reported in *The New York Times* (December 20, 1989, p. A18) that the vote was 199 for no confidence and 1,685 against.

Soviet legislatures is the question period. Deputies, groups of deputies, and legislative committees and commissions have the right to submit written or oral inquiries or questions to the Chairman of the Council of Ministers, individual ministers, and heads of other governmental bodies. The Standing Orders provide that time is to be set aside in the legislative agenda for both the questions and the answers (*Reglament,* 1989, Articles 176 and 177). The last Wednesday of every month was set aside for the question period.

Legislative Committees

Like the old Supreme Soviet itself, the Supreme Soviet committees had little impact on policy-making. Each house had sixteen standing committees, whose assignments covered subject matter areas such as legislative proposals, foreign affairs, agriculture, and health and social security. They received proposed legislation shortly before it was presented to the legislature for approval, but not in time to make any substantial difference. Their brief and infrequent meetings guaranteed that they would be a non-factor in policy-making, a result which the previous structures were designed to achieve.

All evidence indicates that the committees created under the new arrangements will be much more important. The Congress of People's Deputies has the authority to establish committees, but the basic standing committee structure is connected to the Supreme Soviet. Two types of bodies exist: committees (*komitety*) of the whole Supreme Soviet and standing commissions (*postoiannye komissii*) of the two houses of the Supreme Soviet. There are fourteen committees, some of which cover specialized areas such as health, international affairs, defense and state security, and agriculture and food (see Table 6.1). There is also a key committee, on Legislation, Legality, and Law and Order.* This committee receives all legislative proposals and draft laws, determines which specialized committee or commission the bill should be sent to (that committee is designated the "head" committee or commission), and shares with that committee the examination of the proposal or draft. Another committee that has received much attention is one on Glasnost and Citizen Rights and Appeals.

In addition, each house of the Supreme Soviet has four standing commissions. The Council of the Union's commissions specialize in matters that might be seen as having more all-union significance. They cover industry, energy, machinery, and technology development; labor, prices, and social policy; planning, budget, and finance; and transportation, communications, and information technology. The Council of Nationalities' commissions deal with affairs of nationality or regional concern: nationalities policy and interethnic relations; culture, language, national and international traditions, and protection

---

*This committee's name was changed to the Committee on Legislation in 1990. At the same time, a new Committee on Legal Order and the Struggle Against Crime was created. In addition, a legislative commission on the ethics of deputies was established.

TABLE 6.1 Supreme Bodies of State Power of the Union of Soviet Socialist Republics.

The Congress of USSR People's Deputies is the highest body of state power in the USSR.

The USSR Supreme Soviet is the standing legislative, management, and control body of state power in the USSR.

The USSR Council of Ministers—the Government of the USSR—is the highest executive and management body of state power in the USSR.

Congress of USSR People's Deputies

USSR Supreme Soviet

Council of the Union	Council of Nationalities

Presidium of the USSR Supreme Soviet
Chairman of the USSR Supreme Soviet
First Deputy Chairman of the USSR Supreme Soviet

USSR Council of Ministers

Chairman of the USSR Council of Ministers

First Deputy Chairman of the USSR Council of Ministers

Deputy Chairman of the USSR Council Ministers

Ministers of the USSR and Chairmen of USSR State Committees	Chairmen of Union Republic Councils of Ministers

USSR Ministries and State Committees

USSR Constitutional Oversight Committee

People's Control Committee of the USSR

USSR Supreme Court

USSR Procurator's Office

USSR States Arbitration Committee

Committees of the USSR Supreme Soviet

International Affairs Committee

Defense and State Security Committee

Legislation, Legality, and Law and Order Committee

Soviet of People's Deputies and Management and Self-Management Development Committee

Economic Reform Committee

Agrarian and Food Committee

Construction and Architecture Committee

Science, Education, Culture, and Upbringing Committee

Health Committee

Women's Affairs and Family, Mother and Child Protection Committee

Veteran and Invalid Affairs Committee

Youth Affairs Committee

Ecology and Rational Use of Natural Resources Committee

Glasnost and Citizens' Rights and Appeals Committee

Standing Commissions of the Houses of the USSR Supreme Soviet

Planning, Budget, and Finance Commission

Industry, Energy, Machinery, and Technology Development Commission

Transportation, Communications, and Information Technology Commission

Labor, Prices, and Social Policy Commission

Nationalities Policy and Interethnic Relations Commission

Social and Economic Development of Union and Autonomous Republics, Oblasts, and Okrugs Commission

Culture, Language, National and Inter-national Traditions, and Protection of Historical Heritage Commission

Consumer Goods; Trade; and Municipal, Consumer, and Other Services Commission

Commissions of the Presidium of the USSR Supreme Soviet

State Awards Commission	Citizenship Commission	Pardons Commission

SOURCE: Argumenty i Fakty, 1989, no. 47, p. 8. Translated in JPRS-UPA-89-070, December 29, 1989, p. 5.

of historical heritage; social and economic development of union and autonomous republics, oblasts, and okrugs; and consumer goods, trade, and municipal and other services.

Both the committees and commissions are composed of deputies, but the rules provide that only half of the members come from the Supreme Soviet, with the other half chosen from Congress deputies not on the Supreme Soviet. The committees and commissions occupy a central place in the legislative process. A draft or other recommendation for legislation is normally sent to a committee or commission immediately after it has been formally proposed. On the basis of the committee or commission recommendation, the whole body (Congress or Supreme Soviet) decides whether to place the bill on the legislative agenda. At that stage it may be rejected, placed on the agenda for first reading, or sent back to committee or commission, where it might be worked on further by a subcommittee. At the first reading stage a bill may be rejected or adopted in principle. If the latter, it may then be adopted in its final form (after second reading) or it may be sent back to the committee stage for further work.[18]

After the committee or commission has produced its recommendations concerning a bill, it is considered by the whole legislature. But the bill could still be sent back again to committee for further work. The record of proceedings of the Congress and the Supreme Soviet indicates that, indeed, some legislative measures have been bounced back and forth between committee and parliament numerous times.

In case of disagreement between the Council of the Union and the Council of Nationalities on a bill, a different kind of commission is created. This is a "conciliation commission" (*soglasitel'naia komissiia*) made up of equal numbers of members from each house. If an impasse cannot be resolved in this way, it is turned over to the Congress of People's Deputies. The provisions on conciliation commissions are contained in the constitution, Article 117, and are reiterated in the parliamentary Standing Orders (*Reglament,* 1989, Article 146).

In addition to their legislative functions, standing committees and commissions have the right of preliminary review of nominees for ministerial and other posts, and make recommendations regarding these candidates. And they are responsible for oversight of the implementation of laws and other administrative functions of the bureaucracy. Early evidence suggests that at least some of the committees are taking this responsibility seriously (Yasmann, 1989).

Finally, the Standing Orders provide that the Congress, the Supreme Soviet, and both of its houses may establish "investigative, auditing, and other commissions on any question" (*Reglament,* 1989, Article 181). Several "select committees" (to use British parliamentary terminology) of this kind have already been established.

---

[18]The Standing Orders also provide that it can be published for public discussion at this stage.

The Presidium of the Supreme Soviet

The old Presidium of the Supreme Soviet was endowed with a number of significant functions, which allowed it to perform as a combination collective head of state and mini-legislature. But since the Presidium seldom met as a body, those functions devolved upon the Presidium's Chairman. And since the chairman was also invariably a high Party official (the last five chairmen under the old arrangements were Brezhnev, Andropov, Chernenko, Gromyko, and Gorbachev), the Presidium could serve as a convenient medium for transforming Party policy into governmental policy.

The old Presidium was composed of 36 members plus a Chairman, a First Deputy Chairman, and a Secretary. Fifteen of the regular members represented the union republics and were, as a rule, the chairmen of their republic supreme soviet presidiums. The other members included a mixture of well-known and obscure personages in the Soviet political hierarchy. The Presidium had an impressive list of powers and duties granted by the Constitution, such as granting pardons, awarding orders and titles of honor, certifying diplomatic representatives, and issuing interpretations of laws. The most important power, however, was that of issuing edicts. In this capacity the Presidium served as a kind of continually functioning legislature, allowing for the extremely short sessions of the regular legislature, the Supreme Soviet. When there was a need for a legislative-type act having the force of law and the Supreme Soviet happened not to be in session (which was about 98 percent of the time), such a measure could be adopted by the Presidium in the form of an edict (*ukaz*) and would be fully enforceable by the executive branch and the courts. Then the Supreme Soviet, the next time it met, would transform the edict into a statute (*zakon*) in one of its regular unanimous votes. In fact, much of the time in Supreme Soviet sessions was spent in this process of transforming edicts into statutes. In terms of the total volume of Soviet legislation, relatively little of it was adopted initially as statute by the Supreme Soviet. This procedure was normally reserved for basic pieces of legislation, the immediate adoption of which was not a pressing matter, such as the "Basic Principles" of criminal law or civil law, or for routine and recurrent legislation such as that on the annual budget or economic plans. Thus, the basic law-making function was performed by the Presidium, in spite of the constitutional provision giving sole legislative power to the Supreme Soviet. And actually, as suggested, it was not the whole Presidium that typically performed this function but the Chairman, aided by the Secretary and the Presidium staff.

The role of the Presidium was considerably reduced under the structures created in 1988 and was diminished even further with the creation of the presidency in 1990. Since the Supreme Soviet itself was to become a standing legislature, the need for the Presidium to perform legislative functions was, in theory at least, largely obviated. But in the period between the 1988 constitutional changes and the creation of the presidency in 1990, the Presidium retained some of its traditional functions, such as appointing Soviet diplomats to posts abroad and receiving diplomatic representatives from foreign states. And the Presidium was responsible for declaring a state of martial law or emergency when the situation called for it. Moreover, among its powers was ensuring that the constitutions and laws of the union republic conformed with the USSR Constitution and laws. On more than one occasion, under this authority, the Presidium declared acts by union republics to be at variance with the USSR Constitution.

With the creation of the office of the president, however, the functions of the Presidium were drastically reduced. It is now described as a body "set up to organize the work of the USSR Supreme Soviet" (USSR Constitution, Article 118). It makes preparations for the sessions of the Congress of People's Deputies and the Supreme Soviet; coordinates the work of legislative committees and commissions; organizes public discussions of draft laws and other important issues; and ensures the publication, in the languages of the union republics, of USSR laws and other legislative acts.

The Presidium is composed of the chairman of the USSR Supreme Soviet, the chairmen of the Supreme Soviet's two houses—the Council of the Union and the Council of Nationalities—their deputies, the chairmen of the Supreme Soviet's standing commissions and committees, and one USSR people's deputy representing each of the fifteen union republics. This amounts to some 40 people. When Gorbachev was elevated from chairman of the Presidium to the presidency in 1990, his first deputy chairman (a position now abolished), Anatoly Lukyanov, was chosen Presidium chairman.

The Presidency

In Chapter 5, the details of the power of the presidency, which was established by the 1990 constitutional amendments, were reviewed. The position was established to fill a gap created by the diminished authority of the Communist Party and to provide a focus of political power on the national level to cope with the serious social and political problems facing the country. Soviet spokesmen close to the center of power have tended to play down the potential concentration of power that the presidency involves. Supreme Soviet Chairman Lukyanov stated in 1990 that "the president's most important function is to coordinate the work of" other USSR level organs, particularly the Congress of People's Deputies, the Supreme Soviet, and the Council of Ministers (*Pravda,* April 2, 1990, p. 3). And a jurist who helped draft the law on the presidency described the office as "a bridge, figuratively speaking, from legislative to executive power" (B.M. Lazarev in *Pravda,* March 10, 1990, p. 2).

But certainly the office is designed to do much more than serve such a coordinating function. As the presidency's first incumbent, Gorbachev moved swiftly to establish the authority of the office. He directed the efforts to discourage the separatist tendencies of Lithuania and other independence-minded republics. And he used various presidential powers to exert central control over republic and local activities. For example, he signed an edict in April 1990 depriving the Moscow city government of the power to control street demonstrations in the center of the capital. The justification given was the existence of the Kremlin and other high state institutions in downtown Moscow, whose work might be disrupted by demonstrations. But certainly the fact that a new Moscow city council, not controlled by the Communist Party, had recently been elected was not lost on Gorbachev. He no doubt believed that some level of presidential control over the kinds of demonstrations that the Moscow city council insurgents might allow was in order (*The New York Times,* April 21, 1990, p. 1).

To aid the president in his activities, the Constitution provides for the creation of two bodies appointed by the president: a Council of the Federation, which deals with the USSR's nationality problems and policies; and a Presidential Council, "to elaborate measures to implement the main direction of the USSR's domestic and foreign policy and to ensure the country's security" (USSR Constitution, Article 127(5)) The Council of the Federation is headed by the President and includes high state officials of each of the union republics. Officials of smaller ethnic-territorial units and nationalities are permitted to participate in its sessions. The membership of the Presidential Council is completely within the discretion of the President, except that the Chairman of the USSR Council of Ministers is an ex officio member and the Chairman of the USSR Supreme Soviet has the right to participate in the Council's sessions. To his first Presidential Council Gorbachev appointed fifteen members, a combination of important governmental and Party officials (for instance, Politburo colleague Yakovlev, KGB head Kriuchkov, Minister of Foreign Affairs Shevardnadze, Minister of Internal Affairs Bakatin, Minister of Defense Yazov, and others), and other public figures (for example the liberal Kirghiz writer Chingiz Aitmatov, the conservative Russian writer Valentin Rasputin, and the radical economist Stanislav Shatalin).

The two councils have been referred to as "the councils of national security and national accord" (Lukyanov in *Pravda,* April 2, 1990, p. 3). And while they will surely perform these functions, the importance of the Presidential Council in particular is likely to grow as the authority of Party bodies, most significantly the Politburo, continues to diminish.

The Council of Ministers

Analogous to a cabinet in Western parliamentary or presidential systems but of considerably larger size, the USSR Council of Ministers is described in the Constitution (Article 128) as "the highest executive and administrative organ" of the USSR. Also consistent with Western usage, it is referred to as "the Government" (*Pravitel'stvo*) and sometimes now even as the "cabinet" or "governmental cabinet" (*kabinet* or *pravitel'stvennyi kabinet*). Its chairman, the equivalent of prime minister, is head of government. But the USSR

Council of Ministers has long been much too large to serve as a real cabinet. Prior to the changes of the late 1980s the Council had over 100 members. Fifteen of these members chaired the union republic councils of ministers, performing their major functions on a completely different level of government, for the most part outside of Moscow. Even without these fifteen, a body of 95 to 100 members was much too large to meet either frequently or with efficiency. In recent years this fact received official acknowledgment, accompanied by a more realistic assessment of the importance of the Council. A law regarding the USSR Council of Ministers was adopted in 1978 and provided (Article 28) that meetings of the council will take place "not less than once per quarter," which is probably about as often as it actually meets. The more important policy-making and executive organ of the government is the Presidium of the Council of Ministers. Said to have existed since 1953 but given official recognition only with the adoption of the 1977 Constitution, this body is composed of the chairman, first deputy chairmen, and deputy chairmen of the Council of Ministers. It typically numbers about 15 members.

The reason for the large size of the Council of Ministers is the large number of economic ministries included therein, in addition to the traditional ministries found in Western countries, such as foreign affairs, defense, and justice. It is understandable that the central government in a socialist system would have considerable responsibility for running the economy, and in the Soviet Union this responsibility is handled largely through the economic ministries.

A word of explanation might be useful about the structure of ministerial-level departments of the Council of Ministers. There are three basic types of such bodies: all-union ministries, union-republic ministries, and state committees and other departments. All-union ministries are, in theory, more centralized bodies than union-republic ministries, since they exercise direct control throughout the country of the branch of administration within their jurisdiction. Corresponding ministries on the union-republic level do not exist. Union-republic ministries, on the other hand, normally administer their affairs through corresponding bodies of the same name at the level of the fifteen union republics. It is difficult to state a general rule delineating the kinds of ministries that are all-union and those that are union republic. At the time of the adoption of the 1936 Constitution there were few ministries of strictly economic purpose. Heavy industry was put in the all-union category, whereas light industry was union republic. But with the proliferation of economic ministries over time, such a heavy industry–light industry dichotomy has become largely meaningless. From Khrushchev through Brezhnev there was a considerable growth in the number of all-union ministries, suggesting an increase in authority at the national level at the expense of the union republics.

Like ministries, USSR State Committees are identified as "central organs of state administration" and may be all-union or union republic. But whereas ministries are said to be responsible for "branch administration" (that is, a branch of the economy such as the petroleum and gas industry), state committees carry out "interbranch administration," meaning that they are responsible for activities common to several branches of administration. A good example is the State Planning Committee (*Gosplan*).

Under Article 133 of the constitution, the Council of Ministers has the power to issue "decrees" (*postanovleniia*), acts that are considered legal norms, and "resolutions" (*rasporiazheniia*), which are normally of a routine rather than normative nature, pursuant to laws already on the books. This provision is the vehicle for the policy-making power exercised in the name of the Council of Ministers. Sometimes exceedingly important policies are adopted as decrees or resolutions. In the past, an act of particular importance, or one for which special public attention is desired, might be issued as a joint decree of the USSR Council of Ministers and the Party Central Committee. It was not unknown for such a document to serve as the basis for, and to be followed by, edicts adopted by the Presidium of the Supreme Soviet or statutes adopted by the Supreme Soviet itself. Thus, the constitutionally mandated order of things was reversed: Rather than a Council of Ministers' action being adopted "in pursuance of" laws or other acts of the Supreme Soviet or its Presidium, laws sometimes "pursued" Council of Ministers' decisions. In the era of glasnost this practice has been much criticized. And with the creation of the new legislative structures at the end of the 1980s, reformers have sought to curb the power of the Council of Ministers to act on its own.

One of the ways to rein in the bureaucracy is to make its leaders responsible to parliament, and this is being undertaken. The parliamentary practices described previously, including the confirmation of ministers, legislative committee oversight, parliamentary questions to leaders of government, and the vote of no confidence, aim to achieve this end. Another means of limiting a bureaucracy's pervasive power is to cut its size, and this too is said to be in process. At the time that the new Council of Ministers was being proposed and confirmed in 1989, Council of Ministers Chairman Ryzhkov announced that 18 state agencies would be abolished, the number of cabinet posts would be cut, and that appointments to responsible posts would go only to highly qualified candidates. He indicated that in the future a more drastic reduction in bureaucratic organs was in order, that the number of ministries ought to be reduced to about 25, but that this could only be achieved when the economy had been stabilized (*CDSP,* 41, no. 35, 1989, p. 14).

In fact, however, it is not clear how much actual reduction in the bureaucracy has been achieved. It is true that some agencies have been abolished and that the functions of some others have been combined (for example, there were formerly separate ministries of ferrous and nonferrous metallurgy, which have now been combined into one ministry of metallurgy). But some ministries abolished on the national level have been reinstituted on the republic level. And it appears that many of the employees of the eliminated ministries ended up working in other parts of the bureaucracy (Mann, 1989c, p. 10).

The government confirmed by the Supreme Soviet in 1989 did show some reductions in size and complexity in comparison with the past. The Presidium of the Council of Ministers was made up of one chairman (equivalent to the prime minister or premier), three first deputy chairmen, and ten deputy chairmen. All the first deputy chairmen had additional responsibilities in other areas (for example, Y. D. Maslyukov was one of three first deputy chairmen and chairman of the State Planning Committee [Gosplan]). In terms of regular Council of Ministers members, there were 37 ministers, 19 chairmen of state committees, and 4 other officials whose duties gave them Council of Ministers rank. When those holding two portfolios were considered, the Council of Ministers was made up of 86 members, somewhat smaller than the approximately one-hundred-member Council of Ministers chosen in 1984.[19] It is also true that during the Gorbachev years there has been enormous turnover at the top of the bureaucracy. By the end of 1989 virtually none of the ministers in office when Gorbachev took over in 1985 were still on the job. Most analysts agree that, at the very least, this has resulted in more competent personnel in responsible positions to face the tasks of perestroika.

SOVIET GOVERNMENTAL STRUCTURE
BELOW THE NATIONAL LEVEL

Up to now, only the national level of the state apparatus has been considered. There are other levels of government as well. Local governments are organized around the "local soviets of workers' deputies" or local soviets. And since the Soviet Union is a federal system, there are also intermediate levels of government to consider.

For two reasons, the examination of these governmental structures and operations will be brief. First, in structure the subnational governments are in many respects microcosms of the national government. So in that sense a full description would involve considerable repetition of what has been said above. Second, and more important, both the structure and the operation of the subnational units are in a state of transition. The process of political reform under Gorbachev was initiated at the national level and has been partially completed. The next phase is to extend the reform to the republic and local levels, and that process is in its early stages. Therefore, little can be said at this point of a definitive nature. Moreover, if some of the movements for greater autonomy in various parts of the USSR are carried further (see Chapter 12), the Soviet federal system could soon be very different. Thus, a few general remarks are in order until a more settled analysis of subnational government can be made.

---

[19]Both the 1984 and the 1989 figures exclude the 15 chairmen of the union republic councils of ministers, who are *ex officio* members of the USSR Council of Ministers. There is some difference of opinion about the size of the 1989 Council of Ministers. See Mann, 1989c, p. 10.

Federal Structure

As far as units in the federal system go, below the all-union or national level are four levels representing nationality groups that populate given territorial areas. These are the union republic (also called soviet socialist republic or SSR), the autonomous republic (autonomous soviet socialist republic or ASSR), the autonomous province (autonomous oblast), and the autonomous area (autonomous okrug).

As was mentioned earlier, representatives from these units make up the membership of the Council of Nationalities, one of the houses of the Supreme Soviet. The union republics, 15 in number, are the most important and embrace territories in which most of the country's major nationalities are concentrated. Union republics vary greatly both in territory and in population. The largest by far is the giant Russian Soviet Federated Socialist Republic (RSFSR), with almost three-fourths of the total land area of the country and more than 52 percent of the total Soviet population. Thus, the RSFSR is more than twice as large as the continental United States and has as many people as Great Britain, France, and the Benelux countries combined. The remaining union republics range down in size to tiny Armenia, which is approximately the size of the state of Maryland, and Estonia, which is slightly larger but which has a much smaller population.

Unlike units on the three lower levels, union republics possess the theoretical right under the USSR Constitution (Article 72) "freely to secede from the USSR." This right has never been exercised, but as the 1990s began, several republics seemed to be ready to put it to the test. Article 75, a provision not in earlier constitutions, appears to dilute the right of secession in stating that the territory of the USSR "is a single entity and comprises the territories of the union republics" and that "the sovereignty of the USSR extends throughout its territory."

In 1990 the Supreme Soviet adopted a law on union republic secession. It purported to provide procedures that would operate in conformance with Article 72 of the Constitution, but in actuality the law serves to restrict a republic's right "freely to secede." The law requires a referendum in which at least two-thirds of the republic's residents vote for secession; and a transition period of up to five years in which practical matters connected with secession are worked out. If the required two-thirds vote is not achieved, another referendum may not be held for ten years (*Izvestiia,* April 6, 1990, p. 1).

These provisions are not likely to end the aspirations of restive nationalities for greater autonomy. But the adoption of the law, combined with Moscow's economic blockade of Lithuania in response to that republic's declaration of independence in 1990, appeared to have stalled the drive for secession temporarily. Clearly, however, the centrifugal impulses of the various regions are strong and can be expressed in a variety of ways. Several republics have sought to assert their separateness by declaring their laws to have primacy over

USSR laws. When the "mother" republic (the Russian republic or RSFSR), under the leadership of newly elected RSFSR Supreme Soviet Chairman Boris Yeltsin, a Gorbachev adversary, took this step in 1990, the possibility of an eventual breakup of the USSR had to be taken seriously.

It used to be said by Soviet authorities that a union republic possessed three distinguishing characteristics: it is not surrounded on all sides by other union republics; the nationality for whom the republic is named constitutes a "compact majority" of the republic's population; and it has a population of at least one million people. These characteristics would be necessary, it was suggested, should the republic choose to secede from the USSR. In recent years, however, Soviet sources have stopped mentioning these three "objective characteristics," perhaps because the Kazakh and Kirghiz peoples no longer constitute a majority of the populations of "their" republics.[20]

As far as governmental structure goes, the union republics very much replicate the national level. Each has its own constitution and elects a legislature. As was indicated previously, under the 1988 constitutional amendments, this was to be a two-tier legislature as on the USSR level. But this unpopular provision was changed in 1989, and the republics were permitted to decide for themselves whether to have two-tier or one-tier legislatures. Of the fifteen union republics, only the RSFSR chose to have both a Congress of People's Deputies and a Supreme Soviet. The legislature chooses its presidium and a council of ministers, and the supreme soviet chairman is chosen in the manner designated by the republic constitution. Each republic has a supreme court as well as lower courts. Within their areas of jurisdiction, these organs are designed to operate in the same ways as their national-level counterparts.

The autonomous republics (ASSRs) represent concentrations of nationality groupings within union republics. The ASSRs are designed to give a limited amount of autonomy to the medium-sized nationality groups of the country; each possesses its own constitution and its own elected legislature, which appoints its presidium and a council of ministers. Again, the chairman of the legislature is chosen in the manner described in the union republic constitution. These "organs of state" are apparently meant to accord limited attributes of statehood or sovereignty to the ASSRs (Soviet sources refer to the ASSR as a "Soviet socialist national state"). Unlike union republics, however, autonomous republics do not possess even theoretical rights of independence such as the right of secession and the right to maintain foreign relations. They are clearly under the jurisdiction of the union republics in which they are located. Lately the subordination of some of these smaller nationalities to the larger union republics in which they are located has become an important political

[20]According to the 1979 census, the Kazakhs constituted only 36 percent of the population of the Kazakh Republic, with Russians constituting 40.8 percent. The Kirghiz were the largest ethnic group in their republic, with 47.9 percent of the population. The fast recent growth of both the Kazakh and Kirghiz populations suggests that these proportions will change considerably in the next census.

issue. Protests in the late 1980s by residents of the Abkhazian ASSR against their treatment by the Georgian SSR, for instance, manifested a level of ethnic tension that was previously kept under wraps. There are 20 ASSRs, 16 of them located in the RSFSR.

Very little autonomy, even of the theoretical variety, is accorded to governmental units on the two lowest levels, the autonomous province and the autonomous area. Both types of units have elected soviets or representative councils, which name their executive committees as well as the district courts. But in these respects they are no different from regular local governments. Except for the nationality basis for these units, they appear to differ very little from the other administrative subdivisions in the Soviet Union that are run by local soviets. The only exception to this point is the potential ethnic strife connected with some of these smaller units. The whole world learned this, for instance, in 1988, when the Nagorno-Karabakh Autonomous Province sought separation from the Azerbaidzhan SSR and association with the Armenian SSR. The bloody clashes that ensued brought about one of the gravest internal problems faced by the Gorbachev leadership. There are 8 autonomous provinces and 10 autonomous areas.

Local Governments

Local governments may be considered those that do not possess even theoretical statehood or sovereignty. This category would include the two lower units in the federal structure just discussed, the autonomous province and the autonomous area, as well as the strictly territorial units. The last group includes a confusing array of names and types.[21] Suffice it to say that they cover all of the territorial-administrative subdivisions of the country down to the level of the village or big-city district, and that they all have essentially the same structure. It consists of an elected local soviet (council), which typically meets more often than its big brother, the Supreme Soviet, but which still meets rather infrequently. The local soviet elects an executive committee to handle its business during the intervals between local soviet sessions.

It is the chairman of the executive committee of the local soviet that Western journalists often refer to as the "mayor" (for example, the "Mayor of Moscow"). The local soviet possesses full rights to exercise the powers granted to it, such as they are. But traditionally, local authorities in the Soviet Union have had very few powers guaranteed to their exclusive competence.

As the previously unchallenged power of the Communist Party has weakened, and as popular elections have permitted a broader range of political participation, the potential for more assertive local government activity has become evident. As the 1990s opened, popularly elected Soviets in both Mos-

---

[21]According to Feldbrugge and others (1985, p. 482), "local organs of state power" in the USSR include the following units: territory, province, autonomous province, autonomous area, district, city, city-district, settlement, and rural settlement.

cow and Leningrad, for instance, were fashioning economic and social programs far more radical than those endorsed by the all-union authorities.

REFERENCES

BARRY, D., and BARNER-BARRY, C. (1987). *Contemporary Soviet politics.* Englewood Cliffs, N.J.: Prentice-Hall.

FELDBRUGGE, F.J.M., and others, eds. (1985). *Encyclopedia of Soviet law.* Second edition. Dordrecht, The Netherlands: Martinus Nijhoff.

FOYE, S. (1989). Yazov survives contentious confirmation debate. *Report on the USSR, 1,* no. 29, 9-11.

GILISON, J. (1968). Soviet elections as a measure of dissent: The missing one percent. *American Political Science Review, 62,* 814-826.

GIRNIUS, S. (1989a). Sajudis candidates sweep elections in Lithuania. *Report on the USSR, 1,* no. 15, 29-30.

GIRNIUS, S. (1989b). Preliminary results of the runoff elections in Lithuania. *Report on the USSR, 1,* no. 17, 23-24.

KARKLINS, R. (1986). Soviet elections revisited: Voter abstention in noncompetitive voting. *American Political Science Review, 80,* 465-478.

MANN, D. (1989a). The Congress of People's Deputies: The election marathon ends. *Report on the USSR, 1,* no. 22, 3-5.

MANN, D. (1989b). Legislative reform. *Report on the USSR, 1,* no. 52, 1-3.

MANN, D. (1989c). Gorbachev's personnel policy: The USSR Council of Ministers. *Report on the USSR, 1,* no. 46, 8-13.

MANN, D. (1990). Bringing the Congress of People's Deputies to order. *Report on the USSR, 2,* no. 3, 1-5.

MANN, D., MONYAK, R., and TEAGUE, E. (1989). *The Supreme Soviet: A biographical directory.* Washington, D.C.: The Center for Strategic and International Studies.

NARODNYE deputaty SSSR—iuristy. (1989). *Sotsialisticheskaia Zakonnost',* no. 6, 56.

REGLAMENT S'EZDA NARODNYKH DEPUTATOV SSSR i Verkhovnogo Soveta SSSR. (1989). *Izvestiia,* December 28, 1.

ROEDER, P. (1989). Electoral avoidance in the Soviet Union. *Soviet Studies, 41,* no. 3, 462-483.

Soviets appreciate U.S. Congress' ethics. (1989). *Moscow News,* no. 46, 10.

VAN DEN BERG, G. (1978). A new electoral law in the Soviet Union. *Review of Socialist Law, 4,* 356-361.

YASMANN, V. (1989). Supreme Soviet committee to oversee KGB. *Report on the USSR, 1,* 26, 11-13.

Zasedaniia Verkhovnogo Soveta SSSR. (1983). 10th Sozyv, 8th session, 16-17 June. Moscow: Verkhovnyi Sovet SSSR.

ZASLAVSKY, V. and BRYM, R. (1978). The functions of elections in the USSR. *Soviet Studies, 30,* 366-379.

SEVEN
THE COMMUNIST PARTY:
The Loss of Monopoly Power

A Soviet friend was having trouble keeping his apartment in the university housing complex where he lived. He had gotten the apartment because his wife was a student at the university, but now her studies were completed. His work was in a research institute under the jurisdiction of a different government ministry from that of the university, and the university was trying to evict them to make room for university people. The housing problem being what it is, the friend was fighting tooth and nail to keep the apartment. He had appealed to the director of his institute for help and was returning for the last time to try to reason with university officials. "If this doesn't work," he said, "I'll go to the Party." He said this was an air that suggested both assurance and finality. As a loyal Party member in good standing, he was confident that the Party would resolve the matter in his favor (and he was not above using his Party position to this end). Moreover, he looked upon the Party as a kind of court of last resort, the organization that would have the final word. Our friend kept his apartment, with the Party's support.

The incident just related happened over 25 years ago. But it is instructive with regard to two constants of Soviet life over the decades: (a) that influence and connections count; and (b) that Party membership is one of the surest roads to influence and connections. As the Soviet system evolves, it is not likely that status and "knowing someone" will diminish in importance. In fact, in a country such as the Soviet Union, where there is such a shortage of things that people want—housing, automobiles, quality clothing, home appliances, and the like—connections may be considerably more important in everyday life than in a country of relative abundance like the United States. The Russian word for this influence or "pull" is *blat,* and it is a very important word in the language.

Regarding the second constant, the central place of the Party in the system, it appears that the Soviet Union is beginning to change in a basic way. If this is the case, not only will the more mundane aspects of the Party's position, such as the enhanced status and privileges of Party members, be called into question; the change will also affect the career patterns of the country's politicians and even the Communist Party's traditional monopoly on political power.

Our task in this chapter is to examine both the traditional position of the Party in the Soviet system and the evidence of change that is now under way.

PARTY MEMBERSHIP

By the end of the 1980s Party membership in the USSR had reached almost 20 million members, about 6.5 percent of the total population and some 10 percent of the adult population. There was some evidence that Party membership by that time had started to drop off somewhat (Hanson and Teague, 1989). But the Party is still a large and formidable force. It may be surprising to some that Party members constitute such a small percentage of the total population. But this is in line with the Leninist idea of a small, highly disciplined group of revolutionaries who would win the revolution and direct the new state. Lenin's insistence on this kind of party was one of the major factors leading to the split of the Russian Social Democratic Party into the Bolshevik wing, led by Lenin, and the Menshevik wing, led by Martov, who advocated a mass party. Many analysts maintain that it was only the Leninist type of organization that could have achieved success in the Revolution (Anderson, 1963, pp. 90–100). Throughout the Lenin period, Party members made up considerably less than 1 percent of the Soviet population. Gradual growth since then saw the percentage surpass 3 by 1950, 4 by 1960, 5 by 1965, and 6.5 by the 1980s.

There has never been any idea of having the Communist Party embrace the whole Soviet population. Admission standards are rather strict. Persons may join the Party at age 25 or, if they are members of the *Komsomol,* at age 18. Applicants must have recommendations from three Party Members of five-or-more years' standing who have known the applicants for at least a year. Such recommendations presumably are not given lightly, for the Party Rules provide that those making recommendations will be considered responsible by the Party for the impartiality of their endorsement. Persons admitted to the

Party serve a probationary period of one year as candidate members before being accorded full membership.[1]

The document known as the Party Rules is a kind of constitution of the Party. It sets out the general principles of admission to the Party and requirements of members and describes the principles of Party operation as well as its structure and organization. Like the USSR Constitution, it is basically a statement of ideals or seemingly desirable principles rather than an accurate reflection of actual Party operation. According to the Rules, which list numerous duties of Party members, Communists are expected to "master Marxist-Leninist theory," "provide an example of a conscientious and creative attitude toward labor," "firmly and steadfastly put into effect the general line and directives of the party," "take an active part in the political affairs of the country," "boldly lay bare shortcomings and strive for their removal," and so forth. In short, whatever a Party member's full-time job, he or she is expected to be ever active in pursuing the Party's interests as well.

It is not surprising, then, that being a Party member is not every Soviet citizen's desire. It means giving up some portion of one's free time, and for the young and politically ambitious, perhaps virtually all of it. Moreover, the profile of the good Communist suggested in the Rules involves a member's being always "on guard" to detect shortcomings and ready to correct them. Even in a society that has long encouraged the idea that being a busybody is a positive trait, this can get to be something of a bore. In some circumstances Party membership can interfere with a person's ability to perform conscientiously in one's profession. Dina Kaminskaya, a former Soviet lawyer who was involved in the defense of several important dissidents, found that not being in the Party gave her slightly more room for maneuver in some of her professional activities. For instance, she writes that when she found herself almost alone in supporting a colleague whose professional work with dissidents had brought him into disfavor with the authorities, "I thought to myself for the nth time, thank God I'm not in the party" (Kaminskaya, 1982, p. 217).

But for many, the advantages of Party membership—the sense of belonging to the elite, no matter how low one's position, and the chances for job advancement and material rewards that membership implies—outweigh these disadvantages. There has been much talk in recent years of diminishing the privileges that accompany status in Soviet life. And Party membership, whatever the level of one's position, certainly confers some status. Thus, although housing, automobiles, and other things in short supply are now supposed to be distributed in a scrupulously fair manner on the basis of need or one's place

---

[1]Like much else in this book, Party membership, and the rules governing it, are in a state of flux. Many of the generalizations in this chapter, and the references to the Party Rules, apply to the situation up to the middle of 1990. But many changes regarding these matters are under way, including a liberalizing of Party membership requirements and a drastic revision of Party Rules. The draft version of the latter document, which is slated to be adopted at the 28th Party Congress in 1990, is included as Appendix B.

on a list, well-placed people still frequently find ways to circumvent such rules. To some extent, at least, Party membership suggests connections or *blat,* and, as the old Soviet saying goes, *"Blat* is stronger than the government." Regarding jobs, it has simply been a fact of Soviet life that a large number of jobs are only open to Party members. These include key positions in politics, the military, diplomacy, and internal security. Party membership is also an advantage to the person seeking any number of other responsible positions. And of course, with regard to such matters as travel (especially abroad), Party members, as the most trustworthy people, have received preferential treatment.

It is not surprising, therefore, that the Party attracts certain persons who are not "politically active and conscious" and who are not wholly "devoted to the communist cause" (Party Rules, Article 4). The Party is engaged in a continuous campaign, sometimes more intensely pursued than at others, to weed out the unworthy: the lax, the incompetent, those pursuing their own selfish interests. For the last, the Soviet political lexicon contains two appropriate epithets. These happen to be cognate words and are easily translatable: *kar'erist* (careerist) and *opportunist* (opportunist); but the derogatory connotation of these terms is much stronger than in English. In addition to the regular expulsion procedures, the Party from time to time carries out a thorough membership-review procedure to eliminate members who are not fulfilling their Party duties. It was reported in the early 1980s that almost 300,000 Party members had been removed from the Party in the past five years for "acts incompatible with the designation communist" (*Izvestiia,* February 24, 1981, p. 4).

Another aspect of Party membership worth examining is social composition. Available data indicate that the Party is typically a somewhat more elite organization than the governmental bodies, particularly the soviets, examined in the last chapter. Information on social groups in the Soviet Union typically includes only three broad groups: workers, collective farmers, and employees. The last category embraces all white-collar workers up to and including high Party, government, and economic functionaries, as well as intellectuals. Workers and collective farmers comprise almost 74 percent of the Soviet population and about 56 percent of the Party membership (Dobrokhotov, 1986, p. 39).

One of the misleading aspects of this breakdown is that the statistics are based on the status of individuals when they joined the Party and generally do not reflect changes that result from an individual's advancement in occupation or education. Thus, most of the members of the high Party leadership are still listed in the worker or collective farmer categories, their status when they joined the Party many years ago. This practice may hide the fact of a Party membership overwhelmingly composed of persons who are not workers or farmers. And it may also explain the strenuous efforts of the Party since the mid 1970s to recruit more workers and farmers and to reduce the proportion of intellectuals.

Those with partial or complete higher education number about 8 percent of the Soviet population but almost one-third of the Party; those with primary or no formal education constitute more than 31 percent of the Soviet population but less than 10 percent of the Party. Women now number more than 53 percent of the Soviet population but about 27 percent of the Party membership (Dobrokhotov, 1986, p. 39). Finally, a small handful of nationality groups, most notably the Russians, are overrepresented, whereas a number of others, mostly concentrated in the Baltic area and Central Asia, are grossly underrepresented. All these discrepancies increase in the upper levels of the Party hierarchy.

PARTY ORGANIZATION

The lowest level of Party organization is the primary Party organization (PPO). PPOs are normally organized at members' places of work, but they may also be established on a residential basis in villages or large housing complexes. At least three Party members are required to create a PPO. There are more than 425,000 such PPOs, which are said to exist in almost all "workers' collectives" in the country. This is the basic organization to which every Party member belongs, and for most members it is the main point of contact with the Party. Several million members of PPOs serve in leadership capacities as members of PPO committees and bureaus or as PPO secretaries, but by no means all of these persons are full-time Party functionaries. Most are given time off from their regular jobs to perform Party duties. Normally only a PPO with 150 or more members is entitled to have full-time paid workers.

Obviously not all PPOs are equal in size. About 40 percent of the more than 425,000 PPOs have 15 or fewer members, more than 80 percent have fewer than 50 members, and only several hundred have over 1,000 members. The complexity of the leadership organization of the PPO varies with its size. The highest organ of the PPO is theoretically the general meeting of all members, which is supposed to be convened at least once a month. Soviet authorities have acknowledged, however, that in many PPOs this rule is often ignored.

Above the PPO level, the Party is organized on approximately the same territorial basis as the state administration. The levels are the rural or urban district (*raion*), the city (*gorod*) or autonomous district (*avtonomnyi okrug*), the province (*oblast'*) or territory (*krai*), the union republic, and the national Party organization.

As with the governmental structure discussed in the last chapter, there is considerable similarity between the lower and national Party structures. Our emphasis in this chapter will be on national Party structure and operations. We will discuss the central Party organs in some detail, but for now let us merely mention that the main parts of the central Party organization are the Party Congress, the Central Committee, the Politburo (called the Presidium from 1952 to 1966), and the Secretariat (headed by the general secretary of the CPSU). The Party Rules (Article 40) also permit the convening, in the intervals between congresses, of an "All-Union Party Conference" to discuss "urgent questions of Party policy." Such a conference was held in 1988, and will be discussed later.

Organs or positions analogous to these are present at lower levels of the Party system. All levels have their congresses, (called conferences below the union-republic level), their committees, their bureaus, their secretariats, and their first secretaries. At all levels the formal hierarchies of organs are the same: The congress or conference is the highest body, and it elects the smaller committee, which elects the even smaller bureau as well as the secretariat or individual secretaries. And at all levels the actual power hierarchy is the opposite of what the Party Rules and the organization charts suggest. The best way to demonstrate this is to discuss in more detail the relationship between the various Party organs at the all-union level.

THE NATIONAL PARTY ORGANS

The Party Congress

The major Party organs at the all-union level are the Congress, the Central Committee (CC), the Politburo, and the Secretariat.[2] The Party congress is referred to as the supreme organ of the CPSU, but it is so only in a formal sense. As with other bodies of large membership and infrequent meetings, its actual powers are meager. Delegates to congresses represent subordinate territorial Party bodies in numbers determined by the CC CPSU. Those numbers grew continuously until the 1980s and then stabilized at about five thousand (the capacity of the Palace of Congresses in Moscow's Kremlin, where congresses are held). Over the years, the intervals between congresses have gradually been widened through changes in the relevant provisions in the Party Rules. Only recently have congresses regularly been convened at the prescribed intervals. No congresses took place between 1939 and 1952, when they were supposed to be held every three years. From 1952 to 1971 the prescribed interval was four years, with congresses actually being held in 1956, 1959, 1961, and 1971. In 1971 the interval was lengthened to five years, ostensibly to provide the congress with the opportunity of reviewing each new Five-Year Economic Plan before its adoption, but also perhaps in recognition that (except

---

[2]Another central organ is the Central Auditing Commission. This body, whose members are named by the Congress, handles a variety of administrative matters, including the review of letters and complaints from citizens to the Party. It is also charged with auditing Party financial accounts. It appears to be a largely honorary body whose members are somewhat less important in the Party hierarchy than those chosen to the Central Committee.

for the "Extraordinary Congress" in 1959)[3] the Soviet leaders have seldom been able to get around to holding a congress more than once in five years.

If the foregoing suggests that Party congresses are without significance, that impression would be wrong. As a body, the Congress possesses virtually no political power, and this has been the case at least since Stalin consolidated his power in the mid to late 1920s. But congresses do serve as a backdrop for the presentation of some of the important programs and objectives of the Party, and as a forum for the discussion (such as it is) of these matters. They are held with great fanfare, including saturation media coverage just before and during the two week period of the congress. They thus perform the function of mobilizing Party members and the populace at large to follow the direction indicated by the Party leaders. The proceedings of the congress serve, in other words, to provide the "line cues" and instructions as to what the Party leadership considers important for the present and immediate future.[4]

And there are sometimes indications of policy differences within the leadership that surface during congress proceedings. Traditionally the Soviet press has worked hard to cover up such differences, however, and these meetings typically give the appearance of tame, even boring, sessions. Only infrequently, at least since Stalin's day, have congresses broken out of this mold, as a review of several of the post-Stalin congresses will indicate.

The twentieth Party Congress in February 1956 is remembered by students of Soviet politics as perhaps the most spectacular meeting of its kind, because of the sharp break with the past. A major theme of the congress was de-Stalinization, initiated by Khrushchev's "secret speech".[5] Open published attacks on Stalin date from this point. This congress set off a period of "thaw" within the country that spilled over into some of the USSR's East European neighbors such as Poland and Hungary.

At the twenty-second Congress in 1961 (the "Extraordinary" twenty-first Congress in 1959 had been called to review new economic and social policies), the anti-Stalin theme was renewed by Khrushchev and culminated in the removal of Stalin's body from the Mausoleum on Red Square. Another major event was the adoption of a new ambitious Party Program to guide the "comprehensive building of communism" in the USSR over the next 20 years.

The next four congresses (1966, 1971, 1976, and 1981) were held while Brezhnev was at the helm and generally reflected the status quo orientation of what have come to be called the "years of stagnation." By the time of the next congress in 1986, three Party General Secretaries had passed from the scene (Brezhnev, Andropov, and Chernenko), and Gorbachev had been in office for almost a year. By this time it was clear that Gorbachev hoped to make

---

[3]The Congress held in 1959 is officially designated as an "Extraordinary" Congress, called for special purposes before the time interval for the convening of another Congress had elapsed.

[4]The collected speeches and resolutions of the congresses are published in book form and the most important individual speeches in pamphlet form soon after each congress.

[5]This speech was finally published in the Soviet Union in 1989.

major changes in the Soviet system. The twenty-seventh Congress served as a forum for the airing of some of his plans. In his five-and-one-half-hour "Political Report" he touched on all major aspects of domestic and foreign policy. Although he and others called for "radical reform" of the economy, more concrete policy proposals in this area were left vague. He reaffirmed his commitment to glasnost, and when compared with congresses of the Brezhnev era, some increase in openness and spontaneity was noticeable at this meeting.

The twenty-seventh Congress constituted an early stage of Gorbachev's reform effort and, as was suggested, little in the way of concrete policy was laid down. More specific proposals were left for the future. The convening of a Party *conference,* two years later, provided an opportunity for setting forth the details of political, social, and economic reform. This conference will be discussed presently.

An important function that takes place at every congress is the choosing of the Party leadership. Formerly this was a routine activity: Although the congress was supposed to "elect" the Central Committee (which then "elected" the Politburo and the Secretariat), the election was really a matter of approving the list of CC members, and it was carried out so as to insulate the leadership selection process from the mass membership of the Congress as much as possible.

An important psychological way of insulating the top leaders from the rank-and-file delegates to the Congress was the seating arrangement. The top one hundred or so people sat on the stage of the Palace of Congresses in Moscow; the rest of the delegates sat in the "audience" and watched the performance. No less a student of legislative assemblies than Winston Churchill has commented on the psychological importance of the shape and arrangement of representative assembly halls. When the House of Commons was to be rebuilt after being damaged by bombs during World War II, Churchill argued persuasively for retaining the small, rectangular-shaped hall with an aisle down the middle to separate the Government from the Opposition. This, he felt, would help maintain the two-party system as well as the sense of importance of members and of legislative proceedings. He opposed the "semicircular assembly, which appeals to political theorists, enables every individual or every group to move around the center adopting various shades of pink according to the weather changes" (quoted in Lijphart, 1969, p. 85). No doubt Churchill would have recognized the symbolism of the theater arrangement in the Soviet Union as well as the unified, if passive, support of the "audience" for the "actors" that the arrangement suggested.

The twenty-eighth Congress, in July 1990, was a very different affair from its predecessors. In keeping with the turbulent politics of the time (the Party had, just months earlier, lost its constitutionally mandated monopoly position), the twenty-eighth Congress was a stormy, open event that exposed the Party's deep divisions and problems. In a large sense, the Party meeting that paved the way for the events of the twenty-eighth Congress was the nineteenth Party Conference in 1988. It will be discussed first.

The Party Conference

The Party Conference is a body with an ostensibly different function from that of the congress. But its significance as a Party organ has at times been so slight that during large periods of Soviet history no conferences have been convened. Both congresses and conferences predate the Bolshevik seizure of power. By the time of the October Revolution six congresses and seven conferences had already been held (Schapiro, 1971, p. 645).

The original distinction between congresses and conferences had to do with the way delegates were selected: for congresses they were supposed to be chosen by the Party membership, and for conferences by the local Party committees (*Izvestiia,* March 28, 1988, p. 2; *CDSP, 40,* no. 13, 1988, p. 15).

Between 1919 and 1929 nine more conferences were convened, and according to a Soviet source, a relationship between the congress and the conference was established during this time: "The congress discussed and decided issues in principle, while the conference's task was to draft proposals and documents and analyze the situation" (*Izvestiia,* March 28, 1988, p. 2; *CDSP, 40,* no. 13, 1988, p. 15).

With the consolidation of Stalin's power, however, the need for the conference as a Party institution declined. Only two more were held, in 1932 and 1941, after which the provision on conferences was removed from the Party Rules. At the first "Brezhnev congress," in 1966, the Rules were amended again to allow for the calling of conferences in the interval between congresses "to discuss urgent questions of public policy." But more than two decades passed without the convening of a conference. It was somewhat surprising, therefore, when the Party Central Committee in June 1987 decided to call the nineteenth Party Conference for one year later.

This conference turned out to be an event of watershed importance in the development of the Party and the Soviet system. If the twenty-seventh Congress had made it clear that it was Gorbachev's intention to reform the system, it was the nineteenth Conference that promulgated a number of the specific proposals for realizing the reform.

There was some speculation that Gorbachev might use the occasion of the conference to remove and replace members of the leadership, particularly of the Party Central Committee, who opposed reform. In fact this did not happen, perhaps because he lacked sufficient support to push through such a move. Certainly a number of Gorbachev supporters were excluded as delegates to the conference by members of the Party old guard, who controlled the screening process for delegate selection in many parts of the country.

In spite of this, the conference was a meeting of great vitality, far more lively than preceding Party congresses. It lasted four days, less than half the length of the typical congress. The number of delegates, 5,000, made it about the same size as a congress. Only a fraction of the 300 people who registered to speak actually were given time at the podium. But many of the speeches had an air of spontaneity to them, and some clearly surprised at least part of the leadership (for instance, the delegate who called for the ouster of Polit-buro member and Supreme Soviet Presidium chairman Andrei Gromyko and several others).[6] And not all speakers supported the direction events in the country seemed to be taking. Several, for instance, complained that the press, in the atmosphere of glasnost, was too frankly airing the shortcomings of So-viet society.

The conference adopted policy statements, known as resolutions, in a number of areas.[7] These resolutions were based largely on two sources: a docu-ment published about a month before the conference, the "Theses for the nineteenth All-Union Party Conference," and Gorbachev's opening report, "On the Progress in Implementing the Decisions of the twenty-seventh CPSU Congress and the Tasks of Deepening Restructuring."

According to Gorbachev in this speech, among the many questions fac-ing the USSR, the one "key question" was "the reform of our political sys-tem" (*CDSP, 40,* no. 26, 1988, p. 7). These reform objectives, as they relate to Party structure and operations, can be listed in three main categories:

1. To make a clearer demarcation between Party and state operations; to achieve a "separation of functions" between the two. In line with this goal, it was reem-phasized that the Party should not supplant the state in the performance of its duties.
2. To change the structure of the Party apparatus in order to achieve a separation of Party and state functions. In place of a fragmented organization of many Party agencies, closely supervising state organs, an apparatus reduced in size and made up of fewer departments with broader focus was advocated.
3. To stimulate intra-Party democracy and general Party effectiveness through a series of measures, including (a) creating a genuine spirit of openness in which debate and criticism can take place; (b) making more exclusive Party bodies, such as the Politburo, more responsible to larger bodies, such as the Central Committee; (c) limiting high Party officials, including Politburo members and the General Secretary, to no more that two consecutive five-year terms; and (d) holding Party conferences every two or three years and allowing the replacement of up to 20 percent of the members of the Party committees, such as the Central Committee, at such conferences.

These reform proposals are of undoubted importance. Taken together with others recommended at the nineteenth Conference, they constitute the

[6]Gromyko did retire several months later. He died in 1989.

[7]The texts of these resolutions may be found in *Izvestiia,* July 2, 1988, p. 1 and July 5, 1988, p. 1. Condensed translations may be found in *CDSP, 40,* nos. 36, p. 12; 37, p. 10; 38, p. 15; and 39, p. 14.

most far-reaching attempt at change since Stalin put his stamp on the system from the late 1920s onward. But some of the objectives, such as limiting the length of service of Party leaders and preventing excessive Party interference in the operation of state bodies, have been tried before, without notable success.

Moreover, discussions at the Conference of the place of the Party in the political system suggested that little change was intended. Time and again conference statements referred to the Party with such phrases as "the bearer of the programmatic goals of society," and "the vanguard of the people." And one of Gorbachev's conference proposals seemed designed to ensure this result. While rejecting the notion of other political parties as an "abuse of democratization," he recommended that, at each governmental level, the first secretary of the Party committee be chosen as the chairman of the soviet (*CDSP, 40, No. 26,* 1988, p. 14). This, of course, is equivalent to what Gorbachev himself did in October 1988 in becoming chairman of the Presidium of the USSR Supreme Soviet. Thus, the "separation of functions" aimed at would, by this scheme, be defeated by what might be called the "unity of personnel" controlling the top of the Party and governmental organs.

In the aftermath of the nineteenth Conference, then, it was still unclear what the long-term place of the Party was to be. It could be said that the twenty-seventh Party *Congress* represented the "early Gorbachev," when the idea of radical reform was first aired. By contrast, the nineteenth Party *Conference,* led by Gorbachev, produced a concrete package of proposals for reform purportedly aimed at modifying the Party's role and enhancing the authority of soon-to-be-created legislative structures. But in examining the results of the nineteenth Conference in retrospect, one can see the inherent contradiction created by Gorbachev in proposing these new arrangements: Increased power in the new structures meant diminished power elsewhere. By opening the door to this potential result, the traditional position of the Party was bound to be challenged, even as Gorbachev sought to protect it by the measures just discussed. And this, in fact, is what happened, aided by other events that further eroded the Party's position.

The Twenty-Eighth Congress

If the nineteenth Party Conference was the forum for the initiation of the momentous political changes just described, the twenty-eighth Congress can be seen as the occasion when the demise of the Party as the supreme political institution was played out in public. Convened nearly a year ahead of schedule, in July 1990, the twenty-eighth Congress resembled its predecessors in some superficial ways: It was a two week gathering, in the Kremlin's Palace of Congresses, of nearly five thousand Party leaders and delegates from all parts of the country. Beyond these features, however, there were few other similarities.

Much of the time in the Congress was taken up with complaints about the Party's loss of authority and prestige. The target for many of these complaints was Gorbachev himself. Rather than becoming defensive, however, Gorbachev staunchly maintained his centrist position and sought to keep the party unified. With no credible alternative choices, the Congress overwhelmingly re-elected Gorbachev to the position of General Secretary. This time, however, the election was held in the open, at the Congress itself, rather than in secret proceedings in the Central Committee.

Gorbachev got his way on other important matters as well. His choice for deputy General Secretary, the Ukrainian leader Vladimir Ivashko, easily defeated Politburo member Egor Ligachev, Gorbachev's long-time conservative nemesis. Thereafter, Ligachev was left off the new Central Committee and Politburo and decided to retire. The Central Committee that was chosen was largely moderate, very much in Gorbachev's mold. And Gorbachev succeeded in expanding the size of the Politburo by giving seats to the leaders of the fifteen union republics. This appeared to be intended to prevent a conservative coalition from controlling the Politburo. Moreover, as a body unlikely to meet frequently, it was destined to shrink in importance and have less of an opportunity to try to direct government operations. Of the previous Politburo members, only Gorbachev and Ivashko retained membership on the new body. In a decisive move to further separate Party and state functions, the Prime Minister, Minister of Defense, Minister of Foreign Affairs, and Chairman of the KGB lost their Politburo positions. But they retained their places on the Presidential Council (described in Chapter 6), a clear indication of where their principal activities lay.

These victories for Gorbachev were tempered by the reality of the decline in the position of the Party in the last several years, a trend that the Congress did little to halt. Nor did Gorbachev succeed in one of his main goals, that of keeping the Party together. Toward the end of the Congress Boris Yeltsin, recently chosen as President (Chairman of the Supreme Soviet) of the RSFSR, announced his resignation from the Party, as did the leaders of the city councils of Moscow and Leningrad. These acts led to the defection of other prominent progressives from the Party. The Democratic Platform, the Party's insurgent progressive wing, appeared ready to take its supporters into a separate organization, perhaps in coalition with liberal forces already forming outside the Party. So while Gorbachev succeeded in asserting control over the Congress, by its end the future of the Party was much in doubt.

The Central Committee

As was indicated previously, the Central Committee is chosen by the Party Congress. In electing the Central Committee, the Congress in effect vests its supreme power in a smaller leadership body. In theory, the Central Committee plays a very important role, for it provides the main link between the Congress and the even more elite Politburo and Secretariat. And, at least on paper, it is provided with a set of really formidable powers.

According to the Party Rules, the CC "directs the activities of the Party" between congresses, "selects and appoints leading functionaries, directs the work of central government bodies and social organization of working people, sets up various Party organs, institutions, and enterprises and directs their activities, appoints the editors of the central newspapers and journals operating under its control, and distributes the funds of the Party budget and controls its execution" (Article 35). Thus, the Central Committee is given a leading role in directing not only the Party but also the work of all other governmental and social organizations in the country through the Party members in these groups. From what Western scholars know of the operation of the Central Committee, however, it has only rarely risen to the level of playing a really significant decision-making role with regard to these matters.

Meetings of the CC (called plenary sessions or plenums) are required at least every six months by the Party Rules, and until Gorbachev's time that was about how often they were held. More recently, the CC has been meeting three to four times per year. As an aspect of the rationalization of Soviet politics, CC meetings in recent years were often timed to take place just before Supreme Soviet meetings, which also typically were held twice a year. This not only facilitated the coordination of business processed by the two bodies, but it also meant that the considerable numbers of persons who belonged to both organs, many of whom lived great distances from Moscow, could attend both meetings in one trip. Under the constitutional amendments of 1988, the new Supreme Soviet meets for longer sessions. But it appears that the Central Committee plenary meetings are still timed to link up with these sessions.

There are, however, considerable differences between the meetings of the Supreme Soviet and those of the Central Committee. Until the end of the 1980s, as was mentioned in the last chapter, the Supreme Soviet usually met in two to three day sessions accompanied by considerable press coverage of both the important speeches made and the formal actions taken, such as the adoption of laws. It was, relatively speaking, an open proceeding. The CC plenary session, by contrast, is usually completed in one day, and by tradition it has been a more closed affair.[8] The Gorbachev years have given more attention to CC meetings, however, and if the pledges of intra-Party democratization adopted at the nineteenth Conference are carried out, much more will be known about CC operations.

The Central Committee is accorded considerable power on paper. But is it really so important in practice? Yes and no. Yes, symbolically, potentially, and in the sense that enormous authority is exercised in its name. No, in that the Central Committee *as a body* does not and, in its present form, cannot exercise continuous control over Party policy-making and implementation. Let us be more specific about these matters.

The Central Committee is of great *symbolic* importance because it is the

---

[8]In April 1989, for the first time, the complete texts of speeches in a CC meeting were published in the press.

membership body of the top four hundred or so Communists in the country. It includes not only all the members of the supreme Party organs, the Politburo and the Secretariat, but also most of the important leaders of republic and regional Party organizations as well as Party leaders in many other walks of life, from governmental administration to the communications media to the military, the arts, diplomacy, the sciences, and the economy. It brings together, even if for only a few days a year, the most important Party members in the country.

It is of *potential* importance in terms of the power and authority that *could* devolve upon it some day, given the right circumstances. With its considerable theoretical powers, especially regarding the activities of the Party and the selection of party leaders, it is not inconceivable that a nucleus within the Central Committee could unite to oppose the leadership. This opposition could be on matters of policy or personnel, or even on the subject of more genuine participation of the Central Committee in running the Party. The basic principles of Party operation (for example, democratic centralism and the prohibition against "factions") militate against such a development, it is true. But if devolution of political authority were to take place within the Party, the Central Committee is a likely place for it to happen.

There has been one occasion in the post-Stalin period in which the Central Committee appears to have opposed a majority of the Politburo and to have prevailed. As Khrushchev explained it, a majority of the Politburo (at that time called the Presidium) in June 1957 opposed Khrushchev's leadership and demanded his resignation as first secretary of the Central Committee. Khrushchev insisted that he had not been appointed by the Politburo to this position and that body could not oust him. He was able quickly to assemble much of the Central Committee in Moscow and to receive their support, thus affirming his position according to the Party Rules. He was then able to have his opponents, whom he labeled the "anti-Party group," removed from their positions (Pethybridge, 1962).

If this can be looked upon as an example of the exercise by the Central Committee of its authority, it is surely not typical CC activity. Nor does it suggest much actual power in the CC itself. Initiative did not come from the CC. It was clearly manipulated by Khrushchev and his allies. And one looks in vain for repeat performances. When Khrushchev was ousted by his Politburo colleagues in 1964, the Central Committee quietly supported his removal.

Another situation in which the Central Committee might be able to exercise power involves disagreements in the Politburo that fall short of clear attempts to oust leaders from power. Some Kremlin watchers see such disagreements as a more or less constant part of Soviet politics. In such situations, it is suggested, a bloc of Central Committee members siding with one of the contesting factions in the Politburo may succeed in frustrating the adoption of policies favored by the other faction. There is some evidence to suggest that such activity has long characterized CC meetings, but the authorities seek to keep such information secret. Direct evidence of contention at CC meetings, therefore, seldom finds its way into the Soviet press. A rare example was Boris Yeltsin's outburst at an October 1987 plenum against the slow pace of perestroika and against certain other leaders. This behavior led to Yeltsin's dismissal as a candidate Politburo member and as head of the Moscow Party organization (*CDSP, 39,* 1987, no. 45, p. 1, and no. 46, p. 7).

An enormous amount of activity takes place under the third category mentioned above, policies and actions carried out in the Central Committee's name. Authoritative policy can emerge in a number of interrelated forms, from a speech of a Party leader at a CC plenary meeting to a CC plenary meeting decree (*postanovlenie*) to a simple CC decree. The simple decrees are interesting for two reasons. First, they are sometimes issued as joint decrees with the USSR Council of Ministers. This form seems to be used to give added authority to important government programs or regulations. Second, they are issued and dated at times when the Central Committee is not meeting as a body (indeed, they are *not* identified as decrees of the plenary sessions, as some others are), and one must wonder how they come into being. It appears that they are issued *in the name of* the Central Committee on the instruction of either the Politburo or the Secretariat. These decrees of the Central Committee far outnumber the decrees of the Plenum of the Central Committee.

But the very fact that most such Central Committee decrees are not adopted at Central Committee meetings indicates the relative insignificance of the body. Although a much smaller body than the Congress of People's Deputies, it is a kind of Party equivalent of the Congress; its size (normally over four hundred members and candidate members) is prohibitively large for genuine discussion and policy-making, particularly in light of the fact that it meets infrequently and for short periods of time. So it is basically relegated to a position of providing the medium through which Party decisions are channeled by more important Party bodies and officials.

The Party leadership under Gorbachev has pledged to enhance the CC's role, and the responsibility of the Politburo to it. This is best summarized in the nineteenth Conference resolution on "The Democratization of Soviet Society and the Reform of the Political System":

> The conference calls for expanding the participation of members of the CPSU Central Committee in the activity of the Politburo of the Central Committee, for having plenary sessions of the Central Committee hear regular reports and briefings by the Politburo, and for creating commissions of Central Committee members on various areas of domestic and foreign policy.
> . . . The conference supports the proposal for the publication of verbatim records of plenary sessions of Party committees. (*CDSP, 40,* no. 36, 1988, p. 24).

Although the implementation of these proposals would still not place the Central Committee at the center of Party decision-making, it would undoubtedly increase its importance to some extent.

To reiterate a point made earlier, the Central Committee is made up of the most important Party members in the country. In this sense it is both a "talent pool" from which top leadership emerges and a stepping stone to (and, in some cases, down from) the top leadership. This is a point to which we will return later in the chapter in connection with the discussion of political elites.

The Politburo and the Secretariat

At the apex of the Party structure are the Politburo and the Secretariat. Students reading about CPSU structure for the first time are often confused about the relationship between these two bodies and want to know which is the more important and powerful. Answering such questions is not a simple matter. The two organs are charged with different responsibilities. The importance of their functions and the power that results from them are not easily comparable, although at times it appears that they compete for power. As a result of Gorbachev-era changes, the importance of the Secretariat appears to have diminished considerably. This development will be discussed after examining the traditional roles played by these two Party organs.

One way to assess the relative importance of the Politburo and Secretariat is to ask whether membership in one or the other body carries more prestige. It seems fair to say that it would be more prestigious to be a full member of the Politburo than to be a Secretary of the Secretariat. At the same time, the person typically recognized as the single most important official in the country has been the leader of the Secretariat, the general secretary. But the general secretary is also a member of the Politburo and is sometimes even referred to officially as the "leader" of the Politburo. It is more prestigious, then, to have a position on the Politburo *and* on the Secretariat, as several men typically do.[9] Finally, it can be said that losing a position on the Secretariat normally would be considered a demotion, but not the complete collapse of a political career if a seat on the Politburo were retained. Loss of a seat on the Politburo, however, would surely spell political demise.

The provision in the Party Rules on the Politburo and the Secretariat (Article 38) is extremely brief:

> The Central Committee of the Communist Party of the Soviet Union elects a Politburo to direct the work of the Party between plenary meetings and a Secretariat to direct current work, chiefly the selection of personnel and the verification of the fulfillment of Party decisions. The Central Committee elects a General Secretary of the CC CPSU.

On the basis of this bare statement and whatever else analysts have been able to discover about these bodies, it is generally said that the Politburo is

---

[9]The reader should note that with the changes at the twenty-eighth Party Congress, discussed above, this generalization appears no longer to hold.

the policy-making body of the Party and the Secretariat is the administrative or bureaucratic arm. The Secretariat supervises the execution of policy and, as the Rules suggest, handles day-to-day problems, including the selection of personnel to fill Party jobs. The Secretariat may also play an important role in shaping policy when it researches questions subsequently discussed in the Politburo and when it drafts resolutions that are then passed by the Politburo.

There is not a set number of members of either the Politburo or the Secretariat. In recent years the Politburo has been a body of about twenty members, several of whom have only candidate (nonvoting) status (Lowenhardt, 1982; Laird, 1986). The Secretariat, as the administrative branch of the Party, may employ as many as several hundred thousand persons, a figure that includes paid workers in Party organization around the country (Theen, 1981, p. 76).

As one gets closer to the center of power, the information about actual operations becomes vaguer. Not a great deal is known about the conducting of Politburo or Secretariat business. During their tenures as Party leaders, both Khrushchev and Brezhnev gave interviews to Western correspondents about Politburo proceedings (Khrushchev, 1957, pp. 53–57; *The New York Times,* June 15, 1973, p. 3). And at Party meetings Brezhnev and others provided a few further details, which were reported in the Soviet press. Since the death of Brezhnev brief descriptions of Politburo meetings have regularly been carried in the Soviet press. On the basis of this information the following can be said: The Politburo meets in a building in the Kremlin on a regular basis, usually once a week; typically the meeting day is Thursday, with meetings lasting three to six hours; discussions deal with a variety of domestic and foreign policy problems, with a consensus of the whole Politburo eventually being reached; only rarely is it necessary to take a formal vote, but when that happens, a majority vote carries; in some cases the Politburo creates special commissions to study particular problems or to implement particular decisions.

This rather bland description of Politburo proceedings may be typical of some meetings, but it is not likely that things are always so peaceful. Many Western analysts look upon Soviet political structure and tradition as inherently involving more or less continuous conflict among the leaders. Since the most important body is the Politburo, the conflict must surface most often among Politburo members (although not necessarily always at Politburo meetings). But the paucity of information on this aspect of Soviet politics leaves us only with a vague partial sketch rather than a full picture.

One of the much-endorsed principles of Soviet politics is that of "collective leadership" (*kollektivnoe rukovodstvo*), but it has been subject to only partial application in practice. The term embraces the idea that no single person should hold the top posts of Party chief and head of the government (chairman of the Council of Ministers) at the same time. This principle was disregarded by both Stalin and Khrushchev. After Khrushchev's fall the Central Committee resolved that the two positions should not be held simultaneously by the same person.[10] All subsequent leaders (Brezhnev, Andropov, Chernenko, and Gorbachev) assumed the chairmanship of the Supreme Soviet Presidium while keeping the Party general secretary's position. But this did not violate the letter of this resolution, since the Presidium chairmanship was not considered as important as the Council of Ministers chairmanship. But when Gorbachev took the new post of Chairman of the Supreme Soviet in 1989 and the USSR presidency in 1990, he clearly occupied the two most important positions in the country.

Although the Politburo is the prime decision-making body in the Party, few formal decisions are taken in its name. Traditionally, press coverage of Politburo meetings has been minimal. But after Brezhnev's tenure as general secretary, the veil of secrecy surrounding Politburo activities was lifted slightly. In late 1982 regular reports began to be published in the Soviet press entitled "In the Politburo of the Central Committee of the CPSU." These reports have appeared almost weekly since then, usually in the Friday or Saturday issues of certain newspapers (suggesting, as indicated, that the Politburo usually meets on Thursdays). The reports do not really add much to our knowledge of Politburo operations. One Western analyst sees the reports "more as a public relations exercise than as a genuine attempt to inform the Soviet population of the concerns of their leaders" (Teague, 1983, p. 7). Moreover, it is almost certainly true that the Politburo has numerous meetings that are not reported in the press (Lowenhardt, 1988, pp. 11–13, 17).

Secretariat operations are less publicized than those of the Politburo. Its meetings are virtually never announced and it was not until 1971 that it was even indicated that regular meetings were held. At that time Brezhnev stated that the Secretariat, like the Politburo, meets once a week. The normal meeting day is Wednesday, the day before the regular Politburo meeting. In his speech at the Twenty-Sixth Party Congress in 1981, Brezhnev stated that the Secretariat had met 250 times since the Twenty-Fifth Congress. This number is slightly higher than that of Politburo meetings for the same period (236) and amounts almost precisely to one meeting per week. Brezhnev's description of functions of the Secretariat amounted to little more than a reiteration of the statement in the Party Rules: "The selection of personnel, the organization and checking of the execution of decisions, practically speaking, all current questions of Party life—such, basically is the circle of problems handled by the Secretariat of the Central Committee" (*Izvestiia,* February 21, 1981, p. 8).

In terms of formal organization, the Secretariat is headed by the general secretary, who is responsible for the execution of general policy. Under him is a group of "Secretaries of the Central Committee of the CPSU," several of

---

[10] The resolution has not been published openly but is referred to in several sources. See the discussion in *Resolutions and Decisions of the Communist Party of the Soviet Union,* vol. 4, ed. Grey Hodnett, pp. 316–317 (Toronto: University of Toronto Press, 1974) and vol. 5, ed. Donald V. Schwartz, p. 73 (1982).

The Communist Party   133

whom also serve on the Politburo. The Secretariat also contains a number of departments, some traditionally headed by secretaries and others headed by lesser Party functionaries. These departments, which numbered more than twenty until reforms in the late 1980s, covered all of the major areas of economic activity and foreign affairs as well as culture, propaganda and agitation, science and education, governmental administration, and personnel. The staff workers in these departments constituted the large number of central-Party-apparatus employees.

The 1988 reorganization of the Party apparatus has lessened the Secretariat's importance. In September 1988 it was announced that six new commissions of the Central Committee were being created, each one headed by a high Party official. Apparently in line with the idea of giving more of the authority to govern to the actual governmental organs, these commissions were assigned broad areas of responsibility (thus implicitly leaving the particulars to the government). The commissions, which report directly to the Politburo, cover the following subjects: Party construction and personnel policy, ideology, social and economic policy, agrarian policy, international policy, legal policy. When these commissions were constituted later in 1988, they were made up of 20 to 25 members each, mostly from the Party Central Committee or Central Auditing Commission. Part of the rationale for creating the commissions was the push for greater intra-Party democracy. As the resolution naming the commission members put it, the commissions "are called upon to promote in every way the development of the collective principle of Party leadership and the involvement of members and candidate members of the CPSU Central Committee and members of the CPSU Central Auditing Commission on a regular basis in active work in the most important areas of domestic and foreign policy" (*Izvestiia,* November 29, 1988, p. 2; *CDSP, 40,* no. 48, p. 24). Among the commissions' functions are preparing drafts of documents and other materials for Politburo consideration and making recommendations on questions within their areas of jurisdiction.

It is intended that the size of the Party bureaucracy be considerably reduced, as governmental bodies are given a more substantial role in governing the country. Since the bulk of the employees in the central Party apparatus in effect work for the Secretariat, this should mean a reduction in the Secretariat's importance. But several factors suggest that the Secretariat will continue to exercise at least some influence. The number of departments in the Secretariat has been cut from 20 to 9. The departments remaining are Agrarian, Ideological, International, Legal, Party Construction and Personnel, Social and Economic, Administration, Defense, and General. Note that the first six of these correspond generally in subject with the six Politburo commissions. These departments will serve a staff function for the commissions. As the resolution spelling out the reform put it: "In their work the commissions are guided by the corresponding departments" of the Secretariat, and "organizational and technical conditions" for the commissions' activities "are provided by [the Secretariat's] General Department and its Administrative Office" (*Izvestiia,* November 29, 1988, p. 2; *CDSP,* 40, no. 48, p. 24).

All six men originally chosen as chairmen of the commissions were Party secretaries,[11] suggesting that coordination of the activity of the commissions will take place in the Secretariat. The membership of the commissions, by contrast, is quite diverse, and includes numerous officials whose full-time functions are outside of Moscow (Rahr, 1988). Since the commissions are required to meet only every three months, it may be that much of the actual work and decision making will be done in their name by the secretaries and their staffs.

THE PARTY–GOVERNMENT RELATIONSHIP

Much of the Gorbachev-era activity connected with reforming the political system has been aimed at enhancing the role of the government, particularly the soviets, in relation to the Party. One should not conclude from this, however, that Gorbachev is addressing a new problem. The tension between Party and government, the overlapping of functions, and the uncertainty as to which hierarchy should be responsible for what activities have existed since the beginning of Soviet power. And these problems are unlikely to be solved easily by the reforms so far adopted.

Gorbachev describes much of his reform scheme as a return to a Leninist model for ruling the country. This is true in a sense. Lenin's most important position was chairman of the Council of People's Commissars (now the Council of Ministers), although he was, during his time at the helm, the central figure in the Party as well. But even during Lenin's time the need to keep the Party from usurping the functions of the government was recognized.

The standard Soviet position on Party–government relations is that the Party plays a "leading role" and "guides" governmental and social organizations, and that the latter carry out their functions under Party guidance (Barry, 1984, pp. 37–52). This suggests a rather neat division of responsibilities, somewhat reminiscent of the "policy–administration" dichotomy long familiar to students of public administration in the West. But it is clear that to treat policy and administration as completely distinct categories is a futile exercise because of the unavoidable mixture of the two functions in practice. The late Leonard Schapiro, long a student of Soviet affairs, saw the problem clearly as it applied to the Soviet system: "The borderline between policy and administration is

[11]And all but one CC secretary was on the Politburo. This has created the unusual (for the CPSU Politburo) situation in which CC secretaries constituted a majority of the full membership of the Politburo. This suggests that the Secretariat *as a body* may have diminished in importance, but that the secretaries, as administrators of day-to-day affairs, have become more important in Politburo policy-making.

never easy to draw. The party cells in the government machine were supposed to 'guide' but not 'interfere.' But where does guidance end and interference begin?'' (Schapiro, 1971, p. 327).

The concept of *podmena* (''substitution'' or ''supplanting''), Party organs acting in place of governmental organs, is a source of long-standing concern for the Party. Although it has been recognized as a problem since at least 1919 and is prohibited by the Party Rules (Article 60),[12] it has long been a widely discussed phenomenon. Given the pervasiveness of the Party role, it is not surprising that suggestions were made during the public discussion of the 1977 Constitution to give direct legislative power to the higher Party organs. Brezhnev, in his speech at the time of the adoption of the constitution, called such proposals ''deeply erroneous,'' creating ''confusion as to the role of the Party'' and obscuring ''the meaning and functions of the organs of Soviet power.'' As suggested, however, such confusion is understandable, given the extensiveness of Party activity in the Soviet system.

PRINCIPLES OF PARTY OPERATION

One principle of Party operation already noted is collective leadership. This involves a sharing of top Party and government posts, rather than their being held by one person. As was shown, this principle has been subject to somewhat inconsistent application by the Party leadership over time.

Among other principles of Party operation, three that deserve close examination are ''democratic centralism,'' ''criticism and self-criticism,'' and the *nomenklatura* system. As with many other areas of Soviet life, these three traditional bases of Party practice have been subject to potential modification during the Gorbachev era. By far the most important, ''the guiding principle of the organizational structure and of the entire life and activity of the Party'' (Party Rules, Article 19), is democratic centralism. The term is said to embrace four subprinciples, the first two of which might be looked upon as democratic, the last two as centralist.

a. Election of all leading Party bodies, from the lowest to the highest;
b. Periodic reports of Party bodies to their Party organizations and to higher bodies;
c. Strict Party discipline and subordination of the minority to the majority;
d. The obligatory nature of the decisions of higher bodies for lower bodies.

[12]The prohibition on *podmena* seems to have been strengthened in the Party Rules adopted in 1986. In this version of the Rules the prohibition has been placed in a separate article (it had been in Article 42, on lower-level Party organizations). And in addition to the statement on *podmena,* a new stipulation that ''Party organizations operate within the framework of the USSR Constitution'' was added.

Traditionally the actual interpretation of "democratic centralism" has been much more restrictive and "centralist" than the four elements imply. Election of Party leadership bodies has been a *pro forma* exercise in which the leaders themselves provided a single list of candidates to Party committees for approval. As for the periodic reports by leaders to Party organizations, these never served as the occasion for debate or policy development. Moreover, other sections of the Party Rules can be looked upon as essentially negating the democratic elements of the principle. Particularly relevant is a passage from the introduction to the Rules:

> Ideological and organization unity, monolithic cohesion of its ranks, and a high degree of conscious discipline on the part of all Communists are an inviolable law of the CPSU. All manifestations of factionalism and group activity are incompatible with Marxist-Leninist principles, and with Party membership.

In terms of the principle as a whole, then, the most that can be said about its democratic substance is this: On some issues Party members appear to be accorded the right to free discussion "until a decision has been made" (as an earlier formation of the concept of democratic centralism put it; Avtorkhanov, 1966, p. 100). Continuation of opposition on an issue beyond that point would be improper.

In theory at least, Gorbachev-era changes in Party operations ought to affect the way in which democratic centralism works. Making Party operations more open, increasing the responsibility of more exclusive organs to the bodies to which they report (for instance, the Politburo to the Central Committee), and limiting the tenure of responsible Party officials to two consecutive five-year terms could lead to a devolution of organizational power. As was noted previously, all of these points were contained in resolutions adopted at the nineteenth Party Conference in 1988.

Gorbachev noted at that time that democratic centralism had been "largely replaced by bureaucratic centralism" (*Izvestiia,* June 28, 1988, p. 6; *CDSP, 40,* no. 26, 1988, p. 22). Previously he had given direct support to the idea of competitive elections for Party offices, a concept that received much discussion in the months thereafter. This is an example, however, of the difficulty of translating reform intentions into institutionalized practice. Competitive Party elections appear to have been used relatively rarely, and then only at the lower levels of Party organization (Lowenhardt, 1988, pp. 21–22; Brown, 1988, pp. 5–6). Nor is it likely that this will change soon. The prospect of the Central Committee *actually* making choices among competing candidates for Politburo membership does not appear to be an idea whose time has come.

Another principle that is referred to several times in the Party Rules is "criticism and self-criticism." In one passage the term is mentioned in connection with free discussion of Party policy (Article 26) and in another with the laying bare of shortcomings in Soviet society (Article 2i). The principle was obviously created to help the Party check and eliminate abuses of power, both within and outside the Party. But the limitations on free discussion have restricted somewhat the extent to which this device has been implemented. It probably comes into play in criticizing Party operations at the lower levels, but public criticism of high Party leaders, especially at the national level, is rare, unless a campaign against a high Party leader is being orchestrated by his colleagues. If the Gorbachev-era promises of freer intra-Party discussion are realized, however, this could change.

The term *nomenklatura* refers to a list of positions for which Party approval is required before a person holding one of those positions can be removed or a replacement can be named. Every Party organ above the PPO has its *nomenklatura* list. In general, the more important the position, the higher the Party organ on whose list it appears. Many, but by no means all, positions on *nomenklatura* lists are Party posts. Such lists contain, as one writer has put it, "the most important leading positions in all organized activities of social life" (Harasymiw, 1969, p. 506), including high positions in the military, soviets, the administrative apparatus, economic enterprises, the communications media, and the semipublic social organizations such as the *Komsomol* or youth organizations, trade unions, women's organizations, and scientific and cultural societies. Appointment of Party members to *nomenklatura* positions is not required, but communists clearly predominate in such posts.

In this way the Party seeks to maintain control over broad aspects of Soviet society. And greater power flows to the central Party apparatus because its list covers all of the strategic positions in the country. Within the central apparatus, most decisions on *nomenklatura* appointments take place within the Secretariat, which helps to explain why the general secretary's position is such an important one in Soviet politics.

Most analysts agree that although *nomenklatura* implies only Party approval or confirmation of personnel decisions, in fact the Party often takes the initiative in filling positions on the list. Moreover, even lower-level positions in various organizations are subject to Party scrutiny through the so-called "accounting nomenklatura" (*uchetnaia nomenklatura*). Changes in such positions do not require Party approval, but the Party must be kept informed.

Like many systems of rules of this kind, the *nomenklatura* system has given rise to some unintended consequences. A measure of prestige in Soviet society has become whether one's job is "nomenklatured," and by what level of Party organ. It is said that a person on a sufficiently high *nomenklatura* list cannot be subject to criminal prosecution without Party approval. Persons having a *nomenklatura* position may be removed from it for incompetence but appointed to other similar work because they have retained their *nomenklatura* status. This status, once conferred, provides a kind of permanent tenure to those who hold it, and the Soviet press provides occasional examples of persons' going to great lengths to keep from losing *nomenklatura* status.

At times, then, the *nomenklatura* system has been criticized for providing a haven for incompetents. But it is also seen by Western analysts as facilitating the building of power bases within the Party (especially by those who control *nomenklatura* appointments) and producing an inbred and conservative leadership (Harasymiw, 1969, p. 506).

While helping to maintain Party control of the system, then, *nomenklatura* practices seem to inhibit reformist impulses and even restrict the ability of the leadership to implement policy decisions made at the top. Michael Vozlensky (1984), a former Soviet citizen and the author of the authoritative book *Nomenklatura* asserts that "only an outside observer could suppose all power in the Soviet Union to be in the hands of the Politburo. . . . In fact, the Politburo, though immensely powerful, has only a limited field of action. This limitation of its power has nothing to do with democracy and everything to do with the division of labor inside the nomenklatura class." He goes on to suggest that district and local Party leadership groups have control over most *nomenklatura* appointments at those levels and that the Politburo finds it prudent to interfere only rarely in their activities. This puts considerable power in the hands of local Party officials. Vozlensky finds parallels between this aspect of the Soviet system and medieval feudalism: "The nomenklatura is a bastard kind of feudalism; every nomenklaturist is granted a fief, just as every vassal was granted a fief by the crown" (Vozlensky, 1984, p. 71).

It is clear that Soviet leaders have long appreciated the disadvantages of the *nomenklatura* system: its tendencies to keep conservatives (and incompetents) in positions of authority, and thereby to frustrate the implementation of reform efforts agreed upon at the top. But the advantages of Party control achieved through *nomenklatura* seemed to outweigh these disadvantages. And even under Gorbachev there has been a reluctance to attack *nomenklatura* head-on. The move toward competitive election of persons holding responsible posts, not just in the Party but in such jobs as factory manager and scientific institute director, would counter the influence of *nomenklatura* to a considerable extent. But as has been indicated, it is not yet clear how comprehensively genuine elections of this kind will be used. The brief discussion of *nomenklatura* in the nineteenth Party Conference resolution on democratization and political reform, therefore, may amount to more of a hope than a promise. The resolution notes that the *nomenklatura* system "is becoming obsolete" and that the Party's basic method in naming people to leading posts should be founded on democratic procedures: "The final solution of cadre questions should be determined by election results" (*Izvestiia,* July 5, 1988, p. 2; Mann, 1988, p. 3).

PARTY LEADERS: BACKGROUND AND CAREERS

Compared with a president, a prime minister, or a cabinet member in the West, most Soviet politicians are anonymous bureaucrats. But relatively speaking, the members of the Politburo and the Secretariat are the best-known politicians in the country. The names and pictures of the top several leaders appear frequently in the Soviet press in connection with speeches, travel abroad, meetings with foreign leaders, and the like. Thus, a reasonably full picture of their careers and background characteristics can be sketched.

There are basically two ways in which a leadership group of this kind can be described. One is to sketch the broad characteristics and trends with regard to the group as a whole, perhaps over some set period of time. The other is to provide information on individual personalities. The latter approach may be more interesting, but it is also of less long-term interest because of turnover in the membership of the leadership group. Our emphasis, therefore, will be on the group as a whole, with individual leaders mentioned only for illustrative purposes. What is referred to as the top leadership group is composed of full members of the Politburo, who have numbered between 11 and 16 in recent years; the candidate Politburo members, who typically number 6 to 8; and a few more CC secretaries who are not also either full or candidate Politburo members. The top leadership, then, normally comprises 20 to 25 members.

Until 1990, the holding of certain positions seemed to entitle the incumbents to full Politburo membership. Among these were the party General Secretary, the Premier (Chairman of the Council of Ministers), the Chairman of the Supreme Soviet, and the First Secretary of the Ukrainian Party organization.[13] New incumbents to these posts either were already on the Politburo or were elevated to that status on being appointed to one of these posts. The other places on the Politburo (there is no set number of full or candidate members) were held by persons occupying other significant posts: perhaps one or two first deputy premiers, and several first secretaries of union republic Party organizations. Usually heads of government ministries were not important enough as politicians to qualify for Politburo membership, but from the 1970s to 1990 the heads of the Ministries of Foreign Affairs and Defense and of the KGB typically were either candidate or full Politburo members. As indicated previously, substantial changes were made in these practices in 1990: The heads of all union republic Party organizations were given automatic seats on the Politburo; and the holders of governmental posts (Premier, Minister of Foreign Affairs, and so forth) lost their positions on the Politburo.

The status of candidate members of the Politburo is interesting but somewhat ambiguous from the standpoint of career patterns. They are not mentioned in the Party Rules (which state only that the CC selects a Polit-

---

[13] The Ukraine is the second most populous Soviet republic and a key agricultural and industrial area. No other republic has been accorded the more or less permanent representation on the Politburo that its first Party secretary has had almost continuously since the 1930s. Until 1990, the largest union republic, the RSFSR, had no separate Party organization. This was no doubt because the Russians dominated the national Party structure. In 1989 the Party recreated the Russian Bureau of the Central Committee, an organ that had existed in the 1960s but had been abolished for many years, and in 1990 a separate RSFSR Party organization was established.

buro); but on the analogy with the functions of candidate CC members—who are mentioned in the Rules—it would seem that the candidate Politburo members have the right to speak but not to vote in Politburo proceedings.

Candidate Politburo membership can be a stepping-stone to full Politburo membership, although this stage is sometimes skipped. Moreover, a large number of candidate members never attain full Politburo membership. For these people, candidate membership is the high point of their careers. Some slip back to more modest positions rather quickly, whereas others hold candidate membership as a relatively permanent status. P. N. Demichev was appointed a candidate Politburo member in 1964 and held that position for almost 25 years until his retirement in 1988 at age 70.

Only three women have served on the Politburo: Ekaterina Furtseva (candidate member, 1956 to 1957, full member, 1957 to 1961), Aleksandra Biriukova (candidate member, 1988–1990); and Galina Semyonova (1990–). Furtseva and Biriukova have also been the only female CC secretaries. The top organs have always been strongly dominated by members of the three major Slavic nationalities, the Russians, Ukrainians, and Byelorussians, with only token representation of other nationalities. Unlike earlier generations of Soviet leaders, virtually all of the present top leaders have complete higher education. For the overwhelming majority of leaders, this education has been of the highly specialized technical variety. The norm has been to have training in one of the engineering specialties rather than in the humanities or social sciences.[14]

Although most of the leaders spent some time working at their professions, by and large they got into political work fairly early in their lives. For only a few was this political work in organizations other than the Party apparatus, such as the state apparatus or the army. The dominant career pattern for the top political leadership is fairly clear then: Slavic ethnic background (preferably Russian), graduation from a higher educational institution with a technical specialty, early transfer to professional Party status, and a process of working up through Party ranks.

That the major characteristics of the top 20 to 25 leaders can be summed up in so few words is in itself extremely significant. It suggests a deliberate attempt to minimize diversity and to bring like-minded individuals into the top leadership group. One might reasonably ask if this narrowness is suitable for a large and complex system where the leaders have so many political and economic responsibilities. Western analysts who have raised this question have suggested that the leadership pool is kept exclusive to maintain ideological orthodoxy and the prevent "revisionism." The danger is that the kind of leaders who rise to the top under this kind of an arrangement will not have the competence or experience to cope with the increasing demands placed on

---

[14]Lenin, the founder of the Soviet state, studied law, and Gorbachev graduated from the Law Faculty of Moscow University in 1955. But almost no other high Soviet political leaders have had legal training.

them. This approach to elite recruitment may constitute one of the root causes of the Party's present dilemma.

By comparison with ruling bodies in many other countries, the top Soviet Party leadership is a relatively old group (Lowenhardt, 1982, p. 53). The purges of the Stalin period had helped keep down the average age at the top of the Party, but after Stalin much greater stability characterized this group, particularly during Brezhnev's tenure (1964–1982). Under Brezhnev and his successors, dismissal in disgrace has occurred less frequently, but graceful retirement has not quite become institutionalized. Consequently, many leaders seem to try to hang on to power as long as possible. Thus, the average age of full Politburo members (this generalization could be made about other high Soviet political bodies as well) rose from about 50 in 1939, to 55 in 1952, to 61 in 1964, to over 70 near the end of the Brezhnev period. The Brezhnev-era gerontocracy probably approached the limit in terms of average that one could reasonably expect in a collegial body of a dozen or so members, and after Brezhnev's death the average dropped somewhat. In spite of the considerable turnover in top positions in the first year of Gorbachev's tenure as Party general secretary, however, the average age of the twelve full Politburo members elected at the Twenty-Seventh Party Congress in March 1986 was still nearly 65, and by 1990, after considerable further turnover, it had dropped to about 62. Even under Gorbachev, then, the average age of the top leaders has remained quite high.

Until Gorbachev, the tendency in recent years was toward older persons holding the top Party position (General Secretary). The age factor was clearly connected with the remarkable turnover in that post in the early to mid 1980s. While there were only four top leaders during the first 65 years of the Soviet regime (Lenin, Stalin, Khrushchev, and Brezhnev), four also occupied the top post in the 28 months between November 1982 and March 1985 (Brezhnev, Andropov, Chernenko, and Gorbachev). Lenin and Stalin were in their forties when they assumed the reins of power, while Khrushchev and Brezhnev were in their late fifties. Andropov was 68 and Chernenko was 72. None of these leaders left voluntarily, all dying in office except Khrushchev, who was removed by his colleagues at age 70. Mikhail Gorbachev, in assuming the General Secretaryship just a few days after his fifty-fourth birthday in March 1985, became the youngest Soviet leader since Stalin.

Many of the same characteristics of the top leadership just described are to be found at the lower levels of the Party leadership as well. Next to the Politburo, the body most studied as to elite characteristics is the CPSU Central Committee. Since the CC is the main promotion channel to higher Party rank, it is understandable that its members would bear similarities to the top leaders. As with the Politburo, a considerable proportion of CC membership is apportioned on the basis of status. That is, the holding of a position more or less automatically qualifies one for a seat on the CC. For full CC membership such positions include

1. Party: the top 20 to 25 Party leaders discussed previously, all first secretaries of union republic Party organizations, 30 to 50 first secretaries of important regional Party organizations, and the first secretaries of the Moscow and Leningrad Party organizations
2. Government: the chairman and first deputy chairman of the USSR Council of Ministers, the ministers and first deputy ministers of several key ministries, including Foreign Affairs and Defense; the chairmen of several republican councils of ministers, including those of the RSFSR, the Ukraine, Byelorussia, and probably Georgia and Uzbekistan
3. Other: the first secretary of the USSR *Komsomol,* the chairman of the All-Union Trade Union Council and at least one deputy of that council, the editor of *Pravda,* and the president of the Academy of Sciences

To some extent, at least, this process of status appointments also applies to CC candidate members.

This "automatic" membership constitutes less than half of the full members of the CC; the internal politics of the Party, the bargaining and competition among various leadership groups, determines the remainder of the members. Whatever the final composition in terms of individuals, the proportion of various hierarchies represented on the CC has remained fairly constant in recent years: 40 to 45 percent are full-time Party workers, about 35 percent are from the governmental apparatus, about 10 percent from the military and security bureaucracies, with the remainder made up of plant directors, outstanding workers, and people from the arts, sciences, and other fields.

Regarding other background factors, the parallel between the CC and the top leadership is maintained. Women have made up about 4 percent of CC members in recent years (as against about 25 percent of the total Party membership). Although the level of education has not been as high in the CC as in the Politburo-Secretariat, the former is dominated by persons with engineering and technical training. Also, the CC is disproportionately dominated by ethnic Slavs. As to age, the Central Committee naturally has a lower average than do the Politburo and Secretariat. But as in those two bodies, its average age shows a tendency to increase over time. From an average age of 49 in 1952, full members of the Central Committee rose gradually in age to an average of 56 in 1966, 58 in 1971, and 60 in 1976. After drifting higher thereafter, it returned to 60 in 1986 (Tatu, 1986). Moreover, there is evidence to show that the Central Committee's age structure is high when compared with other countries (Nagle, 1977, pp. 77–91).

This bare detailing of dominant background characteristics and career patterns tells only part of the story, of course. Beyond the traits that we have described, political success depends on a person's performance on the job and his or her luck or skill in backing the right policies. Finally, as in any political system, connections are important. A politician must have the astuteness to associate himself or herself with the "right people," those who succeed rather than fail.

Regarding job performance, since so many future leaders come from at least a few years in responsible production assignments, they must have demonstrated at least minimal competence in their professions. Those who got into Party work at an early age likewise probably exhibited some level of political and managerial skill in order to work up through Party ranks. Thus, obvious incompetents would probably not rise very high in Party circles.

Personal connections, developed and cultivated to help one's career, are prevalent in most countries. Yet the peculiar nature of Soviet political processes may make such contacts especially important there. The late Franz Borkenau explained this phenomenon over 35 years ago in a passage that is still basically sound:

> Here, as in most other things, life in the USSR is different only in degree, not in kind, from life everywhere else, and it is just as hard to draw a line between the personal and the political factor. Both have to be taken into account, and especially their interaction. Yet certain peculiarities do attach to the Soviet case. Prominent among them is the institution or practice called *Shefstvo,* which gets its name from the French word *chef,* meaning "leader" or "boss." This system is not confined to the Soviet world, but the absence of political, economic, and intellectual freedom in that world endows it with much greater importance there, making it in effect the only way in which a Soviet citizen can rise to power and eminence. No matter what his pursuit or field, if he is ambitious, he must choose a protector or patron among those already in power, and put himself in the relation of "client" to him and rely upon him for favors indispensable to advancement.
>
> The universality of this practice creates a rather complicated and extensive system of patronage on the various echelons of Soviet power that has to be deciphered before the personal factor in Soviet politics can be given, in each case, its due importance. Difficult though this may seem, it is not always an insuperable task. The very scale on which the *Shefstvo* system functions in Soviet Russia provides the observer with leads aplenty. (Borkenau, 1954, p. 394)

Much analysis by Western scholars about power relationships in the Kremlin ("kremlinology") over the past four or five decades has been based on assumptions about such patron-client relationships. Yet these relationships need not be permanent: A *shef* may abandon his protégé or the latter may turn against the former. Crucial to the downfall or continued success of a Soviet politician may be his or her ability to see the direction things are going and to shift alliances or modify policies. Moreover, seeing *shefstvo* relationships as permanent may mislead the Western analyst in his or her conclusions about the strength of a leader's position or other aspects of Soviet politics. Brezhnev was almost universally seen by Western scholars as a protégé of Khrushchev—which he surely was for a considerable period of time—until he replaced Khrushchev as general secretary of the Party in 1964. Brezhnev obviously had been able to disassociate himself from Khrushchev to some extent and be recognized as a leader in his own right; in contrast, others closer to

Khrushchev, such as Leonid Ilichev and Khrushchev's son-in-law, Alexei Adzhubei, both lost their positions soon after Khrushchev's removal from office.

In addition to everything else, there is surely a measure of luck in the ebb and flow of political careers. Being in the right place at the right time or backing the policy whose time as come (or gone) appears at times accidental rather than calculated. A number of brilliant political careers were helped along when rivals or superiors were removed in large numbers during Stalin's purges. And being connected with the virgin-lands program during times of bumper harvests (as Brezhnev briefly was) could be very good for one's career. But numerous political fortunes have been hurt by association with the much more frequent experience of mediocre or poor agricultural production. Gorbachev's job as Party leader in the Stavropol area, which boasts some of the most well known spas in the Soviet Union, allowed him to make contact with numerous Kremlin leaders coming to the area for rest. One of his patrons through this connection was Andropov, who is thought to have been largely responsible for bringing Gorbachev to Moscow in 1978 (Walker, 1988, pp. 14–17).

THE FUTURE OF THE PARTY

One of the defining characteristics of the Soviet system, throughout its history, has been the Communist Party's monopoly on political power. Yet at several points in this chapter alone, the erosion of the Party's position in Soviet society has been discussed. That so basic an aspect of Soviet life should be brought into question indicates the pervasiveness of change in the USSR in recent years. Regarding the change in the Party's position, two matters remain to be discussed: the factors that have led to this situation, and the direction in which present developments seem to be leading.

Major Factors behind the Challenge to the Party's Authority

On this point, four considerations seem most important. It is clear that these are not independent factors but are interrelated parts of a larger process of political evolution.

Glasnost.   The rapid opening up of Soviet society, beginning about 1987, was obviously of crucial significance. The three other factors to be discussed in this section stem directly from it. The atmosphere of glasnost meant that formerly taboo subjects could now be discussed openly. The process started innocently enough, with writers and other artists being able to publish and produce works that would have formerly been banned, and with a new freshness and candor in the press. But once the smaller barriers were breached, who was to say that other, more sacrosanct subjects could not also come in for criticism, including the previously untouchable image of Lenin and the place of the Party in the Soviet system? When it became clear just where glasnost was leading, Gorbachev tried to put on the brakes by reining in the press and dismissing talk of a multiparty system. But like the sorcerer's apprentice, he seemed to be no longer fully in control.

Ethnic Upheavals.   The long-simmering ethnic tensions in the Soviet Union, which had been reasonably well contained by the authorities until glasnost, came to the surface and were intensified by the openness with which they were acknowledged in the late 1980s (for further discussion of nationality problems, see Chapter 12). The demands for greater autonomy, territorial changes, and even independence by some national groups caused grave problems for the Soviet leadership. And some of the strongest pressures on the Communist Party itself came from the national revival. Nationality interests, particularly in the Baltic republics, in considerable part initiated the call for a multiparty system in the Soviet Union. And the move to abolish the Party's constitutionally mandated monopoly position was first undertaken, at the end of 1989, by Lithuania and Latvia.[15]

The Liberation of Eastern Europe.   The reciprocal influence of developments in the Soviet Union and Eastern Europe can be seen clearly with regard to their effect on the position of the Communist Party. Spurred by developments within the Soviet Union, reformers in Eastern Europe moved to change their political and economic systems, and to reduce Moscow's role in their affairs. When it became clear that the Gorbachev leadership would not interfere in these developments, reform proceeded quickly, and the momentous changes of 1989 were accomplished. Not the least important of these was the successive elimination of the Communist Party's monopoly position in Poland, Hungary, Czechoslovakia, East Germany, Bulgaria, and Rumania. These developments cannot have failed to influence advocates of change within the Soviet Union, both Communists and non-Communists. At the Lithuanian Communist Party meeting in December 1989, when the Lithuanian Party voted to become a party independent from Moscow, one delegate reminded the audience of Gorbachev's words regarding Eastern Europe: "Every nation has the right to choose its own way to develop its social structure." To this the delegate responded: "All European nations includes us. We're no worse than anyone else in Eastern Europe" (*The New York Times,* December 21, 1989, p. A1). This sentiment has spread to other parts of the USSR, as reformers continue to attempt to find the place for their regions, either within or outside of the USSR.

The New State Structure.   In engineering the momentous changes in political structure and the distribution of power described in the last chapter,

---

[15] This was accomplished by deleting from the republic constitutions the reference to the Communist Party as "the leading and guiding force in Soviet society and the nucleus of its political system and of state and social organizations." The wording and numbering of this article (Article 6) was identical in the USSR and in all 15 union republic constitutions until 1989. See Feldbrugge, 1979, pp. 77–78 and 275.

the Gorbachev leadership has called into question the rationale for the Party's central role: If representative bodies are really to be empowered, if they are genuinely to make decisions, why do they need even to be "guided," much less controlled, by some other organization? The creation of the new structures, in other words, carries with it the germ that leads to the destruction of the Party's traditional role in the Soviet system.

Gorbachev sought to prevent this development in various ways: by declaring, for instance, that since the Party was the initiator of the changes, it could lay legitimate claim to remain in charge of the process; and by recommending devices that could keep Party members in strong positions in the new structures, such as setting aside seats in the legislature for social organizations and recommending that the heads of the new soviets be the Party leaders on the corresponding levels. But the legitimacy claim has not proved persuasive, and the devices to maintain Party control have been strongly criticized and, in the case of parliamentary representation from social organizations, have been all but abolished. As the displacement of power from the Party toward the state has proceeded, it has become clear that Gorbachev's more important position is not general secretary of the Party but President of the USSR. It appears that Gorbachev, in creating the powerful presidency, was designing a more secure position for himself as his Party post, and the Party itself, went into decline. That decline was furthered, of course, by the other 1990 constitutional change that accompanied the creation of the presidency: the revision of Article 6 to deprive the Party of its monopoly on political power.

The Direction of Present Developments

With other party and political groupings legalized and organized, the position of the Communist Party can only be further eroded. And the Party itself has lost the monolithic unity once imposed on it from the top. Fissures in the Party have appeared, and it seems inevitable that it will split into at least two factions and probably more, not to mention the hiving off of ethnic Party organizations in the republics.

But the Party has certain advantages that should not be discounted. It remains a large organization with many members. It possesses considerable property and other resources. And it has attracted a membership that traditionally included many of the most active members of society. Moreover, in its new position as one among others, it has made moves to change its mode of operation and to project an image of a more progressive, democratic organization.

One's assessment of the place of the Communist Party in the Soviet system, then, depends on one's perspective: The Party no longer holds a monopoly position, a situation that must pain many communist traditionalists; but it could remain one of the important forces in Soviet politics, and so the direction and extent of internal reform in the Party continue to be important issues.

REFERENCES

ANDERSON, T. (1963). *Masters of Russian Marxism*. New York: Appleton-Century-Crofts.

AVTORKHANOV, A. (1966). *The Communist party apparatus*. Chicago: Regnery Gateway.

BARRY, D. (1984). The *Spravochnik Partiinogo Rabotnika* as a source of party law. In D.A. Loeber and others, eds., *Ruling communist parties and their status under law*. Dordrecht, The Netherlands: Martinus Nijhoff.

BORKENAU, F. (1954). Getting at the facts behind the Soviet facade. *Commentary*, 17, no. 4, 390–395.

BROWN, A. (1988). The Soviet leadership and the struggle for political reform. *The Harriman Institute Forum, 1*, no. 4.

DOBROKHOTOV, L. (1986). The CPSU on the right track. *Soviet Life*, no. 3, 38–39.

FELDBRUGGE, F.J.M., ed. (1979). *The constitution of the USSR and the union republics: Analysis, texts, reports*. Alphen aan den Rijn, The Netherlands: Sijthoff & Noordhoff.

HANSON, P., and TEAGUE, E. (1989). Has Party membership begun to fall? *Radio Liberty Report on the USSR, 1*, no. 15, 16.

HARASYMIW, B. (1969). *Nomenklatura*: The Soviet communist party's leadership recruitment system. *Canadian Journal of Political Science, 2*, 505–512.

KAMINSKAYA, D. (1982). *Final judgment*. New York: Simon & Schuster.

KHRUSHCHEV, N. (1957). *Speeches and interviews on world problems*. Moscow: Foreign Languages.

LAIRD, R. (1986). *The politburo: Demographic trends, Gorbachev, and the future*. Boulder, Colo.: Westview.

LIJPHART, A. (1969). *Politics in Europe*. Englewood Cliffs, N.J.: Prentice-Hall.

LOWENHARDT, J. (1982). *The Soviet politburo*. New York: St. Martin's.

LOWENHARDT, J. (1988). Glasnost in the CPSU. Unpublished paper presented at the 1988 meeting of the Midwest Political Science Association, 14–16 April, 1988.

MANN, D. (1988). The party conference resolution on democratization and political reform. *Radio Liberty Research*, no. 301/88.

NAGLE, J. (1977). *System and succession: The social bases of political elite recruitment*. Austin: University of Texas Press.

PETHYBRIDGE, R. (1962). *A key to Soviet politics: The crisis of the anti-party group*. New York: Holt, Rinehart & Winston.

RAHR, A. (1988). Gorbachev changes party structure. *Radio Liberty Research*, no. 519/88.

SCHAPIRO, L. (1971). *The Communist party of the Soviet Union*. Second edition. New York: Random House.

TATU, M. (1986). The central committee elected at the Twenty-Seventh Party Congress: Halfway toward rejuvenation. *Radio Liberty Research*, no. 106/86.

TEAGUE, E. (1983). A month in the life of the politburo. *Radio Liberty Research*, no. 379/83.

THEEN, R. (1981). The Soviet political system since Stalin. *Problems of Communism*, 30, no. 1, 74–77.

VOZLENSKY, M. (1984). *Nomenklatura: The Soviet ruling class*. New York: Doubleday.

WALKER, M. (1988). *The waking giant: Gorbachev's Russia*. New York: Pantheon.

EIGHT
THE LEGAL SYSTEM:
The Attempt to Create a Socialist Law-Governed State

There is perhaps no aspect of the Soviet system about which educated laymen in the United States have more definite—and negative—views than Soviet law. Armed with some knowledge about the Stalin-era purge trials, the harsh treatment of dissidents more recently, and perhaps other examples of arbitrary practices by Soviet governmental organs, numerous friends and acquaintances have, over the years, asked the authors essentially the same question: "Why do you bother to study the subject? It's clear that there's no law in Russia." There is something to be said for this exaggerated point of view (aside from the typical insistence on equating Russia with the whole of Soviet territory): The Soviet record of protecting human rights and of applying reasonable legal principles in an evenhanded way has often left much to be desired; the legal process was employed to eliminate political adversaries during large parts of the Stalin period (and to some extent both before and after it); during the Stalin era thousands of other "enemies," both real and imagined, were imprisoned or eliminated without benefit of the legal process; and through virtually the whole of Soviet history the authorities have reacted negatively to manifestations of independent thinking and action, and have not hesitated to use or abuse legal mechanisms to neutralize such developments. The overall picture of Soviet law in many respects, then, is not a positive one.

But simply to dismiss the examination of Soviet law on the basis of these considerations would be a mistake for at least two reasons: (1) it would suggest that all of Soviet law has been characterized by the arbitrary practices so far described; (2) and it would exclude the possibility of significant change in the legal system. On both of these counts further analysis is in order.

Most Soviet citizens experience their legal system in terms of the humdrum of banal disputes that is the grist of legal systems everywhere in the world. Unless there is something highly unusual (for a Soviet citizen) in their behavior, they no longer fear the knock on the door at night. Their contact with the legal system is more likely to be of the divorce-court-and-parking ticket variety; it seldom causes more than a ripple in the surface of their day-to-day lives. Correspondingly, it is in this less spectacular aspect of the Soviet legal system that we can recognize law and justice in the forms similar to those with which we are accustomed.

This should not be surprising. Any society as large and highly organized as the Soviet Union cannot be governed entirely on the basis of arbitrary fiat from above. There must be some system of regularized rules to take care of the great majority of disputes: those which are not sufficiently sensitive to be given individual political attention. Otherwise, Soviet leaders would be unable to focus their attention on the relatively small number of disputes that do have significant political implications.

How, then, can one characterize such a system, part arbitrary and part ordinary? Ernst Fraenkel (1941) writing of Nazi Germany, characterized such a system as a "dual state." In some aspects, it can be a "prerogative state" that is governed arbitrarily with no effective limits on the jurisdiction of state organs. In other aspects, it can be a "normative state" in which government is limited by legal norms that delineate the boundaries of permissible government action. The areas of jurisdiction covered by the prerogative state and the normative state are not fixed. Rather they are constantly expanding and contracting as the situation demands. Thus, the period of the Stalinist purges can be viewed as a period when the ambit of the "prerogative state" was greatly expanded. Correspondingly, the current period of reform can be regarded as a period when the "prerogative state" seems to be contracting and the "normative state" expanding to fill the void.

Therefore, in studying the Soviet legal system at any particular point in time, one must take into account the relative strengths of those forces that are characteristic of the prerogative state and those that are characteristic of the normative state. To focus exclusively on one or the other distorts the picture. In addition, to generalize on their relative strength from one point in time to the entire history of the Soviet Union is to construct a highly inaccurate picture of the Soviet legal system.

KEY PRINCIPLES

There are certain principles that can be regarded as hallmarks of the Soviet legal system in that one cannot progress far in the study of Soviet law without understanding them. Three of the most important are: (1) socialist legality, (2) the educational function of law, and (3) the relation between economic planning and law. All of these involve ideas or assumptions that are heavily influenced by the Soviet environment and Soviet history. Thus, they form the basis for some key distinctions between the Soviet legal system and those of Western democracies. A fourth principle, which embodies the major legal innovations and viewpoints on law of the Gorbachev era, is the concept of a "socialist law-governed state." Although it is not necessarily contradictory to the three other principles mentioned, the law-governed state certainly represents a significant departure from traditional legal ideas and practices. In theory, at least, it narrows the gulf of difference between Soviet and Western law.

Socialist Legality

Soviet officials and writers use the words "socialist legality" in more than one way. First, and less important for this chapter, is the use of the term "socialist legality" to distinguish law and justice under the Soviet regime from the "bourgeois legality" that held sway in the territory of the Soviet Union before the October Revolution. Second, "socialist legality" can be defined as "unwavering fulfillment of laws and related legal acts by the organs of the state, officials, citizens and public organizations" (*Iuridicheskii Entsiklopedicheskii Slovar'*, 1984, p. 101). It is the second use of the term that will be examined here.

Observance of the law by Soviet officials, particularly those of the organs of state security such as the KGB (Committee for State Security), has never been as "unwavering" as the foregoing definition suggests. The historical pattern has been for prominent Soviet leaders, beginning with Lenin, to make public statements calling for strict observance of legal norms while allowing or encouraging Soviet government organs blatantly to violate certain of these norms when political expediency demanded it. An early example of this tendency is given by Samuel Kucherov:

> After the seizure of power by the Bolshevists, Lenin had already declared to the Second All-Russian Congress of Soviets on November 8, 1917: "The problem of land may be solved only by the All-People's Constituent Assembly . . . Even if the peasants will further follow the Socialist Revolutionary Party, let it be so . . . Let the peasants from one end and us from the other, solve this question." But when the Bolshevists gained only 175 of the 707 seats of the Constituent Assembly, Lenin dispersed it with the help of the bayonets of sailors and Red Guards. It must be stressed that the elections to the Constituent Assembly were conducted when the Bolshevists were already in power, that they accepted the results of the election in advance and that the forcible dispersal of the Assembly was a clear breach of legality. (Feldbrugge, 1973, p. 620)

The extent to which there has been a gap between words and deeds has changed over time. The nadir was probably the Stalinist purge period, during which the Special Boards of the NKVD sent thousands of Soviet citizens into forced labor camps, frequently on the flimsiest of evidence. Prior to the Gorbachev reform period, the high point of concern with the establishment of "socialist legality" as a working force in the administration of justice came after the Twentieth Party Congress in 1956. Khrushchev had denounced the excesses of the Stalin period and called for reforms that would rule out the possibility of such abuses in the future. The Party Congress had also passed a resolution that charged all Party and government organs with the "watchful guard over legality and the resolute and severest suppression of any expression of illegality, arbitrariness and the violation of socialist order" (Feldbrugge, 1973, p. 621).

Thus, there ensued a period lasting to the early 1960s, when both scholars and political leaders talked about socialist legality in a way that approached the "rule of law" idea in the West: the idea that countries ought to be governed by laws, not by men. But, as the sixties wore on, the pendulum began to swing the other way, and in official pronouncements the idea of "socialist legality" came to be coupled with the idea of "socialist law and order" (*sotsialisticheskaia zakonnost' i pravoporiadok*), which implied that the main thrust of socialist legality should be the firm application by the state of laws aimed at preserving public order. With this as the prevailing view, concern for the niceties of legal protections and procedures tended to recede into the background.

Although socialist legality is supposed to characterize the legal behavior of all Soviet citizens and organizations, up to now the USSR Procuracy has had the principal responsibility for maintaining socialist legality. In spite of the impressive theoretical authority given to the Procuracy, however, it has not always been able to carry out this mandate properly. Reports from the Gorbachev era have shown that procurators themselves have, on occasion, violated legality (*Pravda,* June 19, 1987, p. 1 and June 29, 1987, p. 4). As a result, in 1987 the CPSU Central Committee adopted a resolution: "On Measures to Increase the Role of the Prosecutor's Oversight in Strengthening Socialist Legality and Law and Order." This resolution was aimed at the effectiveness of the Procuracy in enforcing socialist legality by giving greater importance to this aspect of its mandate. The functions of the Procuracy, along with other legal institutions, will be discussed later in this chapter.

The Educational Function of Law

In the Soviet Union, much more than in most Western countries, the law is regarded as an active force in molding individuals. It is *assumed* that both behavior and attitudes can be changed if only the people are brought into contact with the law and the legal system in the proper way. There are three overlapping themes that emerge from Soviet efforts to do this job of legal socialization.

First, and in some ways most basic, is "legal upbringing" (*pravovoe vospitanie*). This refers to the process of legal socialization that begins during early childhood and continues throughout life. Here the emphasis is both on inculcating a knowledge of what the law demands of the individual and on the nurturing of a value system that stresses law-abiding behavior and attitudes. It has as its aim the creation of responsible, law-conscious, and law-abiding adults. Second, and most obvious to a foreigner, is the continuous effort by the media, the adult education system, and the *agitprop* structure to propagandize knowledge of the law among the Soviet people. This theme, referred to as "legal propaganda" (*pravovaia propaganda*) by Soviet writers, focuses on adults and, in effect, reinforces and continues to build on the base created by "legal upbringing."

The third theme, the educational role (*vospitatel'nania rol'*) of the legal process, is not unlike what is referred to as the deterrent role of the law in some Western countries. It is different, however, in some very basic ways. First, there is considerable reliance on the effect on individual Soviet citizens of exposure to actual court processes or trials. Media coverage of court trials is selective, the standard usually being their value for educational purposes. Thus, what the average Soviet citizen knows about actual court proceedings is either what he or she is supposed to know or what he or she personally has experienced from involvement in a trial process. Much of Soviet court procedure is designed with its educational role in mind. For example, some Soviet trials are held in circuit sessions (*vyezdnye sessii*). Circuit sessions are trials that are held in the places of work or residence of the people involved, rather than in courtrooms. Thus, the trial process reaches—and presumably educates—not only the persons directly involved but also their families, coworkers, and neighbors.

Also, the procedural rules that govern Soviet trials allow Soviet judges much more freedom to perform pedagogical roles—lecturing, cajoling, and scolding. George Feifer conveys this relationship between the judge and the participants in the following dialogue between a judge and a criminal defendant:

> The judge clears her throat, flips the pages of the record and finds her place with a stout finger . . .
>   "Have you been reprimanded for truancy at the factory?"
>   "Yes."
>   "Absent from work with no good reason—that is your attitude toward your work, toward your responsibilities. And rebukes for appearing drunk in the factory—did you get any of these?"
>   He does not answer.
>   "Did you?"
>   "I think . . . well, yes."
>   "How many?"
>   "I don't know. I don't remember."
>   "Four?"

"Maybe. I didn't count. Sometimes it was on a holiday, when everyone was drunk."

"Four reprimands! That's an unheard-of attitude toward work and life in our socialist society. Disgraceful! It started with disinterest in work; then drinking and hooliganism—and led from that to stealing; of course it led to stealing, naturally to stealing—do you understand that? Why were you repeatedly late? Why did you continue to violate work discipline in spite of your warnings? You ignored them. You drank on the job. You were truant. And then you stole. Logical." (1964, p. 30)

Popular participation in the administration of justice serves to enhance the educational role of law. Such participation may take a variety of forms. The use of lay judges, known as people's assessors, to hear cases along with the regular professional judge will be described presently. Other kinds of popular participation may be included under the Russian term *obshchestvennost'*. This untranslatable word is often rendered as "the public" or "society," with the adjectival form *obshchestvennyi* as "public" or "social." It refers to the use of Soviet citizens to perform unpaid services that supplement the work of the state bureaucracy. Thus, when a person is accused of a crime or has another kind of legal problem involving adjudication, colleagues at his place of work, acting as a *kollektiv,* might send to court a "social defender," a lay colleague of the accused, to testify as to the defendant's good moral character. If his work record is not good or he has exhibited other negative traits, his *kollektiv* might send a "social accuser" to present the bad side of the defendant's extrajudicial record.

Another form of *obshchestvennost'* is the volunteer people's detachment or *druzhina* (from the word *drug,* meaning "friend") made up of citizens who, in nonworking hours, perform a kind of auxiliary police role, helping the regular police to patrol and keep order in places where the public gathers. Perhaps the best-known form of popular participation of this kind is the comrades' court. These tribunals are not part of the regular court system. They are lay bodies made up of representatives of the *kollektiv* in a place of work or residence. They hear cases that do not involve actual illegality, such as a worker's chronic absenteeism, or a person's slovenliness in the communal areas of an apartment house. A comrades' court has the right to levy minor sanctions against the accused (such as a censure or a small fine) or to transfer the case to the regular court system if the alleged infraction warrants it. But the main function of the comrades' court is an educational one: to achieve desirable behavior in the community at large by mobilizing the force of organized public opinion. Emphasis on these forms of popular participation in the legal sphere reached its high point under Khrushchev. More recently, their role has diminished.

The law, then—and with it court processes and the legal profession—is not only to settle disputes but also to reinforce and elaborate on the messages coming from other sectors of Soviet society. The good Soviet citizen is supposed to be law conscious and law-abiding. With the cooperation of the media and the educational system, this idea is introduced to every Soviet citizen at an early age and continually reinforced in a myriad of ways.

Economic Planning and Law

The fact that the Soviet economic system operates largely within the framework of the government apparatus, with a limited (though growing) amount of private economic activity permitted, suggests a pervasive legal regulation of the economy. There are a large number of forbidden economic activities for which legal sanctions are imposed. Some of them, such as counterfeiting, are also illegal in the West. But others, such as speculation, find no analogue outside the socialist bloc.

Soviet authorities have carried on a long campaign against prohibited economic activities. In fact, it is a sign of their lack of success (as well as a set of corresponding needs in the marketplace) that one of the earliest laws passed as a result of Gorbachev's reform was the Law on Individual Labor Activity (*Pravda,* November 21, 1986, pp. 1, 3). This law expressly permits a limited amount of highly regulated private enterprise in the consumer sector. There are still several economic crimes on the books, however. One of these is speculation, which is defined in Soviet law (Article 154 of the RSFSR Criminal Code) as the "purchase and resale of goods or other articles for gain." Under the criminal law operating from the early 1960s until the 1990s, speculation and some other economic crimes, if committed on a large enough scale, could be punished by the death penalty. Under the Principles of Criminal Law of the USSR and the Union Republics drafted in 1988, it was proposed that the death penalty for economic crimes be dropped, but be retained for several other crimes, including treason, espionage, sabotage, terrorism, murder committed under aggravating circumstances, and the rape of a minor.

The more fundamental way in which law penetrates the economic sphere is with regard to planning. As will be discussed in more detail in Chapter 9, the economic system is still highly centralized, although the current economic reform is designed to progressively shift more and more responsibility to the individual enterprise or farm. The mechanism for achieving optimal economic results is planning, and in a quite literal sense, the plan *is* law. Annual plans and five-year plans are adopted by the legislature as statutes and thereby have an obligatory character.

This does not mean that if plan targets are not fulfilled by a factory its manager will be considered to have broken the law.[1] Nonfulfillment of plan is more a career liability than a legal liability. The adoption of the plan as law denotes both the official character of the plan and the serious intentions of

---

[1]Although, if the factory repeatedly produces poor quality products or does it on a large scale as part of its plan fulfillment, certain managers may be subject to a criminal sanction (Article 152 of the RSFSR Criminal Code).

the leaders with regard to economic performance. The details of plan fulfillment are legalized by converting plan assignments into legal relationships between participating parties. Thus, state economic enterprises (the major pro-
ducers and sellers of goods and services in the USSR) are invested with legal
personality, allowing them to enter into contracts, administer property, and
sue and be sued. These enterprises contract with each other for sale and purchase of goods and supplies necessary to fulfill plan assignments. Breach of
contract and other legal problems between and among economic enterprises
are handled by a system of arbitration tribunals called *gosarbitrazh,* which is
completely separate from the regular court system.

Even employer-employee relationships are based in part on a legal premise. Factory laborers and other workers have work quotas they must fulfill,
and in that sense they are part of the overall economic plan. In addition, in
each plant there is a collective contract (*kollektivnyi dogovor*) between management and labor concerning the mutual obligations of both sides relevant to
fulfilling production plans and other matters.

All able-bodied persons in the USSR are expected to work. Article 60 of
the Constitution provides: "It is the duty of, and a matter of honor for, every
able-bodied citizen of the USSR to work conscientiously in his chosen, socially
useful occupation, and strictly to observe labor discipline. Evasion of socially
useful work is incompatible with the principles of socialist society." Legal
teeth for this constitutional principle are found in the antiparasite laws.

The antiparasite laws have been in existence since the late 1950s and are
aimed at vagrancy, begging, or leading a "parasitic way of life." (Article 209
of the RSFSR Criminal Code). Violations can be punished by a sentence of
up to two years in prison or in corrective labor (up to three years in prison for
repeaters.) Thus, the requirement to work, with legal sanctions for able-bodied
persons who avoid it, remains part of the system. In spite of such legal sanctions, however, avoiding work is still possible. As of the late 1980s, Soviet
sources indicated that there are thousands of tramps and hobos in the Soviet
Union (*Radio Liberty Research,* no. 85/87, p. 2). They survive by living in
places like freight cars and supporting themselves with odd jobs. And, as any
recent visitor to the Soviet Union can testify, beggars have become a common
sight in urban areas in many parts of the country.

Another means of legal or quasi-legal influence in the economic sphere is
through so-called "people's control." Under the new governmental structures
created in 1989, the USSR People's Control Committee (*Komitet narodnogo
kontrolia*) reports to the USSR Supreme Soviet. Its Chairman is an *ex officio*
member of the Presidium of the Council of Ministers. Below the national level,
there are several thousand people's control committees chosen by soviets at
the various levels of the Soviet federal system. Under the law, people's control
organs are charged with carrying out "systematic checkups to verify the implementation of Party directives, Soviet laws and government decisions" (*Izvestiia,* December 1, 1979, p. 2). The duties of the people's control committees

are carried out by professional inspectors. In the past these inspectors were helped by ordinary citizens who volunteered their services. At the end of the 1980s the authorities reached the conclusion that the system of volunteer inspectors was not working, and it was abandoned. The control organs are now to be staffed by professionals, and are intended to work under the supervision of legislative rather than Party organs (Adams, 1989).

The Socialist Law-Governed State

A principle of a different nature from the three just discussed is the concept of the "law-governed state" (*pravovoe gosudarstvo*).[2] As Soviet writers acknowledge, the idea of a law-governed state had its roots in Western law (for example, *Rechtsstaat* in German law, the rule of law in Anglo-American jurisprudence). In the past Soviet scholars were castigated for attempting to employ this "bourgeois" concept (Lampert, 1989, p. 1; *The Christian Science Monitor,* January 19, 1989, p. 2). Thus, it is a measure of the development of tolerance for non-Marxian ideas during the Gorbachev period that the term has come into use, and that the debt to Western jurisprudence can be acknowledged. It is true that Soviet leaders and others often speak of the *socialist* law-governed state, and some writers attempt to link it conceptually with "the founders of Marxism-Leninism" (Iavich, 1988, pp. 23-26). But it is generally acknowledged that the law-governed state is a new concept, and certainly the term was not in general use until several years after the beginning of the Gorbachev period.

The idea of the law-governed state as a new direction for Soviet law seems to have surfaced in 1987 among legal scholars (Iuridicheskaia nauka i praktika v usloviiakh perestroiki, 1987). By that time, the move toward liberal law reform was well under way, but a general term to encompass the reform movement had not emerged. The "law-governed state" came to serve that purpose. The concept was endorsed by the Party leadership in the "Theses" of the nineteenth Party Conference in 1988, and reaffirmed in the Conference's resolution on legal reform (See *CDSP, 40,* no. 21, 1988, p. 8; *CDSP, 40,* no. 38, 1988, p. 15). Since then it has been the subject of great attention in the popular press and the legal literature.

Those who endorse the idea of a law-governed state may have a number of specific legal reforms in mind. But at a more basic level, they envisage the fundamental transformation of the role of law in the Soviet Union. This would involve a change in the traditional relationship between the state and private parties, with the balance shifting more in favor of the rights of private parties. The fact that this shift is so fundamental, such a break with the past, has led to the adoption of a new principle to denote the development. One enthusiastic supporter put it this way:

[2]In some translations (for example *The Current Digest of the Soviet Press*), *pravovoe gosudarstvo* is rendered as "state based on the rule of law."

It is not an empty question: why in particular is it necessary for us to introduce a new term? . . . Weren't there words having to do with strengthening legality, the development of democracy, the broadening of participation of the masses in state administration, etc.? There were all of these. But the main thing wasn't there—the recognition of the higher value of human freedom—specifically freedom, and not only well-being, although this is also very important. There were not effective barriers against sliding back to a regime of personal power. Therefore, the formation of a law-governed state presupposes the introduction of fundamentally new principles of legal and state operation which possess the character of democratic guarantees. (Baglai, 1988)

The emphasis in this quotation on curbing the power of the state and enhancing personal liberties helps one to see the difference between the concept of a law-governed state and the slogan that has traditionally been considered the hallmark of Soviet law, "socialist legality." As was indicated earlier, socialist legality has typically been interpreted to invest great power in state organs, with the admonition that this power should be applied strictly and even-handedly.

The fullest official endorsement of the law-governed state is found in the Theses of the nineteenth Party Conference:[3]

In adding the concept of "law-governed" to the description of our state of all the people, it should be emphasized once more that not only do citizens have a responsibility to the state, the state has a responsibility to its citizens. It must show constant concern for strengthening guarantees of the rights and freedoms of Soviet people. This has to do with the further expansion and enrichment of social rights (to work, rest, education, health care, social security, etc.) . . . It has to do with the creation of the material and legal conditions of the realization of constitutional freedoms (freedom of speech, freedom of the press, freedom to assemble and hold rallies, street processions and demonstrations, freedom of conscience and others). It also has to do with strengthening guarantees of the citizen's personal rights (the inviolability of the individual and of the home, the right to privacy in correspondence and telephone conversations, and others).

The Thesis goes on to add that the changes envisaged will constitute a departure from the past aimed at "resolutely eradicating the distortions and deformations that were a consequence of authoritarian methods of administration that are alien to the socialist system" (*Izvestiia,* May 27, 1988, p. 2; *CDSP, 40,* 21, p. 8).

In addition to such Party pronouncements, much more has been written about the law-governed state by scholars and publicists. Although their views may not be official policy, they suggest areas of both continued concern and of possible further development. As was indicated, the two subjects that have received the most attention are the rights of individuals and the place of the

---

[3]As was indicated previously, support for the socialist legal state was reaffirmed in a resolution at the end of the Conference.

state in the Soviet system. If, as one author put it, "the defense of individual rights is the keystone of the law-governed state" (V. Savitskii in *Izvestiia*, January 5, 1989, p. 6), mechanisms are needed to protect individuals against the exercise of governmental powers. Since "the strongest of the three powers in our system is executive power" (V. Grafskii in *Izvestiia*, January 5, 1989, p. 6), executive power must be controlled. Thus the need for a "separation of powers," which many Soviet writers have advocated, accompanied by a strengthening of the other two branches of government, the legislative and the judicial. The rationale for strengthening legislative power has been discussed in Chapter 6 and will be touched on again presently. It is the courts, however, that are seen as being the main instrument for protecting individual rights; therefore, the courts need to be truly insulated from outside influence, and the opportunity of citizens to use the courts in defense of their rights needs to be expanded.

This, then, is the general line of reasoning of legal scholars in giving concrete meaning to the concept of a law-governed state. The debt to Western (and, more particularly, American) political thought is clear and is sometimes openly acknowledged by Soviet writers.[4] But one important area with regard to the development of a state based on law does not have a direct Western analogue. This has to do with the relationship of the Party to law. The problem of the Party's status above the law has been recognized and examined in the West (see, for example, *Ruling Communist Parties and Their Status Under Law*, 1986). But in the Soviet Union there was long a taboo against openly discussing it. Soviet writers would quote the part of the old Article 6 of the 1977 Constitution, which provided that "all party organizations function within the framework of the Constitution of the USSR," as if all problems were thereby resolved.

In the glasnost era, many subjects, including the position of the Party, have been examined more closely. Thus in discussions about achieving a law-governed state, some analysts have suggested that it is not only the power of the state that needs to be reined in but that of the Party as well:

The root [of the problem of a law-governed state] is that our state cannot be law-governed in the position that it occupies now. Its highest legislative organ does not have full power. A structure beyond the state—the party, or, more accurately, its apparatus—has held the highest power during the course of seven decades. And no one can cover this up. It is noted in party documents. During the whole 70 years of our history the question has been raised of the division of functions between the party and the state. And up to now, until the supervision

---

[4]V. Grafskii, the last person quoted in the text, concluded his observations on separation of powers as follows: "In concluding I would like to refer to a phrase which was used by Madison, the creator of the American constitution: 'Men are not angels'" (*Izvestiia*, January 5, 1989, p. 6).

of legal activity is transferred to the state, there will be no place for talk about the sovereignty of state power. (L. Mamut in *Izvestiia,* January 5, 1989, p. 6)[5]

Views of this kind, however, demonstrate the difference between official policy and the breadth of opinion permitted under glasnost. One of the constant themes of this book is the attempt by the Party to preserve its central role in the system while seeking to manage the momentous changes taking place. The revision of Article 6 of the Constitution, discussed in Chapter 5, may be the first genuine step in bringing the Communist Party and its apparatus under the rule of law.

COURT STRUCTURE

In the Soviet Union, as in most other developed countries, if you have a legal problem, the first thing you must do is get yourself a lawyer. For the person accused of a crime or party to a civil suit, recourse is to the local law office, where one selects or is assigned a lawyer (*advokat*) to represent one's interests and to provide advice.

If the case is one that must be taken to court, it will probably be tried in the people's court of that district. The people's courts hear 90 to 95 percent of all civil and criminal cases of the first instance. If it is one of a limited number of important criminal cases, however, it may be first heard in a court of the next level, a regional court,[6] or if it is adjudged by certain key officials to be a case of extreme importance, it may get its first hearing in the supreme court of that union republic.

If it is a criminal case the court is hearing, it is likely to have been preceded by considerable pretrial activity. The pretrial investigation in Soviet law is typically a thorough one in which most of the advantages are on the side of the state rather than the suspect. Traditionally under Soviet law, it has been almost axiomatic that if a criminal case is brought to trial, the accused will be convicted. Acquittals have been rare, although apparently somewhat more frequent in recent years than in the past (*Izvestiia,* August 10, 1988, p. 3). As a result, people's court judges are often inclined to see the defendant as guilty even before the trial has started. A 1987 survey reported that 43 percent of

---

[5]The legal publicist Yuri Feofanov wrote in 1988 that the Party's position with regard to the law had "engendered distrust in the power of law" among the people. Citing the Russian slogan "zakon zakonom a raikom raikomom" (the law is the law, but the local party committee is the local party committee), he stated that "perhaps the most important" task in regard to creating a law-governed state is "to define the place of the party as the leading force in society. . . . The role of the party, the decisions of its central and local organs, its apparatus absolutely must be coordinated with state power and with law" (Feofanov, 1988, p. 23).

[6]The term "regional court" as used here includes provincial (*oblastnye*) courts, territorial (*kraevye*) courts, courts of autonomous provinces, supreme courts of autonomous republics, courts of national districts, and some city courts (for example, Moscow and Leningrad).

736 judges surveyed said that they always assume guilt even before the trial begins (*Moskovskaia pravda,* May 17, 1987, p. 3). The Chairman of the USSR Supreme Court has deplored this practice as "prosecutorial bias" but has noted that courts are beginning to approach pretrial investigation evidence more skeptically, citing an increasing tendency on the part of courts to demand further investigation or to acquit (*Pravda,* December 5, 1987, p. 3).

Because the pretrial investigation stage is of such crucial importance, abuses of power by the police and investigators have resulted in considerable criticism under glasnost. For example, there have been complaints about unreasonable preventive detention, arrests on insufficient evidence, investigations conducted by unqualified personnel, and coerced confessions (see, for example, *Izvestiia,* May 22, 1987, p. 3 and September 26, 1987, p. 3). Present efforts to rewrite Soviet criminal law and procedure appear to be designed to make such violations of individual rights less likely in the future. One safeguard long advocated by reformists has been the expansion of the participation of defense lawyers in pretrial investigations. After years of advocacy by a small group of liberal jurists, which had seemingly little effect on official views, policy changes came quickly at the end of the 1980s. Most important in this respect was the adoption in 1989 of the USSR Principles of Law on Court Structure. It provides (Article 14) that the defense lawyer is to be given access to his client from the time of detention. This law also contains a number of other innovations. For instance, it spells out an unequivocal presumption of innocence of the accused (Article 14). And it provides that the union republics can adopt legislation requiring a jury trial in cases where the death penalty or over 10 years of imprisonment may be imposed (Article 11; *Izvestiia,* November 16, 1989, p. 1).

Let us follow the path of an ordinary case, one which starts at the lowest level of the system, in a people's court. We will put the reader in the position of a party to the trial. In the Soviet Union, courthouses are not the prominent, often imposing, edifices that they are in the United States. Your trial is likely to be held in a small, sometimes dingy, building on a quiet street somewhat removed from the mainstream of daily activity. If you are not being held in pretrial detention, you take your place on a bench in a dark hallway among others who are also waiting for their cases to be tried. When your case is called, you enter a small courtroom presided over by a portrait of Lenin hanging above a long table with three chairs behind it. The people involved in your case may not be the only ones in the courtroom. There may also be some curious onlookers, probably senior citizens who use the entertainment the court affords to add zest to their retirement years in much the same way that some retirees in the United States religiously follow their favorite soap operas.

Your case will be tried before a court consisting of a judge and two people's assessors. The judge, who presides, is selected by the local soviet one level above the jurisdiction served by the court. His term of office is 10 years and, in theory, anyone over 25 years of age is eligible. As a matter of practice, however, virtually all judges are lawyers. Unlike judges, the people's assessors hold full-time jobs elsewhere. Every *kollektiv* that has more than one hundred members elects one people's assessor. During their five-year terms, people's assessors serve in this capacity for only two weeks per year. The rest of the time they are at their regular places of work. There is little opportunity for a people's assessor to accumulate any great store of legal knowledge or experience, and consequently, unless the assessors are particularly assertive types, they will play a rather *pro forma* role in the hearing of your case. Their symbolic importance is considerable in that they represent the wisdom of the common man—not unlike the jury in Anglo-American legal systems. Currently, there are more than 13,000 judges and 850,000 people's assessors in the Soviet Union (*Pravda,* December 5, 1987, p. 3). There have long been suggestions that in more important cases the number of people's assessors should be increased. As was indicated previously, this was written into the law in 1989.

Soviet court sessions, in keeping with the buildings in which they take place, are much less formal, ritualistic, and impressive than those in the West. There is usually a good bit of give and take between the bench and witnesses It is not all unusual to hear a judge or, less frequently, a people's assessor carry a large portion of the burden of questioning witnesses. They might even scold or lecture on morals and conduct, as in the following exchange between a people's assessor and an alleged victim of an attempted rape:

> "With whom do you live?" It is one of the lay assessors, her spreading breasts resting on the desk, come to life.
> "With my mother!"
> "She gives you permission to stay out until three in the morning?"
> "No."
> "Well, what do you think about such behavior now? About the way you treated your mother—is that the way to treat a Soviet mother?"
> "No, I behaved very badly, of course." (Feifer, 1964, pp. 212–13)

As a result of the relatively unrestrained style of courtroom discussion, the general direction of the opinions of the three members of the court is sometimes quite easy to guess before they retire for deliberation. The conference in which the judge and people's assessors reach their decision, however, is always secret. The decision, which includes both the verdict and the sentence, must be in written form. If there is a minority point of view it is not announced publicly, although it can be written down and attached to the file of a case. The average courtroom hearing for a criminal case is five to six hours and the average courtroom case takes about 88 days from entry on the docket to verdict (*Moskovskaia pravda,* May 17, 1987, p. 3).

If you are being accused of a crime, the case against you will be presented by an official of the local office of the USSR Procuracy.[7] But trying such cases

[7]In petty cases where there is no question of guilt—only of the validity of a confession and proper punishment—this formality can be eliminated and the judge can perform the accusatory task.

is not the only function performed by the Procuracy. It is a huge and highly centralized governmental body that operates on a nationwide basis. All procurators are appointed, beginning with the Procurator General of the USSR, who is appointed for a five-year term by the Supreme Soviet of the USSR. He, in turn, appoints his immediate subordinates for five-year terms, and so on down the line, with all procurators being appointed for five-year terms by those superior to them. Therefore, the local offices of the Procuracy function independent of all local government organization, with all subdivisions and personnel directly or indirectly responsible to the Procurator General of the Soviet Union. The 1979 law on the Procuracy charges the Procuracy with supervising precise compliance with the laws of the Soviet Union. It specifically provides for

1. supervision over the execution of laws by agencies of state administration, enterprises, institutions, organizations, officials, and citizens;
2. supervision over the execution of laws by agencies of inquiry and preliminary investigation;
3. supervision over the execution of laws during court trials;
4. supervision over the observance of laws in places of detention, in places of pretrial custody, and during the enforcement of penalties and other measures of a compulsory nature prescribed by courts. (Feldbrugge and others, 1985, pp. 546–47)

The very breadth of these functions began to be criticized by jurists in the late 1980s because of the potential for abuse in putting such wide powers in the hands of one agency. Reformers would cut back on procuratorial discretion by strengthening the power of courts to monitor the legality of arrests and the decisions of the procuracy to extend the period under which a person could be held by the authorities (Kudriavtsev and Lukasheva, 1988, p. 55).

Let us assume for purposes of discussion that you lose your case. Where do you go from here? In the larger Soviet republics, the judgment of a people's court may be appealed to the next level, the regional court. In the smaller republics in which there are no regional courts, appeal is to the republic supreme court. Correspondingly, if your case were one of those important criminal cases that are heard in the first instance in the regional court, appeal would be to the republic supreme court. In any event, no matter where your case is heard, it is your one and only chance for an appeal in the usual sense of the word.

But the appellate process is not the only way a case may be reconsidered. There is also supervision review (*proizvodstvo v poriadke nadzora*). In this, the president of the people's court or an official of the Procuracy may protest a decision. Frequently, this protest is made at the request of a party to the case, but it can be made independent of the wishes of the parties. Such a protest can also be made in the regional courts, the republic supreme courts, and even the USSR Supreme Court. Thus, a case may go through a lengthy series of reconsiderations in which only the decision of the Plenum of the USSR Supreme Court is truly a final judgment. It should be noted, however, that although such a protracted process is theoretically possible, in practice it is extremely rare.[8]

Finally, a word about the USSR Supreme Court, which plays a much more modest role in the Soviet government than is played by the U.S. Supreme Court. The members of the Court are appointed by the Supreme Soviet of the USSR for a term of 10 years, and the chairmen of the supreme courts of the union republic are *ex officio* members. The Court can act as a whole (the Plenum) or in separate panels of judges (the Civil Chamber, the Criminal Chamber, and the Military Chamber). Under the 1979 Law on the Supreme Court of the USSR, the Plenum of the Supreme Court has two main tasks: to hear appeals from decisions of republican supreme courts and to issue guiding explanations to the lower courts. The latter are published statements concerning the interpretation and application of the law and are written by the Supreme Court Plenum on the basis of an examination of current court practice and judicial statistics. The Civil and Criminal Chambers hear protests concerning cases that come up from the supreme courts of the union republics when these decisions are alleged to violate federal legislation or impinge upon the interests of other union republics.

As was mentioned in Chapter 5, a constitutional amendment adopted in 1988 provided for the creation of a 23-member Committee of Constitutional Supervision chosen by the Congress of People's Deputies. Members of the Committee serve 10-year terms. Although not a court in the narrow sense of the term, the Committee is charged with checking the texts of laws and other legal acts with regard to their conformity with each other and with the USSR Constitution.

THE LEGAL PROFESSION

In the 1930s more than half of all judges and procurators had no legal education whatever. Since World War II, however, the situation has changed drastically. Today it is impossible to enter any branch of the legal profession without higher legal education. Soviet citizens with formal legal training usually pursue one of a number of law-related careers, including notary, advocate, *jurisconsult* (legal advisor to an enterprise, government agency, or other organization), judge, member of the Procuracy, or legal scholar.

Legal education may be pursued either part- or full-time. Full-time study

---

[8]There are people's assessors for every level of the court system who are available to hear cases of original jurisdiction. But when a case goes from a lower court to a higher court by appeal or supervision, only professional judges participate.

is offered at university law faculties and at law institutes. The curriculums of the two differ somewhat, with the institutes being less theoretical. The basic curricula, however, are more similar than different. It is also possible to study in correspondence or evening-school courses designed for part-time students. The correspondence program is administered by the All-Union Institute of Soviet Law Teaching by Correspondence, which has branches in many cities, especially those where there are no institutions of higher learning. The curriculum and examinations in both these part-time programs are the same as those for full-time students. Correspondence students are given paid leave from work to take examinations or to do special projects. Though some Soviet and Western commentators have raised questions regarding the quality of correspondence education, there are many more students in correspondence education or evening courses than there are in full-time programs.

How does one become a law student? First, a person must have completed secondary education. Second, he or she must be under thirty-five years of age and have had two years of work experience. Finally, a successful applicant must have passed the entrance examinations in Russian language and literature (or the local language if classes are conducted in that language), the history of the USSR, and a foreign language. Once the applicants have fulfilled these requirements, selection for admission is competitive, with the available places going to those applicants who have the highest scores in their examinations and the best records from their secondary schools. Once a person has been accepted at a university or institute there is no tuition, and for most university students and all institute students there is a stipend to cover living expenses (Feldbrugge and others, 1973, p. 391).

Graduate work in law is open to those who have completed the basic program of legal education and who have worked for two years after graduation (there are exceptions to the latter requirement). Again, there are competitive examinations, and the aspiring graduate student must present a paper on a research subject. The three-year, full-time graduate curriculum (there is a four-year curriculum for evening and correspondence students) leads to a degree of "Candidate of Legal Sciences." The degree "Doctor of Legal Sciences" is only awarded to mature scholars who have made a significant contribution to research in some area of legal studies.

What career options are open to the newly graduated jurist? Most jurists go into one of several major branches of the legal profession, becoming defense lawyers, jurisconsults, procurators, judges, law teachers, or legal scholars. Each of these represents a distinct career pattern that will be discussed in more detail presently. Jurists can, however, work in a wide variety of other positions. For example, some serve as investigators for the police, the Procuracy, or the KGB. Also, jurists compose the legal staffs of a wide variety of governmental and paragovernmental organizations, ranging from the USSR and republican supreme soviets to trade unions.

Jurists who represent private citizens in court and who give them legal advice are called "advocates." On occasion, an advocate may represent an economic enterprise, but the advocate's main function under the law of 1979, concerning the *Advokatura* of the USSR, is to supply legal services to citizens and organizations. Soviet advocates are organized into associations of advocates that serve specific geographical regions. Each association elects a presidium that governs its affairs.

The advocate is paid according to a fee schedule that is issued by the republican ministry of justice, although in special cases where extra work or special expertise is required, an advocate may obtain permission to charge more than the schedule allows. Fees are low, and many advocates ask a bit more "under the table." This practice is illegal and can lead to disbarment, but is evidently quite widespread.[9] It leads to a certain cynicism about the legal profession among the general population. There have been suggestions that raising the incomes of these defense lawyers should be part of the reform of the legal system, not only to stem abuses, but also to raise the quality of persons choosing to enter this branch of the legal profession (*Pravda,* December 5, 1987, p. 3).

One of the major problems for the advocate in practicing his profession stems from the fact that he has a duty to society as well as to his client. As a legal textbook puts it, "In rendering legal aid, a jurist strives to defend the rights of his client while taking into account the interests of the socialist society and state" (Semenov, 1976, p. 291). This can create problems for the individual advocate in preparing his case. Should he make the strongest possible case for his client, as do American lawyers, or should he present a more balanced view of the issues being litigated? If he does the former, he may be accused of putting his client's welfare above the welfare of society—a serious charge in the Soviet context. On the other hand, it is difficult to engage in advocacy and be balanced and objective at the same time.

In spite of their relatively low status, low pay, and somewhat ambiguous role, there are many excellent and dedicated advocates. Among these are advocates who have worked hard to defend the interests of clients who are highly unpopular, including such political "untouchables" as dissident writers and economic criminals (Kaminskaya, 1982). There have, however, been many recent complaints about the work of advocates. Encouraged by glasnost, citizens have been expressing their dissatisfaction with the qualifications and quality of work of some advocates. Also, they have complained that local offices do not always exist in areas where they are needed.

And defense lawyers themselves are increasingly asserting their dissatisfaction with their ambiguous status and divided loyalties. The move toward establishing an independent lawyers' association, which developed in the late 1980s, was intended in part to address these problems. As a Soviet lawyer put

---

[9] The slang term in Russian for these supplementary fees is *mixt*. A thorough discussion of the practice may be found in Kaminskaya, 1982, pp. 29–30.

it in the *Moscow News,* the association "would help lawyers perform their duties better, be independent and uncompromising in defending rights of citizens, [and] create additional guarantees against the abuses of law by officials" (Makarov, 1988, p. 15). Sensing that in independent association of advocates might take reform of the bar farther than they desired, some authorities sought to bring the country's 27,000 advocates into a much larger association including all lawyers, under the supervision of the Ministry of Justice. The question of how this controversy will be resolved remains open (see *CDSP, 40,* 46, 1988, p. 21; *CDSP, 40,* 51, 1989, p. 23; *The New York Times,* February 26, 1989, p. 12).

Although some advocates do advise or represent economic enterprises, most large economic enterprises employ legal specialists known as jurisconsults. They are jurists whose job is

1. to check on the legality of all the activities of the ministries, departments, enterprises, organizations, or institutions in which they work;
2. to work to strengthen the economic accounting of management;
3. to make sure that all contractual obligations are fulfilled;
4. to defend the legal rights and interests of the management and employees;
5. to engage in legal propaganda (which involves delivering lectures, making reports, working in social-law consultation offices and being constantly available for consultations with employees). (Luryi, 1979; Chudnov, 1977)

Many jurisconsults appear to exert considerable influence over management policy-making as a result of their legal expertise. Jurisconsults have also played key roles in the preparation of economic legislation and in bringing the legal problems of state enterprises to the attention of policymakers in the Party and government.

Unlike the U.S. judiciary, in which a judgeship is often the capstone of a successful legal career, the Soviet judiciary is a career alternative for the newly graduated jurist. Thus, the Soviet judiciary is run along civil service lines, in that it is composed mainly of persons who become judges at or near the beginning of their careers and who are promoted from lower courts to higher courts on the basis of performance. The choice of judicial candidates is supposedly made on the basis of merit. In 1987 the Minister of Justice said that the leadership was making an effort to get rid of judges who were incompetent or abused their offices. He said that those chosen for judicial office would be selected from the best jurists regardless of previous career path (*Radio Liberty Research,* no. 197/87, p. 11).

About 5 percent of Soviet court cases involve judicial impropriety of some sort (*The Washington Post,* February 26, 1987, p. A29). Influence on the judiciary that is exerted by powerful individuals with a personal interest in the outcome of particular cases is one of the prime targets of the current reform. Soon after Gorbachev became General Secretary, commentaries in the

Soviet press began to mention "telephone justice." This refers to a situation in which a judge decides a case, not on the merits, but according to the telephoned instructions of influential people. This includes, but is not limited to, cases in which an individual who exposes corruption or refuses to participate in corrupt practices is prosecuted and convicted of a crime by judges following the orders of the corrupt officials involved. Such practices led to the passage in 1985 of a law punishing officials who persecute people voicing criticism (Article 139–1, RSFSR Criminal Code). In addition, Article 177 of the RSFSR Criminal Code provides that "the levying by judges of deliberately unlawful sentences, judgements, decisions or decrees can be punished by up to 3 years imprisonment" (Ministerstvo Iustitsii RSFSR, 1987, p. 98). If the consequences are particularly dire, the sentence can be increased to 10 years. Further efforts to insulate judges from improper influence were adopted in the late 1980s in the form of laws "On the Status of Judges in the USSR" and "On Liability for Disrespect to a Court" (*Izvestiia,* August 12, 1989, p. 1 and November 12, 1989, p. 2).

Another career option open to the graduating jurist is entry into the ranks of the Procuracy. As with the judiciary, most procurators begin their work in the Procuracy soon after completion of their legal education. Career advancement comes about mainly by promotion within the organization. The overwhelming majority of procurators are Party members. Prior to 1981 the Procurator General was the only jurist who was a member of the Central Committee of the CPSU, a fact which indicates both the relatively high status of procurators within the legal profession and the importance of the Procuracy within the Soviet government. The Party Central Committee selected in 1981, however, had the Supreme Court Chairman among its full members, and the Minister of Justice among its candidate members. Although the incumbents of these positions had changed by 1986, the new incumbents were elected to the same positions, thus indicating an upgrading of their importance relative to the Procurator General.

The academic jurists (teachers and scholars) command the highest status and pay in the Soviet legal profession. These are the jurists who teach in the 4 law institutes and the 45 university law departments, as well as those who engage in research and graduate training in legal research institutes. It is the academic lawyers who have been the most active in the various post–1956 campaigns for legal reform.

Jurists in the USSR have historically chosen career patterns within the legal profession. Seldom have they been found in top political posts. Legal training and practice have not served as the springboard into active political life that they do in many countries of the West, most notably the United States. Although Lenin and several other early Soviet leaders had legal training, General Secretary Gorbachev is the first post-Lenin top leader to have had a legal education. Thus, jurists in the Soviet Union have tended to stick pretty close to the practice of law in one form or another. Their political influence has stemmed largely from their mastery of the fine points of the law and from the fact that many occupy key positions from which they can participate in both the drafting and the administration of the law. With the creation of the new governmental structures at the end of the 1980s, this situation seems to be changing to some extent. Thirty-five lawyers were elected to the Congress of People's Deputies in 1989, several of whom have played key roles in Congress and Supreme Soviet activities (*Sotsialisticheskaia Zakonnost'*, 1989, no. 6, p. 56). Anatolii Lukyanov, who was a student at the Moscow University Law Faculty at the same time as Gorbachev, was chosen Gorbachev's First Deputy Chairman of the USSR Supreme Soviet in 1989 and became Supreme Soviet Chairman in 1990. A candidate Politburo member, he has chaired numerous meetings of the Soviet legislatures and has shown himself to be an effective parliamentarian. With the focus on policy-making apparently beginning to shift from the Party, the opportunities for law-trained persons in responsible positions appears to be growing.

The Gorbachev leadership's emphasis on law reform, as well as its efforts to bring greater rationality to economic operations, have stimulated the demand for law-trained personnel. Although there are about three hundred thousand lawyers in the country, this number is said to fall far short of what is needed. According to Soviet experts in the field, at present there is a demand for about five hundred thousand more lawyers than are available. Consequently, jobs are being left unfilled in practically every branch of the profession. It is calculated that on a population basis, the USSR has only about one quarter of the lawyers of Western countries like West Germany and England (O rasshirenii i uluchshenii iuridicheskogo obrazovaniia i organizatsii iuridicheskogo vseobuchiia, 1988, p. 49).

THE FORM OF SOVIET LAW

The Soviet Union is like most other countries in that it has a very complex system of law—especially if one includes the substatutory rules that can issue from both governmental and semigovernmental sources.[10] In this section only those of the most general significance will be considered in order to outline the form of Soviet law in its broadest dimensions.

At the base of Soviet law is, of course, the USSR Constitution. The statutory law of the Soviet Union takes two forms: the codes and the statutes (*zakony*). There are several varieties of substatutory rules. The most significant are edicts (*ukazy*) of the Presidium of the Supreme Soviet of the USSR (many of which typically have been enacted into statutory law at the subsequent session of the legislature), decrees (*postanovleniia*) originating in the

---

[10]Examples of semigovernmental sources would be the Central Committee of the CPSU and the Presidium of the All-Union Central Council of Trade Unions.

Council of Ministers of the USSR, and legal acts issued by departments and ministries. Finally, there are court opinions. The most important of these emanate from the USSR Supreme Court and the union-republic supreme courts. These bodies may issue both decisions in specific cases and broader "guiding explanations." Although neither of these constitute precedent in the sense that they would in a common-law system, like that of the United States, they are used as guides by lower courts in deciding cases.

Like the legal systems of many continental European countries—and unlike the common-law systems of Great Britain and the United States—the Soviet system of law is built around a comprehensive set of codes. These codes, the basic statutory law of the USSR, cover such areas as criminal law and procedure, civil law and procedure, family law, housing law, land law, labor law, corrective labor law and others. Most such codes are union-republic legislation, meaning that each union republic has its own separate set of codes.[11] This does not mean that the codes differ greatly from each other. Generally speaking, codification is a two-step process. First, the USSR Supreme Soviet adopts All-Union Fundamental Principles in those areas slated for codification. These Principles, shorter and less detailed than the republican codes, set down basic legal provisions to which all republican law must conform. They ensure fundamental uniformity in the republic codes, although allowing differences on matters of detail or on matters involving adaptation to local conditions. For example, the republic of Georgia, unlike the other union republics, permits the making of wine at home. Quite obviously, this permission is related to the fact that the Georgian SSR is the wine-making center of the country.

The practice of enacting comprehensive codes goes back to tsarist Russia. But to keep the law contemporary, there is the need to write new codes from time to time. Although considerable codification took place during the Khrushchev and Brezhnev periods, rewriting of codes has been undertaken more recently as well. The work on criminal legislation mentioned earlier in the chapter is an example.

The second type of statutory act, the statute (*zakon*), is legislation passed by the Congress of People's Deputies or the Supreme Soviet. These statutes may cover important areas of law but are generally narrower in scope than the codes. Examples from the 1980s include the Law on Cooperatives (1988) and the Law on the State Enterprise (1987). One of the aims of increasing the power of state organs under Gorbachev is to enhance the importance of legislative bodies in the law-making process. Since the old Supreme Soviet met for only a short time each year, the statutes that it could adopt were relatively few in number. Longer Supreme Soviet sessions should allow for more genuine law-making by that body.

Far more common in the past was for the Supreme Soviet to transform

---

[11]There are also some USSR codes, such as the Air Code, the Customs Code, and the Merchant Shipping Code.

substatutory law into statutes. Many of the documents adopted by the Presidium of the Supreme Soviet as edicts (*ukazy*) between Supreme Soviet sessions were transformed into statutes by the full Supreme Soviet. This routine exercise required very little time and was part of the reason why Supreme Soviet sessions were so short.

But this practice has come under considerable criticism of late. Jurists have found that many edicts were adopted without consultation with experts and therefore contained serious flaws. The secretive form of Presidium activity, it is felt, contributed to this problem. As one legal expert put it in 1988: "In the course of many years I have attended meetings of the Presidium of the USSR Supreme Soviet, and not once was there any discussion of edicts. Their confirmation at meetings was, it is agreed, merely a ritual." This writer predicts a change in the situation. Because of 1988 constitutional amendments, he believes that Presidium edicts should no longer be normative in character. He favors the adoption of a "law on legislation" to spell out precisely the predominance of statutory law over other kinds of legal enactments (*Izvestiia*, December 9, 1988, p. 3).

Reformers say that enhancing the importance of statutes over edicts should be accompanied by a more open process that includes public discussion of all recommended laws and the participation of legal specialists in the drafting of all legislation. Without this, even the most well intended legislation is bound to be flawed. Among several cases in point is the 1987 law "On the Procedure for Appealing to Court Illegal Acts of Officials that Infringe the Rights of Citizens." Adoption of such a law, as a means of protecting the rights of individuals, had long been advocated by reformers. Article 58 of the 1977 Constitution provides for such court review, but it requires further legislation to implement the right. Many lawyers had urged the adoption of such legislation, but for 10 years their efforts met with no success.

When the law finally came out in 1987, it was adopted without advance notice or discussion and without the opportunity for legal specialists to contribute their views. During the process of its adoption at the Supreme Soviet, the law was criticized by several members of the Supreme Soviet, a highly unusual occurrence at the time. Even more unusual, this newly adopted law was amended at the next session of the Supreme Soviet, even before it had gone into effect. The amendments removed some, but not all, of the flaws that critics saw in the law (see Barry, 1989). But the secret, anonymous process of its creation was deplored by many observers (see, for example, *Izvestiia*, December 9, 1988, p. 3). To the credit of the reformers, they kept pushing for further revisions of this law, and another version, which met most of their objections, was adopted in 1989. It is now possible for a citizen to get court review of almost any allegedly illegal act by government authorities. The exceptions to this provision are narrowly drawn (*Izvestiia*, November 12, 1989, p. 2).

Decrees (*postanovleniia*) adopted by the USSR Council of Ministers and other subordinate acts of governmental ministries and departments are much more numerous than edicts. Dietrich A. Loeber (1970, p. 76) has estimated that there "is one statute for every 50 edicts and 285 decrees." Decrees are the main vehicle for determining the direction of the economic and cultural development of the country and are, therefore, the major device used by the Soviet leadership to exert its will in the form of legal norms. The effect of these legal enactments may be substantial and far-reaching, and yet, as will be shown, their availability to the public leaves much to be desired.

It has long been the conclusion of scholars that a certain number of enactments of Soviet governmental organs are not published. There is a definite requirement that statutes (*zakony*) be published, and it is probably safe to assume that most or all of them are published. Edicts are also supposed to be published as a general rule, but there are provisions for nonpublication if they are not of "general importance" (*obshchee znachenie*) or are not "normative" in character. It is probably safe to assume that most, but not all, edicts are published. Since a majority of Soviet laws passed by the Supreme Soviet up to 1989 originated as edicts,[12] the modus operandi was probably for an edict that the leadership did not wish to have published to be left as an edict that was deemed not to be of "general importance" and not "normative."

Unlike edicts, it is the unusual decree that gets published. There is no specific requirement for publication unless the Secretary of the Council of Ministers decides that publication is necessary. In 1985–6, for example, only 32.5 percent of decrees were published, and a large percentage of these appeared in excerpted form (*Izvestiia,* June 1, 1988, p. 4). Even less accessible to the public are the so-called "departmental acts" (*vedomstvennye akty*) of individual ministries and other agencies, a situation harshly criticized by Soviet scholars and publicists since the advent of glasnost. There are thousands of such acts in force, and their legal effect often extends well beyond the agencies issuing them. Past attempts to organize and systematize this mass of law have been frustrated, in part because some governmental agencies seem to prefer a system of semisecret law (*Izvestiia,* October 17, 1986, p. 3 and September 23, 1987, p. 3).[13]

Because of this situation support is growing for establishing a rule that a governmental act that is not published according to established procedures cannot have the force of law (*Izvestiia,* July 1, 1988, p. 4; August 1, 1988, p. 4; September 23, 1987, p. 3).

[12]*Izvestiia* (June 1, 1988, p. 4) indicated that about two-thirds of all statutes adopted by the Supreme Soviet between 1938 and 1987 were adopted first as edicts.

[13]One Soviet jurist related the following in 1986: "About ten years ago a decision was made to organize a register of legislative acts and departmental decisions. The responsibility was given to the Scientific Center for Legal Information of our institute. . . . Departments showed no interest in this matter. . . . Some departments, such as the USSR State Construction Committee, not only did not send their acts, they wouldn't even allow our workers access to their materials"(*Izvestiia,* October 17, 1986, p. 1).

Another problem with subordinate legal acts is their relationship to statutes, or the lack thereof. Article 133 of the Constitution provides that decrees of the Council of Ministers should be issued "on the basis of and in pursuance of" statutes and other acts of the Congress of People's Deputies and the Supreme Soviet. Yet this hierarchical relationship appears to be frequently ignored. According to one Soviet critic, a statute is adopted and then "the Council of Ministers promptly issues acts at variance with it" (*CDSP, 40,* 31, 1988, p. 2).

So ingrained is this practice that it is difficult to curb, even in the era of perestroika. An example cited by numerous scholars was a decree adopted in December 1988 by the Council of Ministers. A duly adopted statute of earlier that year had created a general framework for the operation of cooperatives in various fields of economic endeavor. The subsequent decree considerably circumscribed the range of activities that could be legally undertaken by cooperatives. This, many felt, was wrong, because it amounted to an "organ of executive and management authority correct[ing] a statute adopted by the highest organ of legislative authority." This, said the critics, goes to the heart of the problem of creating a law-governed state, and perhaps it represents a capstone statement regarding the obstacles the Soviet system faces in attempting to achieve genuine legal reform:

> In forming a law-governed state, we must, we are simply obligated, to reject past conceptions about what constitutes legislation. A law-governed state depends on the distinction, the clear delimitation, between statutes and derivative administrative acts. The priority of the statute is a constant and absolute requirement. Administration is subordinate to legislation. This is a fundamental principle of the law-governed state (statement by eight scholars from the Institute of State and Law, Moscow; *Izvestiia,* February 20, 1989, p. 2).

REFERENCES

ADAMS, J. (1989). USSR People's Control Committee and *perestroika. Report on the USSR, 1,* 47, 1–3.
BAGLAI, D. (1988). Tol'ko zakon! Razmyshleniia o suti pravovogo gosudarstva. *Izvestiia,* September 1, 3.
BARRY, D. (1989). Administrative justice: The role of Soviet courts in controlling administrative acts. In G. Ginsburgs and others, eds., *Soviet administrative law: Theory and policy.* Dordrecht, The Netherlands: Martinus Nijhoff.
CHUDNOV, V.I. (1977). *Polpredy Zakona: O Rabote Iuriskonsul'ta.* Moscow: Iuridicheskaia Literatura.
CONQUEST, R., ed. (1968). *Justice and the legal system in the U.S.S.R.* New York: Holt, Rinehart & Winston.
FEIFER, G. (1964). *Justice in Moscow.* New York: Simon & Schuster.
FEOFANOV, Iu. (1988). Svobodnoiu dushoi zakon blagotvorit'. *Kommunist,* no. 13, 16–23.

FELDBRUGGE, F.J.M., ed. (1973). *Encyclopedia of Soviet Law.* The Netherlands: A.W. Sijthoff.

FELDBRUGGE, F.J.M. and others, eds. (1985). Encyclopedia of Soviet Law. Second revised edition. The Netherlands: Martinus Nijhoff.

FRAENKEL, E. (1941). *The dual state: A contribution to the theory of dictatorship.* Trans.E. A. Shils and others. New York: Oxford University Press.

IAVICH, L. (1988). O sootnoshenii prava a gosudarstva, razvitii i realizatsii idei pravovogo sotsialisthcheskogo gosudarstva. *Pravovedenie,* no. 6, 18–28.

IURIDICHESKAIA NAUKA I PRAKTIKA V USLOVIIAKH PERESTROIKI. (1987). *Kommunist,* no. 14, 42–50.

Iuridicheskii Entsiklopedicheskii Slovar'. (1984). Moscow: Sovetskaia Entsiklopedia, p. 101.

KAMINSKAYA, D. (1982). *Final judgment.* New York: Simon & Schuster.

Khronika Tekushchikh Sobytii, no. 34, December 1974. New York: Khronika, 1975.

KUDRIAVTSEV, V., and LUKASHEVA, E. (1988). Sotsialisticheskoe pravovoe gosudarstvo. *Kommunist,* no. 11, 44–55.

LAMPERT, N. (1989). Legal reform and criminal justice in the Soviet Union. *Soviet Union, 16* (forthcoming).

LOEBER, D.A. (1970). Legal rules: For internal use only. *The International and Comparative Law Quarterly, 19,* 70–98.

LOEBER, D.A., ed. (1986). *Ruling communist parties and their status under law.* Dordrecht, The Netherlands: Martinus Nijhoff.

LURYI Y. (1979). Jurisconsults in the Soviet Economy. In D.D. Barry, F.J.M. Feldbrugge, G. Ginsburgs and P. Maggs, eds., *Soviet law after Stalin. Part 3, Soviet institutions and the administration of law,* pp. 182–196. The Netherlands: Sijthoff & Noordhoff.

MAKAROV, A. (1988). Lawyers' guild planned. *Moscow News,* no. 45, 15.

MINISTERSTVO IUSTITSII RSFSR (1987). *Ugolovnyi kodeks RSFSR.* Moscow: Iuridicheskaia literatura.

O rasshirenii i uluchshenii iuridicheskogo obrazovaniia i organizatsii iuridicheskogo vseobuchiia. (1988). *Sovetskoe Gosudarstvo i Pravo,* no. 10, 47–58.

SEMENOV, V.M. (1976). *Sud i pravosudie v SSSR.* Moscow: Iuridicheskaia literatura.

SMITH, G. (1978). *The Soviet Procuracy.* The Netherlands: Sijthoff & Noordhoff.

NINE
ECONOMIC PLANNING AND MANAGEMENT:
The Central Organization of Scarcity

All of the "private enterprise" systems of the West have a generous component of government participation in the economy. In this sense they are not pure capitalist systems but are "mixed" systems. The composition of the mix between free enterprise and state regulation varies from country to country. But none begins to approach the level of state control over the economy that exists in the Soviet Union. One of the main goals of the economic reform under way is to bring more elements of individual initiative and private economic activity into the Soviet economic system. Even with the significant alterations achieved and promised under Gorbachev, however, central governmental control over the economy remains dominant.

What *is* so different about the Soviet economic system? First and foremost, almost all employees in the Soviet Union work for the government. Legal employment outside of state auspices is allowed under certain circumstances and has received increased encouragement in recent years. Also, a variety of illegal and semilegal activities, constituting the so-called second economy, has existed for many years. All of these will be discussed presently. But the foundation of the Soviet economy, and the ideologically most favored segment, is the socialized, state-run system.

BASIC ECONOMIC ORGANIZATION

Traditionally there have been four types of legally sanctioned organization in the Soviet Union: institutions (*uchrezhdeniia*), enterprises (*predpriiatiia*), cooperatives, and *obshchestvennye* or "social" organizations; only the first two are, strictly speaking, state organizations.[1]

Institutions are of two types, those with administrative or authoritative functions and those without. The first includes the traditional governmental organizations described in Chapters 6 and 8: the soviets, councils of ministers (including the ministries and committees within the councils), the courts, and the Procuracy. The second includes such organizations as scientific and research institutes, schools and all other educational institutions, hospitals, and museums.

Unlike institutions, enterprises have basic economic functions. Most of the production, distribution, sales, and service organizations are organized as enterprises. These range from steel plants and coal mines to clothing stores to hotels to local bus and taxi systems. Each enterprise has some degree of autonomy. It possesses certain property; it may enter into contracts; it may sue and be sued. In legal terminology, it is a "legal person." In addition, the enterprise operates on the basis of "economic accountability" (*khozraschet*), meaning that its performance is judged on the basis of the relationship between the value of what it produces and the cost of its operation.

In spite of this partial autonomy, higher state organs exercise considerable control. Enterprises are created by state charters and are managed under rules approved by the government. Property is "allotted" to them but they do not own it—even jointly—since the state itself (Constitution, Article 13) owns all state property. Moreover, enterprises perform work specified by the government, fulfill governmental plans, and are run by persons chosen by the government. The lagging performance of many Soviet enterprises has led to a widely held view, both outside and inside the USSR, that less central control would increase efficiency. This has affected the course of economic reform over the past several decades.[2] These reform attempts have traditionally been met with great resistance from the central bureaucracy. Since the mid–1970s emphasis has been placed on merging enterprises into "production associations," groupings of enterprises that manufacture related products and are located near each other. The objective of creating these associations, which possess somewhat greater autonomy than do enterprises, is to enhance the efficiency of Soviet industry.

The Gorbachev leadership has made cooperative organizations a major

---

[1] A fifth type of organization came into the picture in the late 1980s: the informal group (*neformal'naia gruppa*). A long effort to define its legal status continues. This variety of organization will be discussed in Chapter 11.

[2] This will be discussed in more detail later in this chapter.

part of its economic reform. The 1988 legislation on cooperatives encourages development of a wide variety of cooperative ventures. Before this law was adopted, the main type of cooperative organization was the *kolkhoz* (collective farm), which has long been a basic unit of agricultural production. A special section of the 1988 law allows the *kolkhoz* to operate with more autonomy. In theory, it was always supposed to be controlled democratically by the "general meeting" of its full membership. In practice, however, this did not happen. For example, collective farm chairmen were selected by Party and governmental officials. Now, with the Gorbachev-era emphasis on *demokratizatsiia,* the selection of chairmen and other crucial aspects of the cooperative's operation should genuinely be in the hands of the members.

The term "social organization" covers a wide variety of associations, including trade unions, sports clubs, unions of writers and artists, and many others.[3] They are voluntary and, like cooperatives, are supposed to be run by their general membership. Like collective farms, however, they have traditionally been controlled in important ways by the Party. With perestroika and the proliferation of political clubs and other special interest groups, many social organizations operate independently from the Party and contend with it for political influence. Because most social organizations are not primarily economic in function, they will not be discussed further in this chapter.

SUPERIOR GOVERNMENTAL ORGANS

The economic ministry is the link between the factory or farm and the central government. At the national level there are two kinds of ministries: all-union and union republic. Economic ministries may be found in both categories. As might be expected in a country where the state has so much control over the economy, the governmental apparatus is full of economic administrators. Over 80 percent of the ministries and state committees presently represented in the USSR Council of Ministers have a primary economic purpose. Many of these are charged with narrow production areas such as oil, coal, metallurgy, and timber. Some change in this area has taken place, however. A part of the economic reform movement of the late 1980s and early 1990s was aimed at reducing the degree of central control over the economy. One of the manifestations of this move was the reduction of the number of narrow economic ministries and the transfer of supervision of some economic activities to the union republics.

Several top economic agencies have broader objectives. The State Committee on Statistics (*Goskomstat*) is charged with the collection of economic and social statistics. In addition to taking the census of population, it prepares

---

[3]Under the new legislation on cooperatives, a cooperative is also identified as a social organization (*Izvestiia,* June 8, 1988, p. 1).

and publishes periodic reports on economic accomplishments and plan fulfill-ment. The Ministry of Finance prepares the annual budget. The portion of the budget that is published for the general public is quite brief, but the Ministry keeps much more detailed budgetary information for restricted use. The State Bank Administration is the apex of the banking system. Among other func-tions, it is charged with enforcing detailed rules on banking and credit that apply to every economic institution in the country. The most important central economic agency, which has no exact counterpart in the West, is the State Planning Committee (*Gosplan*). France may have its *Commissariat du Plan* and Britain its National Economic Development Council, but neither ap-proaches the extensiveness or detail of Soviet planning, and neither has the power of *Gosplan*.[4] *Gosplan* is responsible for the coordination and direction of all economic planning in the country. It works with the USSR ministries as well as the republic-level councils of ministers. They, in turn, deal with the enterprises and other economic organizations.

PARTY CONTROL

Over the years, the Party has been able to exercise a high level of control over economic activities. This has been achieved in a number of ways, several of which have been mentioned previously. Of foremost importance is the selec-tion of leading personnel: Virtually all the important economic administrators, from ministers to managerial personnel at the factory level, have been Party members. This was guaranteed, in part, by the *nomenklatura* system described in Chapter 7. With the changes taking place in the Party's role, and the fre-quently heard attacks on the *nomenklatura* system, it is questionable, however, how stable this aspect of Party control will continue to be.

The Party bureaucracy also plays a role in running the economy. A seg-ment of the Central Committee apparatus, under the jurisdiction of the Secre-tariat, oversees various aspects of economic activity. Formerly this role was strongly institutionalized through the departmental arrangement within the Secretariat. But as described in Chapters 6 and 7, efforts have been made to make the soviets more significant and to reduce the direct role of the Party in governmental operations, and this has been reflected in Party supervision of economic administration. Until 1988 there were within the Secretariat of the Central Committee some 20 departments responsible for various substantive areas that are of interest to the Party. About half of these covered rather nar-row areas of economic activity. In a major reorganization in late 1988, a num-ber of the departments were eliminated. Six new Central Commissions were

---

[4]The distinction is often made between "indicative planning" on the Western side and "imperative planning" on the Soviet side. The former involves guidelines; the latter involves orders.

created, only two of which are directly connected with the economy: (1) a commission on socioeconomic policy and (2) a commission on agricultural policy (*Izvestiia,* October 1, 1988, p. 1).

From various angles, then, the Party's role in directing the economy is being questioned. Glasnost has brought out into the open what has long been recognized but rarely acknowledged within the Soviet system: the awkward situation in which a "ruling party" and a governmental apparatus attempt to operate in the same area of activity. This problem has been discussed elsewhere in this book, but it has particular relevance to economic administration, in which the Party has traditionally sought to exercise close supervision. Under the conventional thinking on this matter, the Party is not supposed to supplant state economic management but to guide and aid it. Excessive Party interference in state operations is called *podmena* ("substituting" or "supplanting"). *Podmena* has long been a matter of concern, and although it is prohibited by Article 60 of the Party Rules, the temptation of the Party to play a large and direct role in the Soviet economy is one of the persistent themes of economic administration. Thus, one of the major problems presently under discussion is as old as the Soviet polity.

Another formal mode of Party participation takes place during the review of plans and budgets. Each autumn, the legislature approves the plan and budget for the coming year. In most recent years, this meeting has been preceded by a Central Committee plenary session at which reports on the plan and budget are made by responsible officials.

THE PLANNING FUNCTION

The Soviet government and economy work within the framework of economic plans of varying time durations. Most well known to outsiders are the Five-Year Plans (the Twelfth Five-Year Plan covered the period from 1986 to 1990, and the Thirteenth will direct economic planning between 1991 and 1995). Five-Year Plans are broken down into annual plans and quarterly plans. And at the actual production level, there are even monthly plans. Finally, the current Soviet leadership is experimenting with planning for a much longer period of time. The "Complex Program for the Development of Consumer Goods Production and the Service Sector for 1986 to 2000" is an example.

In the beginning stages the planning process is referred to as "negotiated planning" or "counter planning" (*vstrechnoe planirovanie*) in that it runs in two directions, from the top down and from the bottom up. The enterprises provide estimates of their production output and input requirements. These are collected, coordinated, and revised by the planning agencies and sent still higher in the planning hierarchy, where a preliminary plan is drafted. Relevant parts of this draft are sent back down to the enterprises, which may comment on and request changes in the plan. In this way, a final plan is developed.

Although the process seems to involve considerable grass roots influence, this has traditionally not been the case. The most important planning decisions have been made at the center, with only minor influence by production units. This led factory managers to circumvent plans or seek devious ways of fulfilling them in order to accommodate the special problems they faced in their production units.[5] Among the most common have been falsifications of production statistics, illegal transfer of funds from one use to another, and the concealment of full production capacity from superiors. Another frequent practice has been to take advantage of the way in which plan targets are stated to fulfill the plans in the easiest manner possible, regardless of the needs of the economy. An oft-quoted passage from a Khrushchev speech illustrates this well:

> It has become traditional to produce the heaviest chandeliers possible rather than just beautiful chandeliers to adorn homes. This is because the heavier the chandeliers manufactured, the more a factory gets since its output is figured in tons. So the plants produce chandeliers weighing hundreds of kilograms and fulfill the plan. But who needs such a plan? . . .
> Furniture factories have plans stated in rubles. Hence they find it best to make a massive armchair since the heavier the chair the more expensive it is. Formally the plan is fulfilled since the furniture makers add various details to the armchair and make it more expensive. But who needs such armchairs? . . . Everybody knows this. Everybody talks a good deal about this, but still the armchairs win. (*Pravda,* July 2, 1959, p. 2)

Practices of this kind, which have frustrated the political leadership for decades, have led to persistent calls for planning reform. More than once during the post-Stalin period the authorities have tried to change the system in order to eliminate such problems. In the two most significant reform efforts, one embarked on in 1965 and the more recent initiatives of the Gorbachev era, the *quid pro quo* has been to give the enterprises more autonomy in operation and material incentives in exchange for increased efficiency. The success of these reforms will be discussed presently.

This description of the process of negotiated planning does not begin to suggest the complexity of the operation. There are over 46,000 enterprises and production associations in the Soviet economy, some 49,000 collective and state farms, and many other economic units, as well as a total work force of over 130 million people. All the essential economic operations of all these organizations and people must be embraced and coordinated by the plan. The complexity of this undertaking demands technological sophistication in the planning process, especially the use of mathematical modeling and the widespread introduction of computers. So far, however, computer production has

---

[5]These methods have been described in a number of books in English (for example, Schwartz, 1968, pp. 56–68).

lagged far behind demand. Moreover, there has been considerable resistance within the planning bureaucracy to the use of such techniques and tools.

In spite of some successes in recent years, the record regarding fulfillment of plans is very mixed. Attempts have been made in recent years to give higher priority in five-year plans to the lagging consumer sector than to heavy industry. But plans and performance do not always coincide. And in practice, the primary emphasis on the growth of heavy industry has remained. Even in this sector, however, recent performance has not been strong. Chronic dissatisfaction with overall economic results is behind the recurring attention paid by Soviet politicians and economists to economic reform.

ECONOMIC REFORM

Soviet leaders are inveterate economic reformers. Although they have not changed the basic socialized nature of the economy, they have carried on a restless effort—especially in the years since Stalin—to create a more successful economic structure. Each new leader has pledged to make progress in combating the country's problems, initiating reforms of varying complexity and magnitude. During the Khrushchev period, the main reform was the change from the "production principle" to the "territorial principle" in economic organization. What this involved was the elimination of many highly centralized, specialized economic ministries and the creation of over one hundred economic councils (*sovnarkhozy*) throughout the country. Each was to have responsibility for almost all economic activities within its region. The main purpose of that reform was to enhance the country's economic efficiency. Khrushchev charged that the centralized ministries had become self-contained economic empires. Economic councils were seen as more rational units for the supply of materials and for overall economic coordination. In particular, they were intended to cut down on transportation costs and other economic inefficiencies. The reform also gave Khrushchev the opportunity to try to outmaneuver his political opponents and to place his lieutenants in strategic positions.

As things worked out, the *sovnarkhoz* reform did not bring about substantial decentralization. Most important economic decisions were still made in Moscow. And it did not result in great increases in economic efficiency. In 1965, within a few months after Khrushchev's ouster, the whole reorganization was scrapped and the system of specialized economic ministries was reinstated. If anything, economic control through the ministries became even more centralized than before. The *sovnarkhoz* arrangement was one of the "hare brained schemes" for which Khrushchev's successors castigated him.

Another development that began during the Khrushchev period did outlive him, however. Under Khrushchev, limited experiments were begun that would give greater responsibility and less central direction to enterprises in order to enhance their economic efficiency and productivity.[6] In September 1965 Khrushchev's successors instituted some related measures reform economists had been advocating. They gave enterprises a greater voice in planning and production decisions, allowing them to keep a greater share of their profits to distribute as incentives to workers. There followed a variety of other decentralizing moves intended to enhance the efficiency of enterprises. The job of implementing the economic reform was entrusted to the economic bureaucracy, including many bureaucrats with a vested interest in the *status quo*. Within several years it was clear that even the more modest goals of the reform had not been achieved, and it was quietly abandoned. Apparently, the leadership concluded that enterprise autonomy and decentralization constituted a greater threat to their political control than they were willing to risk. The next reform was in the mid-1970s. "Production associations" were created to supervise and coordinate the work of groups of enterprises. This amounted to more centralization, since it involved taking power from enterprises and giving it to production associations.

Thus, none of these reforms solved what many Western analysts consider the major problems of the Soviet economy: overcentralization and excessive direct planning controls. Numerous Soviet economists have publicly advocated greater decentralization for many years. There has, however, been sustained resistance to such a move. In large part this has been a *political* decision. From the point of view of the leadership, experiments that might increase productivity have not been worth the political risks involved in decentralization. This resistance has come largely from the middle and upper levels of the political and economic bureaucracy, and even the highest political leaders have had trouble implementing economic reforms when recalcitrant subordinates refuse to cooperate.

Gorbachev's accession to power in 1985 signaled the most serious attempt yet to deal with the conservative bureaucracy. During his years in power a large number of ministers and other top officials have been removed. The country has embarked on what he has called a "radical reform" of the economy. The urgency of the need for reform has been apparent, but perhaps no one paints the picture so vividly as Gorbachev himself. In a 1988 speech to the Central Committee, he noted that if the higher prevailing prices for oil exports and the "totally unjustified increase in the sale of alcoholic beverages" were excluded, over a twenty year period "we had no increase in the absolute growth of national income . . . and it even began to decrease in the early 1980s" (*Izvestiia,* February 19, 1988, p. 2; *CDSP, 40,* 7, March 16, 1988, p. 7).

As Ed Hewett has remarked with regard to the Soviet scene, "[e]conomic reforms are a process, not an event" (Hewett, 1988, p. 20), and it has taken

---

[6]This general idea was called "Libermanism" in the West after Evsei Liberman, a Soviet economist and a strong advocate of reform.

some time for the general outlines of Gorbachev's plans to emerge. It was not until a June 1987 plenary meeting of the Party Central Committee that important specifics became clear. Later that month a new law on the state enterprise, which is an important centerpiece of the reform, was adopted. One of the main objectives of the law is a drastic reduction in detailed central supervision (Hardt and Kaufman, 1987, vol. 1, p. xii). Although the central planners will still provide nonobligatory "control figures," enterprise management will now create its own plans and will operate more autonomously in a wholesale trade network.[7] Although enterprises will be expected to fill certain "state orders," much of their activity will be based on decisions made by the enterprises themselves. The advantage to the enterprise of this autonomy is that the more successful ones will be able to reward their workers. Moreover, workers will also have a managerial stake in their firm's operation. The 1987 Enterprise Law provides that the work force will elect the enterprise director and other senior managers.

There is a down side to this enhanced independence, however. Economic entities are to be completely self-financing. Under the old arrangements, enterprises were not permitted to go bankrupt, and many were heavily subsidized by the state. Now there are provisions for allowing insolvent firms to go bankrupt. In an economic system that traditionally prided itself on the job security of its workers, this aspect of economic freedom will certainly not be popular with workers. This is one of the main problems that Gorbachev faces in building popular support for the economic reform.

The process of economic decentralization will have a ripple effect across the entire Soviet economy. As more responsibility is placed on individual enterprises, there will be less need for large numbers of central economic bureaucrats. The number of ministries will be reduced. These changes, plus further central reorganization, should result in staff cuts affecting thousands of people (Franklin, 1988, p. 5; Schroeder, 1987, p. 313). In a society in which unemployment has never been a major political issue, the impact of these reforms on the popularity of Gorbachev and other political leaders could be significant.

Only the barest outlines of the Gorbachev economic reform can be discussed here. It is to be implemented in several stages lasting well into the 1990s. The hoped-for successes may be slow in coming. And in the meantime, numerous hard political and economic decisions will have to be made. An example is the need for a more rational price structure. Certain goods are heavily subsidized by the government in order to hold down their price to the consumer. Consequently, retail prices on some products have remained unchanged for decades. Over time, these prices have become less and less related to the cost of production, and the level of government subsidies has steadily increased. A meaningful economic reform will need to work on bringing prices and the costs of production closer into line. In many cases, this will mean higher

---

[7]Within limits set by central officials who are in charge of the pricing system.

prices, a change which is never popular with consumers. Abel Aganbegyan, a high economic adviser to Gorbachev, gives a succinct example of the problem:

> [T]he average price of a kilogram of meat is 1.80 rubles, which represents a state subsidy of 3.00 rubles on that kilogram. The same applies to dairy products and to bread which is extremely cheap. As a result the volume of the state budget which the subsidy for food products represented last year was 57 billion rubles out of a total state budget of 430 billion rubles. This is enormous, of course. So many economists, including me, consider it essential to raise the prices of bread, meat and dairy products. (Aganbegyan, 1988, p. 181)

Rational pricing, then, means at least some increases in the cost of basic food products. Recent history in both Poland and the USSR suggests, however, that raising food prices is not a decision to be taken lightly. It will be one of the tests of whether the leadership is determined to carry out real reform.

A final area of the current reform that needs to be mentioned involves efforts to stimulate individual initiative. As was already noted, giving more autonomy to enterprises will allow them to award outstanding workers with higher pay and bonuses. Other reform measures would expand the role for private and cooperative businesses. New legislation was adopted in 1988 allowing a wide variety of cooperative ventures in the production of goods and services. And in 1987 a law on individual labor activity went into effect. This law allows individuals employed in other jobs to engage in small-scale trades during their leisure hours. It also permits students, full-time homemakers, and pensioners to work full-time at such activities.

Some care has been taken by the authorities to make it clear that these innovations are not "unsocialist" appendages to the economic system. The law on individual labor activity prohibits the hiring of outside persons although members of the immediate family may work with the person holding the license (*Izvestiia,* November 21, 1986, p. 2). And the income and profits of cooperatives are heavily taxed in order to make this type of activity more ideologically acceptable. An early version of the tax caused a storm of complaints about the high taxes. As a result, the new tax system was suspended and an effort was made to find a more acceptable level of taxation. It was later decided that each union republic would establish its own taxes on cooperatives (*Izvestiia,* February 23, 1989, p. 2).

Although the aim of the new legislation on cooperatives and individual labor activity is to stimulate the economy, the feeling persists in a large segment of the population that cooperatives and individual economic activities are unsocialist. Numerous instances of foot-dragging and harassment by local officials, who regulate these activities, have been reported in the Soviet press. Moreover, public opinion surveys show that much of the Soviet public opposes the cooperatives, looking upon them as an opportunity for a greedy few to take advantage of the population.

SOVIET ECONOMIC PERFORMANCE

It is clear that there are serious problems in the Soviet economy and considerable dissatisfaction among both the leaders and the public with economic performance. But the genuine achievements of the Soviet economy over the years should also be recognized. An impressive industrial base has been constructed. Until recently, economic growth rates have also been impressive, and a military machine of great force has been created. Although economic plans are chronically underfulfilled for many consumer goods, other plan quotas are often impressively exceeded. In several important areas, production figures have been consistently high. In fact, in certain recent years, Soviet output of a number of products has surpassed that of the United States. These include steel, oil, coal, pig iron, and fertilizers.

Even though the consumer sector has been neglected compared with the rest of the economy, there have usually been improvements in the standard of living from one year to the next. For example, average wages have been rising slightly every year. Prices are not completely stable, but neither is there the raging inflation recently seen in some Western countries. Frequent visitors to the Soviet Union often remark that Russians are better dressed than they used to be, and many Soviet citizens move into new apartments each year. This says nothing, however, about the overall *quality* of consumer goods. Generally speaking, it is fair to say that quality is below the norm in the West. In fact, compared with Western standards of living, all of these accomplishments may appear to be quite modest. The openness of the Gorbachev period has allowed Soviet citizens to vent their frustrations about the consumer economy. Clearly, significant numbers of them are dissatisfied with the situation.

A look at some official data on the Soviet economy and at the conclusions Western economists have derived from these data will give a fuller description of Soviet economic performance. It will also indicate the guarded way in which economic figures are publicized and the incompleteness of the information released.

One example is the Soviet budget. Published budget figures indicate only the barest outline of economic activity. By the late 1980s the Soviet budget was nearing 500 billion rubles in expenditures. Over 30 percent of this amount is obtained from enterprise profits. Less than 10 percent (about 7 to 8 percent in recent years) comes from personal income taxes. Soviet publicists are proud of the fact that the income tax constitutes such a small share of total budget revenues. For many years a mildly progressive income tax, ranging from 0 percent of personal income for the lowest wage levels to 13 percent for salaries of more than 100 rubles per month (with somewhat higher rates for authors, certain self-employed persons, and others deriving income outside the regular wage and salary system) was in operation. A 1990 law introduced progressively steeper tax rates for higher earners (those receiving more than 700 rubles a month), culminating in a 60 percent tax rate on incomes over 3000 rubles per month.[8]

The remainder of budget revenue comes from several other sources, the most important of which are deductions from enterprise profits (which have totaled about 30 percent of budget revenues recently) and the turnover tax. In recent years the latter has provided more than one-quarter of total revenues. Soviet authorities have been reluctant to discuss the turnover tax. This is not surprising, since its existence is one of the main reasons why income taxes can be so low. It is an indirect tax levied largely on consumer goods. Although the rates of turnover tax on individual products are seldom publicized, they are known to be quite heavy on some goods, amounting to 100 percent and more of the wholesale price. This not only serves to raise considerable amounts of revenue for the state, but it is also designed to sop up extra purchasing power in the hands of Soviet consumers and discourage demand for certain scarce products, like passenger cars. For instance, the turnover tax on one model was reported in 1979 to be almost 60 percent of the car's retail price (Welihozkiy, 1979, vol. 1, p. 821).

Until 1988, Soviet leaders claimed that the budget was always balanced. Deficit financing, they asserted, was not practiced. Typically, their figures showed a small surplus of revenues over expenditures. This was viewed skeptically by some in the West (Birman, 1980, 1981) but never acknowledged in the USSR. When the figures for the 1989 budget were released, however, a deficit of over 36 billion rubles was announced. Even this figure was seen as a gross underestimation by some Soviet sources, however, and it was later officially acknowledged that the real deficit was about 100 billion rubles (*Izvestiia,* March 30, 1989, p. 2). When announcing the deficit, the Finance Minister acknowledged that deficits had existed for a number of years.

Whatever credence Western analysts might have placed in other budget figures, they were unanimous in agreeing that defense expenditures were grossly understated. And this is understandable: Official figures for the 1980s consistently put defense spending at well below 20 billion rubles per year, under 10 percent of the budget (by contrast, U.S. military spending in these years approached $300 billion, over one-quarter of the budget). When some of the pervasive secretiveness of Soviet society began to be eliminated, a more realistic picture of Soviet military spending was shown. For 1990, according to official figures, the military budget was to be about 71 billion rubles, which amounted to about 15 percent of the total budget. This ruble figure was reported to be a reduction of over six billion rubles from a year earlier (*Izvestiia,* December 16, 1989, p. 16; November 11, 1989, p. 2). Although even these figures may not provide a complete picture of Soviet military spending, they are much more realistic than those issued in the past.

[8]*Izvestiia,* May 6, 1990, p. 1.

THE SPECIAL PROBLEM OF AGRICULTURE

Several areas of activity compete for the title of "domestic problem number one" in the Soviet Union, but all analysts place agriculture at or near the top of the list. It is a long-standing problem, one that has baffled generations of Soviet leaders and contributed to the demise of a number of political careers. The chronic inflexibility of Soviet leaders regarding any expansion of allowable private initiative undoubtedly contributes to the depth of the problem. It must be said, though, that the USSR starts out with serious inherent disadvantages. Only about 10 percent of the Soviet Union's vast landmass is arable, and much of this is not ideal for farming. One Soviet source has stated that "almost two-thirds of all arable land on the country's state and collective farms lies in zones categorized as suffering at least to some degree from water erosion, and over 40 percent has 'significant' erosion problems" (Pryde, 1972, p. 36). Moreover, undependable weather conditions make crop yields uncertain even on the better land.

As a result, even the best years do not produce great surpluses of food, and in years when natural conditions are particularly bad, a near disaster can result. In spite of these problems, the agricultural situation did not reach its present serious proportions until the 1970s. During the 1960s, the USSR was a net exporter of grain and had to import it only one year. But the 1970s were a turning point in the Soviet agricultural situation. From then on, "reliance on imports from the West became what now appears to be a permanent part of the Soviet foreign trade picture" (Holtzman, 1982, p. 19). In the 1980s food rationing had become common. The leadership has advanced an enormous number of proposals and decrees on agriculture, which suggests the urgency with which they view the situation.

While grain production is only one aspect of the agricultural picture, it can be regarded as a significant measure of success. By 1990 Soviet grain production was targeted to reach 250 million tons per year (*Izvestiia,* June 19, 1986, p. 2). As one Western observer put it, this figure "obviously bears no relation to reality" (Kroncher, 1985). The all-time record crop, in 1978, was only 235 million tons, a figure not approached since then. When less than 200 million tons are produced, it is considered a poor harvest, and the government must resort to imports from the West. Suffice it to say that from 1980 to 1985, the 200 million ton level was not reached once, and large annual imports of grain have constituted a substantial drain on Soviet hard currency holdings. During Gorbachev's years the grain harvests have been somewhat better, passing the 200 million ton level several times but still far below the unrealistic plan targets. Consequently, the need to maintain large imports of grain has continued.[9]

[9]In a notable display of glasnost the USSR Supreme Soviet Committee on Agrarian Problems and Food disclosed in 1990 that from 1971 through 1978 the USSR had bought 483 million tons of grain from abroad, at a cost of 70 billion dollars (*Izvestiia,* May 20, 1990, p. 1).

What is the leadership doing about the agricultural problem? Although it is a considerable simplification, it can be said that the important elements on the input side of Soviet agricultural policy (or any other area of economic activity, for that matter) are investment, exhortation, and organization. The relative emphasis on each of these elements appears to have some relationship to the level of agricultural success.

Regarding investment, the Soviet commitment to agriculture has been enormous, although the results achieved have been decidedly modest, as this quotation from a study by two American specialists makes clear:

> The agricultural sector in the USSR is immense, currently claiming roughly one-third of total annual investment (including housing and services) and employing nearly 30 percent of the labor force. Farm production alone claims about 20 percent of annual investment and of the labor force in comparison with less than 5 percent for each in the United States. Moreover, the USSR farms about one-third more land than does the United States, but the value per hectare in the USSR averages only 56 percent of that in the United States. (Flynn and Severin, 1987, vol. 1, p. 65)

Exhortation has always played a major role in agricultural efforts, and Soviet society is well set up for it. The media, the *kollektivs,* and the various organizations in Soviet society can be efficiently mobilized to call attention to agricultural achievements and problems and to seek mass support for agricultural activities (such as calling for volunteers to help with the harvest). Farmers are regularly urged to make greater efforts. In recent years numerous plenary sessions of the Party Central Committee have been devoted to agricultural problems, as have many speeches of top leaders. A "harvest decree" has given special attention to shortcomings and has proposed changes to improve the situation. Exhortation alone, however, is incapable of solving the problems, and during large parts of the Stalin and Khrushchev eras it was not accompanied by the necessary financial and organizational support.

As was suggested earlier, Soviet leaders have shown themselves to be restless reorganizers, fitfully seeking *the* administrative arrangement that will provide optimal economic results within a socialist framework. This penchant for reorganization has not been so evident in agriculture as in the rest of the economy, but the record shows a considerable amount of organizational evolution, and more change is likely in the future. The present economic organization of agriculture can be traced to the late 1920s and Stalin's drive for collectivization. The collective farm (*kolkhoz*) quickly became the dominant form of agricultural organization. By 1936, more than 90 percent of the peasants had been forced into *kolkhozes*. Although accomplished at great cost in terms of both lives and agricultural production, this "revolution from above" achieved Stalin's end of gaining control over the countryside and eliminating "capitalist elements."

As was mentioned earlier, the *kolkhoz* is a cooperative organization and is supposed to be run democratically by its membership. Although this has clearly been fiction, other aspects of *kolkhoz* operation have historically set it off from regular state-run institutions. For many years, members of the *kolkhoz* were not paid wages but received a share in the profits of their cooperative. The share was based on the level of skill of the worker and the amount of work performed. Peasants living on poorer collective farms, in particular, got a very low level of income. This method of payment has largely been replaced by a regular wage system. Although the average wages of collective farmers are still far lower than those of industrial workers, they are better off than before as a result of this guarantee of regular wages.

Another result of being outside the regular state system was that, until 1964, persons working on collective farms were not covered by the state system of social insurance. A collective farm might have its own social insurance, but the benefits were on the whole inadequate, especially in the poorer *kolkhozes*. Reforms in 1964 and 1970 changed the system, so that now there is a uniform system of social insurance.

In these two respects, the payment of wages and the provision of state social insurance, the *kolkhoz* has become more like the other major agricultural organization, the *sovkhoz* or state farm. But the *kolkhoz* is still technically a cooperative organization and as such is considered to be at a lower stage in the development toward socialism than the state farm, which is state owned.

The *sovkhoz* can be looked upon as a kind of rural enterprise. It is a state institution run by a director appointed by the government. Its employees are paid regular wages. Although created during the 1920s, the *sovkhoz* did not become very important to Soviet agriculture until after Stalin's death in 1953. During the Khrushchev era, the number of *sovkhozes* in the country more than doubled, and the amount of land under their jurisdiction increased greatly. Since Khrushchev, this has continued at a slower rate. By the late 1980s there were about 23,000 state farms, which cultivated over 53 percent of the country's agricultural area. Many of the *sovkhozes* were created from collective farms. Also, many *kolkhozes* were consolidated to make larger *kolkhozes*. As a result, the total number of *kolkhozes* has fallen steadily, from a high of nearly 240,000 in 1940 to about 27,000 by the late 1980s. At that time, *kolkhozes* accounted for about 44 percent of sown land (*Narodnoe Khoziastvo SSSR za 70 Let,* 1987, pp. 208–25).

Another category of land under cultivation is the "personal subsidiary undertakings of the population" (as it is called in the official statistical yearbook). These are, of course, the "private plots" so coveted by Soviet citizens. This land constitutes less than 3 percent of the total sown area, and yet its production figures in certain areas are disproportionately great. In the late 1980s, the Soviet authorities stopped indicating what proportion of basic agricultural products came from the private sector. Prior to that time, the figures were quite significant: over 60 percent of potatoes, about 33 percent of all vegetables, 30 percent of meat and milk, 30 percent of eggs, and 25 percent of all wool. In all, their output amounted to nearly one-quarter of total agricultural production (Waedekin, 1979, p. 11). There is good reason to believe that private plots are continuing to make significant contributions (Waedekin, 1988).

Many nonspecialists in the West associate the private plot exclusively with collective farmers. Such plots, however, may also be provided to *sovkhoz* employees, professional people living in the countryside, and even urban workers (who frequently travel to the country to tend their plots). In fact, it has been estimated that some 35 million such plots exist, supplementing the incomes of over 120 million Soviet citizens (Brunner, 1985, p. 615).

At times the private plot has been viewed as a survival of the past destined to die out with the abundance eventually produced by the collective and state farms. But since this plenty has not materialized, it has remained a necessary feature of the agricultural scene. With Gorbachev's emphasis on individual initiative in all aspects of economic activity, not only the private plot but other forms of agricultural private enterprise seem likely to increase in importance.

To put the current agricultural reform effort into its proper context, it is necessary to go back a few years. The "Food Program" initiated in 1982 was intended as the major contribution of the Brezhnev regime to addressing agricultural problems. This program emphasized the "unified management" of all agricultural activity and provided both investments and incentives to stimulate production. Coordination at the local level was to be handled by district agroindustrial associations.[10] The importance of the agroindustrial associations was diluted, however, by the many central agricultural organs supervising them. To alleviate this problem, there was a major reorganization in 1985: Five ministries and one state committee were abolished[11] and replaced by a single USSR State Agroindustrial Committee (*Gosagroprom*; Doolittle and Hughes, 1987, pp. 33–34; Tenson, 1986).

Substituting one giant central institution for several was not the answer, however, and *Gosagroprom* lasted barely three years. Early in 1989 it was abolished. Put to rest with it, as one Soviet commentator wrote, were any "final illusions that agriculture can be run from afar" (*Izvestiia,* April 11, 1989, p. 1). Some of *Gosagroprom*'s functions were given to several central agencies such as the State Planning Committee and the State Committee on Prices, but the basic purpose in abolishing it was to turn agricultural administration over to the union republics (*Izvestiia,* April 11, 1989, p. 1). To build real incentives into agriculture, they advocated smaller units that could directly

---

[10]The Russian acronym is RAPO.

[11]The ministries of Agriculture, Fruit and Vegetable Industry, Meat and Dairy Industry, Food Industry, and Rural Construction, and the State Committee for the Supply of Production Equipment for Agriculture.

see the results of their efforts. Proposals of this kind have been put forward frequently before, but have always been blunted by the centralizing tendencies of the authorities (Tenson, 1988). The most promising recent version, pushed hard by Gorbachev and begun on a trial basis in the late 1980s, is the leasehold contract (*arendnyi podriad*) system. The key to this experiment, and the feature that distinguishes it from earlier attempts at decentralization, is the provision that allows farmers to lease land for long periods of time. If this scheme is fully implemented and the promised autonomy for the production units is fully realized, it could be "the biggest single change in Soviet agricultural policy since collectivization" (Bush, 1988, p. 2). Although the leasehold contract experiment met resistance from various quarters when it was introduced, Gorbachev succeeded in getting it approved by the Party and formalized into law in 1989.

Assuming the success of the new initiative, what will be the future of the traditional Soviet agricultural organization? Since the land will be leased from *sovkhozes* and *kolkhozes,* they will presumably continue to exist, although perhaps in modified form. Not all rural residents are likely to participate in endeavors involving the amount of work and potential risk that the new arrangement seems to imply. Perhaps these people will remain regular members of the collective and state farms. Obviously many questions remain to be answered. Whatever the particular configuration of the new system, the changes in agriculture in the Gorbachev era appear to be no less far-reaching than those in other parts of the economy.

REFERENCES

AGANBEGYAN, A. (1988). The economics of *perestroika. International Affairs, 64,* 177–185.

BIRMAN, I. (1980). The financial crisis in the USSR. *Soviet Studies, 32,* 96.

BIRMAN, I. (1981). *Secret incomes of the Soviet state budget.* The Hague: Martinus Nijhoff.

BRUNNER, G. (1985). Private farms. In F. Feldbrugge and others, eds., *Encyclopedia of Soviet law.*

BUSH, K. (1988). Fifty-year leases recommended for agricultural teams. *Radio Liberty Research,* no. 390/88.

DOOLITTLE, P., and HUGHES, M. (1987). Gorbachev's agricultural policy: Building on the Brezhnev food program. In *Gorbachev's economic plans.* Washington, D.C.: Joint Economic Committee.

FLYNN, J., and SEVERIN, B. (1987). Soviet agricultural transport: Bottlenecks to continue. In *Gorbachev's economic plans.* Washington, D.C.: Joint Economic Committee.

FRANKLIN, D. (1988). The Soviet economy: Russian roulette. *The Economist, 307,* 3–18.

HARDT, J., and KAUFMAN, R. (1987). Gorbachev's economic plans: prospects and risks. In *Gorbachev's economic plans.* Washington, D.C.: Joint Economic Committee.

HEWETT, E. (1988). *Reforming the Soviet economy.* Washington, D.C.: The Brookings Institution.

HOLTZMAN, F. (1975). *Financial checks on Soviet defense expenditures.* Lexington, Mass: D. C. Heath, Lexington.

HOLTZMAN, F. (1982). The performance of the Soviet economy: Past, present and future. *Occasional Paper No. 160.* Washington, D.C.: Kennan Institute for Advanced Russian Studies.

KAUFMAN, R. (1987) *Overview. Gorbachev's economic plans.* Washington, D.C.: Joint Economic Committee.

KRONCHER, A. (1985). The twelfth five-year plan: Old wine in new bottles. *Radio Liberty Research,* no. 382/85.

Narodnoe khoziastvo SSSR za 70 let. (1987). Moscow: "Financy i Statistika."

PRYDE, P. (1972). *Conservation in the Soviet Union.* London: Cambridge University Press.

SCHWARTZ, H. (1968). *An introduction to the Soviet economy.* Columbus, Ohio: Charles E. Merrill.

SCHROEDER, G. (1987). Prepared statement of Gertrude E. Schroeder. *Economic reforms in the USSR.* Washington D.C.: Joint Economic Committee.

TEDSTROM, J. (1988). The economics of Soviet defense spending. *Radio Liberty Research Bulletin,* no. 4/88.

TENSON, A. (1983). Rates of income tax in the Soviet Union. *Radio Liberty Research,* no. 452/83.

TENSON, A. (1986). New measures to fulfill the food program. *Radio Liberty Research,* no. 14/86.

TENSON, A. (1988). On the eve of great changes in Soviet agriculture? *Radio Liberty Research,* no. 61/88.

WAEDEKIN, K. (1979). Policies and prospects for the private sector of Soviet agriculture. *Radio Liberty Research,* no. 352/79.

WAEDEKIN, K. (1988). Soviet agriculture in 1987 and the private sector. *Radio Liberty Research,* no. 110/88.

WELIHOZKIY, T. (1979). Automobiles and the Soviet economy. *Soviet economy in a time of change.* Washington, D.C.: Joint Economic Committee.

TEN
THE SOVIET CITIZEN:
Worker and Consumer

In the previous chapter we discussed economic operations, achievements, and problems in the Soviet system. Attention to the economic situation of the Soviet citizen was intentionally omitted in order to give it separate treatment in this chapter. Here we take a look at basic aspects of the individual's economic and social status: work, remuneration, standard of living, and typical consumer problems, with particular attention to housing. The concluding section of the chapter examines three areas of citizen preferences that are related to the individual's status as worker and consumer: developments regarding the birthrate, labor turnover, and internal population migration. In each of these areas citizen preferences conflict to some extent with the desires of the political authorities. These conflicts constitute long-term problems for the political leadership.

In an analysis such as this one, comparisons of the economic situation of Soviet citizens with those of other countries, especially the United States, are desirable and useful. The reader should be aware, however, of the problems such comparisons present. In many cases the comparison is best made in terms of money. But the official relationship between the Soviet ruble and the U.S. dollar is a very misleading one. The ruble is not "hard" currency; that is, unlike the U.S. or Canadian dollar, the British pound, the West German mark, the French franc, the Dutch guilder, and other Western currencies, it is not freely convertible on the open market. Although some rubles are smuggled out of the country and may be bought in the West (at lower prices than the official rate), rubles are not supposed to be available outside the USSR. The rate of exchange, therefore, can be and is set by the Soviet authorities at a level as advantageous as possible to the Soviet Union.

For many years the official exchange rate was set at an unrealistically high level. For instance, in late 1989 it was about 100 U.S. dollars to about 63 rubles (a ruble is made up of 100 kopeks); thus a ruble at that time was worth about $1.60. In a surprise move made at the end of 1989, the ruble was devalued drastically for some transactions, mainly for foreigners in the USSR and for Soviet citizens traveling abroad. As a result of this devaluation, instead of the ruble being worth $1.60, its value was set at about 16 cents (*Izvestiia,* October 28, 1989, p. 4). This move, which was not to affect commercial transactions such as exports and imports, is seen as a first step toward making the ruble a convertible currency. Other objectives of the devaluation were to stem the black market trade in foreign currency and to curb the loss of foreign currency as a result of Soviet citizens traveling abroad. The black market rate at the time of devaluation was as high as 10 or more rubles to the dollar. The new official rate, over 6 rubles for a dollar, was much more competitive. As for Soviet citizens traveling abroad, each citizen was allowed to change a maximum of 200 rubles at a Soviet bank into hard currency. That would have amounted to about $320 under the old arrangement, but only $32 after devaluation.

This devaluation amounts to a first step toward convertibility, but many hard steps remain before the Soviet authorities can embark upon full convertibility of the ruble. It has only been since the late 1980s that the possibility of such a move has been discussed openly. The advantage of having a hard currency would be to facilitate international trade activities for the Soviet government, in addition to diminishing the black market demand for dollars and other Western currencies. The downside would be the drop in the value of the ruble when the government was no longer able to set it at an arbitrarily high price. The Soviet authorities will no doubt look long and hard at this matter before introducing a convertible ruble.

A second, less tangible problem of comparison of the economic situation of Soviet citizens with their counterparts in the West involves quality. A single measure of the differences in quality of goods available in the Soviet Union and in the West would obviously be very difficult to calculate. No such measure is available. Most people familiar with the situation agree that the quality of Soviet consumer goods tends to be below the typical Western level. Thus, the reader should keep qualitative considerations in mind when consumer goods and services are compared in the course of the following discussion.

WORK

Of the total Soviet population of approximately 290 million, in excess of 120 million are classified as "workers" and "employees." But these categories include the state sector only. When collective farmers and persons employed in the small private sector are added, the figure totals more than 140 million (Rapawy, 1987, p. 203). Over 60 percent of those employed are involved in production, with the remainder in services. As in other industrialized or industrializing countries, the service industries have been accounting for an increasing percentage of the labor force in recent years. But the Soviet proportion is still much lower than in the United States, where nearly 70 percent of working people were in the service industries in 1987.[1] The disparity is even greater in farming: Over one-fifth of the total Soviet labor force is in farming, as against less than one-twentieth in the United States.

The proportion of women in the labor force is high: 51 percent in 1987 compared with about 44 percent in the United States. As in the United States, certain types of employment are considered "man's work" and "woman's work," although the fields may not be exactly the same in the two countries. A small proportion of women work in construction and transportation, whereas retail trade, banking and insurance, and the health professions are overwhelmingly populated by women. In most areas, however, it appears that women are underrepresented in management and supervisory positions. As noted in Chapter 7, the lack of women in the upper reaches of the party and state apparatuses is even more striking. For example, only two woman have ever been in the Politburo.

The conclusions one can draw about the status of women in professional life, then, are decidedly mixed. The proportion of women in the labor force is high, and in certain professions their numbers far surpass those in the West. The most obvious example is the medical profession. Nearly 70 percent of Soviet doctors are women, compared with about 17 percent in the United States. Moreover, women hold 60 percent of all positions in the Soviet Union occupied by specialists with either higher or intermediate education. But as was suggested, women are generally underrepresented in supervisory positions. And this subordinate job status is reflected in earning power. Alastair McAuley, in his study of working women in the USSR, came to the conclusion that, overall, women's gross earnings in the 1970s were 60 to 65 percent of men's earnings. He found that for the most part these disparities could be attributed to occupational segregation (McAuley, 1981, pp. 96 and 206).

Part of this is no doubt due to the traditional dominance of men in leadership posts. But it may also be attributed to the differing roles played by men and women in Soviet domestic life. One Soviet specialist on family matters determined that a husband's workweek (including housework) is about 50 hours and that of the working wife is 80 hours. Another speaks of women having "literally a double working day—seven to eight hours on their jobs,

---

[1]Much of the data in this chapter comes from the statistical yearbooks published in Moscow. The latest edition available to the authors was a summary volume covering 1917 to 1987, *Narodnoe Khoziastvo SSSR za 70 Let* (1987). Comparative figures on the United States are from *The 1988 World Almanac and Book of Facts,* New York, 1988.

and between four and six at home." Soviet experts associate this heavy burden with a variety of social problems the country is now facing, including an increasing divorce rate and a dropping birthrate in many parts of the country. One writer has even concluded that women are "rebelling" against the status quo of the "patriarchal family, with complete and unconditional primacy of the husband" (Juviler, 1980, pp. 227–251). An early manifestation of this rebellion was the appearance of an underground feminist literature. More recently, the official Soviet press has allowed the expression of remarkably frank views on the subject; the assertion, for instance, that a man's refusal to share household chores amounts to "moral parasitism and sponging" (Voznesenskaia, 1984).

Women are accorded certain benefits under Soviet law. Article 35 of the Constitution prohibits employment discrimination against women, and the criminal law provides sanctions for refusal to hire a woman because of pregnancy. Provisions of the labor law exempt women from heavy work, work in unhealthy circumstances, underground work, and, in most cases, night work.

In spite of these provisions, it appears that in fact women carry on their share of heavy, unpleasant work. Soviet authorities have not published hard information on this subject in recent years, but the 1970 Census indicated that nearly half of all jobs requiring mainly physical labor were held by women (*Itogi Vsesoiuznoi Perepisi Naseleniia 1970 goda,* 1972, p. 165). And even the casual observer in the Soviet Union is bound to note examples of women performing unusually heavy tasks. The frequent sight of women shoveling snow into a piece of snow-removal equipment while the driver, a male, sits and smokes, or the railroad repair gang made up entirely of female laborers are pictures that make the foreigner do a double take.

Although the normal workweek for most of the labor force is a 5-day week with 2 days off, about one-sixth of workers put in a 6-day week. In a sense, the 6-day week is the legally mandated norm, because paid vacations are figured on the basis of the 6-day week. The minimum paid vacation for all workers (except collective farmers) is 15 days—2 weeks and 3 days as calculated according to the 6-day workweek. This vacation time increases with one's length of service. A 7-hour workday goes with a 6-day workweek. Those working fewer days usually work 8.25 hours a day. The average workweek at the end of the 1980s was 40.5 hours, several hours more than in the United States.

This average workweek does not include overtime, which may amount to a considerable number of hours in some Soviet industries. In certain fields, in fact, it is clear that production plans would not be fulfilled without the use of overtime. Soviet workers are paid straight wage rates for overtime rather than time-and-a-half or some other form of enhanced compensation, as is common in the United States. Under Soviet law, overtime work is supposed to be allowed only as an exceptional measure and only with the consent of the trade unions. This appears to provide little protection to workers, however, since trade unions have normally been acquiescent on the matter of overtime work.

With the renewal of sociological research in recent years, a considerable amount has been learned about the general area of worker satisfaction. A number of studies have uncovered quite significant findings on this question. For one thing, workers appear increasingly to be expressing dissatisfaction with the boredom and lack of creativity of assembly-line work. This, of course, is not a uniquely Soviet phenomenon but has been reported recently in numerous Western countries as well. Other findings indicate that (at least at the factories where the surveys were carried out) there is dissatisfaction with unsanitary working conditions, inferior working equipment, the hectic organization of factory life, and the phenomenon of "storming," that is, the practice of crash production at the end of a month, quarter, or year in order to meet plan targets. The level of wages, although an important factor, is by no means the only significant job-satisfaction issue (Yanowitch, 1985).

Another problem area explored in Soviet sociological studies is "socialist competition." This practice was started in the 1920s under Stalin and was revived under Brezhnev. Following the examples of "shock workers" and others with excellent production records, individuals and work collectives "voluntarily" revised their production plans upward and compete against others having similar work assignments. This received much publicity in the early 1970s, and was personally endorsed by Brezhnev. But actual implementation at the production level was another story. In one study it was shown that official figures on socialist competition that had no relation to reality were concocted by the factory administration in order to cope with what were considered unrealistic demands from higher-ups (*Izvestiia,* October 25, 1973, p. 2).

Another aspect of the drive for greater work productivity was the renewed emphasis on "Stakhanovism." Alexei Stakhanov was a Donets Basin coal miner who in August 1935 was reported to have cut 102 tons of coal by hand in a single work shift, about 14 times the regular quota of 7 tons. This achievement, which was staged by local officials by providing Stakhanov with all manner of auxiliary aid, was given wide publicity. Thus began the Stakhanovite movement, involving the recognition of similar achievements in other fields of work and the raising of output norms for regular workers. Stakhanov became an instant celebrity. He was admitted to the Party by a special decree without having to serve candidate status and was elected to the Supreme Soviet. Books were published in his name.

After World War II much less attention was given to the Stakhanovite movement. But in 1970 a revival of sorts took place when Stakhanov, then 64 years old, was designated "Hero of Socialist Labor," the highest civilian award. And in 1985 the fiftieth anniversary of the Stakhanovite movement was celebrated with a reception honoring veteran Stakhanovites at the Central Committee headquarters, hosted by Party chief Gorbachev. Media coverage emphasized the relevance of Stakhanovism for Gorbachev's drive for labor productivity (*Izvestiia,* September 21, 1985, p. 2 and September 22, 1985, pp.

2-3). Gorbachev's endorsement of the Stakhanovite movement is probably an example of the "early Gorbachev," however. As the 1980s proceeded, much more emphasis was placed on economic incentives than on exhortation campaigns. And the fraudulence of Stakhanov's feat was openly acknowledged in the Soviet press (*Radio Liberty Research,* no. 461/88, October 21, 1988, p. 2).

It was mentioned earlier that trade union permission is required for overtime work but that such permission did not appear to be a serious obstacle for a factory's management to overcome. This fact is related to the place and role of trade unions in the Soviet system. During the latter years of the tsars, unions had come to be positively associated with the goals for which workers were striving, and so their retention became a necessary part of postrevolutionary Russia. But in the early 1920s the unions became the focus of a struggle that could have challenged Party control (Daniels, 1960, pp. 119–136 and 156–159), and before the decade was over trade unions had been effectively neutralized as an independent force. It was declared that there was no basic antagonism between unions and management, because the latter was representative of the state, which was a dictatorship of the proletariat, that is, of the workers. Management and unions were to work hand in hand, with all decision-making power in areas related to production on the side of management and the union playing a subordinate role. Under this kind of philosophy, it was clear that the ultimate weapon of trade unions of the West, the union-sponsored strike, was strictly forbidden.

This is not to say that unions have had no role to play. As John Hazard has shown, the unions have come to perform some of the functions normally associated with a Ministry of Labor (which as abolished in the USSR in 1933; Hazard, 1980, pp. 70–71 and 221). Thus, the observance of safety rules is controlled by trade union committees, as is much of the social-insurance system. In addition, the grievance-procedure mechanism, by which an individual worker may appeal decisions of management that affect him or her adversely, involves a commission for labor disputes made up of representative of the local union and management. In such situations it appears that, at least on occasion, the unions genuinely attempt to support the worker's point of view.

Unions also serve as a kind of social focus for workers' lives, managing the factory "club" and other social and cultural events. Twenty-one large national unions are affiliated in one central organization, the All-Union Central Council of Trade Unions (ACCTU). Workers are not required to join a union, but the overwhelming majority do. There are more than 130 million trade unionists in the USSR, making the ACCTU the largest mass organization in the country (*Iuridicheskii Entsiklopedicheskii Slovar',* 1984, p. 307). Membership dues amount to 1 percent of a worker's wages. Membership confers on the worker some minor advantages in the social-insurance system as well as payment or partial payment for stays at health and vacation resorts maintained by the factory. But the unions have only an advisory voice in matters of output and efficiency, which are controlled by management; they have no role in setting wage rates, which are established by the government. References by Soviet spokesmen to unions as "a force to be reckoned with" ("A Force to Be Reckoned With," 1975, p. 41) should be considered in the light of such constraints.

As the glasnost period has allowed increasing frankness in the discussion of Soviet economic problems, the place of unions in the system has begun to be criticized. Independent rival unions have been set up in parts of the country, and regular unions have lost some of their following. A series of coal strikes in the late 1980s led to the creation of workers' councils at the mines, a potential new form of labor organization that could eventually lead to the replacement of the traditional union structure (Teague, 1989).

A further blow to the prestige of traditional unions was the legislation adopted in 1989 that allowed a limited right to strike. This law, "On Procedures for Resolving Collective Labor Disputes," is written narrowly so as to ban work stoppages in the transportation, communications, power, and defense industries, as well as in other fields under certain circumstances (*Izvestiia*, October 14, 1989, p. 1; *CDSP, 41,* no. 41, p. 18). Although the law allows trade union committees to organize strikes, it also permits strike committees and other groups to do so. Under these circumstances, it seems likely that the old trade unions, which were easily controlled by political authorities in the past, will either have to change their ways or be superseded by more independent, less compliant organizations.

One of the benefits provided by some of the larger labor unions in the United States is a supplemental unemployment benefit. No unemployment compensation of any kind is provided in the Soviet Union because unemployment was declared to have been abolished in 1930. Each year the State Committee on Statistics reports full employment. In some overall sense this may be true, but the real picture is more complex. In some parts of the country there is a critical shortage of workers, giving rise to a policy of encouraging retired workers to return to productive labor and of enlisting migrant workers and laborers from other socialist countries to work temporarily in some parts of the Soviet Union. But in other parts of the country there are more workers in certain job categories than there are jobs. Frequently these workers do not want to move to less desirable parts of the country, where jobs in their specialty are available. In the West such workers would be classified as unemployed, but in the USSR, since vacant jobs await them, they are not. Aside from this, there is "frictional" unemployment, that is, workers who are between jobs because of lack of knowledge that jobs exist or lack of knowledge by employers that workers are available. Time lost in such situations has usually averaged about one month in recent years, but a worker receives only two weeks' severance pay.

There is, then, more unemployment in the USSR than is acknowledged. And with the ambitious plans of the Gorbachev leadership for improving the efficiency of the economy, the situation is likely to get worse. As enterprises seek to make their operations more competitive, they can ill afford to keep superfluous workers on the job. Estimates of the number of such workers are as high as 12 to 16 million (Peterson, 1989). To alleviate problems that are bound to arise from this projected unemployment, the Party and government moved in 1988 to establish a nationwide job placement service (Trehub, 1988a).

Wages and Other Benefits

By the end of the 1980s the average monthly wage or salary in the Soviet Union was over 200 rubles (*Izvestiia,* April 29, 1988, p. 1), a rise of over 30 rubles or almost 20 percent from 10 years earlier. The fact that this is an *average* wage means, of course, that not everyone is paid this much. As a matter of fact, income disparities in the Soviet Union are quite great. The minimum wage was increased during the 1970s from 60 rubles to 70 rubles per month, and during the 1980s to 75 rubles.

Ever since the early Stalin period, any notion of equality with regard to wage rates has been clearly disavowed. "Equalitarianism has nothing in common with Marxist Socialism," said Stalin in 1931. Thereafter much steeper wage differentials than had theretofore existed were introduced. In official Soviet wage figures one can observe considerable differences in wage payments among various branches of the economy. Thus, workers in the building industry average about 25 percent more than the average wage, those in transportation 17 percent more, and those in industry 10 percent more. If one examines certain subcategories of these branches of the economy, the salaries are even more impressive: Workers in water transport receive about 40 percent more than the average wage.

There are, of course, a number of categories of workers that receive less than the average wage. The less-favored sectors include agriculture (2 percent less than the average wage), housing and communal services (24 percent), and health and social security (31 percent less).

The wage levels discussed so far involve only *legal* money earnings. To judge from conversations with Soviet citizens, articles in the press, and reports of court cases, a considerable number of Soviet citizens manage to supplement their regular income by a wide variety of illegal or improper practices. These include using state-owned trucks for private business, short-weighting products and keeping the difference, underreporting income from driving a taxi, and engaging in black market activities such as buying foreign currency or blue jeans from foreigners. Such practices as these are illegal, of course. They constitute "stealing of state property" (Articles 89 to 96 of the RSFSR Criminal Code) or "speculation" (Article 154 of the RSFSR Criminal Code).

These laws did not appear to be much of a deterrent during the "years of stagnation" under Brezhnev, and the so-called "second economy" grew and prospered (Feldbrugge, 1984, p. 528). The Gorbachev regime, determined to enhance popular support by increasing consumer goods and services, has moved on two fronts to deal with the second economy. Through the legislation on individual labor activity and cooperatives discussed in the last chapter, the authorities have moved to make legal (and thereby gain a measure of control over) some of the activities previously carried on illegally. Among a wide variety of undertakings that can now be pursued legally are becoming licensed as a taxi driver using one's own car, or running a cooperative restaurant. As Gorbachev himself has put it, these new laws are designed not only to improve the lot of consumers but also to "squeeze out the shadow economy and all kinds of abuses" (*Izvestiia,* June 26, 1987, p. 3; *CDSP, 39,* 26, p. 12). Along with these changes, new legislation was adopted in 1986 providing further penalties for those who derive "non-labor income" from prohibited activities (*Izvestiia,* May 28, 1986, p. 1; Konovalov, 1986). But success in combating the second economy will depend on the ability to satisfy consumer needs through legal channels, and all of the innovations of the Gorbachev years have not yet achieved this. As a result, a variety of underground economic practices, producing income and services for large numbers of Soviet citizens, remain a prominent feature of the Soviet scene.

Aside from the underground economy, there are other, perfectly legal, ways to supplement one's income. These can contribute significantly to the wide disparity in real income among Soviet citizens. Needless to say, the supplements largely go to the more favored members of Soviet society. University professors are among the best-paid people in the country. A full professor holding a doctorate and working at a university receives 450 rubles a month. If he or she heads a department, 50 rubles more is received. A scientist or scholar is better off if he or she can maintain an affiliation with a university *and* a research institute, a fairly common practice. In such a case, a person is entitled to one and a half times one's rate of pay. For instance, a scholar who holds the directorship of a research institute might receive 500 rubles a month for that position and also receive 250 rubles for half-time as a university professor.

The most elite group of scholars are the few hundred who belong to the USSR Academy of Sciences. Full members of the Academy are entitled (in addition to whatever salary they may earn from their regular jobs) to 500 rubles a month tax free for life and a chauffeur-driven automobile. Corresponding members receive 250 rubles per month and the automobile. There are also hundreds of other full and corresponding members of the republican academies of science who receive monthly stipends of 350 and 175 rubles, respectively.[2]

It is no wonder, then, that advanced degrees are valuable commodities in the Soviet Union. It is said that some well-placed Party and governmental

---

[2]Unless otherwise indicated, the information in these passages is based on conversations with former Soviet citizens.

officials have arranged for scholars to write dissertations for them, thus providing the backup security of an academic career to the uncertain future of a political career. A former insider in the Party apparatus reported that at the time when he had direct knowledge of the situation (the 1970s), 63 percent of the CPSU Central Committee members and 73 percent of union-republic central committee members, as well as 56 percent of responsible officials of the state apparatus, held research degrees, with the implication that many of these degrees were based on dissertations written for the recipients (Pravdin, 1974, p. 102).

The middle level of government and Party officials (republican-level minister, USSR deputy minister, department heads in the CC, CPSU, and so on) earn salaries roughly equivalent to that of a university professor but are not eligible for affiliation with a research institute and, therefore, extra pay. Higher-level government and Party officials (heads of republican government and Party organizations, USSR ministers, Central Committee secretaries) earn 600 rubles to 1,000 rubles per month, and the highest officials, the Party General Secretary and the Prime Minister, receive over 1,000 rubles.[3] The salary of the President of the USSR, a new post created in 1990, was set at 4,000 rubles a month. In addition, a number of other benefits were provided, including a lifetime pension of 1,500 rubles a month (*Izvestiia,* May 24, 1990, p. 4).

Nor are these pay levels limited only to scholars and high government and Party workers. Many performers, actors, and artists command high salaries. Mervyn Matthews has estimated that the elite in terms of income (400 to 500 rubles per month and more) amount to some 227,000 people, about 0.2 percent of the labor force (Matthews, 1978, p. 33).

For the truly privileged in Soviet society, the base salary is only the beginning of material advantage. Extra benefits for the most favored, to some extent a feature of the Soviet system since the beginning, developed to their most extreme point during the 18 years of Brezhnev's rule. Special food stores, paid vacations at the finest spots, exclusive medical facilities, advantages in housing, automobiles, country homes, pensions, the education of children—these only begin to suggest the privileges available to certain individuals during what is now called "the period of stagnation."[4]

The existence of such benefits has long been known, both within the Soviet Union and on the outside. What is different about the recent period is the open expression of resentment about privilege by Soviet citizens. A consid-

---

[3]In a 1989 interview Gorbachev stated the following: "Like all Politburo members, regardless of positions occupied, I receive 1,200 rubles a month. Candidate Politburo members receive 1,100 rubles and CC secretaries—1,000 rubles. All honoraria which are credited to me for publication of reports, addresses, and speeches go to the Party budget" (*Izvestiia TsK KPSS,* 1989, no. 5, p. 59). Prime Minister Ryzhkov's salary was reported in 1990 as 1,200 rubles a month (*Argumenty i Fakty,* 1990, no. 15, p. 5).

[4]Among Western writers who describe the system of privileges under Brezhnev are Matthews (1978), Pravdin (1974), Simis (1982), and Zemtsov (1985).

erable part of Boris Yeltsin's reputation as a populist hero came as a result of his attack on elite benefits at the twenty-seventh Party Congress in 1986.[5] As glasnost developed, public criticism became more pronounced. Numerous letters to newspapers have complained about corruption and abuse of official privileges. A 1988 poll conducted by the *Moscow News* showed a strong negative view among respondents when asked about a variety of advantages available to certain levels of officials (Corning, 1988).

The Gorbachev regime appears to be sensitive to this problem but not yet willing or able to confront it directly. Gorbachev and his allies have devoted much attention to the concept of "social justice," a sense of the basic fairness of the Soviet socialist system. They have indicated that this sense of fairness was undermined during the Brezhnev era, resulting in the alienation of a considerable number of Soviet citizens (Teague, 1987, p. 226). And they assert that the reform of the Soviet system that is envisaged, in its economic, political and social aspects, will bring social justice to the population. Since, according to this reasoning, the causes of alienation lie in the period of "stagnation" under Brezhnev, their answer has been to attack the Brezhnev era and some of its more visible symbols of greed. A number of the most corrupt officials of the Brezhnev era have been fired and discredited. Certain others, most notably Yuri Churbanov, Brezhnev's son-in-law, have been tried and convicted for gross misuse of their official positions. But except for some marginal measures to reduce the perquisites available to the present elite (for example, reducing the number of official cars at the disposal of officials, and closing some of the special stores open only to members of the *nomenklatura*; *Izvestiia*, February 4, 1988, p. 2; *The New York Times*, February 4, 1988, p. A5; *Radio Liberty Research*, nos. 311/88, p. 9, and 412/88, p. 9), the privileges available to the elite appear to remain largely intact. Whatever Gorbachev's personal feelings on the matter, the interests of many entrenched officials argue powerfully for maintaining the status quo.

Is the disparity in income and wealth as great as in the countries of the West? Certainly not. Occasionally one reads about a Soviet "millionaire," but such reports are usually in connection with the trial of someone accused of illegal economic activity. The opportunities for huge accumulations of wealth through capital gains, real-estate operations, ownership of large manufacturing plants, and the like, simply do not exist. But in the Soviet context, that of a country that began with a conscious effort to eliminate the vast gulf between the rich and the poor, the disparity is surprisingly great. In spite of a number of leveling features of the Soviet system, such as free education, inexpensive medical care, cheap public transportation, and low-rent housing, money means a great deal. If over 70 years of Soviet power have eliminated classes from the scene, then there still exist several "levels" of population, based on

---

[5]"Yeltsin's birth as a political leader . . . has been recorded with absolute precision. It was . . . on February 26, 1986, at the 27th CPSU Congress" (Tretyakov, 1989, p. 10).

income, wealth, and comfort, and the levels are easily discernible. To some extent the advantages enjoyed by the higher-income citizens can be passed on to offspring. High income appears to be positively correlated with high education, and the children of higher-educated Soviet citizens are more likely to receive higher education than are the children of less educated citizens. For the less-able child of the richer family there is a thriving system of private tutoring to aid in the passing of university entrance examinations. The reported fees are so high that few families of modest income could afford to pay them.

The pension system is consistent with the principle of differing income levels in that it is based on the income earned during the productive years of pensioners. Pensions are paid to retired and disabled workers as well as to dependent survivors of income earners. To qualify for full old-age pensions, men must have worked for at least 25 years and have reached the age of 60; for women the respective figures are 20 and 55 years. For both sexes the age limits are lowered in cases involving arduous occupations or inclement regions of the country. In 1990 the USSR Supreme Soviet adopted a comprehensive pension law that brings together provisions previously scattered through a number of laws. It also contains some new provisions. The size of the pension is based on a percentage of the worker's average pay during high-earning years. The minimum pension is set at 100 percent of the minimum wage (at present 70 rubles per month). Above that level the pension is established at 55 percent of the recipient's average pay during optimal years, and can rise one percent for every year worked beyond the minimum (25 years for men, 20 years for women) up to a level of 75 percent. Other pension benefits are provided for some categories of workers, such as test pilots. And special pensions may be given to persons who have been awarded certain state honors (for instance, Hero of the Soviet Union, Hero of Socialist Labor) and to other citizens "in recognition by the Soviet state of their services to state, public and economic activity, and in the fields of science, culture, education health, physical culture and sport." Such pensions, which used to be called "personal pensions" and were awarded in a covert manner, are now designated "pensions for special services to the USSR" (*Izvestiia,* May 30, 1990, p. 2).

Temporarily disabled workers receive 100 percent of their base pay, and workers with long-term or permanent disabilities receive a percentage of base pay calculated according to their number of years of work. Pensions for survivors of income earners are calculated on the same basis as those for permanently disabled workers.

Until 1965, collective farmers were not covered by state pensions. Collective farms could have their own "mutual-aid" pensions, but only a small percentage of eligible *kolkhozniki* were actually receiving funds. Finally, in that year, the social-insurance principle was extended to collective farms. Although the pension benefits of *kolkhozniki* are somewhat lower than those of other workers, this extension means that virtually all workers in the country are covered by the state pension system.

In terms of adequacy of coverage, however, even Soviet sources have begun to raise serious questions. Soviet specialists have long employed the term "underprovisioning" (*maloobespechennost'*) to describe the economic situation of some portion of the Soviet population, but that was the closest that public discussions came to the concept of poverty until relatively recently. Although there is no official designation of a poverty level for the USSR, there is some consensus among Soviet and Western analysts that 70 rubles per person per month might be an appropriate figure (Eklof, 1989, p. 114). *Izvestiia* revealed in 1988 that more than one-third of Soviet pensioners live on less than 60 rubles a month. Acknowledging that the practice in the past was to "remain shamefully silent" about such matters, *Izvestiia* concluded that "one does not have to be a big specialist to know that it is very difficult to live on 60 rubles a month (*Izvestiia,* August 20, 1988, p. 1).* Increasing public acknowledgment of the problem of poverty has been one of the products of glasnost. And although it is not only people on pensions who constitute the Soviet poor, this group makes up the largest proportion. One of the main reasons for this is that pension levels have increased only modestly since 1956, although overt and hidden inflation has eaten away at fixed incomes (Trehub, 1988b).

A more general assessment of the poor as a proportion of the Soviet population has been made by the British scholar Mervyn Matthews. In a work published in 1986, Matthews comes to the conclusion that the poor numbered "up to two fifths of all workers' and employees' families, and rather more of the population at large" (Matthews, 1986, p. 28).

With an average monthly wage of something over 200 rubles, how well off is the typical Soviet consumer? This can be looked upon in various ways. By any calculation, it appears that the minimum family budget for a family of four well exceeds that figure. In other words, in a family where the principal provider earns only the average wage or less, the working wife is not just a convenience but a necessity. This is no doubt part of the explanation of why a higher percentage of married women in the Soviet Union maintain full-time jobs than is the case in Western countries.

A relatively high percentage of the family budget goes for food. Soviet figures for 1989 indicate that the average family spends more than one-third of its income on food. Other Soviet data, as well as Western estimates, however, suggest that the proportion is considerably higher, perhaps 50 percent or more (*Izvestiia,* January 16, 1989, p. 2; Matthews, 1986, p. 57). On the other hand, the typical Soviet family will spend a considerably smaller proportion of its budget than the American family on such things as housing, transportation, and medical care.[6] What this all adds up to is a substantially different

---

*In 1989 the USSR Supreme Soviet adopted a law "On Urgent Measures to Improve Pension Benefits and Social Services to the Population." Among its provisions was one raising minimum retirement pensions to 70 rubles a month (*Izvestiia,* August 4, 1989, p. 1).

[6]Comparable data on these matters are difficult to find. As a rough comparison on housing, official Soviet figures for 1986 list 2.6 percent as the proportion of family budget spent on

pattern of spending in the Soviet Union, based on a different social and economic setting.

It is time, therefore, to introduce another aspect of the Soviet worker's compensation not yet discussed. This is what official Soviet publications refer to as "payments and benefits from the social consumption funds," which were said to amount to almost 90 rubles per worker per month for 1986 (*Narodnoe Khoziastvo SSSR v 1987 g.,* 1988, pp. 392, 394). This fund covers both direct payments, such as pensions, disability, vacations, and student stipends, and benefits received without direct payment, such as medical care, educational costs, and housing subsidies. Thus, if the typical Soviet family spends considerably less of its disposable income than the American family on housing, it is in part because most Soviet housing is heavily subsidized, and this subsidy is counted as part of the employee's total compensation. But to count the total 90 rubles per month as actual compensation is misleading. It may be reasonable to include medical care, education, and housing subsidies in a worker's compensation, but such direct payments as pensions, disability allowances, and student stipends usually go to people without full-time jobs. These payments certainly are compensation, but not compensation for gainfully employed persons. Therefore, only part of the social consumption fund (and the smaller part at that) should be considered as contributing to workers' incomes (Osborn, 1970, pp. 33–34).

How does the Soviet worker benefit from the social consumption fund compared with so-called transfer payments, that is, social security, welfare payments, and such, in Western countries? Several Western scholars have considered this matter and have concluded that data are not now available to make precise comparisons. But tentative conclusions suggest that for several Western European countries transfer payments as a percentage of total income may not be very different from that in the Soviet Union (Lynch, 1980).

Such benefits aside, how does the Soviet worker's income compare with that of his Western counterparts?[7] Radio Liberty over a number of years has made analyses of earnings and prices in the Soviet Union. Their data are relevant here. As of 1986 the average monthly take-home pay (after taxes) in the USSR and four Western countries (converted to U.S. dollars at the prevailing rates of exchange)[8] was as per the following table (Bush, 1987, p. 31):

"apartment rent, communal services, and maintenance on private homes." U.S. data from earlier in the decade put the figure on housing for an urban family of four persons in the United States at between 18 percent and 22 percent of the annual budget, depending on the level of income involved. On the other hand, the figures on food as a proportion of the U.S. family budget are lower than the Soviet figures, ranging from 19 to 29 percent, depending on the level of income. The data are from *Narodnoe Khoziastvo SSSR za 70 Let,* 1987, p. 385, and *Statistical Abstract of the United States* (Washington, D.C.: U.S. Government Printing Office, 1982), p. 467. After this issue of the *Statistical Abstract,* the figures on family budget ceased to be published.

[7]The reader is reminded of the problems of converting rubles to dollars. Yet if any comparisons are to be made, this conversion seems to be the only reasonable way to approach the matter.

[8]The reader should note that this calculation does not take into consideration the partial devaluation of the ruble in 1989, discussed earlier in this chapter.

USSR	$279.23
USA	$1196.85
Federal Republic of Germany	$1133.02
France	$843.15
United Kingdom	$905.97

STANDARD OF LIVING

Moving from income to expenditures, one finds comparisons equally difficult to make. We have already mentioned that housing costs are considerably lower in the Soviet Union than in the West, and we will have more to say on the quality and availability of housing later in this chapter. Medical and dental expenses for the Soviet citizen are negligible (most Soviet citizens have to pay for drug prescriptions and other medicines, for instance, but for little else), whereas they can be major costs in the United States. The cost of public transportation (five kopecks or less for subways, buses, and trolleys) compares very favorably with similar services in the West. Finally, the price of a good loaf of dark or white Russian bread cannot be approached in the West. But these are only individual examples, and overall they are misleading.

Radio Liberty researchers have attempted a more comprehensive comparison of food and other costs in the Soviet Union and the West. Their analysis is based on a "Weekly Basket of Consumer Goods" containing 23 items—including meats, vegetables, fruits, beverages, dairy products, and grain products—that are available in the West and usually available in the Soviet Union. The items in the food basket are based on an estimated Soviet level of consumption, and the results of the survey for October 1986 for Moscow and four Western cities are expressed in hours of work required to purchase the basket (Bush, 1987, p. 6):

Moscow	51.2 hours
Washington	16.0 hours
Munich	21.3 hours
Paris	24.9 hours
London	17.7 hours

What the overall comparison hides is that although prices on such staples as bread, carrots, and cabbage are generally lower in the Soviet Union than in the West, prices of meat, poultry, dairy products, and fruit are more or less equivalent. The result is that the purchase of this quantity of food places a greater burden on the lower Soviet wage levels.

Theoretically, Soviet consumers should be in a better position than their Western counterparts regarding price inflation. Retail prices are fixed by the state, except for prices at the collective farm markets, which may vary according to supply and demand. By and large, the fixed prices have not changed much in recent years, and at least some price changes appear to be related to goals of the Soviet leadership not directly relevant to internal economic operations. For instance, increases in the price of vodka have been part of the government's drive against alcoholism, and increases in the prices of caviar, champagne, furs, and other products seem to be aimed at discouraging domestic demand in order to increase export potential, especially to hard-currency markets.

That prices are fixed does not mean that there is *no* inflation, however. In addition to the price increases just mentioned, what amounts to hidden inflation can manifest itself in several ways. A frequent practice is to introduce a new model or type of a long-available item and accompany some minor changes with a large increase in price. This technique is used on many consumer goods, from automobiles to vodka. Some goods simply disappear from the shelves for long periods of time, forcing the consumer to purchase more expensive substitutes. Expensive items not available at fixed state prices can often be purchased at higher prices at collective farm markets or on the black market. The ratio between state retail prices and collective farm market prices has been steadily rising for most recent years. Although the kind of inflation described here cannot be documented in Soviet sources or studies by traditional social science techniques, it is real inflation nevertheless. No doubt it is not of the magnitude experienced in Western countries in recent years; but according to many people familiar with the Soviet economy, it is a real problem for heads of Soviet families trying to make ends meet. Moreover, Soviet sources have been acknowledging since about 1987 that real inflation does exist. Estimates vary from the rather low levels cited by "official" Soviet economists—about 2 to 2.5 percent per year—(*Moscow News,* 1989, no. 3, p. 10)—to other Soviet estimates of 8 to 9 percent per year (*Report on the USSR, 1,* no. 37, 1989, p. 28; *The New York Times,* November 3, 1988, p. A1). Nor can the Soviet consumer count indefinitely on restrictions on retail prices. A number of political leaders and economists are convinced that economic reform cannot succeed without significant price increases on certain highly subsidized products, including bread and meat. Such increases, referred to as "shock therapy" by some in the USSR, are certain to be highly unpopular with large numbers of Soviet citizens.

Also characteristic of the Soviet system is what economists call repressed inflation. Repressed inflation occurs when prices cannot rise according to the laws of supply and demand because of the lack of supply (and, in the Soviet case, because of fixed prices). That is, goods in demand are not available for purchase, and a great deal of purchasing power remains unused. A sign of this situation is large amounts of money in savings accounts, which has been very characteristic of the Soviet Union in recent years. In 1989 over 314 billion rubles were held in such accounts, more than double the amount of 10 years earlier. Moreover, the rate of accumulation in recent years appears to be increasing, indicating the large amount of unused purchasing power (*Izvestiia,* October 24, 1989, p. 1; *Narodnoe Khoziastvo SSSR v 1987 g.,* p. 406). A typical way in which the state seeks to cope with this excess purchasing power is by putting extremely high prices on certain items that are in great demand. Of a number of possible examples of this practice, the privately owned automobile is the best.

The privately owned passenger car occupies an interesting position in the Soviet Union for a number of reasons. In the past the government had an ambivalent attitude toward it, at times openly labeling the private car an unsocialist manifestation of privatism. In addition to setting high purchase prices, the authorities have tried to discourage ownership in various ways. These include the unwillingness to provide liability insurance for car owners (which several socialist countries of Eastern Europe do allow their citizens to buy) and sporadic, unsuccessful attempts to provide a car-rental system as a substitute for private ownership. Furthermore, the relatively poor Soviet highway system makes widespread car travel difficult, and the network of filling stations, repair shops, and other service facilities is notoriously inadequate. The difficulties car owners face in getting spare parts are legendary.

The reasons for the underdevelopment of the private-car industry are not difficult to adduce. In addition to ideological considerations, the investments necessary to develop the system would be tremendous, and the authorities have many higher-priority objectives for their investment funds. In addition, a well-developed private transportation system would compete with (and possibly financially undermine, as has happened in the United States) the public transportation system. On purely economic grounds, there is no question which mode of transportation the Soviet authorities see as more rational.

It was not until 1972 that more passenger cars than trucks were produced. The Soviet Union still has an unusually high ratio of trucks to passenger cars on its roads. And even though much progress has been made in providing the public with private automobiles, the USSR, comparatively speaking, lags far behind many other countries.

Yet public demand for passenger cars is long-standing and intense. Although this demand has not been transmitted to government officials via the political process in ways with which we are familiar in the West, there is no doubt that Soviet authorities are aware of it. And notwithstanding the ideological and other considerations mentioned previously, the authorities to some extent have submitted to this pressure by increasing automobile production significantly in recent years. Since the beginning of the Eighth Five-Year Plan in 1966, the Soviet Union has undertaken a major effort to boost car production. During this time they have gone from a production of slightly more than 200,000 passenger cars to more than 1.7 million in 1987 (*Izvestiia,* January 24, 1988, p. 3). Not all of these, of course, have gone to private purchasers. Many are used for official state and Party purposes and as taxis, and an increasing number are being exported, especially to Western countries, in exchange for hard currency. But by 1980 the great majority of automobiles produced were going to private parties; it is here that the car's use to absorb excess purchasing power and to fight repressed inflation comes into play.

Several models of passenger cars are available for purchase by private citizens: the Volga, the Zhiguli (based on the Italian Fiat), the Moskvich, and the Zaporozhets. All are in the subcompact class, but they range in size from the Volga (98 horsepower and about the size of a Ford Tempo) to the Zaporozhets (40 horsepower and about the size of an old Honda Civic). The prices of Soviet passenger cars have risen considerably. As of 1989 the selling prices in the Soviet Union (and the dollar equivalents at the then rate of exchange) of two of these models were as follows (*Izvestiia,* June 19, 1989, p. 2; Bush, 1987, pp. 2, 11, 19):

Model	Price (Rubles)	Price (U.S.Dollars)
Volga 24–10	16,200	25,920
Zhiguli 2108	8,500	13,600

These prices are well above the prices for roughly equivalent vehicles sold in the West. A large percentage of the purchase price, therefore, amounts to turnover tax and is designed to absorb excess purchasing power and discourage demand. Some clue as to the actual cost of production of these vehicles may be indicated by prices charged when they are sold for hard currency. Under these circumstances, the cars mentioned have typically sold at about 35 to 40 percent of the domestic ruble price (*Radio Liberty Research,* no. 380/82, September 20, 1982).

In spite of these prices, the demand for private cars remains extremely high. Autos must be fully paid for at time of delivery and there is a waiting list two to three years long for most models. Even substantial price rises have failed to discourage consumers. Used cars are also extremely high priced. Since they may sometimes be obtained without the long waiting period required for new cars, it is not unusual for a late-model car to sell for substantially more than its original purchase price. Since even the cheapest new car costs over two years of the average worker's salary, it is clear that the high demand for cars is found almost exclusively among the more favored members of Soviet society.

With regard to other consumer durables, supply problems are not nearly so critical. The percentage of families possessing refrigerators, television sets, washing machines, and other appliances has steadily increased, and waiting periods for such items are the exception rather than the rule. Besides the automobile, the other basic commodity in high demand by large numbers of Soviet citizens is improved housing.

HOUSING

To say that the Soviet Union has a housing problem should surprise no one. Nor is the problem one that characterizes the Soviet Union alone. Much of the world is ill housed, and even among the industrialized countries a critical housing situation exists. The Soviet Union has made truly impressive gains in housing construction in recent years. If differences between promises and reality still remain, there is no doubt that many millions of Soviet citizens have recently acquired adequate housing for the first time in their lives.

And yet the problem remains a critical one. Both the leaders and the man in the street agree on this. The great recent efforts in housing construction only began in the 1950s. Prior to that time, the housing record was mediocre at best. And the housing situation inherited by the Soviet regime was a poor one, among the worst in Europe by some accounts (Smith, 1973, p. 406). Added to this was the widespread destruction of housing in the European part of the USSR during World war II. Thus, the present generation has a great deal to make up for in housing construction. And there is no doubt that as the standard of living rises in other aspects of life, expectations as to what constitutes adequate housing rise too.

One index of the housing situation is the so-called "sanitary housing norm," that is, the amount of per capita "living space" supposedly guaranteed by Soviet law to those residing in cities and urban settlements. The minimum norm, first set in the Russian Republic in the 1920s, is 9 square meters (a space about 10 feet by 10 feet square). In spite of the fact that this figure has been written into law for more than six decades, the sanitary housing norm was apparently only achieved for the country as a whole by the early 1980s. And since this is an *average* figure, it is clear that many families in the USSR still live below the norm (Alekseev, 1987, p. 281). The present level of housing space is far more than that achieved in earlier years (6.8 square meters in 1964, 4.7 square meters in 1950) and testifies to impressive recent improvements. The Soviets built an average of over two million apartments per year over the last 25 years, and they annually provide new apartments or improved living conditions for approximately 10 million people. Although the plan targets for housing construction are usually underfulfilled, Soviet authorities claim that they are building more housing than any other country in the world.

It is when one examines more closely a comparative claim such as this one that the Soviet housing situation looks less impressive. If more total housing units are produced in the USSR than elsewhere, the same does not hold with respect to population size. Per thousand population, many Western European countries and Japan have produced more housing units than the USSR in recent years. And in terms of total housing floor space per capita, the results are even more unfavorable to the USSR. Moreover, if one compares the stock of housing per unit of population, the USSR is lower than several East European countries as well as the United States, Japan, and most of Western Europe (Morton, 1979, vol. 1, pp. 791-792; *Pravitel'stvennyi Vestnik,* 1990, no. 14, p. 7).

The Soviet authorities have long promised to solve the housing problem. As far back as 1961, in the Party Program adopted that year, it was stated that by 1980 every family would have its own "comfortable apartment in accordance with the requirements of hygiene and everyday life." When it became clear that this timetable could not be met, the date was pushed back to 1990. When the Party Program was rewritten in 1986, it made the promise for "practically" every Soviet family by the year 2000 (Trehub, 1986, p. 31).

Western observers agree that the quality of housing construction in the USSR is generally inferior to that in the West. Homes built in the early years of the push to solve the housing problem—the late 1950s—sacrificed quality for quantity. Such apartments quickly took on a shabby appearance. Since then, quality has been improved (accompanied by a drop in the construction rate) but is still inferior to most urban housing in the West.

Although most housing is now being built with the standard amenities (such as running water), many housing units still in use lack such facilities. In terms of average size, the housing units built in the Soviet Union in recent years are smaller not only than those in the West but also than those in virtually all East European countries as well. Most housing now being constructed in the Soviet Union is built by the state, about two-thirds of the total in recent years. But this has not always been the case. Until the early 1960s, over half of the housing constructed every year was privately built, and even in the 1970s private and cooperative housing constituted over half of the total housing stock (Morton, 1974, p. 172).

A Gorbachev-era innovation that may increase the proportion of private housing is the scheme adopted in the late 1980s to allow residents to purchase the state-owned apartments they live in. This arrangement would lessen the housing maintenance burden on the state and produce investment funds for social programs, including further housing construction (*Izvestiia,* December 9, 1988, p. 3; *Radio Liberty Research,* no. 538/88, December 9, 1988, p. 10). Much of the private housing at present is the rude one-story structure so prevalent in the Soviet countryside. The predominance of that type of structure in urban areas has long since passed. Great numbers of small private structures have been torn down in recent years, and in many larger cities the building of private homes has been forbidden. As much as the Soviet authorities might have found the private home an ideologically objectionable artifact of the past, however, it remains a much-needed part of the total housing picture. In fact, Gorbachev's plans envisage a renewed emphasis on private and cooperative housing as a major factor in coping with the problem.

Cooperative housing was experimented with early in Soviet history and then abandoned for several decades. During the 1960s it was revived and officially encouraged. The cooperative scheme allows groups of citizens to combine forces and become shareholders in building a multiapartment complex for their own occupancy. Cooperative apartments cost considerably more than state apartments. As was mentioned, the rents in the latter are extremely low, and even with the cost of utilities, tenant payments amount to no more than 4 to 5 percent of the typical family income. State apartments are heavily subsidized. It is said that the state pays two-thirds of the maintenance cost of apartments in addition to financing the initial construction cost (Kamin, 1975, p. 19). A shareholder in a cooperative, by contrast, must make a down payment of 30 percent of the cost of the apartment, which could amount to several thousand rubles. The remainder may be paid over 10 to 20 years in equal monthly shares at an interest charge of 0.5 percent. These monthly payments, which include maintenance costs, are considerably higher than for state apartments. In spite of these higher costs, the cooperative idea has been popular, perhaps because one can avoid the waiting line by joining a cooperative; a wait of perhaps several years will be faced by the ordinary citizen seeking a new state apartment. Cooperative apartments of much higher quality and cost are increasingly being built by members of the various Soviet elites. Such people, who have large amounts of money available, find the cooperative apartment an ideal way to improve housing conditions in a relatively short period of time.

Like other branches of housing construction, cooperative apartment building has usually not met plan targets in recent years. Its share of total housing construction has remained well under 10 percent for a number of years. As comments in the press frequently indicate, in spite of official approval of cooperative housing, support and cooperation by local authorities has not always been what it should be. The Gorbachev regime has stated that cooperative housing should account for over 30 percent of all housing construction by the year 2000 (Trehub, 1986, p. 32). In this and other areas of economic innovation, the leadership will need to go to considerable lengths to get an indifferent or reluctant bureaucracy to cooperate.

CITIZEN PREFERENCES AND GOVERNMENT POLICIES

Birthrates, Labor Turnover, and Migration

The relationship of housing to other economic and social problems has not been widely explored by Soviet scholars. But recent Soviet sociological research has generated information that tends to support the impressionistic views of a number of Western specialists. And the authorities are more open about the relationship of housing to such problems as the falling birthrate, labor turnover, and underpopulation in certain parts of the country.

Soviet demographers are concerned about the drop in the birthrate in the European part of the USSR. Population is growing at a much faster rate in the non-European republics, particularly in Soviet Central Asia. Thus, before the year 2000, ethnic Russians are expected to constitute less than a majority of the Soviet population, and such a shift in population balance would have considerable symbolic significance. Demographers attribute part of the drop in birthrate to inadequate housing. Survey data directed at this problem support the demographers' conclusion.

The housing situation is not the only reason for the low birthrate, of course. For low-income families more children means a general drop in the level of material comforts. The state tries to encourage population increases by various means. Until 1981, a woman received four months' paid maternity leave for each child, and she could take up to one year unpaid leave after a baby was born. In that year, a decree was adopted increasing benefits. Under its terms, a working mother receives 35 rubles a month for a year while remaining home with the child (50 rubles in certain remote parts of the country). Moreover, one-time payments, which used to be awarded only on the birth of the third child, now begin with the first child at considerably higher levels than before (*Izvestiia*, March 1, 1981, p. 1 and September 6, 1981, p. 1). Then there are the well-known awards of "Maternal Glory" for giving birth to and raising 7, 8, or 9 children, and "Heroine Mother" for 10 children. Although the increased benefits in the 1981 decree are notable, it should be emphasized that childbearing incentives have been in existence for many years, while the birth rate has continued to drop. Whether these latest benefits will make a difference remains to be seen.

High labor turnover is a matter of considerable concern to Soviet authorities and planners. From 1940 to 1956, Soviet law made it a crime to leave one's job, and presumably labor turnover was relatively well controlled thereby. Since 1956, workers have been free to change jobs, and although this freedom is of definite benefit to workers, it is of great concern to planners. Since 1957, the rate of labor turnover has stabilized at about 20 percent per year. When compared with an average labor turnover during this period in the United States of about 4.3 percent (Moskoff, 1984, p. ix), one can get some impression of the productivity losses involved. And since a high proportion of job changes are accompanied by changes in occupation, there are enormous costs in retraining as well as in wasted skills. Moreover, these problems are particularly acute in certain parts of the country, most notably Siberia and the Far East, where labor shortages have definitely held up development plans. It is reported that labor turnover in parts of Siberia runs about double the national average (Dyker, 1980).

A third, and related, development is population migration. The two aspects of this problem of most concern to Soviet leaders are the movement from the countryside to the city and the difficulty of persuading people to settle in the less attractive parts of the country. A long-term aspect of population movement has been the rural exodus. Between 1939 and 1961 the proportion of the Soviet population living in cities rose from about one-third to more than half. By the late 1980s the urban percentage had reached about 66 percent. The migration of people from rural areas to the cities, which makes up a great part of this urban growth, has been officially encouraged or condoned, at least until recently. The authorities have long looked upon this development as being naturally related to their high-priority goals of economic growth and urbanization.

This encouragement has been selective, to be sure. For quite a few years the government has tried to prevent migration to the larger cities. As early as 1931, for example, the Party Central Committee adopted a resolution prohibiting the location of new industries in the main urban centers. And in Moscow, Leningrad, and a number of other major cities, regulations have been adopted to prevent out-of-towners from establishing permanent residence. The possibility of obtaining a *propiska* or residence permit in a number of the more desirable localities in the USSR is next to nil unless one has good connections, a profession that is in demand, or a spouse who is already a resident (Morton, 1987, p. 98). This has led many persons to circumvent the law by contracting marriages of convenience with urban citizens in order to gain resident status. The failure of the authorities' efforts is most evident in Moscow, where the population has grown from slightly more than six million in 1959 to about nine million by the end of the 1980s.

But these are measures that have been applied largely to the big urban centers in the western part of the country. It is only in recent years that the authorities have come to understand and react to the more general problems associated with the rural exodus. Aided by data from sociological surveys, they have found that the most desirable rural residents, the young and the skilled, are the ones who tend to leave; that the areas of greatest rural manpower shortage are the ones that are losing the most rural workers; and that the general influx into the cities is adding to the urban problems the country is facing.

By the 1980s the situation had reached a stage that many Soviet leaders must have considered critical. In spite of a crash campaign to train tractor drivers, only a small proportion of those receiving such training remained in agricultural work. And one study showed that three-quarters of the rural youth in a large section of the country left the countryside after receiving higher or secondary education (Tenson, 1980).

These problems characterize many rural areas of the USSR. But they are most critical in a few regions located farthest from the great urban centers of western Russia. The areas of largest rural out-migration naturally include those that are least desirable as places to live and, incidentally, those where underpopulation has long been most severe: Siberia and the Far East.

The Soviet Union has waged a long and largely unsuccessful battle to increase the population in the part of the country east of the Ural Mountains. This large territory is made up of two basic parts, the five Central Asian republics (the Kazakh, Uzbek, Kirghiz, Tadzhik, and Turkmen SSRs) and the three eastern regions of the RSFSR (Western Siberia, Eastern Siberia, and the Far East). It is the three latter regions that will concern us here. Taken together, this vast territory comprises 57 percent of the whole USSR and about 75 percent of Russia (the RSFSR). Yet its 31 million people as of the late 1980s amounted to only 11 percent of the USSR population and 21 percent of the RSFSR population. The main reason for this low population is not hard to ascertain: Life there is difficult and uncomfortable. This problem contributes to the low birthrate for the Russian Republic as a whole, which was only 5.6 percent for the period from 1979 to 1989 as against 9 percent for the entire USSR. On the other hand, in the Central Asian republics there is an indigenous population living in cities that were established in ancient times. These people have strong cultural attachments to that part of the country. There is no problem with keeping them on their land. When attachment to the land is coupled with a cultural emphasis on large families, it comes as no surprise that the Central Asian population growth rate is so high compared with the national average.

In earlier times, before the flush of ideological fervor associated with the Revolution had worn off, the regime sought to populate the unsettled areas by appealing to the patriotic feelings of the citizenry. Komsomolsk on the Amur River in Eastern Siberia, now a city of over a quarter of a million, was originally settled by *Komsomol* members in 1932. The founding of the city was associated with a campaign emphasizing the romantic aspects of capturing the frontier. This appeal, however, has long since lost its effectiveness.

Material incentives have also been tried. Settlement in remote areas has been encouraged by paying higher wage rates to workers in the far north regions, Siberia, and the Far East. In unusual circumstances, such as working on the construction of the northern branch of the Trans-Siberian Railroad (the so-called Baikal-Amur Mainline or BAM, which was completed in 1984), wages and bonuses could amount to five to six times the average industrial wage. But high wages do not necessarily hold workers. The inability to keep workers in these areas has led to the increasing use of the "tour-of-duty" system, in which workers are sent in for short periods of intense work, perhaps for two weeks, and then returned to their homes in more westerly parts of the country (Dyker, 1980).

The whole complex of living conditions, including housing, services, climate, educational opportunities, and other factors, work against attracting new settlers to these areas. The classic Soviet study of labor turnover and population in Siberia is the demographer V.I. Perevedentsev's 1966 book on the subject (Perevedentsev, 1966). Perevedentsev sums up the conditions existing in Siberia by noting that in housing, real wages, retail-trade volume and outlets, medical services, transportation services, level of education and educational opportunities, amount of free time, and average life span, Siberia is worse off than the rest of the RSFSR or the USSR as a whole. What Perevedentsev found in the mid–1960s remains basically true today. Then there are the less quantifiable aspects of life, such as air pollution (which Perevedentsev found to be particularly bad in some West Siberian towns) and the annoyance of biting insects. About the latter he writes:

> One of the most difficult conditions of life for the population in the taiga portion of Siberia, and sometimes in the forest steppe (for example, the Baraba), is the

prevalence of bloodsucking insects—gadflies, mosquitos, and midges, which locally have the generic name *gnus*. During certain periods in many parts of Siberia, the quantity of *gnus* is so great that it is impossible to work in the open air without taking special protective measures. The use of nets and special clothing involves a number of inconveniences, greatly hinders the work, reducing productivity, and unfavorably affects the workers' state of mind. Siberia's major construction projects have special institutions to combat *gnus*. However this effort is extraordinarily difficult, because these insects cover large areas and are very mobile. There is nothing comparable in the western parts of the country with their labor surplus. (*Soviet Sociology, 11,* no. 1, 1972, p. 54)

CONCLUSION

The convergence of these three related problems of low birthrate, labor mobility, and population migration stands out most clearly in areas of greatest underpopulation, such as Siberia. Labor is not attracted to the area because of the absence of basic comforts and amenities that cannot be provided because of the shortage of labor to build them. This is a complex problem that obviously will not be solved soon. Soviet leaders, with all their professed confidence in the future, must sometimes despair of ever bringing these outlying areas into the mainstream of Soviet life. Some Western analysts see in the Gorbachev-era innovations a waning of interest in investing in Siberia (Shabad, 1987, p. 93). That the Soviet authorities would consider a shift in priorities of this kind is indicative of the seriousness of the country's economic problems.

REFERENCES

ALEKSEEV, M. (1987). Soviet residential housing: Will the "acute problem" be solved? In *Gorbachev's economic plans*. Washington, D.C.: Joint Economic Committee.

BRONSON, D., and SEVERIN, B. (1973). Soviet consumer welfare: The Brezhnev era. In *Soviet economic prospects for the seventies*. Washington, D.C.: Joint Economic Committee.

BUSH, K. (1987). Retail prices in Moscow and four western cities in October, 1986. *Radio Liberty Research Supplement,* no. 1/87.

CORNING, A. (1988). Attitudes toward privileges in the Soviet Union. *Radio Liberty Research,* no. 317/88.

DANIELS, R. (1960). *The conscience of the revolution*. New York: Simon & Schuster.

DYKER, D. (1980). Living conditions and labor supply: A key to development in Western Siberia. *Radio Liberty Research,* no. 374/80.

EKLOF, B. (1989). *Soviet briefing: Gorbachev and the reform period*. Boulder, Colo.: Westview.

FELDBRUGGE, F. (1984). Government and the shadow economy in the Soviet Union. *Soviet Studies, 35,* 528.

A FORCE TO BE RECKONED WITH. (1975). *Soviet Life*, no. 8, 41.

HAZARD, J. (1980). *The Soviet system of government*. Chicago: The University of Chicago Press.

HOLLAND, B., ed. (1986). *Soviet sisterhood*. Bloomington, Ind.: Indiana University Press.

Itogi Vsesoiuznoi Perepisi Naseleniia 1970 goda. (1972). Moscow: "Statistika."

Iuridicheskii Entsiklopedicheskii Slovar'. (1984). Moscow: Sovetskaia Entsiklopediia.

JUVILER, P. (1980). The Soviet family in post-Stalin perspective. In S. Cohen, A. Rabinowitch, and R. Sharlet, eds., *The Soviet Union since Stalin*. Bloomington, Ind.: Indiana University Press.

KAMIN, Y. (1975). Soviet living standards rise. *Soviet Life*, no. 6, 18.

KHRUSHCHEV, N.S. (1974). *Khrushchev remembers: The last testament*. Boston: Little, Brown.

KONOVALOV, V. (1986). Stepping up administrative and criminal liability in the campaign against nonlabor incomes. *Radio Liberty Research*, no. 377/86.

LYNCH, B. (1980). A comparison of income from transfer payments in the USSR, the United Kingdom, and the United States. *Radio Liberty Research*, no. 31/80.

McAULEY, A. (1981). *Women's work and wages in the Soviet Union*. London: George Allen & Unwin.

MATTHEWS, M. (1978). *Privilege in the Soviet Union*. London: George Allen & Unwin.

MATTHEWS, M. (1986). *Poverty in the Soviet Union*. Cambridge: Cambridge University Press.

MORTON, H. (1974). What have Soviet leaders done about the housing crisis? In H. Morton and R. Tokes, eds., *Soviet politics and society in the 1970's*. New York: Free Press.

MORTON, H. (1979). The Soviet quest for better housing: An impossible dream? *Soviet economy in a time of change*. Washington, D.C.: Joint Economic Committee.

MORTON, H. (1980). Who gets what, when and how? Housing in the Soviet Union. *Soviet Studies, 32*, 256.

MORTON, II. (1987). Housing quality and housing classes in the Soviet Union. In Horst Herlemann, ed., *Quality of life in the Soviet Union*. Boulder, Colo.: Westview.

MOSKOFF, W. (1984). *Labor and leisure in the Soviet Union*. New York: St. Martin's.

Narodnoe Khoziastvo SSSR v 1987 g. (1988). Moscow: "Finansy i Statistika."

Narodnoe Khoziastvo SSSR za 70 Let. (1987). Moscow: "Finansy i Statistika."

OSBORN, R. (1970). *Soviet social policies*. Homewood, Ill.: Dorsey.

PEREVEDENTSEV, V.I. (1966). *Population movement and labor supply in Siberia*. Translated in *Soviet Sociology, 8*, 1, 2 (summer and fall, 1969); *9*, 3 (winter, 1970–71); *11*, 1, 2 (summer and fall, 1972).

PETERSON, D.J. (1989). Unemployment in the USSR. *Report on the USSR, 1*, 34, 5–10.

PRAVDIN, A. (1974). Inside the Central Committee. *Survey, 20*, 4, 100.

RAPAWY, S. (1987). Labor force and employment in the USSR. *Gorbachev's economic plans*. Washington, D.C.: Joint Economic Committee.

SCHROEDER, G. (1987). U.S.S.R.: Toward the service economy at a snail's pace. *Gorbachev's economic plans*. Washington, D.C.: Joint Economic Committee.

SHABAD, T. (1987). In A. Wood, ed., *Siberia: Problems and prospects for regional development*. London: Croom Helm.

SIMIS, K. (1982). *USSR: The corrupt society*. New York: Simon & Schuster.

SMITH, W. (1973). Housing in the Soviet Union—Big plans, little action. *Soviet economic prospects for the seventies*. Washington, D.C.: Joint Economic Committee.

TEAGUE, E. (1987). Gorbachev's "human factor" policies. *Gorbachev's economic plans*. Washington, D.C.: Joint Economic Committee.

TEAGUE, E. (1989). Embryos of people's power. *Report on the Soviet Union, 1,* 32, 1–4.

TENSON, A. (1980). Vain attempts to bolster the labor force on Soviet farms. *Radio Liberty Research,* no. 203/80.

Trehub, A. (1986). Social and economic rights in the Soviet Union: Work, health care, social security, and housing. *Radio Liberty Research Supplement,* no. 3/86.

TREHUB, A. (1988a). Joint party-government resolution on employment. *Radio Liberty Research,* no. 46/88.

TREHUB, A. (1988b). Poverty in the Soviet Union. *Radio Liberty Research,* no. 256/88.

TRETYAKOV, V. (1989). The Boris Yeltsin phenomenon. *Moscow News,* no. 16, 10.

VOZNESENSKAIA, Yu. (1984). Housework—Soviet women's second shift. *Radio Liberty Research,* no. 448/84.

YANOWITCH, M. (1985). *Work in the Soviet Union: Attitudes and issues.* Armonk, N. Y.: M.E. Sharpe.

ZEMTSOV, I. (1985). *The Private life of the Soviet elite.* New York: Crane, Russak.

ELEVEN
PROBLEMS IN THE POLITICAL PROCESS:
"Loyal Opposition," Interest Articulation, and Dissent

The creation of new state structures and the decline in importance of the Communist Party have resulted in new patterns of activity in many aspects of Soviet life, including policy making. We are observing an effort to establish a balance between the power of the new presidency on the one hand and the other governmental organs, including the legislative bodies, on the other. At the same time, a struggle to find the appropriate role for the bureaucracy is under way. And the functions of newly-emerging parties, in addition to the Communist Party, in developing policy alternatives has yet to be defined.

The reader should understand that a different pattern of policy making operated until the end of the 1980s, one that was superficially simple to understand because of the Soviet leadership's longstanding penchant for denying the existence of conflict and contention about policy aims and processes. This superficial approach masked a considerable complexity, however, as a variety of interests and forces sought to influence policy outcomes.

The objective of this chapter, then, is twofold: to examine the traditional policy process, which was focused on the central Party leadership but involved at least limited input from other sources; and to sketch the beginning of the emergence of the new forces in the political process that have emerged since the end of the 1980s.

How is policy made in the Soviet Union? This is much too broad a question to be answered with one general statement. But the question gets at the essence of the political process in the USSR, and every serious student of Soviet politics must grapple with it. During Stalin's heyday an easy answer to the policy-making question would have been "by Stalin himself," or "at most by Stalin, a few close advisers, and the Politburo." And during this period of the "personality cult," it is clear that Stalin did have enormous personal power and did make numerous decisions more or less on his own. But careful research has shown that even during Stalin's time certain specialists had some effect on policy making in that they provided the information that served as the basis for decisions. (Solomon, 1978, pp. 19–32).

No person since Stalin has held the monopoly of power that he exercised; there has been a wider circle of participants in policy making. And numerous studies have shown that specialists and experts have played salient roles in the adoption of particular policies. The extent of this specialist input varies with the policy at issue and with the political atmosphere at the time when the decision was being made. But some level of participation of this kind has been evident through most of the post-Stalin period.

How, then, can one generalize about Soviet policy making? It is important to distinguish the kind of policy at issue and the number of potential participants in the policy-making process. We would suggest, as a theory rather than as a verifiable statement of fact, two levels of participation: (1) issues on which decisions are made by a small group of persons at the top of the hierarchy plus a few advisers or representatives of strategic elites (such as the armed forces or the secret police), and (2) issues that are open to a wider circle of participants—at least at the stage at which policy alternatives are being recommended. The more important issues would obviously tend to fall into the first category. It is difficult to give an exhaustive list of such issues, but it would include the major features of the budget and the production plans, important personnel decisions, foreign-policy matters, and a scattering of issues across the remainder of the policy spectrum. Examples of the more open policy areas will be given later, but it is important to note that the wider participation mentioned has traditionally been limited largely to recommending policy alternatives and arguing for their adoption. If such recommendations were to be adopted, at least the tacit approval of the top leaders would be assumed. In the context of the new political structures created at the end of the 1980s, there may be reason to question this assumption, a matter to which the discussion will return at the end of the chapter.

The policy process followed in both of these cases is considered legitimate, that is, politics according to the Soviet "rules of the game." There have been, however, other efforts to influence Soviet politics, many of which the authorities considerd to be of questionable legality or downright illegal. These activities can be grouped under the general heading of "dissent" and will be discussed later in this chapter.

LOYAL OPPOSITION

We have put the term "loyal opposition" in quotation marks because the concept does not exist in Soviet politics. "Her Majesty's loyal opposition" is an institutionalized part of the British system, referring to the party out of power in a stable two-party system, and variations on this British institution exist in other countries in the West.

According to the theory on which the Soviet system was based, however, there was no need for more than one party because socialism created a unity of views and an absence of antagonistic interests. The traditions of Soviet politics have involved the prohibition not only of other parties, but also of factions within the Communist Party. Internal "opposition" was something to be repressed, whether it came from within the Party or not. Only at the end of the 1980s, when the Communist Party's monopoly on power was being challenged, did this article of faith begin to be questioned.

As shown in Chapter 7, the 1990s brought not only the elimination of the Communist Party's monopoly position, but also the rise of other parties and splits within the Communist Party itself. If this does not lead directly to the creation of an institutionalized loyal opposition, it is at least clear that some sharing of political power by the Communist Party is in the offing. And in some parts of the country, the prospects are good that the Party will have little role in governing.

But as these developments evolve, it is important to provide a context for understanding them by examining decision-making processes up to the late 1980s.

Decision making by members of the top leadership group has not been the exercise in monolithic unity the Soviet media would have us believe. Leaders disagree over policies, issues, and matters of personality. Most Western analysts have long accepted the "conflict model" of Soviet leadership politics, which stresses the presence of conflict over both personal power and over policy decisions. (Linden, 1966, pp. 1–9). Whether such conflicts involve contention between more-or-less permanent factions (for example, the "reformist" and "conservative" factions), as some kremlinologists contend, or whether the struggle is characterized by shifting alliances that are more fluid than permanent, as others hold, it is clear that the disputes are there.

Some disputes become serious enough that they take on the characteristics of a struggle for power in which one or more leaders lose their positions. These power struggles can have both a policy dimension and a personal dimension. Boris Yeltsin was removed from influential positions (head of the Moscow Party organization and candidate member of the Politburo) in 1987 because he too strenuously and too openly objected to the slowing pace of perestroika. His views on perestroika were combined with an intemperate personal attack on conservative Politburo member Yegor Ligachev. Yeltsin's behavior in this matter was unusual in that he "went public" with some aspects of the dispute with his colleagues. This no doubt contributed to his dismissal, since the traditional style of the Kremlin leadership has been to keep such controversies as much from the public eye as possible.

Most policy issues are settled more quietly, without personnel changes. Many involve disagreement and contention, and without doubt, there is some attempt to organize opinion and persuade the undecided. Such attempts do not constitute "loyal opposition" in the usual sense of that term. They do suggest, however, that the rules of the game allow some latitude for organized advocacy of policy positions at the top layers of the political elite.

If this assumption is sound, where do these disputes take place, who participates, and what are the policy matters at issue? When ultimate power resided in the CPSU, the top of the Party hierarchy was the focus of power. To the extent that the party continues to play a role, the following can be said. Since the Politburo is the top policy-making body of the Party, it is clear that most or all important policy issues receive a hearing there. Such issues are probably framed beforehand by smaller groups of Politburo members. At one time they may have been discussed in a preliminary way in the Secretariat meeting as a group. But the Secretariat seems to have lost this function. Indeed, by the end of the 1980s meetings of the Secretariat were seldom held. The responsible CC secretary and staff probably do preliminary work on the issue in question, and the secretary may, in addition, have discussed it with the General Secretary. It is this early initiative and exposure to issues that, among other advantages and powers, gave the secretaries, and particularly the General Secretary, their strategic position. The ability to present the issues, to set the agenda for Politburo meetings, and perhaps to come to the meetings with prepared draft resolutions on agenda matters provided the General Secretary considerable advantage over colleagues not on the Secretariat. Party chief Khrushchev tried to take further advantage of his Politburo (then called Presidium) colleagues by holding expanded Politburo meetings to which various experts and specialists were invited. Because Khrushchev's high-level antagonists were inhibited about speaking freely and criticizing the leader's policies in front of so large a group, Khrushchev was thereby able to gain even more leverage over the rest of the Politburo. This is seen as one of the factors that led to Khrushchev's ouster by his colleagues.

Some matters may also be taken up in the governmental hierarchy, perhaps going from a minister to the Chairman of the Council of Ministers, with discussion thereafter in the Presidium of the Council of Ministers. From there the Chairman might transfer the issue to the Politburo, of which the Chairman is also normally a member. The fact that policy proposals may emanate from two hierarchies, perhaps in drastically different forms, probably enhances the possibility of contention, which is to be expected among the powerful, ambitious persons at the top of a political system.

Disagreements can, and apparently do, take place at Politburo meetings.

Since these meetings receive only superficial coverage in the Soviet press, there is virtually never any public reference to such problems. But differences sometimes show up in the speeches made by the various leaders at public functions and in newspaper articles that appear in papers "representing" various factions. In the past such differences were rarely expressed in direct terms. The "esoteric communication" of policy differences was the stuff of kremlinology. As the Soviet press has become more open, these differences more frequently come to light.

The Central Committee may also take a hand in policy determination, although it is not likely that this happens often. The top fifteen to twenty leaders in the Politburo can easily see the dangers of having the four hundred or so members of the Central Committee come to the conclusion that *their* body should be the forum for regular policy formation. More likely, the short infrequent CC meetings are used to *inform* CC members of Politburo policy determinations, thus keeping the policy initiative clearly in the Politburo. The occasional use of the CC as a forum for the resolution of policy disputes cannot be entirely ruled out, however. Some publicity has been given to such occasions in the past and since there is minimal press coverage of CC meetings, no one but a CC member knows with any certainty what goes on in CC meetings.

The policy matters that the Politburo discusses are numerous and cut across all areas of Soviet life. Many involve economic matters, from relatively long term decisions about the next Five-Year Plan to short-term concerns about the size of the current grain harvest and whether to import more wheat from the West. In other areas, similar long- and short-term problems probably get put on the Politburo agenda: In foreign policy, what strategy to pursue to enhance Soviet influence in Western Europe, and how best to acquire necessary products through foreign trade; on the domestic front, how to deal with the rising juvenile crime rate, and what stand to take on nationalistic protests taking place in several Soviet republics. In all these areas and a multitude of others the Politburo probably reaches a consensus on the main lines of policy, and that consensus is then translated into policy execution through the Party or governmental apparatus, whose leaders are represented in the Politburo membership.

On some of these general policies, and particularly on the details of proposals designed to implement the policy decisions reached, there is a wider circle of potential participants. Occasionally it even appears that "outside" participants initiate proposals that lead to basic policy changes. A case in point is the whole complex of economic reforms instituted by the Gorbachev regime in the late 1980s. It is clear that a large number of economists and other specialists provided some of the concrete ideas on which parts of the reform were based. If the actual Politburo deliberations on policy matters are largely hidden from public view, a bit more can be said about examples of extra-Politburo participation in the policy process.

The foregoing suggests that the Politburo, when it reaches consensus, pretty much gets its way in policy formulation. Although that has traditionally been the case, a more complex picture of policy-making has emerged lately, as power and authority have partially shifted to the Soviets. The Party leadership has attempted to continue to play the role of policy initiator. But numerous examples from the short period of existence of the Congress of People's Deputies and the new Supreme Soviet show that these bodies do not always endorse the leadership's proposals. The new legislative bodies have become the forum for airing the views of a multiplicity of interests.

INTEREST ARTICULATION

Interest articulation has long been an important concept in political science. It has been used much more frequently in the analysis of Western political systems than in the analysis of the Soviet political system, but it is also useful in the latter context. Students of interest articulation examine the expression of varying points of view on political issues and the avenues by which they come to influence policy making. Certain people or organizations are seen as being voices for various points of view; they seek access to the policy-making process through their positions in the political hierarchy or their contacts in the hierarchy.

Even if the term "interest articulation" is not used, Western analysts of the Soviet system apply the concept in their analyses: Thus, that the Minister of Defense was brought into the Politburo in 1973 was widely, and no doubt rightly, interpreted as giving the military a more direct voice in policy making at the highest level. The same applies to the appointment of the Minister of Foreign Affairs to the Politburo and the elevation of the Chairman of the KGB from candidate to full-member status at the same time. Since then, the persons occupying these positions have often held either candidate or full Politburo membership, and this has meant that the bureaucracies they represent have a direct voice in the highest policy areas.

In this sense, every member of the Politburo can be said to represent one or more hierarchies or constituencies. One of the notable characteristics of the Politburo is its nationality composition. At all times, the overwhelming majority of members are from the three major Slavic nationalities, and this presumably assures that the predominant interests of these groups have a strong influence on policy making. But a small number of "representatives" from one or another of the minor Soviet nationalities have also gained full or candidate Politburo status. In this way, then, each member of the Politburo could be identified with at least one interest that he or she presumably represents.

But interest articulation is normally used to suggest a broader access to policy making than merely having a given interest represented among the top leadership. The methods and results of interest articulation can be demonstrated by means of case studies of policy making that show, to the extent possible, who participated, at what level and in what way, and how this participation can be related to the resulting policy. Assuming complete access to relevant information, one could theoretically do a case study of any and every example of Soviet policy making. As has already been emphasized, however, getting accurate information about policy making in the Soviet Union is a great problem. Therefore, we will have to content ourselves with the relatively small number of case studies and other analyses that have been made. In the analysis that follows we will employ the framework developed by American political scientist Gabriel Almond for analyzing interest-group activity. It posits five types of interest articulation: associational, individual, anomic, nonassociational, and institutional (Almond and Powell, 1978, pp. 170–174). It should be noted that Almond's interest articulation paradigm was not created with the Soviet Union in mind.

Does the attempt to examine interest articulation imply the examination of *interest-group* activity? It certainly would if we were discussing U.S. politics or that of another Western country. But there are considerable problems in applying the interest-group approach, which was developed first in the context of American politics, to the Soviet scene. When one thinks of interest-group activity in American politics, it is first and foremost the "associational" interest group that comes to mind. The associational type is "designed specifically to represent the goals of particular groups" and includes such bodies as "trade unions, ethnic associations, organizations for particular businesses or industries, associations organized by religious denominations, and associations organized to promote particular causes, such as civic reform or foreign policy" (Almond and Powell, 1978, p. 174). In the Soviet Union the possibility of establishing such groups has been severely restricted by the Party's traditional monopoly on political operations. In the case of formal organizations that might develop into associational groups (for example, the writers' union, the trade unions, the artists' union), the level of Party control has been such that they have not been allowed to speak in a unified, independent voice. Within the dissident movement of the 1960s and thereafter, perhaps the beginnings of genuine interest articulation could be found. But the authorities always moved, at some times with more vigor than at others, to break up and eliminate such groups. It has only been with the advent of the Gorbachev era that the development of organizations analogous to traditional interest groups of the West has seemed possible.

As the opportunities opened up by glasnost became apparent to the Soviet population, groups of various kinds came into being (Tolz, 1987). These were neither the secret or semisecret dissident organizations referred to earlier (although some members of these groups were former dissidents) nor the officially sanctioned organizations such as the *Komsomol* or the creative unions. Rather, they were aggregations of citizens interested in a wide range of issues, from particular concerns such as ecology, the interests of a single nationality, or enthusiasm about computers, to a broader agenda that might include a comprehensive program of political reform. The Soviet press, in discussing these organizations, often refers to them as "informal" (*neformal'nye*) or "grass roots" (*samodeiatel'nye*) associations.

In retrospect it seems natural that such groups would emerge from an atmosphere of glasnost, but their proliferation and the intensity of their concerns caught the Soviet authorities off guard. The quandary the leadership faces is that of preserving the enthusiasm for reform that such organizations promise while at the same time preventing the undesirable consequences that might result from giving these organizations too free a hand.

The thinking and actions of the leadership on this matter have gone through several stages. An early stage was that of the 19th Party Conference in 1988. One of the "Theses" adopted by the Party Central Committee prior to the Conference acknowledged that these new associations had sprung up under perestroika and seemed to encourage their development. It condemned attempts "to limit their independence and give them orders," asserted that "measures must be devised to enhance their role in the political process," stressed the need for a law to outline the legal basis of such organizations, and stated that only "one political criterion" needed to be followed: "any public activity that is conducted within the framework of the Constitution and is not at variance with the interests of the development of the Soviet socialist society deserves recognition" (*Izvestiia,* May 27, 1988, p. 2; *CDSP, 40,* 21, p. 9).

The "Resolution" dealing with this matter adopted at the Conference itself over a month later was somewhat less expansive in tone, expressing a more sober and reflective view of the potential problems such groups could cause. While it called the rise of the new associations a "positive phenomenon," it condemned "any activity directed at undermining the socialist foundations of society." And it asserted the centrality of the Party in further developments in this area: "For its part, the Party will aid in every possible way so that the social organizations can comprehend their place in society." And in this same passage it emphasized the "historically established one-party system in our country" (*Izvestiia,* July 5, 1988, p. 2).

But as the Party itself has declined in importance, this attempt to assert Party control is of little relevance. In the meantime, the number of informal groups, including those calling themselves political parties, has grown tremendously. A general law on groups and associations has long been promised, but reaching agreement on the provisions of such a law has been difficult.* Regulation of group activity is based on several legal acts controlling public demonstrations and parades, and the provision in Article 7 of the USSR Con-

---

*A proposed law "On Public Organizations" was published in the Soviet press for public discussion in June 1990. Under the provisions of this draft, some measure of state control over such organizations is envisaged by requiring that the bylaws of all organizations be approved and registered by the government. A public organization may be ordered by a court to be disbanded if it is found to have violated the law or the provisions of its bylaws (*Izvestiia,* June 4, 1990, p. 2).

stitution (as revised in 1990) that all parties and other organizations are to "operate within the framework of the Constitution and Soviet laws" and that organizations "having the aim of forcibly changing the Soviet constitutional system and the integrity of the socialist state, undermining its security, or kindling social, national, or religious strife are not permitted."

As the impulses toward the development of associational interest groups continue, other forces of interest articulation in the USSR have been observable for some time. Individual self-representation in the Soviet Union might involve submitting a complaint about treatment by a government official to the legal authorities or writing a letter to a newspaper. Although both kinds of action are taken, sometimes with success for the initiator, such activity can hardly be considered a major aspect of policy making.

Anomic interest groups include the temporary aggregations of people who join in a demonstration, riot, or similar activity. Spontaneous acts of this kind have been rare in the Soviet Union until recently, or at least they have been little known to the outside world. Since Gorbachev came to power, however, such events, and their coverage by the press, have become more common. The riots in December 1986 in Alma-Ata, the capital of the Kazakh Republic, after a Russian replaced a Kazakh as head of the republic's Party organization, brought the severity of ethnic tensions in the country to public consciousness. Continuing disturbances in the Armenian and Azerbaidzhan republics since the late 1980s demonstrate how difficult to solve some nationality problems are. And manifestations of seething ethnic problems in several other parts of the USSR suggest that anomic activity is becoming part of the Soviet political scene.

Nonassociational groups include ethnic, religious, regional, class, and status groups, whereas institutional groups may be found within armies, bureaucracies, parties, legislatures, and similar organizations that are established for purposes other than interest articulation. There is some evidence of interest articulation from both these sources in the Soviet Union, but whether it involves interest-*group* activity is open to question.

In the pre-Gorbachev era numbers of Soviet Jews favoring emigration and groups of Crimean Tatars pressing for the return of their homeland took on some of the characteristics of nonassociational interest groups. The same was true of several religious groups. More recently, ethnic group activity has taken on renewed importance, as was indicated earlier in this chapter. But nonassociational interest groups, by their nature, tend to have a sporadic, unorganized character. It is when they transform themselves into formal organizations (into associational groups, in the terminology of Almond and Powell) that they can have the greatest potential effect on policy. It is precisely such formal, autonomous organizations that make many Soviet leaders nervous.

Until recently, most of the concrete examples of interest articulation described by Western scholars could be categorized as institutional in nature. These involved individuals or collections of individuals who, on the basis of their occupations and the knowledge and access gained therefrom, were able to participate in the policy-making process in various ways. Some Western analysts doubted that these examples constituted interest *group* activity, and a debate developed in the literature about how they ought to be characterized (Griffiths, 1971, pp. 340–342; Odom, 1973, pp. 318–320). Whatever the appropriate terminology, however, the instances of documented institutional interest articulation are many and varied.

The activities of educational personnel in modifying Khrushchev's proposals for educational reform in 1958 were analyzed, as were the roles played by various groupings in effecting the repeal of large parts of this educational policy. The participation of economists in the adoption of the economic reform of 1965 and the role of scientists in reorganizing the Academy of Sciences were examined. A number of studies looked into the roles of Soviet jurists in policy-making, from their work on the reform of family law to their influence on the norms of civil, criminal, and penal legislation, to their resistance (partially successful) to the so-called antiparasite laws. Other studies examined Party *apparatchiki,* security police, the military, industrial managers, and writers as interest groups. Still other writings commented on the role of collective-farm chairmen in effecting the abolition of the machine-tractor stations, the work of a set of "noninstitutionalized ad hoc environmental lobbies" in achieving stricter pollution standards, and the efforts of nationality and religious groups in pressing their demands on policymakers (Schwartz and Keech, 1968, p. 840; Stewart, 1969, p. 29; Judy, 1971, p. 209; Graham, 1967, p. 133; Barry and Berman, 1971, pp. 321–330; Friedgut, 1976, p. 524; Kelley, 1976, p. 570).

Research in the 1980s showed that regional Party leaders who have presented their views at Party congresses have been reasonably successful in getting local projects added to national investment plans. Howard Biddulph concluded in studying such Party Congress lobbying that increased efforts by regional leaders in this area has helped to legitimize their role in the process (Biddulph, 1983, p. 28). And of course, it is not only through speeches at Party and government meetings that such regional interests are promoted. General and specialist newspapers and journals have long been vehicles for interest articulation of this kind. For example, a grandiose plan to divert water from Siberian rivers in order to cope with water shortages in Central Asia and Kazakhstan was debated in the press for years, with the Central Asian lobby vigorously leading the prodiversion side. And a broadly based, if not fully formalized, "West Siberian energy coalition" lobbied successfully through a variety of access points during the Brezhnev period (Chung, 1987).

What seemed to be common to all these studies of institutional group influence on the policy process was the acknowledgment, tacit or explicit, that the Party leadership set the ground rules for such participation. It allowed the discussions to be initiated, sought to control the limits of debate on issues, and signaled when such discussion should end. Moreover, it was assumed that the Party leadership retained ultimate veto power over any policy proposal, no matter how widely discussed.

Under these conditions, the Party had little to fear from policy recommendations from outside sources. When institutional interests began organizing into associational interest groups, however, which is what happened at the end of the 1980s, the picture changed drastically. At that point, the introduction of a significant measure of pluralism into the system began.

DISSENT

When people speak of the dissident movement in the Soviet Union, they have in mind a phenomenon originating almost entirely in the 1960s. A scattering of expressions of dissent before that time have been documented, but the movement achieved widespread recognition in the outside world only after the 1950s. Its rise at that time seems to have been related to the partial liberalization of the late 1950s and early 1960s and to frustrations growing out of the return to greater limitations on expression that followed Khrushchev's removal (Wishnevsky, 1984).

In the West much attention was given to dissident activity during the 1970s and 1980s, as the unequal struggle continued between a relatively small number of dissenters and a Soviet state apparatus determined to keep them under control. The dissident movement continued to exist into the later 1980s and 1990s. But because of the "Gorbachev phenomenon," which has allowed considerably more public airing of diverse views, including matters that were formerly beyond the scope of open discussion, the line between permitted interest articulation and the advocacy of causes that the regime considers inappropriate has become harder to ascertain or predict. This problem will be discussed further presently.

In large part the dissident movement had its origins in the field of artistic expression, especially that of literature. There are several reasons for this. Among the various ways of expressing dissenting views in the Soviet Union, the written word has often been the most important. So it is not surprising that some writers would be among the dissenters. But the link between literature and dissonant political views is more basic. Throughout most of Soviet history the authorities have gone to great lengths to control literary expression, and their efforts have been largely successful. Officially published fiction and poetry have been by and large supportive of the regime. If little inspired literature has been produced, at least it has not posed a significant political threat. But a relatively small number of writers and other artists have not conformed to the dictates of official policy. They have sought ways around it.

Literature and poetry can be vehicles for the subtle expression of political and social views. They have long provided an outlet for critical assessments of aspects of Soviet life that could not be criticized directly. A poem resounding with double meanings or a play about a foolish king portrayed in a way to remind the audience of a current or past Soviet leader might be published or performed, and its underlying significance would not be lost on the Soviet public. "Getting it past the censor" has a long tradition, going well back into prerevolutionary Russia. This is not to say that anything and everything can be published in this way, or that writers and poets have not been criticized for what they have published. The ambit of acceptable literary expression has been subject to periodic contraction and expansion throughout Soviet history. For instance, Solzhenitsyn's novella about prison-camp life, *One Day in the Life of Ivan Denisovich,* could be published in the relatively relaxed year of 1962. But aside from a few short pieces, nothing else by the author was published in the Soviet Union for over 25 years. And Solzhenitsyn was severely criticized for this writings, including *One Day,* after the period of reaction had set in later in the 1960s. Many other writers have been similarly censured when caught beyond the bounds of the permissible. The worst of times for Soviet citizens in general have also been the worst of times for Soviet writers: During the heyday of Stalinism a large number died in prison or labor camps or were shot.

Historically, Soviet leaders seem to have had an inordinate fear of the power of literature to serve as a catalyst in activating antiregime sentiment. Khrushchev was supposed to have said, regarding the Hungarian Revolution of 1956, which was ruthlessly suppressed by the Soviet Army: "If ten or so Hungarian writers had been shot at the right moment, the revolution would never have occurred" (Barber, 1974, p. 17). And as Solzhenitsyn himself has put it, "a great writer is, so to speak, a second government. That is why no regime anywhere has ever loved its great writers, only its minor ones" (Solzhenitsyn, 1967, p. 415).

Thus, although the writers have had a bit of latitude in expressing mild criticism of the system, they have had their frustrations as well. Fear of reprisal or discouragement at rejection of work submitted for publication has led many to write works in strict conformity with the dictates of official cultural policy. Others have taken to writing "for the desk drawer," that is, producing work that could not be published because of its political or social content and that might be shown at most to a few friends. Writing "for the drawer" had long been practiced in Russia, but only in the 1960s did some such writings make an emergence of sorts in the form of *samizdat.* The word *samizdat* means "self-published." It is an ironic usage, modeled after the acronym *gosizdat,* the term used in the name of official state publishing houses. *Samizdat* refers to underground publications, typescript and mimeographed copies of writings that circulate unofficially among various groups and individuals in the Soviet Union. Some of the contributors to *samizdat* are writers and artists, and a good bit of the early *samizdat* was poetry and fiction. But the bulk of *samizdat* has long since been nonliterary, consisting largely of articles, essays, and other statements about political, economic, social, and religious life in the USSR.

A watershed event in the relationship between dissent and literary expression was the Siniavskii-Daniel trial of February 1966. Andrei Siniavskii and Yuli Daniel were Soviet writers whose works were smuggled out of the Soviet Union and published abroad under pseudonyms. The writings gained a considerable following. Whether or not they were anti-Soviet in character (as the prosecution charged in the trial), they *were* beyond the bounds of approved Soviet literary expression and would not have been published within the Soviet Union. Siniavskii and Daniel were finally identified by the Soviet authorities as the authors and were tried under Article 70 of the RSFSR Criminal Code, "Anti-Soviet Agitation and Propaganda." Their celebrated trial and subsequent prison sentences stirred liberal sentiment both within the country and outside. Many Soviet dissidents date their participation in the movement from the time of the trial. The unofficial record of this trial, prepared by the young writer Alexander Ginzburg, became a leading *samizdat* document. When Ginzburg and others were tried and sentenced in 1968 for their dissident activities, their trial caused even more protest. It was shortly afterward that publication of the foremost *samizdat* journal, *The Chronicle of Current Events,* was begun, and the dissident movement was launched in earnest.

One of the marks of the dissident movement at its height was its great diversity. People dissent and protest for different reasons, and a great number of causes and interests have expressed their views through these means. If the movement was begun largely by those interested in freedom of expression and other democratic rights, it quickly spread to other disaffected groups, such as religious believers of various kinds, members of minority ethnic groups, women's organizations, free trade-unionists, and even extreme Russian nationalists, who promote a program of strong Russian chauvinism containing overtones of racism and anti-Semitism.

Even within these broad groupings diversity exists. Three who have long been well-known dissenters are the writer Aleksandr Solzhenitsyn, the late physicist Andrei Sakharov, and the historian Roy Medvedev. They have all been preoccupied with freedom of expression and intellectual freedom, among other legal and political rights. But their orientations are vastly different. Medvedev is a Marxian socialist who offers a "Leninist" critique of the Soviet system. He advocates a democratic socialism that, he asserts, could be created by eliminating the abuses of the system inherited from Stalin. Sakharov's views were more reformist than Marxist and closely paralleled those of Western European liberals and social democrats. Solzhenitsyn thoroughly rejects Marxism-Leninism but is not completely comfortable with Western-type democratic views either. He believes that Russia is not yet ready for democracy and favors a kind of benevolent authoritarianism during the period of development toward democracy.

These three have paid for their dissent in various ways. Solzhenitsyn was seized by Soviet authorities in 1974 and expelled from the country. He now lives in self-chosen isolation in Vermont. Sakharov was banished from Moscow in January 1980 under an administrative procedure of dubious legality. He was forced to live in Gorky, a city closed to foreigners 250 miles east of Moscow. Only in December 1986 was he permitted to return to the capital. Medvedev was allowed to stay in Moscow but his works could not be published and he was subjected to various forms of harassment by the authorities.

Under Gorbachev the treatment of these three individuals has changed greatly. Medvedev was elected to the Congress of People's Deputies and the Supreme Soviet in 1989 and thereafter his Party membership was restored. He has assumed a centrist position in support of Gorbachev and has rejected the need for a multiparty system. His long-banned indictment of the Stalin years, *Let History Judge,* was finally published in the Soviet Union. As indicated, Sakharov was allowed to return to Moscow under Gorbachev, and later was permitted to travel abroad. He was elected to the Congress of People's Deputies, and while he offered qualified support to the Gorbachev regime, he also criticized actions that he thought ran counter to democratization, such as the overconcentration of power in Gorbachev's hands. He became a leader of the opposition organization, the Inter-regional Group, and, right up to the end of his life in December 1989, he advocated the removal of the constitutional provision (Article 6) on the Communist Party's leading role.

While Medvedev and Sakharov were being restored to positions of honor, Soviet officialdom remained hostile to Solzhenitsyn. A campaign by intellectuals to secure his rehabilitation was openly opposed by Politburo member and top Party ideologist Vadim Medvedev (no relation to Roy) in 1988. In spite of this, however, several of Solzhenitsyn's long-banned works were published in the Soviet Union in the next months, the most important of which was the prison camp chronicle *Gulag Archipelago.* The Writers' Union in 1989 repealed its resolution of 20 years earlier that had expelled Solzhenitsyn. And offers to restore the exiled writer's citizenship have been openly made (Dunlop, 1989, p. 1; *Moscow News,* 1989, no. 28, p. 11). The cases of Medvedev, Sakharov, and Solzhenitsyn indicate how far the official response to dissent has evolved over time. But these men were among the best-known dissenters. It is necessary to look at the official response to dissent more broadly.

Official Responses to Dissent

The responses of the authorities to the dissident movement have varied over the years, both as to the means used to address it and with regard to the severity of the treatment of individual dissidents. Several of the more publicized trials, which, as was suggested, seemed to give the movement momentum in the early Brezhnev years, have been mentioned. Many other trials, which received far less publicity or none at all, sent scores of other dissidents to prison or labor camps. And a variety of measures of "extrajudicial repression" silenced many more. Many of the signers of early protest letters either lost their jobs or were threatened with dismissal. Anyone who persisted in dissent after a warning would at least face this prospect. A variety of forms of long-term harassment were also used, including repeated house searches, frequent summonses for questioning, and constant following and surveillance by secret-police operatives. Nor were the defense lawyers in the political trials immune from sanction for zealous advocacy on behalf of their clients. The Moscow lawyer Boris Zolotukhin was expelled from the Party and removed as head of a legal consultation office after his defense of Alexander Ginzburg. Other defense lawyers have been treated to like forms of harassment.

Samizdat publications have been subjected to varying levels of harassment over the years. The authorities seemed particularly intent on stamping out the more well known underground periodicals. Perhaps the most famous of these, the *Chronicle of Current Events,* was edited by a variety of individuals from its inception in 1968 until it ceased publishing in 1982.

For those whose actions appeared inappropriate for judicial repression, enforced incarceration in psychiatric hospitals was used. Several books by dissidents, including Vladimir Bukovsky's *To Build a Castle: My Life as a Dissenter* (1978), Leonid Plyushch's *History's Carnival: A Dissident's Autobiography* (1979), and Peter Grigorenko's *Memoirs* (1982) provide vivid accounts of experiences in psychiatric hospitals. This practice, which has analogues in prerevolutionary Russia, sometimes has been accompanied by the compulsory administration of drugs.

Attempts by the regime to suppress dissent gained momentum in the late 1970s and early 1980s. The crackdown at this time is thought to have been connected with the USSR's hosting of the Moscow Olympics in 1980 and perhaps with the low level of Western protest against the treatment of dissidents as a result of the distractions of Iran and Afghanistan. Whatever the explanation, the intensification of repression appears to have been part of a cyclical pattern of governmental response to dissent. This suggests both that the Soviet leadership has been attuned to world public opinion relative to its treatment of dissidents and that it has not found a completely successful policy for containing the dissident movement.

Another regime practice for dealing with troublesome dissidents has been banishment from the country. As was indicated, Solzhenitsyn was simply arrested and forcibly deported to the West in February 1974. A number of others, including the late Andrei Amalrik, Valerii Chalidze, Pavel Litvinov, and Zhores Medvedev, were "invited" to leave, with the clear implication that long prison sentences faced them if they refused. After departure they were deprived of Soviet citizenship. Alexander Ginzburg, Valentyn Moroz, Anatoly Shcharansky and others who were serving prison sentences for dissident activities were taken from prison and sent directly to the West (sometimes in exchange for convicted Soviet spies being held in the West). Such banishment has been successful in removing important dissidents from the scene and has helped weaken some of the protesting groups. In the same way, allowing some of the most vocal dissident Jews to emigrate has undoubtedly eased the pressure that the authorities feel from this area.

The Gorbachev regime's treatment of dissidents represents a considerable break with the past. In attempting to open up and broaden participation in Soviet society, Gorbachev has succeeded, to some extent, in neutralizing the dissident movement. A number of causes that were earlier pushed anonymously, through *samizdat* or other means, have been brought into the open under Gorbachev. The line between permissible political activity and impermissible dissent has become blurred. This suggests a greater willingness on the part of the authorities to allow questioning and protest of official actions. But it also indicates that a clear policy on these matters has not yet developed. Even under glasnost no form of political advocacy will be allowed to operate without limits. So the policy toward dissent that emerges will come over time, through trial and error. Indications of this are evident as the Gorbachev-era reforms continue to unfold.

Thus, many works by authors, Soviet and foreign, that were formerly banned (Solzhenitsyn, Boris Pasternak, George Orwell, and Vladimir Nabokov are among many names that could be mentioned) have been published in the USSR since the late 1980s. The same can be said of the works of numerous poets, playwrights, and filmmakers. But the doors have not been thrown open to the publishing of all dissident views. And free rein has not been given to *samizdat*. Sergei Girgoryants succeeded in publishing his unofficial magazine *Glasnost'* for a few months in 1987–88, but he was then arrested briefly and his printing equipment was confiscated. Without the equipment, or a lawyer willing to press for its return, his short period of unofficial publishing ended. Also, the leadership made it clear that cooperative publishing ventures would not be permitted under the general legislation that permitted private citizens to set up cooperative businesses.

The editors of official publications have a good deal of leeway in editorial decision making, but they are still closely watched by political officials, who are ready to interfere if they deem it necessary. Glasnost liberated many such publications from the torpor of the past and instilled a vitality in the official media that is without precedent in Soviet history. Even Gorbachev, however, has at times has called for restraint by the press, pointedly reminding editors that they remain under the control of the political authorities (see, for example, *The New York Times,* September 27, 1988, p. A4).

When the weekly *Argumenty i Fakty* published a poll in 1989 that did not list Gorbachev among the most popular members of the legislature, Gorbachev sought the resignation of the newspaper's editor. Not only did the editor not quit, but numerous journalists and editors called publicly for an end to official harassment of journalistic activity. Examples of this kind demonstrate that the authorities are no longer able to exercise the unquestioned power over the press that they once enjoyed. The principle of press freedom may not be firmly established in the Soviet system, but neither is the level of regime control of the past.

While emigration from the USSR has not become unrestricted, the number of Jews, Germans, Armenians and others allowed to leave has increased under Gorbachev in comparison with the years immediately preceding his ascent to power. The same applies to Soviet citizens seeking to leave the country on short visits: More are able to go but it remains very much a privilege allowed or denied by the regime rather than an individual right. The improper use of psychiatric incarceration,including its application to political dissidents, has been acknowledged in Soviet publications (*The New York Times,* November 22, 1988, p. A9), and although this practice appears to have diminished considerably under Gorbachev, reports of its use can still be found ("Overview," 1988, p. 5).

More changes in the direction of greater tolerance of diverse views are evident. Virtually all jamming of foreign radio broadcasts ceased in the late 1980s, and numerous people identified as political prisoners were released in the same period. Many former dissidents have been praised in the open press, including some of those convicted in show trials. The trials themselves have been condemned in some publications as part of the negative phenomena of the Brezhnev "years of stagnation." And a revision of some of the laws applied in dissident trials has been adopted.

Still, all in all, the picture of Gorbachev's management of dissent is a mixed one. Glasnost and attendant policies have opened up the political system to an unprecedented airing of views. The further implications of these developments, as well as the announcement by the regime of other pending reforms, promise even more liberal treatment of what have long been known in Russian as *inakomysliashchie* (those who think differently). But the record so far indicates that liberalization and concession have only stimulated demands for further reform. The Soviet leaders face a genuine revolution of rising expectations from a large number of formerly suppressed or alienated interests. Many of these propose agendas that go well beyond what the current leadership appears prepared to tolerate. It is one thing to allow a frank portrayal, in a book or film, of the terror of the Stalin period. It is another to permit the analysis and criticism of the establishment of Soviet power, including the "holiest of holies," Lenin. It is one thing to make concessions in republican constitutions with regard to the official language of that republic. It is another to allow independence for one or more of the republics.

Where, then, will Gorbachev's policy toward dissent finally come to rest? Our conclusion on this matter is similar to those in Chapters 6 and 7 concerning the likely limits on the reform of political structures and operations. All of Gorbachev's actions suggest that while he is prepared to allow a wider latitude for expression of nonconformist views, he will only very reluctantly permit the airing of views likely to challenge Moscow's ultimate monopoly on political power. The record shows, however, that partial measures are likely to be met with demands that would dilute this monopoly, and sooner or later he or his successors will have to counter these demands with sufficient force to neutralize them or face the course that seems inevitably to lie ahead: independence for those parts of the Soviet federation that choose it, and a pluralistic, non-Communist-dominated system for the heartland that remains.

REFERENCES

ALMOND, G., and POWELL, G. (1978). *Comparative politics*. Boston: Little, Brown.

BARBER, N. (1974). *Seven days of freedom: The Hungarian uprising, 1956*. Briarcliff Manor, N.Y.: Stein & Day.

BARRY, D., and Berman, H. (1971). The jurists. In H. Gordon Skilling and Franklyn Griffiths, eds., *Interest groups in Soviet politics*. Princeton, N. J.: Princeton University Press.

BIDDULPH, H.L. (1983). Local interest articulation at CPSU congresses. *World Politics, 36,* 28.

CHUNG, HAN-KU. (1987). *Interest representation in Soviet politics: A case study of a West Siberian energy coalition*. Boulder, Colo.: Westview.

DUNLOP, J. (1989). Solzhenitsyn begins to emerge from the political void. *Report on the USSR, 1,* 36, 1.

FRIEDGUT, T.H. (1976). Interests and groups in Soviet policy-making: The MTS reforms. *Soviet Studies, 28,* 524.

GRAHAM, L. (1967). Reorganization of the USSR Academy of Sciences. In Peter H. Juviler and Henry W. Morton, eds., *Soviet policy making*. New York: Holt, Rinehart & Winston.

GRIFFITHS, F. (1971). A Tendency analysis of Soviet policy making. In H. Gordon Skilling and Franklyn Griffiths, eds., *Interest groups in Soviet politics*. Princeton, N. J.: Princeton University Press.

HOUGH, J.F. (1972). The Soviet system: Petrification or pluralism? *Problems of Communism, 12,* no. 2, 31.

JUDY, R. (1971). The economists. In H. Gordon Skilling and Franklyn Griffiths, eds., *Interest groups in Soviet politics*. Princeton, N. J.: Princeton University Press.

KELLEY, D.R. (1976). Environmental policy-making in the USSR: The role of industrial and environmental interest groups. *Soviet Studies, 28,* 570.

LINDEN, C. (1966). *Khrushchev and the Soviet leadership 1957–1964*. Baltimore: Johns Hopkins University Press.

ODOM, W. (1973). The Party connection. *Problems of Communism, 22,* no. 6, 12.

OVERVIEW–1 July–30 September 1988. (1988). *The Bulletin* (North Atlantic Assembly), 48.

SCHWARTZ, J., and Keech, W. (1968). Group influence and the policy process in the Soviet Union. *The American Political Science Review, 62,* 840.

SOLOMON, P. (1978). *Soviet criminologists and criminal policy: Specialists in policy making*. New York: Columbia University Press.

SOLZHENITSYN, A. (1967). *The First Circle*. New York: Harper & Row.

STEWART, P. (1969). Soviet interest groups and the policy process: The repeal of production education. *World Politics, 22,* 29.

TOLZ, V. (1987). Informal groups in the USSR. *Radio Liberty Research,* no. 220/87.

WISHNEVSKY, J. (1984). The fall of Khrushchev and the birth of the human rights movement in the Soviet Union. *Radio Liberty Research,* no. 382/84.

TWELVE
SOCIAL PROBLEMS I:
Nationality and Religion

In this chapter and the next two we will consider several of the major social issues facing the USSR after nearly seven decades of Soviet rule. The Soviet Union is composed of a multiplicity of nationalities and religious groups. Many of them were inherited from a Russian Empire that had conquered diverse peoples. In the United States and Canada everyone but Native Americans immigrated from their ancestral lands, leaving behind visible reminders of their ethnic heritages. The people of the USSR, in contrast, are very likely to live on the land their forebears occupied for centuries and to come into daily contact with reminders of their religious and cultural heritages. One need only look at the mosques of Uzbekistan or the churches and monasteries of Armenia to understand how these traditions could not possibly be ignored or forgotten by the people living there. Out of the clash between these traditions and the Soviet loyalty expected by the central leadership in Moscow grow many problems, both practical and ideological.

Fervent ethnic loyalty and religious belief were supposed to disappear under socialism. According to Marxism-Leninism, the proletarian movement would develop international consciousness, overcoming national differences and antagonisms. Religion, an "opiate" that served to keep the exploited classes submissive, would also disappear once changes in the economic system made it unnecessary. It is now clear that neither ethnic antagonism nor reli-

237

gious conviction were eliminated in the more than seventy years of Soviet history.

In spite of apparently genuine efforts by Lenin to curb Great Russian chauvinism, the dominance of ethnic Russians has continued to be one of the basic facts of life in the Soviet Union and forms the basis for much of the rebellion we have currently been witnessing there. This is a tribute to the remarkable persistence of national identity among the non-Russian ethnic groups. Until recently, the Soviet authorities felt that they had even stronger ideological justification for dealing harshly with religious denominations than with ethnic nationalism. Their persistently negative policy toward religion, however, failed to stamp out either religious belief or practice—though it did drive much of it underground. With the reform and, most notably, glasnost, there has been a revival of religious observances that the Soviet authorities have been impelled to both acknowledge and—to a remarkable extent given past history—sanction.

THE NATIONALITY PROBLEM

Recently, the nationalities question in the Soviet Union has acquired exceptional salience. The Party realizes that the decisions made in connection with this problem are enormously important for the fate of the reform and the future of our country. ("The Nationalities Policy of the Party under Contemporary Conditions," *Pravda,* August 17, 1989, p. 1)

Igor Shafarevich, the well-known Soviet mathematician and dissident, wrote over fifteen years ago: "Of all the urgent problems that have accumulated in our life, the most painful seems to be that concerning relations between the various nationalities in the USSR. No other question arouses such explosions of resentment, malice, and pain—neither material inequality, nor lack of spiritual freedom, nor even the persecution of religion" (Shafarevich, 1975, p. 88). At the time, in the heyday of Brezhnev, this depiction of the situation was scarcely the orthodox one, however accurate it proved to be in the long run.

Until recently, Soviet authorities claimed that the nationality question was solved, that "national antagonisms have been done away with" and that "national equality is now an integral part of Soviet life" (Gafurov, 1976, p. 45). Needless to say, such claims are no longer being made. The rise of separatism in the Baltic republics and ethnic violence in places like Armenia, Azerbaidzhan, and Georgia have created a situation in which it is clear that such claims are blatantly untrue. For the Soviet leadership, nationalities policy has become largely a matter of (at best) managing unrest or (at worst) trying to ward off disaster.

Marxist-Leninist ideology teaches that the true internationalism of the doctrine eliminates national antagonisms and, until recently, Soviet official-dom treated this belief as though it were an accomplished fact. In fact, in the revised Party Program adopted a year after Gorbachev came to power, one finds this statement: "The nationalities question, inherited from the past, has been successfully resolved in the Soviet Union" (*Izvestiia,* March 7, 1986, p. 5). By the time of the Nineteenth Party Conference in 1988, the leadership was talking about "negative phenomena that accumulated over the decades" and "had been neglected and ignored for a long time" not having been "properly assessed by the Party." Quite accurately, the resolution continued: "Perestroika, democratization and glasnost have revealed these phenomena" (*Documents and Materials,* 1988, p. 147).

The position paper quoted at the beginning of this section is even more frank about the importance of the problem, especially with regard to its potential for subverting the reform. By their own admission (*The Washington Post,* January 4, 1990, p. A28), Gorbachev and his associates did not initially anticipate the potential of various of their reform measures for aggravating the nationalities problem. To some extent, they may have been blinded by the rhetoric with which they had been bombarded all their lives, even though evidence of deep ethnic antagonism must have been available to them.

Long before the reform began, frank conversations with Soviet citizens often contradicted the media's glowing tributes to ethnic toleration. When a Russian girl said to the authors several years ago, "We dislike the Georgians and the Georgians dislike us," she was voicing a variation on a theme we heard numerous times in our travels through the USSR. And the release of both greater information and pent-up ethnic resentments during the reform period has brought the magnitude and implications of the problem to the attention of both the Soviet people and the world.

Soviet Ethnic Diversity

What lies behind the strong ethnic sentiments in the USSR? Answering this question involves an analysis of the dimensions of the problem and the main lines of government policy. With more than 100 different nationalities, the Soviet Union is truly a multinational state. Some 130 distinct languages are recognized, and the equality of all languages and national groups is proclaimed. National diversity, however, is not actually as great as these numbers imply. Several of the smallest groups number only in the hundreds.[1]

[1]The last four censuses in the USSR were done in 1959, 1970, 1979, and 1989. Much less information was made public from the 1979 census than was the case with regard to the previous two. In addition, the 1989 figures that have been released to date are preliminary. In some cases, therefore, we have had to rely on 1970 data. The 1970 census data included in this discussion are from *Itogi Vsesoiuznoi Perepisi Naseleniia 1970 Goda* (Moscow: "Statistika," 1973). Unless otherwise indicated, the 1979 census data are from "The All Union Census of 1979 in the USSR: A Collection of Reports Prepared Before and After the Census by the Staff of RL Research" (*Radio Liberty Research Bulletin,* September 1980). The 1989 data are from Sheehy (1989b). In all cases, the most recent data available at the time of writing have been used in the text.

The number of nationalities has tended to drop over time, with smaller groups being assimilated into larger ones. It is the larger groups that constitute the core of the nationality problem in the USSR. According to the 1979 census, there were 23 ethnic groups in the country with over a million members. These included the 15 nationalities for whom the union republics are named, as well as the Tatars, Germans, Jews, Chuvash, People of Dagestan, Bashkirs, Mordvins, and Poles. Of the last 8, only the Tatars had over 2 million members. Our discussion will be limited to the Tatars, the 15 titular nationalities of the union republics, and the Jews, who constitute a particularly interesting population category. Together, these 17 nationalities account for more than 90 percent of the total Soviet population.

These 17 nationalities vary substantially in relative size and rate of growth. (See Table 12.1.) The generalizations one can make are strong and clear: By and large, the ethnic groups that can be classified as European are growing slowly (that is, well under the national average), whereas the Asian and Caucasian nationalities, particularly the Moslem groups, are growing at a rate far above the national average. This means that population growth is much more rapid in the southern parts of the USSR, namely Central Asia and the Caucasus region.

The biggest ethnic group is the Russians. In 1989 the 145 million Russians comprised 50.8 percent of the Soviet population. This figure was down from 52.4 percent in 1978, and it seems virtually certain that by the year 2000 the Russians will no longer constitute a majority in the USSR. This development is not only symbolic but also points to a time when the Russians will find it increasingly difficult to maintain their dominant position among the other, rapidly growing groups within the country. One of the ways in which this dominance has been maintained is through the settling of large numbers of Russians in non-Russian areas of the USSR. Although over 81 percent of Russians lived in the Russian Republic in 1989, this was a drop of 1.3 percent in only a decade. Earlier there had been a trend among Russians to move to the borderlands. This is not the explanation for the drop, though, since this trend seemed to reverse during the 1980s, with ethnic Russians leaving the southern republics in particular. What seems more important at this point in time is a very low birthrate among ethnic Russians and, perhaps, the tendency of some people who had previously claimed Russian nationality for practical reasons, to feel freer to claim their true nationality as a response to the current surge of national assertiveness. (Sheehy, 1989b, p. 5).

After the Russians come the Ukrainians, with over 44 million people in 1989. This second major Soviet nationality is similar to the Russians in language and cultural traditions, but there has long been considerable hostility between them, because of Russian efforts at domination. Over 72 percent of the Ukrainians live in the Ukrainian Republic. To indicate something of the size and significance of this republic, it is about one and one-half times as large as Poland, which is the largest East European country. The Ukraine con-

TABLE 12.1 Major Soviet Nationalities, 1959, 1970, and 1979 (In Descending Order of Size in 1979)

	NUMBER OF PERSONS OF GIVEN NATIONALITY (IN THOUSANDS)			Number of Persons of Given Nationality in thousands) Preliminary 1989	PERCENTAGE INCREASE OR DECREASE			RANK BY 1970–1979 GROWTH
	1959	1970	1979		1959–70	1970–79	% Increase or Decrease	
Total population of the USSR	208,827	241,720	262,085	285,689	15.8	8.4	9.0	
Russians	114,114	129,015	137,397	145,072	13.1	6.5	5.6	12
Ukrainians	37,253	40,753	42,347	44,136	9.4	3.9	4.2	14
Uzbeks	6,015	9,195	12,456	16,686	52.9	35.5	34.0	2
Byelorussians	7,913	9,052	9,463	10,030	14.4	4.5	6.0	13
Kazaks	3,622	5,299	6,556	8,138	46.3	23.7	24.1	6
Tatars	4,968	5,931	6,317	—	19.4	6.5	—	11
Azeris	2,940	4,380	5,477	6,791	49.0	25.0	24.0	5
Armenians	2,787	3,559	4,151	4,627	27.7	16.6	11.5	7
Georgians	2,692	3,245	3,571	3,983	20.5	10.0	11.6	8
Moldavians	2,214	2,698	2,968	3,355	21.9	10.0	13.0	9
Tajiks	1,397	2,136	2,898	4,217	52.9	35.7	45.5	1
Lithuanians	2,326	2,665	2,851	3,068	14.6	7.0	7.6	10
Turkmen	1,002	1,525	2,028	2,718	52.2	33.0	34.0	3
Kirghiz	969	1,452	1,906	2,531	49.8	31.3	32.8	4
Jews	2,263	2,151	1,811	—	-5.2	-15.8	—	17
Latvians	1,400	1,430	1,439	1,459	2.1	0.6	1.4	16
Estonians	980	1,007	1,020	1,027	1.8	1.3	0.7	15

SOURCE: Based on Sheehy, 1979, pp. 10–11; and Sheehy, 1989b, p. 2.

tains much of the USSR's best farm land and many of its important industrial centers.

The other nationalities are considerably smaller than these two giant ethnic groups. The third major Slavic nationality, the Byelorussians, has over 10 million people. In recent years, however, it has been surpassed as the third largest nationality by the Uzbeks, who numbered more than 16 million in 1989. The Uzbeks, along with the four other major nationalities of Central Asia, the Kazakhs, the Tadzhiks, the Turkmen, and the Kirghiz, amount to some 35 million people—about 12 percent of the Soviet population. What is significant about this is that the Central Asian population has increased over 250 percent since 1959, a growth rate not approached by any other major Soviet nationality or related group of nationalities. Except for the Tadzhiks, who are a Persian people, all these nationalities share a common Turkic stock. More important, all five have a common Islamic religious heritage.

Another major Moslem ethnic group is the Azerbaidzhanis (also called Azeris), who live mainly in the Azerbaidzhan SSR in the Caucasus Mountains between the Black and Caspian seas. Their growth has been equally impressive: over 200 percent between the 1959 and 1989 censuses. The Tatars also have a strong Islamic religious tradition. Although there are over six million Tatars in the USSR,[2] they do not qualify for union-republic status because their centers of population are located in the central parts of the country rather than on the periphery. Over one and one-half million Tatars live in the Tatar ASSR, whose capital is the city of Kazan on the Volga River; most of the remaining members of this ethnic group reside in other parts of the RSFSR.

Although classified together with other Tatars for census purposes, the Crimean Tatars are distinct in terms of language and culture. This group, which numbers some 300,000, lived for centuries in the Crimea. For a time, the Soviet authorities accorded their region autonomous republic status. But in 1944, amid accusations of collaboration with the Nazis, the whole Crimean Tatar population was deported and resettled in other parts of the USSR. The Crimean Tatar autonomous republic was dissolved. Since the 1950s this group has persisted in petitioning and demonstrating both for the return of their homeland and for restoration of their autonomy. Although they were absolved of collaboration with the Nazis in 1967 and have achieved other minor concessions from the regime, including the settlement of several thousand of their number in the Crimea, their major goal has been rejected: in 1988 a special government commission turned down their demand for restoration of autonomous republic status (Fisher, 1978; Carerre d'Encausse, 1979, pp. 191–197; Sheehy, 1988).

The two other major nationalities of the Caucasus, in addition to the

---

[2]Unlike the previous figures, the data on the Tatars had to be taken from the 1979 census, because 1989 figures were not yet available when this was written. The same applies to the data on the Crimean Tatars.

Azerbaidzhanis, are the Armenians and the Georgians. These two groups have some similarities to the Moslem nationalities in culture and way of life, but they have long Christian traditions. Their recent population growth rate has been above average but not so high as that of the major Moslem ethnic groups.

Just under five and a half million people are members of the major Baltic nationalities: the Lithuanians, Latvians, and Estonians. Their growth rate has been uneven, higher in traditionally Catholic Lithuania, lower in traditionally Protestant Latvia and Estonia. A large proportion of the recent growth of these union republics is a result of in-migration by other Soviet citizens, mostly Russians. Lithuania, Latvia, and Estonia are among the newest union republics in the country, having been involuntarily annexed by the Soviet Union in 1940 under a pact with Nazi Germany.[3] The Moldavian SSR also was established in 1940. It was formed from the Moldavian Autonomous Republic and Bessarabia, which was annexed by the USSR from Romania in that year. Whether Moldavians constitute a distinct ethnic group from Romanians is a disputed matter. The Soviet authorities claim they do, but many others assert that they are basically ethnic Romanians.

The Soviet Jews are in a different situation from the other major nationality groups in several ways. Judaism, which is considered a religion by most people in the West, is officially designated a nationality in the Soviet Union. But it is a nationality that does not have a recognized territory worthy of the name, as do most of the other major nationalities. It is true that there is the Jewish Autonomous Province, a territory surrounding the town of Birobidzhan in far eastern Russia near the Chinese border. This province was created in 1928, but relatively few Jews settled there. In 1970 only 11,000 Jews lived there, 6.6 percent of the province's population. This is thought to be the lowest percentage of a titular nationality within its own territory (Katz, 1975, p. 365). Most Soviet Jews live in the RSFSR or the Ukraine, with smaller numbers in the other union republics, predominantly in urban areas.

Another distinguishing feature of Soviet Jews is that they are the only major nationality whose numbers have declined in recent years.[4] To some degree, this decline was noticeable before the large Jewish emigration to the West began in the early 1970s; thus, emigration is only a contributing factor, not the whole story. It is also important to note that in census taking, documentary proof of nationality is not required. This has permitted many Jews to identify themselves as being of other nationalities, hoping it will help them escape discrimination. Thus, some estimates put the actual number of Soviet Jews at over 2.5 million, rather than the 1.8 million listed in the 1979 census.

During the decade of the 1970s Soviet authorities allowed substantial

[3]This forced annexation is the legal basis for the current Baltic succession movement.

[4]Two large nationalities not discussed here who also lost population, both from 1959 to 1970 and from 1970 to 1979, are the Mordvins and the Poles. See Ann Sheehy, "The National Composition of the Population of the USSR According to the Census of 1979," *Radio Liberty Research*, no. 123/80, March 27, 1980, pp. 10–11.

numbers of Jews, Germans, and Armenians to leave the country. Of these, the Jews constituted the largest number. The size of Jewish emigration varied considerably from year to year, with the number of "refuseniks" (those denied permission to leave) apparently related to the state of Soviet-American relations. Some 240,000 Soviet Jews emigrated from the USSR during the 1970s, with 51,000 leaving during 1979 alone. But after that year emigration was abruptly curbed. It became virtually nonexistent in the mid–1980s, reflecting the generally poor relationship between Moscow and Washington, but rose again under Gorbachev as the atmosphere improved.

Nationality Policy and Russian Dominance

Preservation of the cultural and ethnic traditions of the various Soviet nationalities has, to a limited extent, been traditionally encouraged. The same is true of their languages. Neither effort, however, has met the demands of nationalist dissidents who fear the gradual loss of their ethnic identity through Russification. In a further effort to defuse the discontent of many of the more demanding ethnic groups, considerable effort has been made over the years to diminish the economic differences among the major nationalities. But here also, there have been charges that too little has been done and that the Russians are giving priority to retaining their primacy.

To some extent these accusations have a basis in fact. All efforts to placate the ethnic minorities have been compromised by the fear on the part of the central authorities that too many concessions could endanger the cohesion of the USSR. The growth of overt ethnic unrest during the Gorbachev years has made it clear that fears about the cohesion of the USSR were justified.

Soviet policy has never embraced the concept of the melting pot. In fact, the boundaries of Soviet political subdivisions are drawn on a largely ethnic basis. What are the chances that the various peoples of the USSR will eventually melt into some kind of Soviet nationality? At this point in history, they look rather slim—at least in the forseeable future. Soviet leaders have occasionally talked about such a development, a *sliyanie* (merging) of the various nationalities, which would accompany the achievement of a mature communist society. It is clear, however, that there is presently far too little popular identification with the Soviet state to overcome the strong ethnic loyalties of its inhabitants. In fact, this concept of *sliyanie* has been so politically unpopular that since Khrushchev Soviet leaders have avoided reference to it, and Gorbachev has explicitly rejected it. Rather he has tended to refer to the cultural "flourishing" (*rastsvet*) of the Soviet nationalities (Nahaylo, 1989).

A more realistic goal in the short term might be a process identified as *sblizhenie,* which implies the drawing together of nationalities and the achievement of socioeconomic equality while preserving national uniqueness (Jones and Grupp, 1984). This implies some sort of confedcration, rather than the closer ties of a federation. The current leadership seems ready to accept some variation on the theme of confederation as the most achievable solution to their current problems, because of the overwhelming evidence that ethnic loyalty is as strong as or stronger than their attachment to the Soviet Union.

Ethnic identification is formalized in Soviet law by more than territorial boundaries. Each Soviet citizen over age 16 has to carry an internal passport that lists nationality. Because this document must frequently be shown to authorities for identification or on special occasions, such as for registration when one moves to a new city, the nationality of every Soviet citizen is readily ascertainable.

Linguistic differences are also a crucial factor. For all practical purposes, Russian is the national language of the Soviet Union. Virtually all of the 145 million Russians as well as over 16 million other Soviet citizens consider Russian their native tongue. Another 61 million state it to be their second language. Thus, at least 82 percent of the Soviet population speak Russian fluently. Soviet authorities cite these figures to demonstrate the significance of Russian in binding together the union. They also usually cite Lenin on the impermissibility of forcing minorities to study Russian. But in spite of this caution, there is considerable pressure to learn Russian and to use it in preference to one's native language. Many governmental and economic activities are conducted almost exclusively in Russian, even in the non-Russian republics. The same is true of the Soviet armed forces and much of higher education. Currently there is considerable dispute over whether Russian should be legally declared the means of all-union and interethnic communication.

The message, although nowhere spelled out in so many words, has always been clear: If you want to get anywhere in life, learn Russian. Thus, being equipped with knowledge of Russian can be considered a positive achievement for any person of a minority nationality. Those Soviet citizens who complain about the process of linguistic Russification do not object to the acquisition of the Russian language *per se*. Rather, they fear its destructive effects on the native languages and cultures of nearly half of the Soviet population. In fact, the issue of what should be the primary publically used language in the non-Russian republics has been high on the agendas of the various popular fronts and separatist groups which have arisen in the reform period.

In spite of the pressure to learn Russian, many have tried—both officially and unofficially—to preserve and to use the other native languages (Dailey, 1989). According to the 1989 census, in 14 of the 15 major nationality groups at least 80 percent speak the nationality language as their native tongue.[5] For all but the Ukrainians, the figure is above 90 percent. The bilingualism that has been created among non-Russians is generally strongest among European nationalities, (for example, for 54.7 percent of Byelorussians and 64.4 percent of Latvians, Russian is a second language) and weaker in

---

[5]The exception is the Byelorussians for whom the figure is 70.9 percent.

Central Asia[6] and the Caucasus (the corresponding figures are 27.8 percent for the Turkmen and 33.1 percent for the Georgians). It is fair to say, however, that linguistic Russification of most of the major nationalities in the country is increasing from year to year (Karklins, 1980).[7] For obvious reasons, the nationality that has the lowest percentage of persons who freely speak a second language of the USSR is the Russians. Only about 3 percent of Russians claim this ability.

In addition to language, one of the obvious ways in which Russians influence other ethnic groups is through their presence in the various republics. (See Table 12.2.) As of 1979, the Russians constituted the largest nationality group in 2 of the 15 republics, their own and the Kazakh SSR.[8] As of 1989, they constituted over 10 percent of the population in 8 of the 15 union republics and over 30 percent in 3 (excluding the RSFSR). But an even more important generalization has to do with the dynamics of population developments in the republics, which is also demonstrated in Table 12.2: In each of the European republics the proportion of Russians has grown as of the 1989 census; in each of the Asian and Transcaucasian republics the Russian proportion has dropped.

In the European part of the USSR, where large numbers of Russians have moved to the non-Russian republics, the magnitude of this in-migration has been a source of ethnic tension. In fact, it has been a major contributor to the upsurge of nationalism in Latvia and Estonia. Many Russians have also moved to the other republics. More Russians were living in each of the five Central Asian republics in 1979 than in 1970, but in each case these increases were more than offset by the high birthrates of the native population. Moreover, since the 1979 census, Russians and other Slavs have been leaving the southern non-Slav republics in large numbers, in what one analyst calls an "imperial retreat" (Sheehy, 1987b; Sheehy, 1989b).

Of course, political control is not indicated by the mere number of Russians in a given republic, but there are other ways to measure the disproportionate influence of Russians. Although Russians constitute little more than 50 percent of the population, more than 60 percent of all Party members are Russians. As of early 1990, 8 of the 13 Secretaries of the CC CPSU (62 percent) were Russian, as were 9 of the 12 full members of the Politburo (75 percent). In all, 18, or 72 percent, of the top 25 members of the Party hierarchy

----

[6]A major exception is the Kazakhs of Central Asia among whom 60.4 claim a good knowledge of Russian as a second language. Aside from the Latvians, this is the highest percentage in any of the union republics.

[7]There are exceptions. In the period between the 1979 and 1989 censuses there was a decline among Byelorussians, Uzbeks, Tajiks, and Lithuanians. Much of this may have been a function of the padding of the earlier figures, rather than an actual drop (Sheehy, 1989b).

[8]By the late 1980s the Kazakhs may have come to outnumber the Russian population in Kazakhstan, although official census figures do not yet show this. See Sheehy, 1987a.

TABLE 12.2 Percentage of Titular Nationality's Population and Russian Population in the 15 Union Republics of the USSR, 1959, 1970, 1979, and 1989

	TITULAR NATIONALITY				RUSSIANS				
	1959	1970	1979	1979 Rank	1959	1970	1979	1989	1979 Rank
RSFSR	83.3	82.8	82.6	1	83.3	82.8	82.6	81.3	1
Ukraine	76.8	74.9	73.6	1	16.9	19.4	21.1	21.9	2
Byelorussia	81.1	81.0	79.4	1	8.2	10.4	11.9	13.1	2
Uzbekistan	62.1	65.5	68.7	1	13.5	12.5	10.8	8.3	2
Kazakstan	30.0	32.6	36.0	2	42.7	42.4	40.8	37.6	1
Tajikistan	53.1	56.2	58.8	1	13.3	11.9	10.4	7.6	3
Turkmenistan	60.9	65.6	68.4	1	17.3	14.5	12.6	9.5	2
Kirghizia	40.5	43.8	47.9	1	30.2	29.2	25.9	21.4	2
Azerbaidzhan	67.5	73.8	78.1	1	13.6	10.0	7.9*	5.6	2
Armenia	88.0	88.6	89.7	1	3.2	2.7	2.3	1.6	3
Georgia	64.3	66.8	68.8	1	10.1	8.5	7.4	6.2	3
Lithuania	79.3	80.1	80.0	1	8.5	8.6	8.9	9.3	2
Latvia	62.0	56.8	53.7	1	26.6	29.8	32.8	33.8	2
Estonia	74.6	68.2	64.7	1	20.1	24.7	27.9	30.3	2
Moldavia	65.4	64.6	63.9	1	10.2	11.6	12.8	12.9	3

*The Armenian population of Azerbaidzhan in 1979 was virtually identical with that of the Russian population.

SOURCE: Based on Sheehy, 1980, p. 15; and Sheehy, 1989b.

(that is, full or candidate Politburo members or CC Secretaries) were Russians.[9]

In the union republics other than the RSFSR, the dominance of Russians is not as evident as it is at the all-union level. The Party first secretary has usually been a member of the native ethnic group. But the second secretary has usually been a member of one of the three major Slavic nationalities—most often a Russian. The same is true with regard to the head of the republican KGB or security police. By contrast, members of non-Slavic nationality groups are not often represented in the political hierarchies of republics other than their own. But if these critical positions have commonly been controlled by Russians or other Slavs, the native nationalities have held on to all of the other posts of significance that they could. This has frequently given rise to complaints from Moscow of "localism," meaning that the leaders of the indigenous nationalities overemphasize local interests to the detriment of national interests. Currently, Moscow seems to be trying to appoint first secretaries of the titular nationality of the republic who have no links to the previous political leadership in that republic. Often they have been people who, prior to their appointment, were working in Moscow or outside the country in diplomatic posts (Mann, 1989).

Regional Economic Differences

Tensions between political leaders with a local perspective and those with a national perspective have economic as well as cultural and political dimensions. Soviet economic development, despite current problems, can be fairly said to have been very impressive since 1917. This is evident in all regions of the country. But because the USSR has always been composed of territories and national groups at different stages of economic development, this growth did not result in the equalization of economic status for all groups. In spite of the perennial efforts of the central authorities to close the development gap among the republics, the picture is a mixed one, with the gap apparently widening on some measures relevant to regional wealth.

What this has meant is considerable economic variation from region to region with obvious effects on the lifestyles of the residents. The overall picture of regional differences is quite clear: The European republics (with the exception of Moldavia) consistently rank higher than the Asian and Transcaucasian republics on most of the measures of wealth, including per capita income produced, per capita money in savings accounts, and per capita trade

---

[9]If one considers the members of the three major Slavic nationalities, the Russians, Ukrainians, and Byelorussians, in these bodies, the figures are also impressive. These three groups accounted for 72.2 percent of the Soviet population in 1979. But as of early 1990, they comprised 92 percent of full Politburo members, 92 percent of CC Secretaries, and 88 percent of the top 25 members of the Party hierarchy.

turnover. The Baltic republics are the most affluent, followed by the other European republics (including the RSFSR, but excluding Moldavia), then Armenia and Georgia, with the Moslem republics at the bottom.

To the extent that level of education, opportunity for higher education, and the number of trained scientific workers are related to present and future economic well-being, the Central Asians will continue to lag behind their fellow Soviet citizens. On all of these measures, the Central Asian ethnic groups (with the Moldavians) rank near the bottom. Having said this, it is important to note that there is another perspective: The growth rates in per capita income in the Central Asian republics, even though below the national average, have been higher than those in most developed and developing countries for the same period. These people, however, are not likely to judge their economic status against the rate of development of foreign countries, about which they know little. Rather, they compare themselves to their fellow Soviet citizens. Consequently, the failure to achieve economic equality (coupled, of course, with the antagonisms growing out of Russian political and cultural domination) seems to be at the root of the intensified national feeling that has led to unrest and even violence.

Thus, one major demand of many of the nationalist movements has been for greater control over local land and resources. A step in this direction was taken when the Supreme Soviet voted to grant the three Baltic republics greater economic autonomy beginning January 1, 1990 (*The Washington Post*, November 28, 1989, p. A27). This law gave these republics more control over their financial systems, banks, factories, and other state-run enterprises. Moscow retained control over the armed forces stationed there, as well as oil and gas lines and "other facilities that have national importance."

There is, however, a limit to how far the current leadership is willing to go. Threats of secession by political groups in the Baltic republics have evoked a response that has economic dimensions. To a great extent during the Soviet period, the economies of the 15 republics have become intertwined. Thus, one of the main arguments used by Gorbachev and others is that the secession of any of the republics would constitute an economic disaster for the republic involved. Obviously, the secession of many of the currently restive republics could also have a serious impact on the economic health of the Soviet Union—and, not incidently, on the prospects for success of the economic reform.

Nationality Problems in the Gorbachev Period

In December 1986 the head of the Kazakhstan Party organization, a Kazakh named Kunaev, was dismissed after nearly 25 years in office. His replacement, a Russian named Gennadi Kolbin, who had no previous connection with the Kazakh Republic, was brought in by Moscow to clean up the corruption and inefficiency of the Kunaev years.[10] Kunaev had been a full member of the Politburo and a crony of Brezhnev. But more important for the nationalistic incident that took place, he was a Kazakh. In Alma-Ata, the capital of the republic, his fall touched off rioting by thousands of Kazakhs, which had to be put down by force (Brown, 1987). The event signaled a nationalistic awakening in an ethnic group previously considered to be quite docile and compliant (Olcott, 1987, p. 249). The Gorbachev regime seemed to have been caught off guard by the intensity of the reaction to firing Kunaev. Thereafter, while it treated some of the rioters harshly, it tried to make some concessions to Kazakh sensitivities, such as increasing the importance of the Kazakh language in the republic (Brown, 1988).

This was only the first in a series of major nationalist disruptions. Gorbachev's idea that glasnost and democratization are important in furthering the economic development of the USSR has encouraged many, including ethnic groups, to press their political interests. And glasnost has made information about nationalist protests increasingly available, thus changing people's ideas about what was possible and whether it would be tolerated. On the other hand, democratization has given nationalist groups a forum, but one which they do not always consider adequate to further their need for self-rule.

Much of the ethnic enmity of groups in the USSR can be classified into two major categories. First, there is a great deal of resentment, even hostility, toward the Russians. This tends to be expressed in defiance directed toward Moscow and attempts to adopt local policies making life more difficult for Russians living in non-Russian republics.[11] Also, with over one hundred nationalities in the country, some having lived in close proximity to each other for centuries, there are many long-standing problems between non-Russian groups. Thus, the second category consists of clashes between minority groups, mostly on the periphery of the Soviet Union. These have usually been between majority groups in neighboring political subdivisions or between majority and minority groups within a political subdivision.

The second category includes one of the most publicized and violent ethnic disturbances of the 1980s. This was the one between the Armenians and

[10]At the time of his appointment, Kolbin was the only Party leader at the republic level who was not a member of the titular ethnic group of that republic (Teague, 1986). Subsequently, a Kazakh was named second Party secretary, thus reversing the traditional arrangement. In 1989 Kolbin was promoted to chair the USSR People's Control Committee. He was replaced by a Kazakh. The new second secretary was a Slav (possibly Ukrainian) who had worked in Kazakhstan since finishing his higher education (Mann, 1989).

[11]For example, in 1989 the Estonian parliament passed a law that gave teeth to the republic constitutional provision making Estonian the official language in Estonia. Everyone whose work involved communication with the public was required to learn Estonian within four years. This was clearly directed at Russians living in Estonia, who had not previously had to learn Estonian in order to work and live there (*The Washington Post,* January 19, 1989, pp. A35, A38; Dailey, 1989).

the Azerbaidzhanis, which brought the region known as Nagorno-Karabakh to world attention.[12] It started as a dispute between two minority groups, but with the passage of time and the central leadership's largely ineffectual attempts at a solution, it increasingly involved hostility toward Moscow and a rise in separatist sentiment. The dispute began when the Armenians demanded control over Nagorno-Karabakh, a territory within the borders of the Azerbaidzhan SSR, three-quarters of whose population was Armenian.

When the Bolsheviks established power in Armenia after the Revolution, Nagorno-Karabakh was given to Armenia, along with the region known as Nakhichevan, which is located on the southwestern border of Armenia, where the latter borders on Iran and Turkey. The neighboring Turks, who are Moslems and traditional enemies of the Armenians, objected to largely Christian Armenia enhancing its territory at the expense of Moslem Azerbaidzhan. This opposition persuaded the Soviet leadership to change its mind, and the granting of these territories to Armenia was never finalized. In 1921 Nakhichevan became part of the Azerbaidzhan Republic. It has no common border with Azerbaidzhan, but its population is largely Azerbaidzhani. In 1924 it became the Nakhichevan Autonomous Republic (of the Azerbaidzhan SSR). In the same year Nagorno-Karabakh became an autonomous province within the Azerbaidzhan Republic.

Although the Armenians resented having the Nakhichevan territory put under the jurisdiction of Azerbaidzhan, their major complaint has been about Nagorno-Karabakh, because of the large Armenian population there. They have contended for a number of years that the Azerbaidzhani leadership has discriminated against Nagorno-Karabakh in numerous ways. When glasnost gave them an opening to express this resentment more forcefully, large numbers of Armenians took to the streets. Starting in October 1987, a series of demonstrations took place, first in the Armenian capital of Erevan and then in Nagorno-Karabakh, demanding that the territory be incorporated into the Armenian Republic. This led to retaliation from the Azerbaidzhanis, most notably rioting in the Azerbaidzhan city of Sumgait in February 1988; 32 people, mostly Armenians, were reported killed. Thereafter, a number of bloody clashes, some involving loss of life, took place in the region, parts of which spent periods under martial law.

The Armenian Republic legislature voted in June 1988 to incorporate Nagorno-Karabakh into the Armenian SSR. The central government rejected this proposal, fearing both the likely reaction of the Azerbaidzhanis and the precedent they would set for other dissatisfied ethnic enclaves in the country. The upheavals continued, accompanied by the displacement of hundreds of thousands of Armenians and Azerbaidzhanis fleeing from their homes to take

---

[12]The following is based largely on contemporary accounts in such publications as *The New York Times, The Washington Post, CDSP,* and *Radio Liberty Research.* A series in the latter by Elizabeth Fuller, written in 1987 and 1988, was particularly useful. Background information is based in part on Walker, 1980, especially pp. 372–373.

refuge in safer locations (Reese, 1988). Then the magnitude of the problem was compounded by the devastating earthquake in Armenia in December 1988, and continuing ethnic enmity complicated efforts to deal with the aftermath of this terrible natural disaster.

Moscow has maintained tenuous control in the region, mostly through the use of armed force. For about a year Nagorno-Karabakh was even put under the direct administration of the central authorities. The Party chiefs of the two republics were fired and replaced in May 1988, along with a number of other less important local leaders. Greater investment in the economy of Nagorno-Karabakh was also promised. But a permanent political solution to the underlying problems has proven elusive.[13]

The ethnic restiveness of the Baltic republics has so far taken a less violent form. But it has been no less important in the evolution of Soviet nationality problems. The enmity of the Lithuanians, Latvians, and Estonians has been directed principally at the authorities in Moscow, who are seen as an occupying power in the lands. This matter was previously discussed in Chapter 5 in connection with the constitutional amendments of 1988. It should be noted, however, that while the focus of that immediate controversy was certain constitutional provisions, the underlying reasons for the problem were essentially ethnic and territorial in nature. The Estonians, Latvians, and Lithuanians had been airing grievances in public for months when the constitutional issues came to the fore. A high point in public demonstrations in these republics came in August 1988, on the anniversary of the 1939 Nazi-Soviet pact, which allowed the USSR to take over the independent states of Estonia, Latvia, and Lithuania. What spilled out in the airing of views at this time was a number of complaints, not only about the Soviet version of history, which held that the Baltic republics willingly joined the USSR,[14] but also about the treatment of Baltic peoples and about the administration of their territories since they were annexed to the Soviet Union.

The most extreme demands were for secession from the USSR. These led to the Lithuanian secession crisis in 1990. The more moderate ones emphasized a number of particular measures aimed at increasing republican autonomy and, thus, reducing the level of Moscow's control. One of the more emotional aspects of the region's complaints against Moscow was the number of Russians living in these areas, which has caused the indigenous ethnic groups to resent and fear continuing Russification. Charges began to be made that "migrants" (Russians) were responsible for shortages and other ills in the region. And demands that the "migrants" be resettled in Russia were also voiced (*Moscow News,* 1988, no. 51, p. 4).

[13]In this connection, Soviet sources report that during the years 1987 to 1988, more than 300 civilians and 18 soldiers were killed in ethnic clashes, primarily in the Caucasus and Central Asia. During the same period, about 5,000 civilians and 800 soldiers were wounded (*The Washington Post,* January 7, 1990, p. A20).

[14]Subsequently, the Soviet legislature conceded the illegal nature of the annexation.

The problems exemplifed by these two disputes are not isolated instances. The fact is that the nationality problem has become a highly significant one for the USSR and the future of the reform. Almost every major ethnic group has come forward to proclaim some kind of ethnic grievance. The organizational form known as a "popular front," a broad-based coalition of persons united by ethnic concerns, was created first in the Baltic republics and thereafter appeared in other parts of the country.

This movement toward unrest and the assertion of ethnic demands has also included the Russians. Glasnost provided the opportunity for Russian nationalism to come out into the open. This phenomenon embraces a range of concerns, from simple patriotism and the desire to preserve Russian historical monuments to more extreme views, such as the restoration of totalitarian controls over society and a neofascist program that includes enmity toward everything and everyone not Russian, but particularly toward Jews. The best-known organization endorsing extremist policies is *Pamyat'* (Memory), a mass organization said to have sympathizers in important places in the government and Party hierarchy, including the KGB (*Russian Nationalism Today,* 1988). Important institutional responses to this development include the formation of the Russian Caucus in the Supreme Soviet, the establishment of a separate RSFSR Communist Party organization, and the creation of a Russian Academy of Science (*The Washington Post,* April 29, 1990, D2).

Ethnic Problems and the Reform

Perhaps no issue shows the mixed results of glasnost as much as that of nationality. As Tatiana Zaslavskaia, a well-known Soviet scholar, has put it: "The first steps of democratization, expressed in the broadening of glasnost and individual rights and freedoms, engendered not only democratic but also chauvinistic, nationalistic, antisocialist and even fascist groups. Their organizers encouraged people to use force, and they have, causing enormous moral harm to perestroika. The development of such phenomena is akin to letting a dangerous genie out of the bottle" (*Izvestiia,* December 24, 1988, p. 3).

Now that the genie is out, what can the authorities do? One thing is clear: They can no longer ignore the nationality issue. It has the potential to blow apart the union. As a result, it has risen to the top of the agenda of the reform leadership, rivaled only by economic issues. For example, the Nineteenth Party Conference in 1988 gave ethnic issues central attention. One of the seven resolutions adopted at the Conference's conclusion, "On Inter-Nationality Relations," provided an assessment of past Party mistakes and a promise to address the problem realistically (*CDSP,* 40, no. 37, 1988, p. 11). This was followed in 1989 by a CC plenum on interethnic relations and a completely new Party "platform" statement on nationalities policy (quoted previously).

Solving the problem will not be easy. Since many of the issues are cross-cutting in their effect, a concession or gain for one nationality becomes a slight or loss for another. Thus, any change in the present status of Nagorno-Karabakh will antagonize the Azerbaidzhanis, as well as encourage rebellion among others similarly situated. On the other hand, the status quo is unacceptable to the Armenians and they are not about to stop trying to change it. On another level, the richer republics believe that their affluence is being too drastically affected by policies that redistribute resources to poorer (and by implication, less deserving) parts of the USSR. They want this practice altered, a proposal opposed by the poorer republics (*CDSP,* 40, no. 45, 1988, p. 4). The most that can be said on the positive side is that the subject is now being addressed realistically and in the open. This can be seen as the first step toward finding a lasting solution. What that solution might be, however, is far from clear, given the enormous complexity and potential for disaster that characterize this policy problem.

RELIGION

The nationality problem is complicated by the issue of religion (Bociurkiw, 1985). Thus, for example, manifestations of Lithuanian nationalism and separatism have been associated with Roman Catholicism; a major factor common to the indigenous peoples of Soviet Central Asia is their Islamic heritage; restrictions on Soviet Jews have historically included strict constraints on the practice of the Jewish religion. At the same time, Soviet religious policy can be regarded as a distinct matter on which the leadership has pursued a number of objectives over the years (Bociurkiw, 1986).

Until recently, official attitudes toward religion were based on "the historical memory, the ideological legacy, and the authoritarian aspirations of the regime" (Bociurkiw, 1973, p. 39). Briefly stated, these three factors involve: (1) the close connection of the Russian Orthodox Church with tsarist autocracy and its early opposition to the Bolsheviks; (2) the Marxist antagonism toward religion, and the brand of Soviet atheism that grew out of this ideological precept; and (3) the regime's effort to suppress or neutralize any competing focus of loyalty that could not be easily integrated into the political system.

Out of the interplay of these three elements, Soviet policy toward religion was formed. The general direction of official policy was negative, but it vacillated between extreme hostility and reluctant toleration. In part, this inconsistency had to do with differences among Soviet officials about the proper stance toward religion. The "fundamentalists" favored an intense antireligious campaign against all groups in order to rid the country of religion as soon as possible. The "pragmatists" advocated a more selective approach, favoring religious groups that would cooperate with the regime and punishing those that would not (Bociurkiw, 1973, p. 41). This attempt to "sovietize" religion was aimed at legitimizing the regime in the eyes of Soviet believers.

Both these tendencies were evident in the official policy toward religion, and to some extent, they competed for ascendancy. Thus, there was an ebb and flow in the zealousness with which antireligious policies were pursued. A wholesale offensive against religion during the 1930s was followed by a policy of accommodation during World War II in the interests of unifying the country. The Khrushchev years saw a resumption of antireligious activities, marked by the closing of many churches and the initiation of systematic "scientific atheistic" indoctrination. In the post-Khrushchev period this campaign subsided somewhat, and during the early Gorbachev period an attempt at accommodation, particularly with the Russian Orthodox Church, was made. Finally, in 1989 there was a major breakthrough to a dramatically more tolerant policy.

The hostility toward religion of successive Soviet regimes inevitably caused religious groups to compromise and accommodate in order to survive. Reluctantly, most organized religions in the Soviet Union accepted this. A common practice of Soviet authorities, for instance, was interviewing compliant spokespersons of various faiths and airing their pro-regime views for both internal and foreign consumption. Thus, the Moslem mufti who stated that "the crowning glory of nature is man, and the crowning glory of all laws existing on earth is the USSR Constitution" had thereby earned some concessions from the authorities in his and his coreligionists' efforts to pursue their faith (Kurodoev, 1984, p. 9). And the 1986 message of the compliant Holy Synod of the Russian Orthodox Church was that the Soviet system "creates real conditions for Christians and other religions and non-religious people to cooperate for the good of their society" (Walker, 1986, p. 216).

During this period of repression, the major legal document defining the place of churches in the Soviet system was a 1929 resolution of the All-Russian Executive Committee (significantly amended in 1975), which mandated the registration of religious associations (Pospielovsky, 1984, vol. 2, p. 493). Registration indicated official recognition by the state. Unregistered groups were considered illegal and were subjected to varying degrees of harassment by the government. The largest registered group, the Russian Orthodox Church, reportedly had at least thirty million adherents. The Orthodox hierarchy studiously avoided clashes with state authority. The Patriarch and other leaders gave sermons supporting political and social policies of the state and rebutted charges from abroad of government suppression of religion. They silenced, suspended, or transferred parish priests who were too outspoken. When these measures did not succeed, the state stepped in to silence priests through harassment, arrest, and prison sentences.

The Russian Orthodox Church has the largest number of adherents in the country, but there are other important denominations. Determining the number of believers of any religious group is difficult, since complete official figures have not been available.[15] Some partial data published in 1987 (*CDSP,*

---

[15] And even if they were, given the treatment of religion throughout the Soviet period, their validity would be seriously in doubt.

39, no. 50, 1987, p. 12) indicate that as of 1986 there were at least 15,036 religious societies in the USSR. The religions with more than 350 recognized congregations each were (in descending order) the Russian Orthodox Church, the Catholic Church, Islam, Judaism, the Evangelical Christian Baptists, the Pentecostalists, the Seventh Day Adventists and the Jehovah's Witnesses. It was also officially estimated that 10 to 20 percent of the Soviet population were believers. According to the same data, the most important function (measured by number of services) performed by these religious societies was the holding of funerals (1,179,051). After that came baptisms (774,747)[16] and weddings (79,840).

A conservative estimate of the number of Russian Orthodox believers is 30 million. This is a substantial number—half again as many as the number of Party members in the USSR. But some put the total even higher. Based on the size of Sunday offerings, spokespersons for the Orthodox Church assert that 30 to 50 million people regularly attend services. Even less conservative estimates go as high as 100 million (Ellis, 1986, pp. 173–177). The Georgian Orthodox Church and the Armenian Church have maintained close relations with Russian Orthodoxy. Both are more closely linked, however, with the ethnic self-consciousness of their respective nationalities. It is estimated that two-thirds of the 3 million Georgians and 60 percent of the 3.5 million Armenians are actively religious.

The number of Moslems is also hard to estimate. One source puts the figure at about fifty million (*The Washington Post,* September 25, 1988, p. C1). If this is true, it means that the Soviet Union contains one of the world's largest Moslem communities, with numbers greater than the Moslem population of any of the Arab nations of the Middle East. The Moslems are concentrated in Soviet Central Asia and the Caucasus region, areas that border on both Iran and Afghanistan. This is important because "Islam is more than a religious belief: it is a way of life, a culture, a means of national expression" (*Radio Liberty Research,* 1976, no. 58, p. 1). Recent years have seen a resurgence of religious commitment, especially among Moslem youth, which has been fueled, in part, by Iranian messianism and religious propaganda from Afghanistan.

Roman Catholics are said to number about 4 million, a large percentage of whom are in Lithuania (Ellis, 1986, p. 176). Lutherans, mostly living in Estonia and Latvia, are estimated at 850,000. The Baptists are divided into three groups, the members of the All-union Council of Evangelical Christians and Baptists, the Pentecostalists, and the so-called "Initsiativniki." All the religious groups discussed up to this point have been among those recognized

---

[16]One of the surprises of 1989 was the admission by both Gorbachev and his wife, Raisa, that they had been baptized as children. They did not, however, baptize their daughter, explaining that "times have changed" (*The Washington Post,* July 6, 1989, p. A22). Gorbachev's mother has always been an openly practicing Christian.

by the government. The split among the Baptists, however, has involved a distinction between "legal" and "illegal" groups. The first group, the "registered Baptists," has been officially recognized by the state authorities. They number about 500,000 and are concentrated in a few areas in the RSFSR, the Ukraine, and several other republics. Estimates on the other two groups go as high as 600,000.

The Pentecostalists have a history in Russia that dates back to the beginning of this century. As of 1986 they were officially reported to have 843 congregations (*CDSP*, 39, no. 39, 1987, p. 12). It is said that some 30,000 Pentecostalists have tried to emigrate from the USSR to obtain religious freedom, but few have been allowed to leave. A visible symbol of this desire was the so-called "Siberian Seven," members of two families of Pentecostalists from Siberia who staged a sit-in at the U.S. Embassy in Moscow in June 1978 in hopes of persuading the Soviet government to allow them to emigrate. They remained in the U.S. Embassy for nearly five years, after which the Soviet authorities allowed them to leave the country.

The "Initsiativniki" came into existence in the early 1960s when an "Action Group" (*Initsiativnaia Gruppa*) of dissident Baptists led a withdrawal from the registered Baptist Church. At that time, the Khrushchev regime was taking a particularly hard line against religion, harassing those who engaged in such practices as "unhealthy missionary tendencies" and illegal baptisms of children. The Initsiativniki continued to be an illegal group and were subject to much state persecution. The split is said to have brought about reform within the registered Baptist movement, resulting in greater democracy in the conduct of church affairs (Simon, 1974, pp. 154–175).

The plight of religious Jews in the Soviet Union has gotten a great deal of coverage in the Western media. As of 1986 there were a little over 100 congregations, as compared to a reported 450 as recently as 1956. The number of practicing Jews in the country is, according to official sources, about 60,000 (out of a population of 1.8 million in 1979), but Jewish sources estimate the number to be higher. There are said to be some 50,000 Buddhists, who live in eastern Siberia, and an undetermined number of members of congregations of Seventh-Day Adventists and Methodists, as well as adherents of the Reformed Church and other denominations. In addition, there have been a number of other unregistered sects besides the two Baptist ones mentioned, including the Jehovah's Witnesses, Ukrainian Catholics, True Orthodox Christians, and others (Lucey, 1983, p. 300).

The Council on Religious Affairs, a state agency, has had jurisdiction over all church matters. Until recently, it developed policies that it imposed on the leaders of recognized churches, such as the Russian Orthodox Church, in exchange for privileges denied to unrecognized religious groups. For the latter, there was a variety of types of harassment, including the prosecution of church leaders who organized religious instruction for children. A sign of the increased tolerance for religious belief that has characterized the Gorbachev years came in 1988. A scientific-consultative commission was set up under the Council on Religious Affairs. Significantly, it included representatives of religious organizations in its membership. Soon after it was established, the members were asked to review a proposed Law on Freedom of Conscience and to submit suggestions and amendments.

In spite of treatment that was often very harsh, religion did not die out in the Soviet Union. In fact, it seems that a religious revival has taken place in recent years (Goble, 1990). In addition to the little old ladies in black shawls, the typical churchgoer described in countless travelers' reports, more young people are attending services. Increasing numbers of intellectuals and other highly educated Soviet citizens have acknowledged religious beliefs. Reports of known Party members and soldiers in uniform worshipping in church have been published. Thus, it seems that many Soviet citizens, from all walks of life, have practiced a double life of public conformity to regime values and private religious piety. *New York Times* correspondent David Shipler wrote of a young Komsomol activist, both of whose parents were Party members, who visited a church, lit a candle, and prayed every day after school. Her response to the question of how she could reconcile the seeming contradictions between her political participation and her practice of religion: "'It's easy,' she said brightly. 'At the komsomol committee, when they ask if I believe in God, I say no'" (Shipler, 1983, p. 266).

Why does religion seem to be growing in importance for large numbers of Soviet citizens? No single factor explains its revival, but some important contributors are (1) the pageantry of religious ritual as compared with the drabness of civil ceremonies; (2) a search for new values by many Soviet citizens; (3) the feeling that practicing a religion constitutes a kind of antigovernment protest which stops short of overt dissent;[17] and (4) an effort to find a link between the present and a rich cultural heritage that has strong religious content.

As in many other areas of Soviet life, the attitude of the government during the early Gorbachev period was somewhat more tolerant and realistic than that of its predecessors. Numerous small concessions were made—such as the broadcast of Orthodox Christmas and Easter services over Soviet television (*The New York Times,* April 11, 1988, p. A3; *Report on the USSR, 1, 3,* 29). In 1988 considerable attention was given by the state to the one-thousandth anniversary of the adoption of Christianity on Russian soil. This included a meeting of Gorbachev and the leaders of the Russian Orthodox Church—an event almost unprecedented in Soviet history. At this meeting Gorbachev indicated that new legislation on religion was being prepared that would be based on "the Leninist principles regarding religion" (Antic, 1988a,

---

[17]This should diminish in importance if the new policies on religious freedom and toleration continue.

p. 3).[18] Shortly thereafter, the government repealed several decrees that limited religious activities. For example, bell ringing and charitable work were permitted again, as was religious education (Antic, 1990a; Antic, 1990b). Such concessions, however, fell far short of permitting completely free religious worship.

More sweeping in its potential impact is the Law on Freedom of Conscience introduced for discussion in 1988. In its draft form, it included several key points: (1) churches would have the right to exist as legal entities; (2) religious education would be permitted; (3) churches could register without interference or approval by political authorities; and (4) an alternative to military service would be permitted for believers with pacifist convictions (Beeching, 1989; Antic, 1989b).

Much more dramatic than legislative initiatives was the visit of Gorbachev to the Vatican in 1989. Initiated by the Soviet leadership, this was the first time that any leader of the Soviet Union had met with the Pope (Antic, 1989c; *The Washington Post,* December 12, 1989, A1). A number of important policy changes were associated with this historic event. First, the two leaders agreed to establish diplomatic relations. Second, Gorbachev formally renounced the militant atheism that has characterized the Soviet Union since its inception, proclaiming the right of all believers to practice their religions. Third, the Ukrainian Catholic Church, brutally suppressed by Stalin in 1946, was legalized. Combined with the new Law on Freedom of Conscience, these policies have dramatically changed the legal status of religion in the Soviet Union. Whether their practical implementation will mark as rapid and decisive a change remains to be seen.

This flexibility on the part of the Gorbachev regime emphasizes a willingness to permit religious activities that aid (or at least are seen as not detracting from) the goals of the Soviet system. It also signals a recognition that, if the current policy of seeking greater integration with the rest of Europe is to be successful, religious freedom is a prerequisite. Compared with the explosion of nationality strife and the manifold shortcomings of the economy, the persistence of religion seems to be a problem that the authorities can accomodate rather easily. Moreover, religion is a matter that is seen as important by large numbers of Soviet citizens. Past regime policies could not help but have had negative effects on citizen satisfaction and feelings of support for the regime. Seen in this light, the ever-pragmatic Gorbachev regime's attempt to find a more flexible accommodation with the country's religious communities appears consistent with its other goals. The major remaining question is whether this new freedom of religious expression will moderate or exacerbate the strife currently associated with the nationality problem, since these two are so closely associated.

---

[18]As a sign of increased tolerance by the state, the Soviet press reported that 1,610 religious associations were registered in 1988, compared with 104 the previous year (*Moscow News,* 1989, no. 15, p. 8).

REFERENCES

ANTIC, O. (1988a). Gorbachev meets with leaders of the Russian Orthodox Church. *Radio Liberty Research,* no. 218/88.

ANTIC, O. (1988b). The charity program and the role of the churches. *Radio Liberty Research,* no. 516/88.

ANTIC, O. (1988c). Policy toward unofficial religious groups under Gorbachev. *Radio Liberty Research,* no. 138/88.

ANTIC, O. (1989a). Draft Law on Freedom of Conscience. *Report on the USSR, 1,* 13, 17–18.

ANTIC, O. (1989b). Gorbachev's road to Rome. *Report on the USSR, 1,* 49, 8–9.

ANTIC, O. (1990a). The church in 1989. *Report on the USSR, 2,* 4, 15–16.

ANTIC, O. (1990b). Sunday schools in the Soviet Union. *Report on the USSR, 2,* 13, 11–13.

BEECHING, M. (1989). Kharchev discusses draft law on religious freedom. *Report on the USSR, 1,* 32, 3.

BOCIURKIW, B. (1973). The shaping of Soviet religious policy. *Problems of Communism, 22,* 3, 37–51.

BOCIURKIW, B. (1985). Institutional religion and nationality in the Soviet Union. In S.E. Wimbush, ed., *Soviet nationalities in strategic perspective,* 181–206. London: Croom Helm.

BOCIURKIW, B. (1986). The formulation of religious policy in the Soviet Union. *Journal of Church and State, 28,* 3, 423–438.

BOITER, A. (1976). Religious samizdat in 1975. *Radio Liberty Research,* no. 40/76.

BROWN, B. (1987). The fall of Kunaev. *Radio Liberty Research,* no. 7/87.

BROWN, B. (1988). Kazakhstan in 1987—The year after Alma-Ata. *Radio Liberty Research,* no. 5/88.

CARRERE d'ENCAUSSE, H. (1979). *Decline of an empire: The Soviet Socialist Republics in revolt.* New York: Harper and Row.

DAILEY, E. (1989). Report on the status of non-Russian languages in the USSR. *Report on the USSR, 1,* 30, 26–28.

Documents and materials, nineteenth All Union Conference of the CPSU. (1988). Embassy of the Union of Soviet Socialist Republics (Special issue of *Soviet Life*).

ELLIS, J. (1986). *The Russian Orthodox Church: A contemporary history.* Bloomington, IN: Indiana University Press.

FISHER, A. (1978). *The Crimean Tatars.* Stanford, CA: Hoover Institution Press.

GAFUROV, B. (1976). The USSR: Equality of nations. *Soviet Life, 2,* 45.

GOBLE, P. (1990). Soviet myths about religion crumble. *Report on the USSR, 2,* 10, 8–9.

JONES, E. and GRUPP, F. (1984). Modernization and ethnic equalization in the USSR. *Soviet Studies, 36,* 159–184.

KARKLINS, R. (1980). A note on "nationality" and "native tongue" as census categories in 1979. *Soviet Studies, 32,* 415–421.

KATZ, Z. (1975). *Handbook of major Soviet nationalities.* New York: Free Press.

KURODOEV, V.A. (1984). *Religiia i tserkov v Sovetskom obshchestve.* Moscow: Izdatel'stvo Politicheskoi Literatury.

LANE, C. (1978). *Christian religion in the Soviet Union.* Albany: State University of New York Press.

LUCEY, P. (1983). Religion. In James Cracraft, ed., *The Soviet Union today,* 295–303. Chicago: Educational Foundation for Nuclear Science.

MANN, D. (1989). Gorbachev's personnel policy: The non-Russian republics. *Report on the USSR, 1,* 48, 8–13.

NAHAYLO, B. (1989). Gorbachev disavows merging of nations. *Report on the USSR,* *1,* 5, 23–26.

OLCOTT, M. (1987). *The Kazakhs.* Stanford, CA: Hoover Institution Press.

POSPIELOVSKY, D. (1984). *The Russian church under the Soviet regime 1917–1982.* 2 vols. Crestwood, NY: St. Vladimir's Seminary Press.

REESE, W. (1988). Refugee problem in Transcaucasia assumes alarming proportions. *Radio Liberty Research,* no. 530/88.

Russian nationalism today. (1988). A Special Edition Radio Liberty Research Bulletin, December 19, 1988.

SHAFAREVICH, I. (1975). The nationalities question in the USSR. In Alexander Solzhenitsyn and others, eds., *From under the rubble,* 88–99. Boston: Little, Brown.

SHEEHY, A. (1980). The national composition of the population of the USSR according to the census of 1979. *Radio Liberty Research,* no. 123/80.

SHEEHY, A. (1987a). Do Kazakhs now outnumber Russians in Kazakhstan? *Radio Liberty Research,* no. 65/87.

SHEEHY, A. (1987b). Migration to RSFSR and Baltic republics continues. *Radio Liberty Research,* no. 478/87.

SHEEHY, A. (1988). Gromyko Commission rejects autonomy for Crimean Tatars. *Radio Liberty Research,* no. 248/88.

SHEEHY, A. (1989a). Gorbachev addresses Central Committee Plenum on nationalities question. *Report on the USSR, l,* 39, 1–4.

SHEEHY, A. (1989b). Russian share of Soviet population down to 50.8 percent. *Report on the USSR, 1,* 42, 1–5.

SHIPLER, D. (1983). *Russia: Broken idols, solemn dreams.* New York: Times Books.

SIMON, G. (1974). *Church, state and opposition in the USSR.* Berkeley, CA: University of California Press.

SOLCHANYK, R. (1986). Does Gorbachev have a nationalities policy? *Radio Liberty Research,* no. 112/86.

TEAGUE, E. (1986). Russian appointed to top party post in Kazakhstan. *Radio Liberty Research,* no. 465/86.

WALKER, C. (1980). *Armenia: The survival of a nation.* London: Croom Helm.

WALKER, M. (1986). *The waking giant: Gorbachev's Russia.* New York: Pantheon.

THIRTEEN
SOCIAL PROBLEMS II:
Alcohol, Drugs, Crime, and Official Corruption

We, and many Westerners who have lived in Moscow, have always felt safer on the streets of Moscow than on the streets of almost any major American city. Why? Until recently there has been little in the mass media or in our own experience to lead us to feel otherwise. Crimes against persons, like plane crashes and other such distressing events, used to be ignored by the Soviet press. Thus, one had to visit the courts or personally experience a crime to become aware of the fact that crime is reasonably common in the Soviet Union. Glasnost has changed all of this and, with it, the notion that Soviet urban streets are safe.

The streets of Moscow have never been free of obvious manifestations of another serious Soviet social problem: alcoholism. Heavy drinking is not a purely Soviet phenomenon, though there is evidence that there has been a gradual increase in alcohol consumption during the Soviet period.[1]Heavy drinking among Russian men is a tradition that dates back to a time long before the Bolshevik Revolution. The cultural image of the "real man" as a person able and willing to drink both heavily and frequently has proved exceptionally difficult for the Soviet government to eradicate, despite the serious losses in productivity and the other problems that it creates.

---

[1]For example, between 1955 and 1984 the yearly alcohol consumption rate rose two and one half times (Treml, 1987, p. 2).

On the other hand, although the alcoholism problem is more serious than it is in the United States, the narcotics problem, though growing, remains far less serious. In fact, until very recently, the only overt indication of a drug problem was a very small number of published articles concerning drug use and the passage in 1974 of an edict by the Presidium of the USSR Supreme Soviet, "Concerning the Strengthening of the Fight Against Drug Addiction" (*Biulleten' Verkhovnogo Suda, SSSR,* 3, 1974, pp. 43–46).

Along with alcoholism and drug abuse, crime and official corruption are, to a greater or lesser degree, social problems common to the entire developed and urbanized world. Although it has always been clear that there had to be crime in the Soviet Union, until the advent of glasnost it was difficult to assess the magnitude of the problem. Thanks to Soviet investigative journalists and greater official candor, a more complete picture is beginning to emerge, both about crime and about the correctional system to which convicted criminals are entrusted. The discussion of both, in the third section of this chapter, will draw on traditional sources and on the wealth of new information which has recently become available.

The form of crime most widely publicized during the early Gorbachev era was the large-scale official corruption of the Brezhnev era. What the Soviet press calls the "period of stagnation" was characterized by wholesale bribery, graft, embezzlement, favoritism, and other abuses by a large number of public officials, ranging from obscure local Party operatives to the son in law of Brezhnev. Not only did this contribute to the economic mess that the reformers hope to eliminate, but it also created entrenched pockets of crime-based privilege that have proved very difficult to dislodge. In addition, since much of this is directly related to deeply held attitudes, beliefs, traditions, and basic characteristics of the economic system, the success of the drive against official corruption is closely tied to the wider effort to revamp the entire Soviet political, economic, and social culture.

All of these problems present serious—and potentially intractable—challenges to the reformers currently in charge of the country. In the following four sections, we will take a more detailed look at the magnitude and consequences of each, as well as the basic policies the Soviet government has adopted to try to deal with them and the way in which these policies have been implemented.

ALCOHOLISM

Alcoholism and drunkenness have long been significant social problems in Russia.[2] Recent reports (Miroshnichenko, 1988, p. 23; *Report on the USSR,*

---

[2]This discussion will focus mainly on the Russians. There are other Soviet nationalities among whom drinking is not nearly such a problem. For example, those ethnic groups closely associated with Moslem traditions (which demand abstinence) are not free of the problem but are affected to a much lesser extent (*CDSP, 41,* no. 17, 1989, pp. 29–30).

September 8, 1989, p. 45) put the number of drinkers at 150 to 160 million, including 35 to 40 million problem drinkers. The more serious consequences include alcohol-related crimes, public disorder, loss of productivity, illness, suicide, and death. In spite of this, however, drunkenness has traditionally been regarded with a high degree of tolerance by the majority of the Russian people. An indication of this is the fact that under the criminal law of tsarist Russia, being drunk could be an extenuating circumstance. The lack of similar tolerance on the part of the Soviet leadership is shown by the fact that intoxication is a circumstance aggravating responsibility in the RSFSR Criminal Code (Article 39).[3]

What Walter D. Connor (1972) has called "the Russian drinking culture" is a gender-associated phenomenon. Historically, drunkenness in men has been taken for granted, whereas drunkenness in women has been condemned. Men cannot abstain without risking slurs on their manhood (or in the case of one of the authors, on the adequacy of American men); "real men" are expected to drain their glasses with every toast and immediately be ready for more. Women have been more free to choose moderation or abstinence.

In recent years, however, drinking among women has become more of a problem. This has led to increasing official concern because of its effects on the infant mortality rate and the conviction that alcohol abuse among mothers is contributing to an increase in birth defects. In 1983 a Soviet sociologist wrote that 12 to 15 percent of Soviet alcoholics are women and claimed that the incidence of female alcoholism was growing more rapidly than the incidence of male alcoholism (Townsend, 1984, p. 2).

For men and women alike, there has been little social pressure to abstain. Until the Gorbachev era, even media propaganda stressed the importance of moderation, as though total abstinence were too utopian to be worth considering as a goal. One of the things that has distinguished the most recent reform effort in this area is an emphasis on total abstinence as the only viable alternative. This has, however, been criticized both inside and outside the Soviet Union as unrealistic.

Juvenile drinking has also been of concern to Soviet authorities. Just before Gorbachev came to power, a Soviet authority stated that 90 percent of alcoholics began drinking before the age of 15 and that 33 percent started before the age of 10 (Vosnesenskaya, 1984, p. 1). There have always been regulations that govern the sale of alcoholic beverages to minors, but they have constantly been violated, in part because of the pressures on distributors and salespersons to fulfill their part of the state plan. Thus, the following comment by the manager of a food store in Moscow:

> Now as before, the regulations for the sale of liquor are being violated. You probably think that Masha standing at the counter in the wine department has

---

[3]Unlike most other aggravating circumstances, the court has some discretion as to whether to regard drunkenness as an aggravating circumstance.

no conscience? And that I have none either? We do have a conscience, and we also have children. We do not want them to become drunkards. But we have our plan, and we want to receive a bonus. If we have not fulfilled the plan by the end of the month, do you think they make up the deficit? They give us vodka. As far as the plan is concerned there is no difference between milk and vodka. (Voronitsyn, 1978, p. 3)

As it turned out, such economic imperatives,[4] as well as public outrage at the hardship caused by the crackdown on alcohol sales, forced Gorbachev to admit at least partial defeat and increase liquor supplies in late 1988—but more on that later.

The connection between milk and alcoholic beverages has another dimension: "breast-milk alcoholism" (*Izvestiia,* July 4, 1984, p. 3). Many children begin imbibing alcohol via the breast milk of their drinking mothers. This is compounded by the fact that many Soviet parents feed alcohol to fussy babies to quiet them at night. An infant's introduction to alcohol is later reinforced by adult examples and the mass media until for many Soviet children there arises the belief that it is impossible to be a proper adult without drinking.

Most Russians drink their vodka straight and rapidly; sedately sipping mixed drinks is not in the Russian tradition. They tend to drink to get drunk, hardly pausing long enough to taste what they are drinking. As if drinking to get drunk were not enough, the occasions on which heavy drinking is considered appropriate are many. There are, of course, the events that are celebrated with alcoholic beverages all over the world: a wedding, a birthday, the birth of a child, a new year. Soviet citizens, however, also drink to celebrate occasions that other cultures normally do not regard as occasions for drinking, such as a first payday. In addition, Russians drink in honor of holidays, like Sunday, International Women's Day, Red Army Day, and so forth. Besides these, there are the holidays that are more limited in scope but treated as excuses for drinking by many people: Builders' Day, Miners' Day, Chemical Workers' Day, and all the other days set aside in honor of somebody or other. Thus, for those who are of a mind to drink, it is usually easy to find an appropriate occasion—frequently.

And for some it is not necessary to find an occasion. They simply drink when and where they wish. This is a particular problem in the workplace. In a survey conducted immediately after Gorbachev began his drive to curb the Soviet drinking problem (*CDSP, 37,* no. 38, 1985, p. 23), it was found that 19.9 percent of the men and 11.9 percent of the women were willing to admit that they drink on the job. Half of the respondents saw nothing wrong with drinking before coming to work. When the researchers questioned the people whose job it was to deal with this problem, almost a quarter were of the opin-

---

[4]Including a continued tendency for local officials to use vodka sales to meet plan goals on a last-minute basis (*Izvestiia,* August 1, 1988, p. 4).

ion that the problem was getting worse. Both the experts and the workers agreed that there was tacit acceptance of such behavior and that drinking—with or without a pretext—was growing more common. Vladimir Treml, the leading U.S. authority on the Soviet drinking problem, estimates that labor productivity could be increased 15 to 20 percent if alcohol abuse could be eliminated (Winter, 1987, p. 2).

Given such attitudes toward drinking, it is little wonder that the USSR ranks among the leaders of the world in the consumption of intoxicating beverages. A careful statistical study by a Western scholar places the USSR fourth in the world in per capita consumption of all alcoholic beverages (Treml, 1982, p. 70). This estimate excludes illegally made, home-brewed alcoholic beverages, which constitute a considerable proportion of Soviet alcohol consumption. Moveover, in spite of Soviet efforts to deal with the problem, the rate of increase in alcohol consumption has been among the highest in the world.[5]

Some Soviet scholars have examined the production losses that could be attributed to alcohol abuse. The possible magnitude of the problem was indicated by a report of the USSR Anti-Alcohol Committee, which stated that approximately 37 percent of male workers were alcohol abusers and approximately 1 percent per day of all male workers missed work because of drinking (Binyon, 1983, pp. 58–59). Particularly serious are the effects of payday and holiday drinking. At a group of Leningrad factories it was found that 90 percent of the absenteeism and 85 percent of the late arrivals occurred on the day after a payday or holiday. On Mondays productivity was approximately 12 to 15 percent below productivity on other working days. In addition, drinking was a contributing factor in about one-fourth of all industrial accidents. Accidents and injuries doubled on paydays (Binyon, 1983, p. 59). Even agricultural production, chronically a problem area in the Soviet Union, is affected. For example, drunken tractor drivers are a major problem.

Alcohol consumption is also a factor in divorce and in family disputes over finances. A substantial portion of the Soviet family budget goes for alcoholic beverages which, unlike wine in Italy and France, are not commonly considered part of meals. This does not take into account the consumption of *samogon* (home-brewed alcoholic beverages). Even Soviet authorities do not have an accurate picture of the situation with regard to *samogon* (Treml, 1987, pp. 15–16). Illegal home brewing is not the only crime which is alcohol-related. A high proportion of all crimes committed in the Soviet Union are committed by intoxicated persons, and this has been steadily increasing in spite of the alcohol reform (*CDSP, 41,* no. 16, 1989, pp. 22–23).[6] Also, drunken persons are prey for those who are both sober and unscrupulous.

To summarize, the problem of alcohol abuse is a serious one in the Soviet

[5]Approximately 50 percent since 1965 and 100 percent since 1955 (Treml, 1982, p. 68).

[6]This is related to the fact that home-brewed alcoholic beverages have gradually replaced those no longer available in the stores.

Union. And because of traditional Russian attitudes toward drinking, it is one that is particularly difficult to eradicate. This is a matter of grave concern to the Soviet government, which has devoted substantial resources to the prevention of alcohol abuse and to the rehabilitation of chronic drunkards. Until recently, the measures that have officially been favored have been based on the premise that drinking behavior is totally under the control of the individual. Therefore, alcoholism has been treated as a habit that develops from drinking increasing amounts over time. Given this assumption, authorities have tried to discourage drinking in general, to change traditional attitudes toward alcoholic beverages and drunkenness, and to help those who have acquired the habit to break it.

In 1985 the new Gorbachev regime embarked on a massive campaign to discourage the drinking of alcoholic beverages, particularly hard liquor. Simultaneous decrees of the Central Committee of the CPSU, the Council of Ministers of the USSR, and the Presidium of the Supreme Soviet of the USSR were published on May 17, 1985. They initiated a series of measures aimed at discouraging the use of hard liquor and stopping the production of *samogon*. Among other things, the penalties for being drunk in public, driving drunk, drinking on the job, giving alcohol to minors, and producing, marketing, or storing *samogon* were increased. In addition, the drinking age was raised from 18 to 21, the opening of liquor stores on working days was delayed three hours, and the production of vodka and other hard liquor began to be gradually reduced. It was further announced that certain fruit-based alcoholic drinks would be completely banned in the future. On the plus side, the government added some "sweeteners." For example, it promised to begin increasing the production of soft drinks, juices, jams, and fresh fruit.

A few months later the government intensified the campaign by raising the price of vodka 25 percent and announcing that a majority of distilleries would be closed or changed to food production. In addition, the price of baking yeast (which is commonly used to brew illegal liquor) was raised. All of these changes were accompanied by considerable media hype and educational efforts. Initially, there seemed to be some real successes. Production of alcoholic beverages was cut sharply. In 1986 per capita consumption of legally produced alcoholic beverages fell to half the 1984 level. Crime, traffic accidents, injuries and deaths, workplace and home accidents, and industrial absenteeism all dropped. Even the crude death rate fell. In 1987 it was reported (*Izvestiia,* May 12, 1987, p. 3) that for the first time in 10 years, average life expectancy had reached 69.

By late 1987, however, there were signs that progress was slowing, if not being reversed. The major contributing factor was a dramatic increase in *samogon* production. Arrests for home brewing went up and many people who had never done so before began brewing alcoholic beverages. In 1988 alone, approximately 427,000 people were charged with making *samogon*; about 325,000 stills and 4 million liters of *samogon* were seized (*CDSP, 41,* no. 16, 1989, p. 23). This trend toward home brewing is particularly notable in urban areas. It is also lucrative. As of 1988, it was reported that the "street" price of a 3-liter bottle of *samogon* was 70 rubles—a very large sum when one considers average salaries (Miroshnichenko, 1988, p. 21). Along with this, there was an increase in poisonings from the consumption of adulterated *samogon* and the crime rate began to rise parallel to the increase in *samogon* production (*Pravda,* June 2, 1987, pp. 1,3; Trehub, 1987). There were also reports of the development of organized crime activity in this area (Miroshnichenko, 1988, p. 21.

Since the production of *samogon* is illegal, it is difficult to find out exactly how much is being produced. One reliable indicator, however, is the sale of sugar, a major component of *samogon*. Between 1985 and 1988, sugar sales rose so sharply that by 1988 it was necessary for the authorities in many localities to ration sugar (see, for example, *Izvestiia,* April 8, 1988, p. 2). In addition, it was reported by the Ministry of Justice that 119,000 kilograms of sugar had been stolen in the first nine months of 1987 (*Radio Liberty Research,* January 8, 1988, no. 13/88, p. 5). Finally, there were 60 percent more court cases involving sugar speculation in 1988 than there had been in 1987 (*Izvestiia,* April 19, 1989, p. 6).

In response to this upsurge of home brewing, the USSR Supreme Soviet Presidium issued a decree, "On Liability for *Samogon* Brewing" (*Pravda,* June 2, 1987, p. 3). It imposed an administrative fine of 100 to 300 rubles for possession or manufacture of home-brewed alcoholic beverages or of home-brewing equipment. Intent to sell is not necessary and the fine can be imposed directly by the police. If there is a repeat offense within a year, it is considered a crime and the offender can be sentenced to corrective labor for up to two years or fined from 200 to 500 rubles. This supplemented already existing criminal penalties for possession and manufacture of *samogon* with intent to sell. Finally, the authorities expressed concern about the ineffectiveness of education and prevention efforts, as well as the need to offer more social alternatives to drinking, especially for young people.

The basic method of coping with the problem of changing people's attitudes toward drinking has been education and propaganda. The educational effort begins in school. In 1984 the USSR Deputy Minister of Health announced a stepped-up program to fight childhood alcoholism (*Pravda,* June 20, 1984, p. 6). First, a new program was instituted, starting at age seven, to educate schoolchildren about the dangers of alcohol. Second, a similar program was begun in vocational-technical schools. Finally, drug abuse clinics were established specifically to treat teenagers. Adults became the target of lectures, consultations with physicians, personal exhortations by propagandists, plays, movies, posters, pamphlets, and tape recordings. As an extension of this effort, a new journal, *Sobriety and Culture,* began publication in 1986.

There is little evidence that any of this has been very successful. Prior to the present antialcohol campaign, most educational efforts depicted alcohol

as an unmitigated evil. At the same time, however, the emphasis was on moderation, rather than on total abstinence. Current educational efforts have
abandoned this posture. The emphasis is on total abstinence. Most Soviet specialists think that this goal is totally unrealistic and that there should be a slow,
patient effort to inculcate the value of moderation in drinking. Because of the
sense of urgency stemming from the relationship of the antialcohol campaign
to other elements of the reform, such as productivity, however, the advocates
of moderation are not being listened to by the leadership (Treml, 1987, p. 18).
Finally, there was unmistakable symbolism in the fact that the Twenty-seventh
Party Congress in 1986 was dry—at least in public.

The Achilles heel of all previous antialcohol campaigns, however, has
been the role of alcohol production and consumption in the country's economy.[7] In spite of their efforts to change consumption habits, it has always
been clear that the attitude of the Soviet leadership with regard to alcohol use
has been, at best, ambivalent. Sales of alcoholic beverages yield tax revenues
that contribute significantly to the state treasury. At the beginning of Gorbachev's tenure in office, the government's earnings from alcohol were approximately 10 percent of the national budget (*The Washington Post,* May 17,
1985, p. A 26). In 1988, during an interview, the Deputy Minister of Finance
said that the turnover tax on vodka was 94 percent of its price (*Moscow News,*
October 16, 1988, p. 8).

Shortly after the Gorbachev alcohol reform began, there began to be
complaints about its economic impact. For example, in November 1986 an
official of the Georgian Republic complained that limits on the production of
wine and vodka had significantly reduced the wine-making republic's plans
for sales and profits. At the same time, however, the republic's plan for payments into the USSR treasury and for turnover tax receipts had stayed the
same. This had created a revenue shortfall of 345 million rubles. He expressed
continued support for the reform, but called for a reordering of financial and
budgetary relationships (*Izvestiia,* November 21, 1986, p. 5).

By 1988, Soviet authorities were beginning to feel a substantial financial
crunch. The first three years of the campaign had cost the Soviet treasury 37
billion rubles in revenue from alcohol sales (Miroshnichenko, 1988, p. 21). In
his speech to the February plenum of the Central Committee (*Pravda,* February 19, 1988, pp. 1–3), Gorbachev asserted that previous growth rates in the
Soviet economy had been attributable entirely to two sources: high world oil
prices and increasing sales of alcohol to the Soviet population. Without these,
he asserted, there would have been virtually no growth in national income for
almost 20 years. Thus, he concluded, the alcohol reform was taking a serious
financial toll on an already stressed economy.

---

[7]This seems also to be a factor in the tendency to back off from some of the more harsh
aspects of the current campaign. Public opinion has also seemed to play a significant role due to
the rise of democratization—especially contested elections and the more precarious position of
the CPSU. Thus, the situation is much more complex than previously.

So, in 1988 there emerged a picture of an embattled Gorbachev. First, he was being blamed for the long lines that ordinary Soviet citizens had to endure to get even a bottle of vodka for a birthday or wedding. In some cases, the lines contained a thousand or more people and became unruly, causing injury or even death (*CDSP, 40,* no. 6, 1988, p. 16). Added to this was a budgetary deficit which was becoming more and more of a problem. According to some Soviet press sources, sales of illegal vodka were at least equal to sales of legal vodka and that, consequently, consumption remained at precampaign levels (*Report on the USSR,* September 8, 1989, p. 46). Finally, there were other serious indications that the reform was not working very well. There were increases in public drunkenness, alcohol-related crimes, and illness and poisonings due to the ingestion of dangerous or lethal alcohol substitutes.

Gradually, signs of accommodation began to emerge. In 1988 it was announced that in Moscow alone almost three hundred additional stores would be permitted to sell alcoholic beverages in order to cut back on the long lines.[8] In September the USSR Council of Ministers lifted some of the all-union restrictions on the sale of a few alcoholic beverages, allowing beer, wine, champagne, and cognac to be sold in grocery stores, thus relieving some of the pressure on liquor stores. Finally, in October the Central Committee acknowledged that there were serious shortcomings in the alcohol reform and called for a "normalization" of liquor sales and an increased emphasis on educational and prevention programs.

It was, in short, an admission that the first major program of the Gorbachev reform had failed. It had created more problems than it had solved, the most serious of which was probably the budgetary impact of sharply decreasing legal alcohol sales (*The Washington Post,* November 25, 1988, p. A38). In addition, for at least some politicians facing contested elections, the level of public anger about the effects of the reform on their lives might have been equally daunting.

What the reform leadership had come to terms with, then, was the fact that alcoholic beverages are both profitable and popular. If the government treasury did not gain from this source of income, there were plenty of home distillers who would and did. For the moment, at least, this seemed to be more important than the fact that the cost of alcohol abuse is extremely high—both for individuals and for the nation. The reform was probably doomed to fail from the start for many reasons, the most important of which was that it failed to address the issue of why alcohol consumption is so popular in the Soviet Union. A basic cause seems to be the difficulty, general drabness, and boredom of Soviet life. Alcohol is the escape mechanism of choice for large segments of the Soviet population.

[8]At that point, it was estimated that the average Moscovite was spending 70 to 90 hours per year standing in line to purchase alcoholic beverages and that control over these lines was occupying about four hundred policemen and volunteer police aids daily (*CDSP, 40,* no. 40, 1988, p. 29).

Drinking provides a pastime, no matter how destructive, to persons who have little other opportunity for diversion in their lives. This is particularly true in the rural areas of Russia. Starting in 1985, there were repeated calls for more measures to provide the Soviet people with recreational and cultural alternatives to drinking, but success in this area was limited and did not have a significant impact. For the moment, the leadership seems inclined to accept slower progress toward moderation in alcohol consumption. It has settled for an approach that emphasizes the alternatives to escape via the bottle. One of the keys would also seem to be the creation of more and better addiction treatment services.

For the person who abuses alcohol in spite of all prevention efforts, there is treatment, and about five million alcoholics are currently being treated in the USSR (*Report on the USSR,* November 10, 1989, p. 32). In line with the traditional opinion that chronic drunkenness is learned behavior (rather than an illness), Soviet treatment has tended to stress (1) the use of drugs, vitamins, and hypnosis to detoxify and negatively condition the patient toward alcoholic beverages; (2) psychotherapy and autogenic training[9] (3) work therapy to make the patient able to cope more effectively with daily life outside the treatment institution; and (4) early treatment at the work site. Increasingly, however, glasnost has permitted specialists to question the assumptions underlying current treatment programs and to call for changes that reflect the theory that alcoholism is a health problem rather than a behavior problem (see, for example, *CDSP, 40,* no. 32, 1988, pp. 7,24; *Soviet Life,* February, 1990, pp. 51–55).

In urban areas the first institution the drunken person encounters might be the "sobering-up station" of the local militia. These receive drunks off the streets, get them cleaned up, give them symptomatic treatment, and furnish a place to sleep it off—all for a nominal fee. This, of course, is not treatment; it is brief custodial care. For treatment, the alcoholic may be cared for in any of several medical and rehabilitative institutions, either on an inpatient or an outpatient basis.

A recent innovation is the establishment of fee-charging treatment centers called "narcological units," where a person may seek treatment anonymously to avoid the label "alcoholic," a designation that could mean problems, especially at work. In an effort to put greater emphasis on early treatment, "narcological departments" have been established at construction sites, enterprises, and agroindustrial complexes. At these centers individuals can get treatment for one to two months while continuing to work as usual. Part of the person's paycheck is deducted to cover treatment expenses and the rest is sent to his or her family. During the treatment period, patients stay at the hospital when they are not working and receive a combination of medici-

---

[9]A form of therapy usually combining relaxation with suggestion and autosuggestion.

nal, psychotherapeutic, and physiotherapeutic treatments.[10] The overall rate of success is difficult to ascertain, but there is little reason at present to assume that it is any better or worse than in other countries with major alcoholism problems.

Alcohol abusers who create substantial problems for the authorities, either by criminal activities or by noncriminal forms of social disruption, can be committed by a people's court to compulsory treatment in special institutions under the jurisdiction of the Ministry of Internal Affairs. These institutions, called *profilaktorii,* or treatment-labor institutions, were first created by a 1967 decree of the RSFSR Supreme Soviet. The system was expanded in 1972 by a decree of the Central Committee of the CPSU and the Council of Ministers of the USSR. Finally, in the mid-1970s an RSFSR Supreme Soviet decree established a system of treatment-labor institutions in which alcoholics could be confined for as much as two years.

Recently, there have been accusations that these institutions are little better than penal institutions (see. for example, *CDSP, 40,* no. 32, 1988, p. 7; *CDSP, 40,* no. 47, 1988, pp. 28-29). Reports of considerable inmate unrest have been traced to the fact that these institutions emphasize confinement over treatment, including such features as barbed wire, punitive solitary confinement, and limits on visits. In addition, the recidivism rate seems to be very high; judging from a few scattered figures it can be estimated at 60 to 70 percent. Finally, when individuals are released back into the community, their personal documents show that they have spent time at a treatment-labor institution, and this constitutes a "blemish" on their record. A few experimental programs permit a much higher level of personal freedom for the inmates but do not seem to address other serious problems, such as the effectiveness of the treatment offered.[11]

To summarize, the Soviet government is using a wide variety of measures to cope with a serious social problem that has proved too deeply ingrained to be solved quickly or easily. It is certainly clear that all efforts—past and present—to solve the alcoholism problem have, at best, met with limited success. The 1985 reforms were more comprehensive than any tried within recent memory. They also seemed designed with past setbacks in mind. In the end, however, their successes were very limited, and it could be argued that they caused more problems than they solved. In any case, the leadership was finally forced to give in to a potentially devastating combination of public discontent and financial pressure. And then there was the ominous fact that as alcohol consumption declined, illegal drug use rose steadily and rapidly.

[10]The Soviet government is also experimenting with treatment centers that permit the alcoholic to live at home, but that provide very strict supervision (Kondratenko, 1990).

[11]Along with suggestions that health authorities be given a much greater role, there have been more concrete developments. One has been the willingness to send people to the West to study new treatment methods, and another has been the establishment of some programs modeled after Alcoholics Anonymous (*Radio Liberty Research,* November 11, 1988, no. 496/88, p. 7, and November 25, 1988, no. 518/88, p. 17).

DRUG ABUSE

Until the advent of the Gorbachev regime and its policy of glasnost, it was difficult to research the problem of drug abuse in the Soviet Union because virtually no data were available to indicate the nature and magnitude of the problem. Since glasnost, the Soviet media have published much more information, making it possible to get a far clearer picture of the Soviet narcotics problem.

First of all, how widespread is drug abuse in the Soviet Union? According to the USSR Ministry of Internal Affairs (MVD), as of 1989 there were 121,700 known narcotics abusers in the Soviet Union. The MVD regarded 60,000 as seriously ill and said that 1,240 had been subjected to compulsory treatment (*Izvestiia,* September 5, 1989, p. 6). This does not, of course, include drug users who have not been identified by the authorities. Estimates of this group vary but are much higher. Another recent MVD estimate sets the USSR drug addiction average at 28 per every 100,000 people (*Izvestiia,* May 12, 1989, p. 8).

Although these figures are small by United States standards,[12] Soviet authorities have been alarmed by several factors. First, there are indications of a rapid increase—possibly as much as 50 percent per year. As in other parts of the world, the incidence and spread of drug addiction is difficult to measure because abusers will go to great lengths to avoid being identified. Second, addiction is heavily concentrated among youth and young adults. Recently, the Novosti press agency reported that 80 percent of Soviet drug users are under 25 (*Report on the USSR,* April 7, 1989, p. 32). Third, Soviet efforts to deal with the problem have been largely ineffectual. There have even been reports of Party officials being fired because of their failure to deal effectively with the increase of drug abuse in their jurisdictions.

The problem of drug addiction involves two categories of drugs: prescription drug abuse and "street" drug abuse. The latter category—which is by far the more serious problem—includes narcotics manufactured in underground laboratories, as well as the more common plant narcotics. About 90 percent of Soviet addicts use homemade concoctions made from poppy or hemp. To date, the use of heroin, LSD, and marijuana seems to be relatively rare in the Soviet Union (*Report on the USSR,* April 7, 1989, p. 32).

Medicinal narcotic drugs can easily disappear into the illegal market because of violations of the rules for inventorying, storing, prescribing, and dispensing them. The thieves are usually medical personnel. During the first eight months of 1989, about 1,130 crimes involved theft of drugs and violations of the regulations on storage, record keeping, and sales (*Izvestiia,* September 5, 1989, p. 6). The conditions facilitating such thefts are many, but some are as

---

[12]The U.S. Drug Enforcement Administration has estimated that there are 500,000 heroin addicts, 11 million cocaine users, and 18 million marijuana users in the United States (*The Washington Post,* July 20, 1988, p. A13).

simple as a shortage of metal safes and files. In some regions of the country, 30 to 40 percent of abusers are using medicinal drugs (*Izvestiia,* February 29, 1988, p. 4). This problem is particularly acute in urban areas in the RSFSR, such as Leningrad and Moscow, where it is more difficult to obtain the raw materials to make plant-based drugs. In 1987 *Izvestiia* (November 23, 1987, p. 4) reported that 35 percent of the drugs being used illegally in Moscow were from medical institutions and that 73 medical employees had been prosecuted during the previous 10 months for crimes related to drug abuse.

In addition to the drugs that are being redirected from medical uses, there is a substantial amount of illegal drug production in the USSR. Although the most serious problem still involves agriculturally produced narcotics, the home-laboratory production of illegal narcotics seems to be increasing. In 1987 homemade narcotic substances constituted 30 percent of the drugs being used in Moscow. This represented an enormous increase over the 2 percent three years previously (*Izvestiia,* November 23, 1988, p. 4). In many cases the methods used are very sophisticated, even allowing the extraction of mind-altering chemicals from over-the-counter pharmaceuticals (*Izvestiia,* February 29, 1988, p. 4).

A major thrust of the antidrug campaign that began in 1986 was an effort to curtail the agricultural production of narcotics. Given the size of the country and the difficulty of some of the terrain, this effort is probably doomed to have only a limited impact. There are, however, scattered reports of successes. For example, during the first eight months of 1989, the Minister of Internal Affairs reported that 1,442 fields of illegal drug plants and 2,700 hectares of wild crops had been destroyed in the Central Asian republics and Kazakhstan (*Izvestiia,* September 5, 1989, p. 6). Similar reports have come from other Soviet republics. Because of the importance of this problem, recent efforts to control the growing of narcotics-producing crops have included a decision to forbid the planting of opium poppies in the Soviet Union (*Izvestiia,* October 6, 1987, p. 2). This is a very serious move given the current economic situation, since it means that opium-based medicines for legal use will have to be imported.

This is not the only way in which authorities have been trying to prevent illegal drugs from reaching abusers. There is already evidence of a network of underground drug dealers that, although it is modest by American standards, represents a new problem for Soviet authorities. They have had some success in dealing with this criminal element. For example, a 1986 national antidrug operation, known as "Poppy–86," led to the arrest of 300 drug traffickers and 4,000 sellers of raw drugs. But as time has passed, the financial incentives to enter the drug business have grown. For example, approximately ten years ago the cost of a kilogram of illegal opium was 5,000 to 6,000 rubles. By 1989, it was about 100,000 (*Izvestiia,* September 5, 1989, p. 6).

A related development is the spread of "drug dens." The maintenance of "dens of debauchery" (*pritoni razvrata*) is a crime under Article 226 of the RSFSR Criminal Code. Although this provision does not specifically mention narcotics, it is placed between two articles that do and seems to be used by authorities to combat the increasing tendency of drug abusers to gather indoors in apartments. Moscow authorities reported in 1987 that 62 percent of arrests for drug possession and use were being made in people's apartments (*Izvestiia,* November 23, 1987, p. 4). That same year 15 criminal cases had been brought against persons running such "drug dens."

Some of the earliest information about the Soviet drug problem began to surface as a result of the war in Afghanistan. Afghanistan is a major producer of hashish and opium. As the war dragged on, evidence began to accumulate that there was a substantial drug problem among Soviet soldiers serving in Afghanistan. Interviews with Soviet army defectors indicated that hashish use was widespread among Soviet troops (see, for example, *The Washington Post,* January 3, 1988, p. B5). Later, Soviet sources reported that some soldiers had used various narcotics prior to going into battle or before other high stress assignments (*CDSP,41,* no. 5, 1989, p. 17). And there have been reports that Soviet veterans were turning to drugs to help deal with their war memories (*Radio Liberty Research,* no. 21/88, p. 13).

Another aspect of the Asian connection is the serious narcotics problem in Soviet Central Asia and Transcaucasia. The use of narcotics is traditional among Soviet citizens of Moslem heritage. In fact, many Soviet Central Asians used to regard narcotics as a commonplace and all-purpose medicine (*Izvestiia,* October 3, 1986, p. 6). In the 1986 riots in Alma-Ata that followed the removal of the Kazakhstan party boss and his replacement by an ethnic Russian, as well as the 1988 riots in Azerbaidzhan, there were allegations that many of the rioters were under the influence of drugs. Since then, there have been regular reports of narcotics seizures and drug crackdowns in these republics. Some have even involved corrupt government officials (see, for cxample, *Report on the USSR,* October 20, 1989, p. 30).

What is the profile of the "typical" drug abuser? Some insight can be gained from a survey carried out in the Georgian Republic (*CDSP, 39,* no. 8, 1987, pp. 9–10). The overwhelming majority were male (91.7 percent) and under the age of 35 (86.4 percent). Most (83.7 percent) had secondary, incomplete higher, or higher education. A large proportion (46 percent) had criminal records related to drug abuse. Over half (61.6 percent) had above-average family incomes. There were, however, a considerable number of troubled family histories. For example, 78.5 percent said their fathers had abused alcohol, and 77.8 percent had brothers who were also drug abusers. Most (72 percent) also used alcoholic beverages. Three-fourths (74.5 percent) had been abusing narcotics for three or more years. Hashish was the most frequently used drug, and its use was said to be fashionable. In fact, prestige was cited by one-fourth as the reason they began taking hashish. Two-thirds said they were motivated by the desire to "get high." Many (35.9 percent) reported spending more than 500 rubles a month for narcotics, and another 44.1 percent spent more than 300 rubles. Much of this money was acquired through criminal activities.

As in the West, there is a strong link between the use of illegal narcotics and other types of crime. According to *Izvestiia* (November 23, 1987, p. 4), it can require 170 to 200 rubles a day to satisfy a drug habit in the Soviet Union.[13] Thus, addicts resort to crimes such as burglary, and robbery to raise the funds needed to purchase the illegal drugs they need. According to the Soviet press, there are places in which approximately half of apartment burglaries are perpetrated by addicts (*Izvestiia,* February 29, 1988, p. 4). In addition, illegal drug use can also lead to crimes that are not exclusively directed at obtaining money to buy narcotics. For example, in 1986 TASS reported that two addicts hijacked a plane and killed two passengers before being killed themselves (*The Washington Post,* September 23, 1986, p. A22).

Under Article 224 of the RSFSR Criminal Code, the sentence for buying, selling, or manufacturing narcotics can be as severe as 10 years in prison. If there are aggravating circumstances, the sentence can increase to 15 years with confiscation of property. Incarceration, however, is obviously no solution and—according to the Soviet press—treatment is seldom successful (*CDSP, 39,* no. 2, 1987, p. 6; *CDSP, 40,* no. 13, 1988, p. 10; *CDSP, 41,* no. 5, 1989, p. 18). According to the law, however, any addict who refuses voluntary treatment can be sent to a closed institution for compulsory treatment.

Treatment centers are in short supply, often in poor physical condition, and overcrowded. They also frequently have an atmosphere more like that of a prison than a hospital. All of this is very frustrating for the Soviet medical profession, which has the ability to do better, given adequate resources. For example, where facilities are adequate there is a reasonably good recovery rate (*Izvestiia,* February 29, 1988, p. 4). This situation is, however, a reflection of the more pervasive shortage of resources in the economy, as well as a punitive attitude toward drug abusers. In the specialized treatment centers that do exist, a major handicap is the shortage of doctors and the inadequate qualifications of those physicians who do work with addicts. The effort to remedy this situation is hampered by an official policy favoring the harsh treatment of addicts and regarding them primarily as "socially dangerous persons" (*CDSP, 40,* no. 13, 1988, p. 10). Anonymous treatment, therefore, is virtually impossible, and as a result even those who are treated successfully often find that when they try to reenter society they have no jobs. In addition, they are thrown back into the same environment in which their narcotics habit got started.

A new law, targeted at the teen addict, promises the establishment of "preventive educational centers" (*The Washington Post,* January 7, 1987, p. A18). These will be run by the police and will accept addicts aged 16 to 18 who have refused to enter voluntary treatment programs. While undergoing rehabilitation, the inmates will work for wages. The penal atmosphere is attested to by the fact that running away will result in a prison term of up to one year. This new development, plus the resources problem faced by the voluntary treatment centers, seems to indicate that Soviet authorities are inclined to treat narcotics addiction more like a crime than like an illness.

[13]It is virtually certain that this figure is higher now.

In short, the Soviet authorities seem to be giving the drug abuse problem a much higher priority than ever before. The problem has been neglected for so long, however, that they seem to be fighting an uphill battle. On the other hand, they are not facing a problem of the proportions faced by American authorities. As a society that has been, relative to the West, very highly controlled, they have been able to stem the flow of illegal narcotics more effectively. Recently, they reported the confiscation of about 42 tons of narcotics per year (*Izvestiia,* February 29, 1988, p. 4). If the Soviet Union continues to open up, however, the inflow of illegal drugs may increase significantly.

As in the West, the major problem is dealing with the factors that lead persons to drug addiction. As was indicated earlier, drug abuse is concentrated in the teen and young adult population. It is apparently rare among those over 40 years of age.[14] At least some of the growth in the drug abuse problem seems to be fallout from the campaign against alcoholism. As liquor became more difficult to obtain, many people turned to narcotics (*Is It Easy To Be Young?* Riga Film Studios, 1987).

Idleness and Western influences have also been cited as contributing factors. One Soviet newspaper (*Moskovskaya Pravda*) published a letter from a girl who said that she and her friends smoked narcotics because it was "fashionable." This aura of respectability may be enhanced by the fact that, according to a survey carried out in Georgia, drug addicts include an increasing number of the children of professionals. Also drug pushers are frequently respectable members of the community, like doctors (*Radio Liberty Research,* no. 313/86, p. 4). Finally, in 1986 *Izvestiia* reported that some addicts get their start through "simple curiosity."

CRIME AND THE PENAL SYSTEM

As in most societies, it is teens and young adults who commit a disproportionate number of crimes—especially crimes of violence. And crime seems to be mainly a masculine occupation. Female criminals are a decided minority and tend to commit nonviolent crimes. Finally, there is evidence that the propensity to commit crime (except in the case of certain economic crimes) is strongly associated with lower educational achievement and occupational status.

What is the magnitude of the crime problem? There is a problem endemic to criminological studies everywhere in the world: Are the crime statistics reported by the police an effort to project a desirable image of police work rather than a reflection of the actual crimes committed and criminals apprehended? There is evidence that this happens in the Soviet Union. Historically, however, a more serious problem has been the extreme secrecy with which crime statistics have been treated in the Soviet Union. Most crime statistics have been treated as state secrets, and those that have found their way

---

[14]In part, this may be due to a lessened life expectancy among drug abusers.

into print have been so incomplete and without context that few conclusions, if any, could be drawn from them. Despite glasnost, this is still a problem. There are, however, signs of a change. In 1988, the USSR Ministry of Internal Affairs began reporting crime statistics to domestic and foreign reporters. Although quite limited in comparison with similar data released in the West, this represents an improvement.

Particularly revealing were data released in 1989 which showed a significant growth in crime during recent years. As the explanation accompanying this information put it, "data of this kind are published for the first time in many decades" (*Izvestiia,* February 14, 1989, p. 6). The information showed that per capita crime had grown by 17.8 percent from 1987 to 1988, with the largest increases in several categories of violent crime. In 1989, according to the MVD, there were almost 600,000 more crimes than in 1988. And again serious crimes increased more sharply than others (Staff, 1990, p. 1; *Report on the USSR,* February 23, 1990, p. 44). The statement of the MVD spokesperson who released the 1987 to 1988 information indicates something about the transformation of official attitudes on the subject: "The published data may shock many people. But it is better to know the true situation. . . . In the end, only society as a whole can combat crime, the root of which lies in many problems that have been neglected" (*Izvestiia,* February 14, 1989, p. 6).[15] According to Soviet sources, the main causes of crime include drunkenness, drug addiction, and mercenary motives. Also increasing is juvenile delinquency and recidivism among juveniles. In fact, one-third of all crimes in 1988 were committed by persons under 30 years of age (*CDSP, 41,* no. 6, 1989, p. 15).

A form of crime about which information has only lately been available is organized crime. As recently as August 1985, the Minister of Internal Affairs was publicly denying that organized crime existed in the USSR (*CDSP, 37,* no. 39, 1985, p. 1). Now it is known that there are several thousand organized crime groups in the USSR (Staff, 1990, p. 1) and that organized crime has been around at least since the Brezhnev years. The press has even used the name "mafia" to label it. Some media reports have suggested that at least some of these criminal organizations maintained ties with organized crime figures outside the Soviet Union, particularly in Italy (*Radio Liberty Research,* no. 323/88, p. 9; *Report on the USSR,* June 23, 1989, p. 32).

Although Central Asia has been a major focus of organized crime activity (see, for example, Critchlow, 1989), it is growing rapidly in European urban centers, like Moscow and Leningrad. The reasons for this include the recent

---

[15]Although there seems to be a consensus about the rise in crime, there are differences in interpretation. Commenting on these figures, a Soviet law professor and USSR People's Deputy, A. Iakovlev, observed that the crime rate was much higher during the Brezhnev years and that the current rise is a rebound from a much lower crime rate attributable to the 1985 antialcohol campaign. He thinks that this rebound can be traced to the gradual development of enough *samogon* production to permit a restoration of pre–1985 levels of alcohol consumption (*Pravda,* May 10, 1989, p. 3).

restrictions on the legal sale of alcohol, as well as the deteriorating economic situation. Also, there has been a sharp increase in protection rackets aimed at certain groups, such as taxi drivers, and at cooperatives, such as restaurants (*Radio Liberty Research,* no. 485/88, p. 13; *Pravda,* March 23, 1989, p. 6). In turn, beleaguered businessmen have demanded police protection at a time when police resources are already stretched thin, due to inadequate resources and the extra burden stemmming from rising crime and violent ethnic unrest.[16] Because of the inability of most police departments to take on this extra duty, some cooperatives have set up their own security systems, offering much more attrative pay and working conditions, thus luring away some of the best personnel from regular police units.

Much other Soviet crime is also similar to crime elsewhere, but some types are of particular interest because of what they indicate about Soviet society and government. Those that will be discussed here are hooliganism and economic crime.

Hooliganism is defined in the RSFSR Criminal Code as "intentional actions rudely violating public order and expressing a clear disrespect toward society" (Article 206, RSFSR Criminal Code, 1987). The term "hooliganism" derives from the name of a notorious Irish family of nineteenth-century London and came into use in Russian legal literature before the 1917 Revolution. It was not until after the 1917 Revolution, however, in the 1922 Criminal Code, that it became an official crime. Now hooliganism is a widely discussed topic in Soviet popular and scholarly legal literature and, apparently, a frequently adjudicated crime. In fact, hooliganism (together with property crimes) is one of the two most frequent reasons why a person ends up in jail; premeditated murder comes next (*CDSP, 41,* no 11, 1989, p. 22).

Soviet authorities view hooliganism as a very serious matter, claiming that approximately half of those persons involved in instances of petty hooliganism sooner or later commit serious crimes. Thus, they see the struggle against hooliganism as a key element in the fight against crime. Hooliganism is also closely related to the seemingly insoluble problem of alcoholism. No matter how harsh the treatment, it seems unlikely that hooliganism will drop significantly until the prior problem of alcohol abuse is dealt with more successfully. This may be another reason why the Gorbachev regime began its reform effort with a far-reaching battle against alcoholism. Unfortunately, it seems to have found the problem more intractable than it had originally supposed.

Economic crimes used to present a particular problem to authorities, because all economic activity was supposed to be under the control of the government and most economic resources were supposed to belong to "the people." In such a milieu, the type of individual entrepreneurship that is widely consid-

---

[16]Police units from other parts of the USSR have been sent in to try to quell the violence in such areas as Nagorno-Karabakh (*Report on the USSR,* July 14, 1989, p. 32).

ered praiseworthy in the United States could be criminal. In fact, increasing success in individual economic endeavors tended to bring increasingly severe penalties, culminating in the death penalty for persons who were exceptionally successful. Now that the regime is trying to encourage individual initiative, the whole notion of economic crime is undergoing a reassessment.

Many activities which used to be illegal are now legitimate business activities. There are others, such as graft, embezzlement, and swindling, that would be illegal, or at least unethical, in many other legal systems. Paradoxically, however, the reformers have been put in the rather difficult position of sorting out this situation and of deciding which activities to legalize and which to leave illegal. Then, of course, they have had to try to change people's attitudes. This has been a particular problem with reference to the cooperative sector, where popular perceptions of much successful cooperative activity are influenced negatively by their similarity to previous types of criminal activity.

The use of the death penalty in the fight against crime seems to have diminished during the earlier part of the 1970s. But the late 1970s and 1980s apparently saw a significant increase in death sentences which were imposed frequently, but not exclusively, for economic crimes. The coming of economic reform led many Soviet commentators to debate whether capital punishment was any longer appropriate, given the fact that many reform efforts encouraged the sort of entrepreneurship displayed by, say, speculators. Using the opportunities afforded by glasnost, some legal experts argued the general abolition of the death penalty on the ground that "human life is sacred and no one—not even the state—should have the right to take it away" (*CDSP, 40,* no. 2, 1988, P. 10). In this they were unsuccessful.

Death-penalty cases used to involve spectacular instances of economic crime. In the final analysis, however, the more serious threat to the Soviet economy is probably posed by crimes of a much more modest nature, such as petty pilfering, small-scale embezzlement, and the hoarding of scare goods for resale. It has been reported that about 30 million Soviet citizens engage in illegal businesses which have a financial return of 100 million rubles (*Report on the USSR,* January 19, 1990, p. 30). This kind of crime is hard to detect and prosecute successfully, not only because any one infraction seems very insignificant, but because it is widespread—so widespread that it is considered acceptable by a broad segment of the populace. This is possible because most people are unaware of how minor crimes can add up to serious economic loss for the state. Also, to many Soviet citizens, "socialist" property belongs to everyone and therefore to no one. If it seems necessary—and Soviet citizens are continually in need of things of one sort or another—it can seem to them that they are justified in helping themselves from "the common pot."

When a crime is petty or when, in the opinion of the authorities, it does not represent sufficient "social danger" to be worth prosecuting, the accused may be turned over to a comrades' court or released "on surety" to his or her collective. This usually happens only in cases of first offenders who give evidence of acknowledging their guilt and resolving to reform. The rationale is that the social pressure exerted on the accused will be sufficient to prevent further wrongdoing, and it seems reasonably successful with this kind of criminal. But using the collective to influence the behavior of lawbreakers is relatively rare.

Most adult offenders go on to a trial at the People's Court level and to some form of criminal punishment. Although the courts have a fairly wide range of options, they have tended to sentence most adult criminals either to correctional tasks or to deprivation of freedom. Other punishments, such as fines, dismissal from office, and exile, have been available but seldom used. One of the unforseen side effects of democratization has been a sharp increase in complaints that the police and courts have become too "soft on criminals" and that the rights of victims and potential victims are thus being neglected (see, for example, *CDSP, 1,* no. 19, 1989, p. 9; Peterson, 1989b).

"Correctional tasks" is a punishment that does not involve isolation from society. Convicted persons can even serve their sentences while working at their regular jobs. In fact, this is the form of correctional task used in the overwhelming majority of cases. In certain situations, however, the court can and does require offenders to work at a job that is different from their regular employment and perhaps even outside their vocational or professional competence. During the period of the sentence, money is deducted from their pay and they are closely supervised. Also, the time of the sentence is not counted as part of the person's labor record for purposes of seniority, pension, and other social-insurance provisions. It is simply noted in their record that they served a correctional-tasks sentence.

Deprivation of freedom is a much more severe form of punishment, involving incarceration in a penal institution. The maximum term of imprisonment is 15 years.[17] Soviet correctional institutions have inherited a particularly bad reputation from the Stalin era. Currently, the best source of information is the Soviet press. More complete press coverage began in 1987 with letters to the editor (see, for example, *Literaturnaia Gazeta,* April 15, 1987, p. 11) and was followed by investigative reporting. In the following description of the correctional system, we will combine the formal, legal characteristics of the system with Soviet press reports in an effort to present as accurate a picture as possible.

There are three basic types of penal institutions: corrective-labor settlements, corrective-labor camps, and prisons. Since the latter contain a relatively small proportion of the correctional population,[18] we will concentrate on the first two.

---

[17]The only exception is commutation of a death penalty as an act of clemency. In such cases, a sentence of up to 20 years, deprivation of freedom is possible.

[18]Conditions in prisons (which can be called prisons or detention centers) can be grim (see, for example, *Pravda,* August 30, 1989, p. 6). They have not, however, gotten as much press coverage as other types of penal institutions.

Settlements were created in the 1960s for people who were clearly on the road to rehabilitation and were designed to aid them in the transition to freedom. In 1977 a new type was created for persons who had committed crimes of negligence, and in 1985 another new type was created for persons whose crime was less than a felony and whose sentence was five years or less. These settlement colonies have a regime which is very different from that in other types of penal institutions. They do not have guards, fences, or barbed wire. Men and women share the facilities, and marriage between inmates is permitted. Prisoners may also be allowed to live in family units and travel without supervision inside a limited area. They can wear civilian clothing, have money and valuables, and receive parcels and letters. This regime is thought to aid in combating recidivism and to make inmates more productive during their time in custody. There are also indications that the ones created in 1985 were intended to relieve overcrowding in ordinary-regime corrective-labor camps (Davydov, 1986).

Corrective-labor camps come in four degrees of harshness: (1) ordinary regime, (2) intensified regime, (3) strict regime, and (4) special regime. Prisoners are assigned to them according to their past records and the seriousness of their crime. First offenders who are convicted of crimes viewed as "not grave" are sent to ordinary-regime camps. At the other end of the spectrum, special-regime camps are intended for convicts adjudged "especially dangerous recidivists" and for those with commuted death sentences. There are, of course, also differences in living conditions, with progressively stricter regimes implying increasing limits on the number of visitors inmates may have, the number of packages they may receive, the number of letters they may send, and their freedom of movement within the institution. Prisoners in special-regime camps are housed in cells, the rest are in dormitories. The amount of food allowed prisoners is supposed to vary according to climatic conditions, the kind of work being done, and each individual inmate's attitude toward the labor required of him or her. At least one Soviet reporter (*Izvestiia,* August 7, 1988, p. 3), however, found that these regulations are not always followed by camp administrators. In fact, during recent years the press has been extremely critical of the way in which these camps are administered. That much of this criticism is justified is indicated by the fact that 821 correctional officials were proved to have treated inmates with illegal cruelty during 1988 (*Report on the USSR,* June 30, 1989, p. 34). During the first five months of 1989, another 263 employees were accused of criminal acts (Peterson, 1989a, p. 4).

Work is officially seen as having a healthy influence on the convict's personality. Also involved is a substantial annual contribution to the economy of 2 billion rubles worth of agro-industrial equipment and 1.5 billion rubles worth of consumer goods (Peterson, 1989a, p. 4). It is the work requirement that has been the subject of some of the most severe criticism appearing in the Soviet press. Corrective-labor camps have plans to fulfill. In some cases, "labor takes primacy above all other interests—irrespective of its corrective effect, and only for the sake of fulfilling the . . . plan" (*CDSP, 40,* no. 32, 1988, p. 5). Recently, this situation has been aggravated by the fact that labor camps are being included in the economic accountability (*khozraschet*) system.

At the same time, the prison population is decreasing as a result of amnesties and other factors, and the remaining prisoners tend to be of the hard-core type (Peterson, 1989a). This situation puts tremendous pressure on correctional administrators to be highly productive at the same time they are dealing with an increasingly difficult correctional population. Thus, not only have correctional officials been tempted to react in illegal ways, but the general level of violence in correctional institutions is rising steadily, with reports of hostage taking, assaults, and murders.

In addition to the situation just outlined, there are many other factors that hinder even good-faith efforts by camp administrators to maintain well run, effective corrective institutions. These include administrative difficulties, simple incompetence, abuses, and a lack of cooperation on the part of even the less troublesome inmates. Noncooperation stems mainly from negative attitudes, such as a lack of interest in studying,[19] or from the dynamics of the informal group structure that develops among the inmates. Group leaders, more often than not, are the incorrigible inmates, and their attitudes can be very infectious. Press reports have repeatedly characterized the camps as universities for crime.

In all of this, however, the Soviet penal system is not particularly unusual. Anyone who takes a close look at the penal system of any country meets with similar tales of incompetence, bureaucracy, inmate subcultures, and unrealized rehabilitative goals. Whether the difference in degree is sufficient to amount to a difference in kind is a function of whom you choose to believe about what actually happens within the walls of Soviet correctional institutions. There are indications, however, that government authorities are sufficiently concerned to make penal reform a part of the larger reform of the legal system which is currently under way.

Release from a corrective-labor colony may come after an inmate has served his or her entire sentence, or it may come earlier. There is provision in the law for conditional early release after half a person's sentence has been served. The decision is supposed to be made on merit, although there seems to be some disagreement among Soviet jurists on how to apply the criteria of merit. "Exemplary conduct" is a term subject to many interpretations. A recommendation for conditional early release can be made jointly by the colony administration and a public inspection commission. The final decision is made by the local court. In practice, the key role is played by the colony administration when it decides whom to recommend for consideration. Per-

---

[19]Inmates who do not have work skills are required to take vocational-technical instruction. Those without eight-year education must study in the colony school in order to complete their education. Exceptions are made for convicts who are over 40 years of age and in poor health.

sons so released appear to be subject either to no supervision or, at best, minimal supervision by a public organization or collective. On the other hand, "especially dangerous recidivists" are automatically subject to supervision by the police. A 1985 amendment to Soviet corrective-labor legislation excluded from early release or commutation of term persons who are sentenced for crimes posing a special danger to society. Examples of such crimes are banditry, theft of arms, and gang rape.

The ultimate test for any correctional system is the recidivism rate. Among persons sentenced to correctional tasks, the overall rate is relatively low. Of course, this reflects both the type of criminals who would be most likely to be sentenced to correctional tasks and the fact that they are not exposed to the brutalizing effect of inmate subcultures. Relatively little detailed information has been available concerning recidivism rates among persons released from corrective-labor camps or settlements. Scattered press reports, however, suggest that the recidivism rate is unsatisfactory—particularly since a series of recent amnesties. A 1989 report which does not differentiate on the basis of type of correctional experience places the current overall recidivism rate at about 30 percent (*CDSP, 41,* no. 32, 1989, p. 27).

Among the reasons for recidivism are the effect camp life has on convicts and the reception they get when they try to return to society. An ex-convict, writing in the newspaper *Literaturnaia Gazeta* (April 15, 1987, p. 11), commented on the brutalizing effect of camp experiences: "Having served his sentence, an individual simply is in no position, is not prepared to abide by the norms of life which are accepted in the outside world." To some extent, this may contribute to the reluctance of many to welcome ex-convicts back into their communities and workplaces. For example, as of 1989 more than seventy cities had restricted the ability of ex-convicts to settle there; they are also not allowed to live in border zones and special closed areas. Even juveniles from Leningrad with parents living in that city were no longer welcome there (*Moscow News,* May 8–15, 1988, p. 4). Finally, it is often difficult for ex-convicts to find people willing to hire them, both because of their past crimes and because they often have no appropriate job skills. This has been aggravated by the increasing number of businesses brought under the economic accountability system, a factor that has made Soviet managers more selective in hiring.

Most recidivists are persons who have been convicted of hooliganism or property offenses, such as theft. Murderers in the Soviet Union, as elsewhere, are unlikely to repeat their crime because crimes such as murder are usually committed in the heat of passion and are highly related to circumstances that are not likely to be repeated. On the other hand, stealing is quite likely to be a calculated act and is much more prone to develop into a "profession" for some persons. Thus, the typical recidivist tends to have a background of recurrent and frequent violations of the law—perhaps mixed with a strong propensity toward alcohol or drug abuse. As a result, some recidivists may spend substantial portions of their lives inside correctional institutions. They tend to be leaders within the inmate subculture and, thus, to do their part in perpetuating recidivism from generation to generation of convicts—much to the frustration of police, court, and penal authorities.

OFFICIAL CORRUPTION[20]

Along with the campaign against alcoholism, one of the first major policy initiatives by Gorbachev was a determined effort to wipe out the official crime and corruption that had flourished in the lax atmosphere of the Brezhnev years. Strictly speaking, Gorbachev did not originate the drive against corruption; Andropov did. Andropov did not, however, stay healthy long enough to carry it very far forward. His successor, Chernenko, made some effort to continue, but his poor health and subsequent death also interfered. Thus, it was Gorbachev who took this initial effort and built it into a major drive to make the Soviet government more honest and responsive to public needs.

Although a certain amount of corruption could be found in Soviet government before Brezhnev, under his rule it flourished. Part of the tacit agreement which kept him in office was that, in return for their support of Brezhnev, Party and government officials could pretty much run their jurisdictions as they wished. Brezhnev simply looked the other way. The situation that emerged was described by *Izvestiia,* the official government newspaper, as follows:

> In their "fiefdoms," their rules, systems of relations and laws of hierarchy flourished. In an atmosphere of unrestrained glorification of a top leader who was susceptible to flattery, these lower-ranking leaders did whatever they wanted, taking refuge behind inflated numbers, inflated plans and inflated achievements. Absolute rule, toadying, bribery and open extortion, flouting of the law, clannishness and nepotism, corruption and the embezzlement of state property came to life and thrived. (trans. *CDSP, 40,* no. 1, 1988, p. 5)

This kind of behavior extended from local leaders and enterprise directors right up to the personal secretary and son-in-law of Brezhnev himself.

Behind it, however, was more than pure greed. Certain aspects of the Soviet system encouraged such behavior. Therefore, when Gorbachev inherited this mess, he not only had the job of getting rid of corrupt officials, he also had to deal with structural and attitudinal factors that permitted, and even encouraged, such behavior. The most important of these can be grouped

---

[20]The material discussed in this section will be limited to corruption on the part of persons holding government or party positions and to the pattern uncovered in the campaign against corruption begun by Andropov and continued by Chernenko and Gorbachev. For a broader treatment of this subject written by a Soviet emigrè, see Simis, 1982.

roughly into two categories: (1) characteristics of the current Soviet economic system and (2) entrenched attitudes, beliefs, and traditions.

At the heart of the first set of factors is the generalized attitude—held by many, if not most, Soviet citizens—that corruption is a necessary evil. They think (with justification) that it is the only way to make the economic system work. There are two major reasons for this belief. First, the Soviet economy is chronically plagued with shortages. This means that people with control over scarce resources can (and, in a sense, must) pick and choose who gets them and who does not. The temptation to make these choices on the basis of bribes or other favors is obvious. Stealing hard-to-get items and reselling them is another temptation. Thus, *Pravda* (August 31, 1987, p. 8) reported the case of Dubrovskii, who worked at a motorcycle plant. He stole scarce spare parts and sold them to motorcyclists for three times their usual price. A fellow worker became aware of this and arranged with two police officers to catch him red-handed. They demanded a bribe of 20,000 rubles, threatening him with 15 years in prison. They got 16,000 rubles. This example not only points out the possibilities mentioned previously, but also illustrates how easily corruption can (and has) infected the law-enforcement officials charged with uncovering and prosecuting such crimes. In fact, it has been reported that over 100,000 policemen (15 percent of the total Soviet police force) have been fired for corruption (Staff, 1990, p. 2). Another type of situation has to do with the fact that some basic necessities, such as adequate housing, are also always in short supply. The head of a local department of housing took more than 30,000 rubles in bribes from city residents promising to move them higher on the waiting list for apartments. They never got what they paid for and it took authorities several years to catch up with him as he moved from locality to locality, using forged documents (*CDSP, 39,* no. 22, 1987, p. 18).

A second characteristic of the economic system that tempts local officials to become involved in corrupt practices is the power over their lives and careers held by the central planners. Gosplan has a tradition of inflexibility in its dealings with factory managers and collective farm chairmen. At the same time, the pressure on these administrators to meet Moscow's expectations can be enormous. Clear-cut examples are seldom found in Soviet press reports, because the pressured officials tend to become involved in networks of interrelated crimes, such as complicated webs of bribery, in their effort to obtain the resources necessary to meet or exceed plan targets. Thus, it can be difficult to distinguish those who resorted to bribery to fulfill their plans from those who did so out of greed or ambition. Friends and relatives often assert that the accused were forced to engage in corrupt practices, but these excuses are usually dismissed out-of-hand by Soviet authorities who have found it easier to deal with the problem of individual criminals than with problems in the system (see, for example, *CDSP, 39,* no. 12, 1987, pp. 18–19).

The second set of factors that contribute to widespread official corruption has to do with attitudes, beliefs, and traditions. In short, they involve "the human factor," which Gorbachev acknowledges is more difficult to reform than any other aspect of the system. Most serious is the belief, nurtured by Brezhnev, that gifts, favors, or special treatment are the natural privileges of those in power. Thus, a bribe is regarded as a gift, and a privilege is justified by the importance of conserving a busy official's time and energy. With this mentality, there is a natural tendency to push the limits. Soon not only the important officials but also their spouses, children, friends, and associates are leading lives of privilege far out of proportion to their contribution (if any) to society.

When this privileged status comes under attack, as it has in the current era of reform, these officials will often resort to extreme measures to protect themselves. One of the techniques used by many, especially in Central Asia, has been to appeal to nationalism. For example, the riots that took place in Alma-Ata, Kazakhstan, in late 1986 were a response to the fact that the Party head, a Kazakh, had been replaced by a nonresident Russian. The main reason for the change was to try to bring in someone who was not involved in the widespread web of corruption then existing in Kazakhstan. Local leaders who might otherwise have been candidates were either potentially involved themselves or were constrained by traditions of kinship loyalty from moving decisively to solve the problem. Thus, when faced with a vigorous new Party leader in the Gorbachev mold, those who had something to lose resorted to nationalist appeals to try to thwart the reformers in Moscow (*CDSP, 39,* no. 1, 1987, pp. 4–6; *CDSP, 40,* no. 30, 1988, p. 5).

This was part of a larger effort by the Gorbachev regime to try to clean up flagrant corruption by placing nonindigenous officials in posts usually held by members of the indigenous nationality (Brown, 1987b). This was ultimately defeated by the upsurge of nationalism as a major political issue. When the import of nationalist sentiment became clear, the reformers began to appoint members of the indigenous nationality who had been working either in Moscow or abroad for a significant period of time and thus were less likely to be part of corrupt networks. That no one is immune, however, is made clear by the fact that even nonindigenous officials have been involved in corrupt activities (see, for example, *Pravda,* October 24, 1986, p. 3; *Report on the USSR,* November 24, 1989, p. 22).

One of the major characteristics of the sort of corruption involved was the filling of important government and Party posts by people on the basis of nationality, personal relationships, personal loyalty, and kinship. For example, one oblast Party first secretary in Turkmenistan was accused of selecting people for top Party and government posts because they came from his home region (Brown, 1987a, p. 3).

In spite of concerted efforts over the last several years, the Moscow reformers have found that practices such as bribery and favoritism continue to exist—even in places where the effort to root them out has been most intense (see, for example, *Pravda,* August 4, 1987, p. 2). It is hard to escape the conclusion that a kind of inertia exists in which the web of corruption and related interpersonal relationships is so intricate that it is virtually impossible to trace all of its threads. In some places this has given rise to highly developed criminal organizations (sometimes referred to in the Soviet press as mafia) that are far more difficult to eliminate than relatively unsophisticated instances of individual or group corruption. And the corruption has crept into law enforcement, presenting the reformers with a flawed apparatus for carrying out their anti-corruption policies (Knight, 1988).

The most dramatic example of corruption uncovered to date has been the Uzbek case, which was characterized by *Moscow News* (April 10–17, 1988, p. 13) as "the biggest in Soviet postwar history in terms of the sums stolen and the political, economic and social damage caused." In 1988 the senior investigator who had been working on this case since 1983 (just after Brezhnev's death) saw no end to the job, even though the prosecutions in the case have resulted in the conviction of numerous officials, including Yurii Churbanov, the son-in-law of Brezhnev.

Much of the difficulty that this investigation has encountered has come from people who are not implicated in the corruption but who resent the fact that outsiders have been brought in to "meddle" in the affairs of Uzbekistan. They also complain that the campaign has given their republic a bad name. Thus, not only do the investigators face corrupt officials and organized crime, they also face a largely hostile indigenous population, many of whom see the corruption as stemming in part from unreasonable demands by the central planners that the republic produce large quantities of cotton. Thus, Uzbeks with something to hide find it easy to use nationalistic animosities to hinder the work of those who are trying to fight local corruption (*The Washington Post*, June 16, 1989, pp. A29,A34).

The Uzbek case, then, illustrates most of the factors that are characteristic of the official corruption to be found in many other places in the Soviet Union. Most of the contributing factors discussed earlier in this section come into play in one way or another. This is why the problem is such a difficult one to solve. In fact, all of the problems covered in this chapter present difficulties which are so formidable that they raise the question of whether anything even approaching success will be achievable in the foreseeable future. The most that can be said at present is that the Gorbachev regime is trying to attack them with vigor and conviction, within the limits of what is possible on a practical level. Whether this will lead to a significant improvement remains to be seen.

REFERENCES

Binyon, M. (1983). *Life in Russia*. New York: Pantheon.

Brown, B. (1987a). The anticorruption campaign in Turkmenistan. *Radio Liberty Research,* no. 49/87.

BROWN, B. (1987b). The progress of restructuring in Uzbekistan. *Radio Liberty Research,* no. 246/87.

BROWN, B. (1988). Corruption reported flourishing again in Uzbekistan. *Radio Liberty Research,* no. 492/88.

CONNOR, W.D. (1972). *Deviance in Soviet Society.* New York: Columbia University Press.

CRITCHLOW, J. (1989). The growth of organized crime in Uzbekistan. *Report on the USSR, 1,* no. 7, 16–17.

DAVYDOV, G. (1986). The legacy of the Andropov "reforms." *Radio Liberty Research,* no. 330/86.

KNIGHT, A. (1988). Corruption and the law enforcement organs. *Radio Liberty Research,* no. 384/88.

KONDRATENKO V. (1990). Alcoholism: The hidden disease. *Soviet Life,* 1, 51–52.

MINISTERSTVO IUSTITSII RSFSR (1987). *Ugolovnyi kodeks RSFSR.* Moscow: "Iuridicheskaia literaturea."

MIROSHNICHENKO, L. (1988). Vo chto obkhoditsia trezvost'? *Ogonek,* no. 39, 20–23.

PETERSON, D.J. (1989a). The zone, 1989: The Soviet penal system under *perestroika. Report on the USSR, 1,* no. 37, 1–6.

PETERSON, D.J. (1989b). Much ado about crime. *Report on the USSR, 1,* no. 37, 9–11.

SIMIS, K.M. (1982). *USSR: The corrupt society.* New York: Simon & Schuster.

STAFF, (1990, March). Crime, police, and Soviet society. *The Woodrow Wilson Center Report,* pp. 1–2.

TOWNSEND, D. (1984). Soviet concern about alcoholism among women. *Radio Liberty Research,* no. 321/84.

TREHUB, A. (1987). Is Gorbachev's antidrinking campaign losing its kick? *Radio Liberty Research,* no. 323/87.

TREML, V. (1982). *Alcohol in the USSR: A statistical study.* Durham, NC: Duke University Press.

TREML, V. (1987). Gorbachev's antidrinking campaign: A noble experiment or a costly exercise in futility? *Radio Liberty Research Supplement, no. 2/87.*

VORONITSYN, S. (1978). Alcoholism among Soviet youth. *Radio Liberty Research,* no. 291/78.

VOSNESENSKAYA, YU. (1984). Alcoholism among children and teenagers. *Radio Liberty Research,* no. 307/84.

WINTER, S. (1987). An interview with Vladimir Treml on alcoholism in the USSR. *Radio Liberty Research,* no. 317/87.

FOURTEEN
SOCIAL PROBLEMS III:
Family Policy

This third chapter on social problems brings together three related subjects: (1) the status of women, (2) current policy dilemmas with regard to sex and reproduction, and (3) the situation of children and youth. The problems that women face in Soviet society are well recognized by both Soviet leaders and social scientists (see, for example, Azarova, 1989). Despite the legal and theoretical equality of women in Soviet society, the day-to-day reality of Soviet women's lives reflects significant inequalities which can and do make life very difficult for the average Soviet woman. Finding a remedy for these women's problems, however, is another matter, because the barriers to true equality are based on deeply held cultural and social beliefs. On the other hand, the importance of women in the work force is seen by the current leadership as so compelling that finding workable solutions to these problems has a definite urgency. Women are needed, at least at their present level of employment outside the home, just to keep the economic machine going, as well as to fuel the additional productivity which will be necessary to make economic perestroika a reasonable success.

Women are also needed, however, to bear and raise the next generation of Soviet workers. In this sense, the population policies of the regime (which are related to long-term work force needs) have clashed with their short-term work force needs. A tired, overworked woman faced with the demands of what amounts to two full time jobs—one in the home and one in the workplace—is seldom eager to add to her work load by bearing many children. Thus, the incentives offered by the government in an effort to increase average family size have had little impact in those parts of the country where population growth is seen as most desirable because of a shortage of workers.

The female role in the work force has also been seen by some as related to problems of Soviet youth, in the sense that women are still seen as having the major (if not exclusive) responsibility for raising the next generation. Thus, there has been official concern that mothers' work loads were contributing to behavioral problems among children and youth (see, for example, Gorbachev, 1987, p. 117). Soviet sociologists and others have pointed out, however, that the changing and often troublesome Soviet youth culture is attributable to a number of factors other than the phenomenon of working mothers. What makes these interconnected topics particularly noteworthy is the degree to which they are now being frankly and openly acknowledged in the Soviet Union. Whether this will eventually result in a dramatic change in the lives of Soviet women and their children remains to be seen. In any case, it may contribute to an effort to address a complex of policy problems connected with the problems of Soviet children and youth, some of which are uniquely Soviet but many of which have their counterparts in other industrialized countries.

Finally, there is an overarching set of problems connected with sex and reproduction. Again, they are problems that are not uncommon in other parts of the world: infant mortality, prostitution, homosexuality, and venereal diseases. Until recently, the Soviet leadership has approached social problems connected to sexual activity and reproduction with a considerable amount of denial. Such problems were not supposed to exist in "the workers' paradise;" therefore they did not. With the advent of glasnost, however, there has been an increasing willingness to acknowledge that such problems do in fact exist and that they require a policy response. The emergence of AIDS and the experience of other countries in trying to control AIDS have added a certain urgency to this policy debate. So far, the Soviet Union has, relatively speaking, been only mildly affected by AIDS compared to places like the United States. To avoid the sort of AIDS epidemic found in other countries, however, it has been necessary for the Soviet government to rethink most of its traditional policy positions with regard to sexual behavior.

Before we turn to these problems, however, we will first consider the status of women in the USSR, then we will consider some important issues related to policy making in the areas of reproduction and sexual behavior, and, finally, we will address the needs of children and the dilemmas which today's youth are posing for their elders.

WOMEN

Women's Work: The "Double Shift"

I think that one of the most wonderful forces for stability and good that I have seen in the Soviet Union are the Russian women.

President Ronald Reagan, Moscow Summit, June 1, 1988

One of the major objectives of the current Soviet reform process is to increase the productivity of the Soviet work force. At first glance this may not seem like a "women's issue." Women, however, constitute slightly over 50 percent of the Soviet work force, as well as 61 percent of people having secondary specialized or higher education and 40 percent of all scientists and researchers (Koval, 1989, p. 24). These numbers make it clear that any factors which impair the productivity of employed women will have a significant impact on overall economic performance. In this connection, the primary issue facing Soviet policymakers is how to accommodate women's responsibilities on the job with their responsibilities to their families. Neither is expendable, since the "irreplaceable contribution of women to both production and reproduction militates against measures which would seriously circumscribe their roles in either domain" (Lapidus, 1982, p. xxxv). Throughout the Soviet period, however, the stress associated with balancing those two roles (popularly known as the "double shift") has had a major impact on the quality of the lives of women and on their ability to do their best in either capacity.

On the job, for example, women have relatively high rates of absenteeism, due to chronic fatigue and related health problems, as well as to the fact that they usually take responsibility for children who are sick.[1] They are also less likely than men to have time for advanced training and overtime work. Such factors contribute significantly (though not exclusively) to the fact that women are underrepresented at higher levels throughout the Soviet economy, as well as in political and professional life. The many demands on the time and energy of Soviet women when combined with the chronic housing shortage (which often forces young couples to live in dormitories or with parents) tends to discourage women from childbearing. In the poignant words of one Soviet career woman: "I was sure that if I had a child, my life would turn into a domestic hell and, what would be hardest for me, I would lose my qualifications as a specialist" (Grigoryeva and Sonova, 1984, p. 16). Particularly in the urbanized and industrialized western areas of the Soviet Union, this has led to concerns about a shrinking work force.[2]

The personal impact on Soviet families is also substantial. Currently,

---

[1]This alone costs the Soviet Union approximately 168 million working days per year (Pukhova, 1987, p. 103).

[2]As of 1988, population growth was below replacement in the RSFSR, the Ukraine, Byelorussia, Lithuania, Latvia, and Estonia (Arutyunyan, 1988).

Soviet policymakers are particularly concerned about the high divorce rate and the fact that most working parents are able to spend very little quality time with their children. In 1988 a poll showed that the average Soviet working mother spends less than 30 minutes a week communicating with her children; the average father spends 6 minutes. Further, this situation was seen by a prominent Soviet sociologist as a cause of juvenile delinquency (Bohr, 1989, p. 13).

The founders of the Soviet state, citing Marxist theory, held that the entry of women into the work force would have a liberating effect on women and thus was a desirable goal. To reach that goal, however, not only would women have to be given access to job opportunities outside the home, but they would also have to have much of their domestic work done by others. During the period after the revolution, political turbulence and economic problems forced the postponement of these services. It did not postpone, however, the need for female labor. Necessity dictated that Soviet women play an active role in the economy while somehow managing to get their housework done.

This imbalance has never been adequately redressed. The result is that, over the years, women have had greater job opportunity than ever before, but have been severely limited in their ability to take advantage of it. The "economic priorities that resulted in the underdevelopment of the service sector and of consumer industries, as well as the failure to fully socialize child-care and household functions or to alter the allocation of roles within the family" resulted in the creation of a dual burden of responsibility in the daily life of Soviet women (Lapidus, 1978, pp. 5-6).

Thus, the current proponents of economic reform are faced with two interrelated problems in their efforts to raise productivity. First, they must deal with the prospect of continual shortages in the work force, aggravated by a slowing of population growth to below replacement in the urbanized, industrialized areas where workers are most in demand. Soviet experts have estimated that "the simple reproduction of the population" will necessitate the encouragement of anywhere from a three- to a five-child family.[3] In Soviet Central Asia, where there is a labor surplus, the value placed on the extended traditional family leads workers to resist moving to more industrialized parts of the country where they are needed. This is related to the second problem, the fact that raising Soviet productivity to world standards cannot adequately be done by a technological "quick fix." More workers, especially educated, skilled workers, are absolutely necessary. These workers, however, must, in the short

---

[3]An exception would be Soviet Central Asia where, since 1950, the population has tripled. At least one Soviet expert projects a 400 percent increase in population in that region during the next 60 years (*The Current Digest of the Soviet Press, 39,* no. 47, 1987, p. 26). The high birthrate in Central Asia is a problem which Soviet policymakers have been reluctant to confront, since measures to limit population growth could be seen as having racial or ethnic overtones. Recently, however, the government of Tajikistan announced the beginning of a propaganda campaign to persuade Tajik families to limit the number of children they produce (Sheehy, 1987).

run, include significant numbers of women of childbearing age. In the long run, they must also include the children whom these women are capable of bearing.

Virtually all Soviet women either work or are full-time students, though the figure for Soviet Central Asia is lower than for most of the rest of the country. In Estonia, for example, almost 95 percent of all able-bodied women are employed (*Izvestiia,* March 2, 1988, p. 1). What is life like for the working woman in the urbanized, industrialized parts of the Soviet Union? First and foremost, it is difficult, since married women are usually responsible for just about all of the housework and child care—as well as full-time jobs. Also, for most, it is a life of limited opportunity.

Beginning in the mid–1960s, Soviet scholars have documented the fact that, like women elsewhere in the industrialized world, Soviet women are over-represented on the lowest rungs of the economic ladder (Arutyunyan, 1988). They tend to hold relatively unskilled jobs, have limited upward mobility, and receive smaller paychecks than men.[4] Even when their qualifications equal or surpass those of their male colleagues, they tend to be classified into lower paying positions than equally qualified males. For example, 48 percent of men with specialized secondary or higher education hold managerial positions; only 7 percent of comparably educated women do (Koval, 1989, p. 24). In addition, many of their jobs involve working conditions which are potentially physically harmful, causing Soviet critics to charge that the existing protective legislation is neither adequate nor properly enforced (Pukhova, 1987, pp. 100–101).

Much emphasis is placed on protective legislation for women, because Soviet policymakers have traditionally proceeded from the assumption that there are biologically based, sex-linked differences in job ability and preferences (see, for example, Lukin, 1986). Thus, the validity of differentiating between "men's work" and "women's work" is seldom questioned. Correspondingly, in contrast with feminist writers in the United States, Soviet commentators have accorded relatively little importance to differences in the socialization of male and female children. The emphasis is on creating working situations which accommodate the "anatomical-physiological peculiarities of the female organism and likewise . . . the moral-ethical temperament of women" (Lapidus, 1982, p. xxiv).

There is, however, a gap between policy and practice (Mihalisko, 1989). A significant amount of the heavy physical labor in several key industries is performed by women. Also, women constitute most of the manual workers in several agricultural sectors. Many of the measures intended to protect the health and safety of women are seldom implemented. Why do women not

---

[4]On the average, women earn 30 percent less than men do (Koval, 1989, p. 24). Soviet commentators have called attention to the fact that low pay tends to cause the "feminization" of certain jobs. Specifically mentioned in one article was the fact that in the Soviet Union medicine is a low-paying field overwhelmingly staffed by women, while in the West it is a high-paying field overwhelmingly staffed by men (Zakharova, Posadskaia and Rimashevskaia, 1989).

claim their legal rights? Often significant benefits go with jobs involving heavy labor. For example, people in such jobs often get larger paychecks or priority status for scarce housing (*Izvestiia,* September 15, 1985, p. 3).

Nonetheless, biological rationales are used, not just for policies like limiting the weight a woman can be required to lift but also to exclude women from certain jobs. Thus, biology is frequently cited as a reason why women are underrepresented in certain occupations and at certain levels. Recently, however, there has been increasing recognition that the lower economic status of women is a result of social, as well as biological, factors. Consequently, there have been calls for social reform. At the twenty-seventh Party Congress Gorbachev noted the need for more measures to aid Soviet women in combining motherhood with employment. Among the suggestions for improvement were increased opportunities for women to work part-time or at home, longer paid maternity leaves, and the building of more day care centers.

None of these, however, address one of the major problems of working women. The concepts of "men's work" and "women's work" carry over to housework, practically all of which is considered to be "women's work." Thus, the fact that women carry most of the burden of housekeeping and child care is regarded as perfectly natural by most Soviet men. The result is that women spend more than twice as much time on housework as do their husbands (who tend to ignore official encouragement to do "their share"). Estimates of the amount of time spent on housework by working mothers with small children have gone as high as 32 hours a week (Voznesenskaya, 1984, p. 2). Also, it has been reported that men have at least 10 more leisure hours a week than women (Boguslavskaya, 1988, p. 16). Although many Soviet commentators see increased male help as the most desirable solution to a critical problem, changing traditional male attitudes and behavior will not be easy.

All of these factors combine to make it very difficult for a married woman with children to follow the kind of career path that eventually leads to leadership positions. Even in fields like medicine, which are dominated by women, the most prestigious posts are almost invariably held by men. The president of the Committee of Soviet Women has asserted that only 12 percent of the top executives and chief engineers in Soviet industry were women (Pukhova, 1987, p. 102). She also noted that while women constituted 40 percent of all scientific workers, only 2 percent were full or corresponding members of the Academy of Sciences.

Turning to the political arena, although women constitute a majority of the members of local governing bodies (Boguslavskaya, 1988, p. 22), only two have reached top national leadership posts in recent history.[5] As of 1989 there was one woman in the Politburo (Alexandra Biriukova, a candidate member

[5]Ekaterina Furtseva was a Politburo candidate member from 1956 to 1957 and a Politburo full member from 1957 to 1961; Furtseva was also the only female CC Secretary until Alexandra Biriukova was named to the Secretariat in 1986. Biriukova achieved candidate Politburo membership in 1988.

and Deputy Chairman of the Council of Ministers of the USSR). Women have fared only slightly better at the middle levels of the CPSU, constituting 7 percent of all provincial and regional committee secretaries (Bohr, 1989, p. 15). In an article in *Kommunist,* the official journal of the CPSU, the president of the Committee of Soviet Women called for women to make stronger efforts to remedy this inequity (Pukhova, 1987. p. 102). One reason for this situation appears to be the willingness of Soviet women to accept the paternalism of male political leaders. Others include the burdens of housework and motherhood, traditional attitudes toward women, and a lack of political ambition on the part of most women.

Given all of this, it may seem strange that there is no significant feminist movement in the Soviet Union. What feminist impulse there is seems to be limited to a relatively small group of women and is significantly different in many ways from Western feminism (Mamonova, 1984; Holt, 1985). The most widespread women's organizations, the Women's Soviets (*zhensovety*), have—to date—tended to concentrate on activities which reinforce traditional female roles, particularly in the family (Browning, 1985). An example is helping women with their shopping chores by arranging for stores to bring their merchandise to places of work. In this sense, though their aid is valuable, they perpetuate the influences which discourage women from aspiring to leadership positions in government and the economy.

Women's Work: Marriage and the Family

> If you wish—we are obligated to renew the one cult that is possible in our country—the cult of the family.
>
> *Albert Likhanov, President, Organizing Committee*
> *Lenin Soviet Childrens' Fund (Pravda,* August 13, 1987, p. 6.)

If the burdens of marriage, family, and job are so great and if the job is the least negotiable of the three (as it currently seems to be for most Soviet women), why do more women not opt for the single life? In most societies there is considerable pressure to legitimize heterosexual relationships via marriage, and the Soviet Union is no exception. Factors such as tradition, status, and family expectations all play a part. In addition, however, official ideology tends to regard married people as more "morally stable," and thus dependable, than unmarried people (Alexandrova, 1984). This means that single persons can suffer significant social, economic, and political discrimination.

Correspondingly, it is very difficult for a Soviet woman to choose to remain childless. To the outside observer, one of the most delightful things about Soviet life is the genuine and uninhibited affection for children that most Soviet people demonstrate. In addition, as has been pointed out earlier, the Soviet government is very concerned about a shrinking work force and is not subtle in conveying this concern to women of reproductive age. It is a measure of the seriousness of the problems associated with childbearing and rearing that the women of this child-loving culture have made the single-child family the norm in the urban, industrialized parts of the country.

In spite of all the pressures exerted, however, marriage and the family have been the areas in which many Soviet women have decided to limit their responsibilities. In recent years a rising level of female education and employment have been matched by lower marriage rates, marriage at an older age, fewer children, and more divorces. This situation, combined with the need to increase the birthrate, has made the government susceptible to pressures to give special privileges to mothers with several children. And such mothers have recently been making demands for even more formal and informal privileges. In the latter category, we find a mother asking why "not a single food store posts a sign saying that mothers with several children will be given their groceries without waiting" (*Izvestiia,* November 4, 1985, p. 3). There have also been complaints about the implementation of special benefits legislation: "If there are benefits for families with several children, why aren't they advertized? For example, I learned about the reduction in parents' income tax only this year and purely by accident" (*Izvestiia,* November 4, 1985, p. 3).

Such complaints (and, of course, awareness of the very real problems of these women) have led the Soviet government to pass a series of measures during the 1980s which increased benefits for the working mother. In 1989 women were given the right to partially paid maternity leave for up to a year and a half. Unpaid maternity leave may be taken for up to three years. The partial pay, however, is 35 rubles a month, which is considered inadequate by some (*CDSP, 40,* no. 34, 1989, p. 31). In spite of this, an overwhelming majority of new mothers have taken advantage of these provisions to stay home with their children. In addition, the establishment of day care facilities has been given a higher priority.

Particular problems are posed by the single-parent family. Since women still outnumber men by a considerable margin, many women decide to have children out of wedlock, because they become convinced that they are not going to marry and they want children. These women now constitute a majority of single mothers and usually have only one child. All single mothers are entitled to certain benefits, including financial assistance and preferential access to day care and housing. There are also, however, single parents who have more than one child.

In 1986 the government adopted a resolution "On Additional Measures of Assistance to Low Income, Single Parent Families Having Three or More Children." Starting in 1987, the children from these families are supposed to be provided with free school, athletic and Pioneer uniforms, and free breakfasts. Also, they are allowed to attend Young Pioneer camps free and they and their parents are allowed to take free vacations. The resolution established a minimum child support payment of 20 rubles a month per child, deductible from the earnings of the noncustodial parent. If this minimum cannot be met, the child support payment can be supplemented by local governments (*Izvestiia,* October 21, 1986, p. 2).

Most recently, in 1987 the USSR Supreme Soviet expanded benefits for working women who are pregnant or have small children. It was specifically stated in the legislation that the intent of the legislature was to lighten the burden of the "double shift." The law establishes the right to part-time work of women who are pregnant, have children under eight, or are caring for sick family members. It also mandates the transfer to lighter work of pregnant women or women with infants, if their medical condition warrants it. Finally, a woman on leave to care for an infant may do additional part-time work at home without losing the partial pay associated with the leave.

All of these measures were adopted on a national level. In 1988, however, the Estonian Republic exempted large low-income families from paying income taxes and reduced by 40 percent the taxes of large families with higher incomes. When combined with previously existing tax reductions established by the national government, this means that large families in Estonia will now pay less than one-third of the normal income tax, regardless of income level. This is part of a larger demographic strategy formally adopted by the Estonian government. It also includes measures such as exempting mothers with several children or with children under three from having to stand in lines in railway stations, stores, and theaters (*Izvestiia,* March 2, 1988, p. 1).

Of particular concern to Soviet authorities in recent years has been a high divorce rate. Currently, the rate has stabilized at from 0.5 to 3.5 divorces for every 10 marriages.[6] Almost 70 percent of these divorces are initiated by women (Arutyunyan, 1988). *Izvestiia* (February 1, 1987, p. 4) has asserted that every year 1.4 percent of all the married couples in the Soviet Union divorce. Some Soviet commentators tie this tendency to family size—the larger the family, the less likely a divorce. The clear message is that larger families are more stable, and thus more desirable. The impact of divorce on children has also been an issue emphasized by the CPSU: "Each year more than 700,000 children lose one of their parents as a result of divorce" (Pukhova, 1987, p. 103).

Another obvious reason for an increasing divorce rate is the amount of stress experienced by families because of the "double shift." For example, the writer of a letter to a Soviet medical newspaper complained that nurses "have no time for family life." She continued, "We work around the clock, two nights running and three 12-hour days in a row, with virtually no days off. Some of us are on the verge of divorce" (*CDSP, 37,* no 27, 1985, p. 17). In another newspaper (*Izvestiia,* October 8, 1986, p. 3), an estranged husband complained about the way he was treated in his own home (shared with his in-laws). An editor of the newspaper responded: "Aren't you husbands and fathers the people who turn women into something you later don't like? Didn't you burden us with the responsibility for all of the housework?"

[6]The exact figure varies with the region of the country.

Even in intact families there is a tendency for many mothers to try to shift part or all of their child care responsibilities to other people or institutions. As a Soviet journalist put it: "'Visiting mothers' are now making their appearance alongside the 'visiting fathers'" (*CDSP, 38,* no. 14, 1986, p. 30). Grandmothers and single relatives undertake part or all child-rearing tasks for some of these women. For others, state-run institutions, such as boarding schools, offer a solution. In some cases, such substitute parenting might be perfectly adequate, but often it is substandard. There is evidence of official concern about these developments: "Society gets people who are broken, shattered and embittered—who haven't been taught to build full relationships with others" (*CDSP, 38,* no. 14, 1986, p. 29). Such concerns might have contributed to the decision to establish the benefits outlined earlier in this section.

REPRODUCTION

During most of the Soviet period, official policy and social custom have combined to make sex a forbidden topic in public discussion. Laws prohibited sexual explicitness in the media, as well as in movies and the theater. This puritanism goes back to Lenin, whose writings cautioned against sexual excess. In recent years, however, it has become apparent that this conspiracy of silence about sex has not prevented many Soviet men and women from engaging in extramarital sexual activity. As of 1987, almost 10 percent of all children born in the Soviet Union had single mothers. This represents an upward trend in illegitimate births since 1980 of about one percentage point (Bohr, 1988, p. 2).

The highest percentage of illegitimate births involve mothers who are under the age of 20 (7.1 percent of all births in this age group). Looked at another way, 16 percent of all unmarried women bear children before they are 20. Most of these children (86.3 percent) are firstborns (*CDSP, 37,* no. 39, 1985, pp. 11–12). Many Soviet commentators have seen this trend as evidence of a need for better sex education in the schools. Until recently, however, such courses were not part of the school curriculum. Only in 1983 was a sex education course made compulsory for all eighth graders. Subsequently, a required course on "The Ethics and Psychology of Family Life" was developed for ninth and tenth graders. Soviet policymakers hope that these educational measures will cut down on the number of pregnancies among young unmarried women.

Another very important factor in this upward movement in the number of illegitimate births is a shortage of available and effective means for preventing pregnancy. According to a recent estimate, approximately 80 percent of the population uses ineffective methods of contraception (*Ogonek,* August, 1988, p. 19). Contraceptive devices are a scarce commodity in the Soviet Union. When they can be found—which may be as little as 10 percent of the time—they are often poorly made, leading couples to doubt both their safety and their effectiveness. Also, the lack of any well organized program for distribution and education means that there is widespread ignorance about methods of contraception and the proper use of birth-control methods. Consequently, most couples do not practice birth control or, at best, only practice it occasionally.

To date, Soviet authorities have seemed ambivalent about mounting concerted efforts to increase the availability and improve the quality of birth control devices. At least part of the problem may stem from the fact that the government is trying to raise the birthrate, particularly in industrialized areas where there is a shortage of workers. One indication that they may be getting ready to do more in the future, however, is the fact that in 1987 the Collegium of the USSR Ministry of Public Health recommended that more resources be devoted to family planning and increasing the use of modern birth-control methods.

Abortion

Abortion is the primary method of birth control; for each live birth there are approximately two abortions.[7] This makes the Soviet abortion rate one of the highest in the world.[8] About 80 percent of these abortions involve the failure of some method of contraception (*CDSP, 39,* no. 44, 1987, p. 15). There was a period in Soviet history, from 1936 to 1955, when abortion was illegal. After it was legalized, the rate rose steadily until the late 1960s. Subsequently, it dropped off slightly but has remained high. Currently, it is estimated that about one-fifth of women of child-bearing age undergo an abortion in any given year (*Ogonek,* August, 1988, p. 18). Only 15 to 18 percent of the women in the USSR have never had an abortion. The average woman has had about three and about 15 percent have had several in a single year (*CDSP, 39,* no. 44, 1987, p. 15). Finally, about 90 percent of first pregnancies end in abortion (*Report on the USSR,* February 3, 1989, p. 37).

Such statistics are of particular concern to policymakers, since abortions can cause subsequent difficulty in carrying a baby to term and giving birth. Illegal abortions often result in death, sterility, or permanent disability. Both physicians and people without medical degrees can incur penalties for performing illegal abortions. The penalties are increased in cases involving more than one abortion, death, or other "grave consequences" (RSFSR Criminal Code, Article 116). The woman having the abortion is not considered to have broken the law—even if she performs it herself (*CDSP, 38,* no. 30, 1986, p. 30).

---

[7]The abortion rate is probably much higher among the Baltic and Slavic portions of the population because it is low among Central Asians for religious and cultural reasons.

[8]According to the World Health Organization, about 25 percent of the abortions performed around the world each year are performed in the Soviet Union, even though the Soviet Union has less than 6 percent of the world's population (*Ogonek,* August, 1988, p. 18).

Between 50 and 80 percent of the abortions performed are illegal (*Ogonek,* August, 1988, p.18), 70 to 90 percent involving women terminating first pregnancies who want to avoid having people know about the unwanted pregnancy (*CDSP, 39,* no. 44, 1987, p. 15). In recognition of this fact, there are plans to develop a network of clinics able to perform abortions anonymously (*CDSP, 40,* no. 7, 1988, p. 24). Many illegal abortions have been intended to circumvent legal limitations on the circumstances under which a legal abortion may be performed. In 1988 the abortion regulations were eased, extending the legal termination period from 12 to 28 weeks and allowing a larger number of reasons for abortion. One of the newly approved reasons is the youth (physiological immaturity) of the prospective mother.

Abortions are relatively inexpensive in the Soviet Union. If one wishes to arrange for special treatment, however, they may cost more. Currently, 50 to 70 rubles seems to be the going rate for "back door" abortions at medical facilities (*CDSP, 39,* no. 44, 1987, p. 16). Since these involve a form of bribery, they can also be classified as illegal abortions, although they are much safer than those performed outside medical facilities and may even be safer than some legal abortions. One reason why a woman might want to pay this much is the fact that frequently legal abortions are performed without effective anesthesia. In 1987 in response to this problem, the Collegium of the USSR Ministry of Public Health instructed the union republic ministers of health to punish doctors performing such operations without anesthesia.

If one were to draw a portrait of the typical Soviet woman getting an abortion, she would have the following characteristics (Moffett, 1985b): First, she would be married. The overwhelming majority of women seeking to terminate pregnancies do so for reasons such as crowded housing conditions, inadequate child care facilities, marital problems, and job pressures. This leads to the second characteristic; she would be employed. Almost all Soviet women over 16 are employed or are full-time students. For either financial or professional reasons, pregnancy can cause an unwelcome interruption in employment. Third, she would have had at least one previous abortion. Given the extent to which abortion is the dominant means of birth control, multiple abortions are common.

Currently, there are definite indications of a recognition that this situation cannot continue. There also seems to be the acknowledgment that trying to restrict or abolish abortions is not the answer. The political leadership needs to develop a way to offer the Soviet people safe, comfortable, and effective birth-control devices, as well as a system for encouraging their proper use. This seems to be the direction in which Soviet policymakers are beginning to move (*The New York Times,* February 28, 1989, p. A3).

Prostitution

During the early Soviet period there were criminal laws aimed at prostitutes. In the 1930s, however, the claim was made that since the causes of prostitution had been eliminated by the Revolution, it was no longer a social problem. Thus, there was no need for laws outlawing prostitution (*CDSP, 40,* no. 8, 1988, p. 23). This remained official policy until quite recently.[9] Until 1985, legal silence was matched by media silence. Then, beginning with an article in the prestigious *Literaturnaia Gazeta,* the press began to publish articles on prostitution that were clearly intended to call public attention to what was perceived by the editors as a serious problem (Konovalov, 1986).

One of the complaints was that none of the criminal codes of any of the union republics forbade the sale of one's body (for example, prostitution). Thus, while authorities could utilize various other articles to bring charges against a small number of prostitutes,[10] there was no way they could punish prostitution. The fact that it was a significant problem can be illustrated in various ways. For example, one newspaper reported that a single Moscow police official had, over the course of 15 years' work in his precinct, accumulated records on more than 3,500 prostitutes (*CDSP, 39,* no. 11, 1987, p. 1). These women ranged in age from 14 to 70 and tended to be down on their luck for a variety of reasons, ranging from advancing age to alcoholism. In many cases, their clients became the victims of related crimes, such as robbery.

There are roughly two strata of prostitutes. The higher stratum is composed of young, good-looking women who are able to attract the most desirable clients. In the Soviet Union this means foreigners and Soviet men with access to foreign currency or scarce consumer goods. These women are usually referred to as "foreign currency" prostitutes, although they are said to call themselves "good-time girls" (*putanki*). In 1986, for example, Moscow authorities detained 726 women for staying or attempting to stay overnight in foreigners' living quarters (Konovalov, 1987a, p. 4). Foreign currency prostitution can be quite lucrative. Recently, two Moscow prostitutes were found to have accumulated nearly a half-million rubles from foreign currency transactions (*CDSP, 40,* no. 8, 1988, p. 23).

Prostitutes in the lower stratum depend on Soviet citizens at the less privileged end of the social spectrum; truck drivers, soldiers, and persons passing through railway stations. They get paid in rubles and have a more modest lifestyle. In some cases, however, they can do quite well. The newspaper, *Nedelia* (Week), published a story about a "Moscow Madam" who charged from 100 to 150 rubles for an evening with one of her girls (*CDSP, 39,* no. 11, 1987, p. 5). On a good evening, the madam made 400 to 500 rubles. But this lower stratum also includes women who hang around railway stations looking for chances to sell themselves for as little as five rubles—or even a drink of cheap liquor.

---

[9]In the mid–1960s and early 1970s there was an effort by various government agencies to gain the power to combat prostitution, but it proved ineffective. The major thrust of the Soviet Criminal Law, to date, has been directed at those who induce others, especially minors, to become involved in prostitution, not at the prostitutes themselves (Konovalov, 1987a, pp. 1–2).

[10]For example, there are laws against running "dens of debauchery," infecting others with venereal diseases, leading a parasitic way of life, and conducting illegal currency transactions.

In 1987 the Presidium of the RSFSR Supreme Soviet passed a decree against prostitution. This was not, however, the criminal law which many wanted. Rather, it imposes administrative penalties for engaging in prostitution. For the first offense offenders are given a warning and a fine of up to 100 rubles. For subsequent offenses in the same year, there are fines of up to 200 rubles. The decree also authorizes medical examination of prostitutes for purposes of detecting and treating venereal diseases. Persons suspected of prostitution can be called to a police station and given an official warning, detained, and searched for items (unspecified) which might be subject to confiscation.[11]

Although this was widely regarded as a step in the right direction, it did not satisfy those who wanted criminal penalties for prostitution, nor did it eliminate prostitution (*CDSP, 40,* no. 8, 1988, pp. 23, 31). In 1988 a group of sociologists did a detailed study of prostitution in the Georgian Republic and concluded that, while the new administrative measures might aid in the fight against the spread of venereal disease, it was necessary to find out more about the root causes of prostitution in order to combat it effectively. They concluded that "prostitution is a result of the differences between women's aspirations for self-affirmation and self-fulfillment and the reality of their lives," noting: "What does a young woman in the big city encounter? A modest salary and also, right under her nose, 'the good life' " (*CDSP, 40,* no. 8, 1988, p. 22).

Their report contained information about the women who engage in prostitution. Most of the 532 women they studied were under the age of 30 (70.1 percent) and included 85.5 percent who were divorced or had never been married. Three-fourths had completed secondary school and 91.9 percent were currently employed or had been previously. Quite obviously, most of these women had other alternatives. Why, then, turn to prostitution? A majority felt that they needed to supplement their incomes. The financial lure of prostitution is illustrated by another study which asked pupils at 10 Moscow secondary schools which occupations were most lucrative. Prostitution tied for ninth place (from the top) with the jobs of director and sales clerk. Whether the desire for supplementary income stems from need or from greed, it is clear that a materially improved life is a primary goal. The top three things prostitutes bought with their money were clothing, cosmetics, and food. Some also spent it on their children and on housing.

One of the reasons why Soviet policymakers have become so concerned about prostitution is the threat of spreading venereal diseases and AIDS.[12] As one Soviet journalist expressed it: "It is common knowledge that prostitutes are among the main transmitters of the AIDS virus" (*CDSP, 40,* no. 8, 1988,

---

[11]Another change in the Administrative Law Code of the RSFSR (Article 164.3) which was made at the same time indicated that the items subject to confiscation are ones which have been purchased from, traded with, or acquired from foreigners.

[12]AIDS is a sexually transmitted disease, but is not a venereal disease.

p. 23). Another commentator saw the issue more broadly, but the bottom line was still AIDS: "Drug addiction, drunkenness and prostitution march hand in hand, and behind them looms the specter of AIDS" (*CDSP, 39*, no. 42, 1987, p. 11).

Sexually Transmitted Diseases: AIDS

The traditional Soviet reluctance to discuss sexual topics has led to a paucity of information about sexually transmitted diseases. According to a prominent Soviet medical researcher (Konovalov, 1987b, p. 2), only two types of venereal disease are a problem in the Soviet Union: gonorrhea and syphilis. Aside from the obvious high-risk groups (for example, prostitutes and the promiscuous), a high and growing proportion of those known to have venereal disease are minors. Obviously, members of the high-risk groups can also be minors, but it is not clear how much overlap there is. Also, many people try to treat themselves to avoid being identified by the authorities.

Secrecy is of particular concern to prostitutes, since transmitting venereal disease is a crime punishable by two years' deprivation of freedom, two years' corrective labor, or a fine of up to 200 rubles (RSFSR Criminal Code, Article 115). Knowing transmission or repeat offenses, as well as transmission to a minor, are more harshly punished. The Criminal Code also makes it a crime to evade treatment for a venereal disease once the person has a medical diagnosis. The punishment alternatives are two years' deprivation of treatment, two years' corrective labor, or a fine of up to 200 rubles.

At present, however, venereal diseases are of much less concern to public health authorities than the possibility that a serious AIDS problem might develop in the Soviet Union. The Soviet press first began to mention AIDS in 1985.[13] The first verified case of AIDS in the Soviet Union was registered in 1986 (*Izvestiia,* March 19, 1987, p. 3). These early media reports dealt with AIDS as a disease affecting foreigners, mainly Westerners. Some asserted that AIDS was a product of American laboratories and was being used by the U.S. government as a form of biological warfare (see, for example, *Literaturnaia Gazeta,* October 30, 1985, p. 14). Such reporting diminished over the next two years, perhaps because several prominent Soviet scientists repudiated such assertions and criticized them as "irresponsible" (*Izvestiia,* October 31, 1987, p. 6).

Currently, the number of Soviet citizens with AIDS is so small as to be insignificant compared with, say, the number of AIDS victims in any major American city. It is clear that Soviet policymakers are reacting to the threat of AIDS, rather than to any existing epidemic. This fact, in and of itself, may insure that AIDS remains much less of a public health problem than it would

---

[13]In Russian, AIDS is called SPID (pronounced "speed"). As in English, it consists of the initials for "acquired immunological deficit syndrome" (*sindrom priobretennogo immunnogo defitisita*).

have been had the political leadership not made a decision to move so quickly and decisively. AIDS will almost certainly, however, eventually become a greater public health problem than it is now.

Unlike the situation in the United States, relationships between homosexuals were not originally a major source for the spread of the AIDS virus. Rather, the first sources of contagion were prostitutes and the poor sanitary practices and conditions in Soviet medical facilities. Only later did homosexuals and intravenous drug users become a major conduit (*The Washington Post,* January 11, 1990, p. A25).

Ironically, the fact that the Soviet Union was such a closed society for so long gave it some protection against the type of undetected contagion that characterized the spread of AIDS to the United States and other more open societies. At a time when the AIDS situation in the United States was already being called an "epidemic," there was virtually no incidence of AIDS in the Soviet population. Foreigners, particularly transients, were the major avenue for the introduction of AIDS. The fact that the "upper crust" of prostitution is composed of "foreign currency" prostitutes points to the danger. These prostitutes prefer foreign men to Soviet men because of the ability of foreigners to give them precious foreign currency and desirable foreign goods. Usually, however, they also have Soviet men among their clients. In addition, when they become older and less attractive, they tend to turn to the general Soviet male population. Thus, AIDS got its start primarily by this sort of transmission, and it is not surprising that the first official AIDS death in the Soviet Union was the death of a Leningrad prostitute with many foreign clients (*The Washington Post,* November 11, 1988, p. A27).

When the AIDS virus is present in larger numbers in the Soviet population, the spread of the disease among Soviet citizens (rather than from foreigners to Soviet citizens) will become more of a problem. There is a problem, however, that the industrialized Western countries have not had: Disposable syringes and other single-use medical equipment are not widely available to the Soviet medical profession, and sterilization practices in many Soviet hospitals are notoriously lax. The lack of an adequate supply of disposable medical equipment has made it impossible for medical personnel to avoid the reuse of equipment which comes into contact with bodily fluids and therefore presents a definite danger to people being treated for other medical conditions (*Ogonek,* July, 1989, pp. 7–8). Thus, it came as a horrible shock in early 1989 when it was reported that 27 infants had been infected with the AIDS virus by contaminated syringes in a provincial children's hospital; four mothers had also contracted the virus from breast-feeding their infants. Subsequently, there have been other reports of infection in medical facilities by medical equipment, primarily syringes. By 1990 half of all HIV positive people in the USSR were children (*Report on the USSR,* March 2, 1990, p. 37).

Soviet policymakers reacted by giving a very high industrial priority to the production of disposable syringes. This is not, however, going to help the situation in the short run. To encourage medical personnel to be more careful about contagion, the people responsible for these incidents were fired and criminal investigations instituted in some cases. In addition, both private citizens (*Ogonek,* July, 1989, pp. 7–8) and public officials (*Report on the USSR,* August 18, 1989, p. 28) began urgently trying to obtain foreign currency to buy disposable syringes and other medical equipment in the West. Thus, by the time the AIDS virus has a chance to infect larger numbers of the Soviet population, they hope to have the means to prevent its spread through the use of inadequately sterilized equipment in medical facilities. Similarly, they have established a monitoring system for donated blood. The potential effectiveness of many of these measures, however, is being compromised by the poor state of the economy.

There is a tendency for the press to imply that AIDS is more readily transmitted if the sexual relations are promiscuous or "perverted" (see, for example, *Izvestiia,* June 16, 1987, p. 3). This implies something more moralistic than the statistical probability of a person with a homosexual or promiscuous lifestyle catching AIDS and is a holdover from the prudish days when sex was a taboo subject. There are signs, however, of a realization that it is dangerous to lull people with a conventional lifestyle into a false sense of security: "As experience has shown, the virus is perfectly comfortable in the body of a highly upstanding person. Drug abuse and homosexuality are not essential to its spread" (*CDSP, 39,* no. 33, 1987, pp. 17–18).

A major factor in the U.S. struggle against AIDS has been the acknowledgment that it is very difficult to persuade people to abstain from sex, even when the danger of AIDS is present. This has led to an effort to encourage people to practice "safe sex"—in other words, to use condoms. Currently condoms are the most readily available form of birth-control device in the USSR. This is relative, rather than absolute. In absolute numbers, it has been estimated that, given the number being produced as of 1989, there were approximately three per year for each Soviet male (*Pravda,* February 21, 1989, p. 3).

If they can be found, Soviet condoms are inexpensive. They are not, however, of very high quality. The primary problem seems to be that, to date, they have been of such poor quality that they deserve their nickname, "galoshes" (Moffett, 1985a, p. 6). Thus, it is necessary for Soviet industry to increase both the quantity and quality of condoms before they can be used as a major AIDS prevention method. Until recently, there was relatively little media attention given to this form of AIDS prevention (*The Washington Post,* April 29, 1990, p. A29). Rather, the emphasis has been on the advantages of a moral lifestyle and the reaffirmation of family values (*Izvestiia,* March 19, 1987, p. 3).

Since February 1987, an information, testing, and research campaign to combat AIDS began. At the same time, the government took more drastic steps. The Presidium of the USSR Supreme Soviet passed a decree entitled

"On Measures to Prevent Infection with the Aids Virus" (*Izvestiia,* August 26, 1987, p. 2). This decree established mandatory AIDS testing for all citizens of the USSR, as well as foreigners who were in the Soviet Union. The Ministry of Public Health was empowered to establish the regulations governing this process. In cases of refusal to be tested, the resisting individual could be compelled to be tested with the help, if necessary, of the police. Foreigners and stateless persons refusing tests could be expelled from the Soviet Union. Under this legislation, if an individual knowingly puts another person in jeopardy of getting AIDS, he or she is subject to imprisonment for up to five years. Intentionally infecting another person with the AIDS virus is punishable by up to eight years in prison.

In the Soviet Union those infected with AIDS, like drug addicts, must be officially registered. An eminent medical authority has described the process as follows (*Izvestiia,* June 16, 1987, p. 3): When a persons is suspected of having AIDS, he or she is not immediately registered. Rather, the individual is hospitalized and medical personnel carry out a complete diagnostic process designed to rule out the possibility of some other reason for the symptoms. Only after the AIDS diagnosis has been carefully verified does official registration take place. As a result, there is usually a two-week period between identification as a possible AIDS victim and official registration. As part of the identification process the government has established a large number of diagnostic centers. It is not clear how many of these will honor a request for anonymity.

Finally, like the United States, the Soviet Union has a problem with exaggerated fear of, and hostility toward, the victims of AIDS, as well as members of high-risk groups. For example, a youth newspaper printed the following comment from a reader: "I fully endorse the . . . view that AIDS is a cleansing agent for humanity that will rid it of drug addicts, homosexuals, and prostitutes" (*CDSP, 39,* no. 45, 1987, p. 27). In the same issue, another reader criticized the fact that some people were blaming AIDS on Africans and showing prejudice against them as a result. More frightening was a letter from a 15-year-old girl and her friends:

> Enough idiotic advice! "Don't have casual sexual encounters!" . . . We don't have the strength to resist these pleasures. Besides, is this AIDS so dangerous? Maybe it's just being used to scare us. In that case, it's a cheap trick, and we're not going to fall for it.

YOUTH: THE PERESTROIKA GENERATION

> [The Pioneers] behaved in a simply unpredictable manner. After the words, "Are there other proposals?", the delegates began to make noise: "There are! We have something to say; we protest!"
>
> *News report, IX All-union Rally of Young Pioneers*
> *(Pravda, December 13, 1987, p. 3)*

This is the generation that will build and consolidate perestroika—if any will. At least some of its members seem already to have learned a bit about glasnost, and perhaps even democratization. Not the least of what these particular Young Pioneers learned was that they could have an impact. Although they were not successful in getting their proposals adopted, their underlying complaint was heard. A Pioneer named Lena expressed it thus: "We want pioneers to participate in the regional councils (*sovety*) of the pioneers, and not just old ladies." They got their wish. After the rally, the adult leadership recommended that Pioneers be included in the governing structures of regional and local Young Pioneer organizations.

As the reporter pointed out, this did not give them the right to elect their own leaders, but it gave them some representation and, perhaps, a feeling that they had a bit of influence on their own organization. If they are to be the perestroika generation, to bring the reform to fruition, they must have the chance to practice open discussion, taking the initiative, and being responsible for their own actions. These are necessary for both democratization and economic progress. As the reporter put it: "It is necessary to let the children have the most democratic forms of self-government, to teach them civic responsibility, and to teach them to live and work with independence and initiative."

Infancy and Early Childhood

I am deeply convinced, that childhood must become one of the major priorities in the life of our society.

Albert Likhanov, President Organizing Committee
Lenin Soviet Children's Fund (Pravda, August 13, 1987, p. 3)

For the current generation of Soviet youth, their very entry into life was fraught with hazards. After a long period during which the Soviet Union steadily and successfully reduced infant mortality, in the 1970s deaths at birth or during the first year of life began to rise in an alarming manner. The reaction of the Brezhnev regime was to stop publishing statistics on infant mortality. This lead to considerable speculation in the West about what the true figures might be. With the advent of glasnost, infant mortality statistics began to be published again and, more important, there ensued a lively discussion in the press about why so many infants were dying before reaching their first birthday and about how to remedy the situation.

In 1970 there were 25 deaths per 1,000 live births. By 1980 the number of deaths had risen to 27.3. This figure had, according to official sources, been reduced to 22.3 by 1989. There was evidence, however, that the real figure might be as high as 25.5. In any case, Soviet policy makers have recognized this as a problem which they need to address as rapidly and effectively as possible. The major key to a solution seems to lie in an understanding of the variations across the union republics. The infant mortality figures for the Central Asian republics are significantly higher than for the rest of the Soviet Union. The highest figure, 54.2, was for Turkmenia, while the lowest figure, 10.7, was for Lithuania (Peterson, 1990).

Some of the reasons given by Soviet commentators for these high figures[14] have included unsanitary and inadequate medical facilities, substandard medical care, poor maternal health (including drug, alcohol, and cigarette use), air pollution, and genetic problems (*Literaturnaia Gazeta,* April 15, 1987, p. 13). In Soviet Central Asia, there are additional problems (Khakhalin, 1989). These include marriage between close relatives, polluted water supplies, hospitals unable to maintain sanitary conditions due to a lack of running water or hot water, and a prevalence of infectious diseases, such as hepatitis and intestinal infections (*Pravda,* August 31, 1987, p. 4). Also blamed is the agricultural use of toxic chemicals.

In an article on Uzbekistan, *Pravda* (February 7, 1987, p. 3) cited an instance were eight newborns died in an outbreak of toxemia and septicemia attributed to poor sanitation. It added that the hospital administrators had attempted to cover up the situation. In one city a Party investigation revealed that when hospital records were examined closely, the district's infant mortality rate quadrupled. As a result, a much larger proportion of Uzbekistan's funds for public health have been allocated to obstetrical and pediatric services. In addition, the Soviet leadership has taken several other decisive steps to correct these problems throughout Central Asia. The most dramatic has been a program to recruit medical personnel and send them to Central Asia to treat infants and to train local medical personnel. Other specialists are being sent to study the causes of infant mortality and develop recommendations.

On a national level, a higher proportion of health care capital investment Is being devoted to obstetric and pediatric medical facilities. Efforts are also being made to increase production of the equipment necessary. The latter poses an additional problem, however, since Soviet industry does not produce many types of equipment currently considered standard in obstetrical practice, at least in developed countries (*Pravda,* August 10, 1987, p. 4; Likhanov, 1987, p. 12). This means that precious foreign currency must be spent to import equipment such as heart monitors and ultrasound machines. In the past, obstetrical equipment has had a low priority for Soviet planners, causing considerable frustration in the Soviet medical profession.

Staff size is being increased in neonatal and pediatric facilities, and the number of pediatric specialists being trained is also increasing. In addition, work loads for medical personnel are being decreased. There has even been the suggestion, made in a popular weekly newspaper, *Nedelia,* by a group of obstetricians that the medical personnel on duty receive a bonus for every

---

[14]The corresponding figure for the U.S. is 10.4 and for Sweden and Finland it is a low 6.9 (Peterson, 1990, p. 5).

healthy baby born and have their pay docked for every "substandard" case (*CDSP, 39,* no. 18, 1987, p. 19).

Related to the problem of infant mortality is the more general problem of the health and safety of Soviet children. In 1987, only 25 to 30 percent of the children in the USSR were considered completely healthy (*CDSP, 39,* no. 47, 1987, p. 26). More recently, a Soviet authority put the proportion of sick children at 53 percent of all schoolchildren (*Radio Liberty Research,* no. 507/ 88, November 18, 1988, p. 15). There are many reasons for this situation. For example, pollution and workplace toxicants are being cited as reasons for the ill health of many children. For example, air pollution has been blamed for high levels of bronchial asthma among children in Bashkiria, and work in Central Asian tobacco fields by nursing mothers and children has been blamed for anemia and hypotrophy (*Izvestiia,* October 15, 1987, p. 3).

There have also been complaints (see, for example, *Izvestiia,* January 6, 1987, p. 2; *Pravda,* October 14, 1988, p. 5) about the provisions which the state makes for the care and education of handicapped children. Although special schools exist, the number is so small that distance effectively precludes much, if any, contact between the institutionalized child and his or her family. Because of this, some families try to undertake the care and education of their handicapped child themselves. According to one family that did this (*Izvestiia,* April 15, 1986, p. 3), virtually no help is available from the state to alleviate the family's burden. Although no plans for remedying the situation have yet been made public, a certain degree of governmental receptivity might be implied from the fact that several such complaints have appeared in the official newspapers of the Soviet government and the CPSU.

Finally, there is the problem of child labor. In 1988 the USSR Procuracy sent a protest to the Ministry of Education and the State Agro-Industrial Committee regarding violations of the occupational safety and health laws (*CDSP, 40,* no. 3, 1988, p. 11). This was a result of hundreds of serious or fatal accidents each year involving child laborers and the fact that the number of such accidents was steadily increasing. For example, in 1986 approximately 35,000 children under the age of 14 were hospitalized for work-related injuries. Each year, about 50 children out of every 1,000 suffer work-related injuries, some fatal. Occasionally, criminal charges are even brought against the adults involved—884 in the first six months of 1987. In addition to the action by the Procuracy, a National Center for Preventing Injuries in the Home and to Children has been set up in Moscow. Finally, there is a movement toward passing legislation that forbids child labor, at least in particularly hazardous situations (*The Washington Post,* October 18, 1988, p. A1).

In 1987 (*Pravda,* August 8, 1987, pp. 1,3) the CPSU Central Committee issued a resolution on the care of abandoned and orphaned children.[15] A number of organizations and government institutions were ordered to study the

---

[15]Related resolutions were passed in 1984 and 1985.

situation and develop ways of improving the upbringing of such children. Most notably perhaps, the CC created the Lenin Soviet Children's Fund[16] and a related weekly publication called *Family* (*Sem'ia*). At the same time, the Soviet press and television were painting a bleak picture of the situation of orphans and abandoned children and calling for reform.

There are approximately 1 million such children in the Soviet Union. Over 300,000 live in children's homes. The rest are under the care of guardians (primarily relatives) and in foster care (*Izvestiia,* July 7, 1987, p. 3; Likhanov, 1987, p. 5). Since 1976, there has been a 33 percent increase in the number living in children's homes. Only about 5 percent of these children are orphans in the true sense of the word. The rest have at least one living parent (*Sovetskaia Kultura,* October 20, 1987, p. 8). In most of the latter cases, either the children have been taken away from unfit parents for reasons such as alcoholism, drug addiction, and sexual abuse, or they were abandoned. In theory, these parents are required to pay support, but often this cannot be enforced. For example, many new mothers give false names when entering maternity homes and then leave the child behind, sometimes without even completing the proper paperwork to release the child for adoption.[17]

When an infant is abandoned or orphaned, it is usually placed in an infant's home, where it stays until age three. Then it is supposed to be moved to a special home or boarding school for older children, but there are not enough to completely fill the need, leaving about two thousand "overage" children in infant's homes (*Kommunist,* no. 8, 1987, p. 83). Some of these children are also placed in regular boarding schools. Conditions in institutions for orphaned and abandoned children have been severely criticized by child care experts, who have been calling for the upgrading of existing institutions and the construction of new ones. The government has begun to provide increased funding for this purpose (Likhanov, 1988). In addition, the first priority set by the new Lenin Soviet Children's Fund was to use 2.95 million rubles to improve staffing in infants' homes (*Izvestiia,* November 13, 1987, p. 3). Finally, in the academic year 1987–88, seven teacher training institutes started programs specifically designed to meet the staff needs of children's homes and boarding schools.

In 1988, in response to a proposal by the Lenin Soviet Children's Fund, the USSR Council of Ministers approved an ambitious program to change the basic nature of the government's program for children left without parental care (*Pravda,* August 25, 1988, pp. 1–2). It involves the creation of children's towns composed of clusters of family-style children's homes plus necessary auxiliary facilities, such as educational and sports facilities. Each children's

---

[16]A similar organization, the Lenin Fund for Aid to Children's Homes, was created in 1924 but ceased to exist in 1938. This organization was designed to care for the children left homeless during the period of the Revolution and civil war (Likhanov, 1988).

[17]Many are the children of prostitutes who get pregnant in order to get better treatment from local authorities (*CDSP, 40,* no. 8, 1988, p. 31).

town would accommodate 150 to 200 children. Obviously, given current economic difficulties, such an ambitious program will not be carried out quickly. At present, plans call for the building of 30 fully furnished and equipped children's homes by 1991. Since these are to be distributed among 14 union republics, it is safe to assume that the plan for children's towns represents more of a hope for the future than a present reality.

Child care problems are not limited to orphans and abandoned children. As in the West, there is a tremendous need for good facilities to care for the children of working parents. In the past, one of the primary solutions to this problem has been the grandmother. Currently, however, Soviet grandmothers are likely to be working themselves. In a recent Moscow survey, 62 percent of women of retirement age were choosing to continue working (*CDSP, 37,* no. 11, 1985, p. 18). Only 20 percent were willing to quit to take care of grandchildren. Even in their retirement years, increasing numbers of Soviet women are becoming involved in community and social activities, rather than devoting their lives to raising their grandchildren. This can cause considerable frustration, and even hostility, among their beleaguered children. But, objectively, it is hard to blame them, given the fact that most of them faced the "double shift" during their working years. This means, however, that the number of day-care places which might have been adequate in the past will be increasingly inadequate in the future.

More than half of all preschoolers—about 17 million or 58 percent—attend some sort of day-care institution with another 1.5 million waiting for admission (*Pravda,* July 1, 1988, p. 4). In some regions, the number is close to 80 or even 90 percent (*Izvestiia,* March 9, 1985, p. 1; *CDSP, 37,* no. 39, 1985, p. 12). The fee paid by their parents covers roughly 20 percent of the cost (about 500 to 600 rubles). In 1984 a graduated system of payments was instituted (*Izvestiia,* March 25, 1986, p. 3). Families with earnings below 60 rubles per person pay nothing, from 60 to 80 rubles the cost is 12 rubles 50 kopeks, and everyone else pays more. The maximum is 20 rubles. Although this was meant to introduce an element of equity, it has also succeeded in greatly increasing the paperwork of day-care administrators and has caused some new inequities. Consequently, there have been calls for further reform.

Other problems have arisen as a result of the fact that only some of the day-care facilities are supervised by educational authorities. Many, for example, are under the supervision of an industrial enterprise. This creates problems for those trying to enforce health, safety, and staffing standards. In particular, where the day-care center is within an industrial enterprise that needs workers, the responsible authorities may tolerate overcrowding and other problems in order to keep the mothers of the children in their work force.

This appears to be an area in which there is ample room for individual initiative. As early as 1986, some people in Riga founded a business to help women organize day care in their homes. They were able to make this work part of a woman's official work record and to offer a salary of 160 rubles a month. When they advertised for women who might want to do this, they got approximately 200 phone calls—about half from parents looking for day care.

Students and Teens

By the end of the Brezhnev years, Soviet youth seemed to be overwhelmingly alienatedfrom the government, the Party, ideology, and politics (Binyon, 1983, pp. 173–187). There were many reasons for this (Trehub, 1988). Among them were the corruption and hypocrisy of that period, the lack of political alternatives, cynicism about the official ideology, and the fact that political activity seemed to have very little meaning other than furthering one's self-interest. This was reflected (and continues to be reflected) in a diminishing desire to participate in the Komsomol, the major political organization for Soviet teenagers and young adults. This estrangement was noted by Gorbachev in his address to the twentieth Congress of the Komsomol (*Pravda,* April 17, 1987, p. 2). The gap remains; during the year immediately after the Congress, Komsomol membership dropped by 2.5 million (*Pravda,* April 25, 1988, p. 4). Also, there are indications that a similar malaise is gripping the Young Pioneer organization (*Pravda,* August 2, 1988, p. 3).

In place of the Komsomol, Soviet teenagers and young adults seem to have turned to a large and growing number of unofficial youth groups (*neformal'nye ob''edineniia molodezhi*). The most popular of these have no overt political purpose, though some may be seen as containing an element of social protest. They are organized around their members' enthusiasm for music—particularly rock music—and sports. Other, less numerous unofficial groups do try to influence policy. These include environmentalists, conservationists, and pacifists. Finally, groups, such as nationalistic,[18] vigilante, and motorcycle groups, are potentially or actually disruptive

Unofficial youth groups are not new; they began appearing in the early 1960s and were well established by the 1980s (Tolz, 1987).[19] What is new is their current high growth rate and the fact that they are playing an increasingly important role in Soviet political and social life. Structurally, they range from informal circles of friends with a common interest to highly organized groups with well-defined activities and goals. They are often cited as proof that official youth organizations, like the Komsomol, are not doing their job properly, because they are too bureaucratic and formalistic (see, for example, *Pravda,* March 30, 1987, p. 4).

---

[18]Clandestine nationalist youth groups which are seen as threatening by the central Soviet government have been uncovered in the Ukraine and in Byelorussia (Solchanyk, 1987; Nahaylo, 1987a; Nahaylo, 1987b). There are also nationalistic youth groups which operate in the open (see, for example, Mihalisko, 1988; Drohobycky, 1988).

[19]These groups are not invariably youth groups. Many have been formed by adults, as well. There are also those which cross generations in their membership. This discussion, however, will be confined to those which are most important to contemporary Soviet teenagers and young adults.

This is probably true to some extent, but it discounts the tendency for young people to want to take an active role in creating their own social world, separate from the influence and direction of older generations. For Soviet youth, as for the young people of most of the Western world, music, appearance, and behavior have been major vehicles for carving out their own place in society and making the rest of society sit up and take notice. In the recent past, Soviet young people have tried to imitate the young people of Europe and (perhaps primarily) the United States, exerting great effort to find out what was up-to-date in "the outside world" and then trying as best they could to incorporate it into their own lifestyles. This led to a craze for jeans (preferably American and with designer labels). More recently, punk and hippie dress and hair styles have made an appearance. Fans of heavy-metal music can be seen dressed in leather and chains. At first the government tried to discourage these trends, seeing such Western influences as corrupting and anti-Soviet.

More recently, as the Soviet government has become increasingly relaxed about such things, there has been a tendency for many young people to become interested in exploring their own ethnic and cultural heritage and in building a lifestyle which reflects their Soviet (or Russian) roots. This has various implications. For example, more and more young people have stopped assuming that the best had to come from outside the Soviet Union. In a letter to *Komsomolskaia Pravda,* a member of a "family rock commune" makes the following declaration: "We revere the ideas of October, we admire the genius of Lenin, and we hope to revive the spirit of bygone times . . . and to drive out Western trends, fashions and symbols, replacing them with our own" (*CDSP, 39,* no. 39, 1987, p. 7).

Many of the more extreme manifestations of this tendency have aroused alarm. Particularly troublesome to the older generation has been the development of Soviet heavy-metal music, together with the outlandish outfits and behavior which often characterizes heavy-metal musicians and their fans (*metallisti*). Some members of the leadership have been openly critical of this preoccupation with rock music (see, for example, *Pravda,* February 18, 1988, pp. 1–4). At the same time, however, organizations such as the Union of Composers and the Moscow Komsomol have begun to sponsor rock music events.

Soviet rock music is not limited to heavy metal. Under the more benign Gorbachev regime, it has flowered, taking on a range of forms. Given the extremely hostile official attitude toward rock music in the recent past, almost any type of rock music can still be seen as making an implicit political statement. Some rock groups, however, are more explicitly political, singing about the attitudes of contemporary Soviet youth toward societal and political problems, such as the impact of Afghanistan on Soviet youth (*The Washington Post,* January 25, 1988, p. C2). Also, the new toleration for rock music has affected the musicians, not always favorably. In the words of a Leningrad jazz critic: "Sometimes a concert was doomed to succeed on the basis of the fact that it was forbidden. . . . It's not so easy to attract attention through artistry alone" (*The Washington Post,* May 16, 1988, p. A22).

It should not be assumed that all Soviet youth welcome these developments. In fact, many young people are at least as hostile to such "outlandish" behavior, dress, and music as any middle-aged bureaucrat. One particularly notorious group holding these opinions is a loosely knit vigilante group which has been dubbed the *liubery,* after the name of the Moscow suburb where it originated.[20] According to the popular magazine *Ogonek (Iakovlev,* 1987), the *liubery* make nightly trips into the center of Moscow to find and beat up punks, hippies, heavy metal fans, and motorcyclists. As one of them put it: "Hippies, punks and heavy metal fans disgrace the Soviet way of life. We want to clean them out of the capital" (Iakovlev, 1987, p. 20). More recently there have been reports of the *liubery* engaging in racketeering, such as demanding protection money from persons selling their produce at markets (*The Washington Post,* February 12, 1989, p. A1).

The *liubery* are not the only disruptive youth group in contemporary Soviet society. Motorcyclists (*rokkery*) are another group of young people about which there are constant complaints in the press (see, for example, *Pravda,* August 23, 1988, p. 6; *The Washington Post,* October 4, 1988, pp. D1–D2). In this case, rowdy behavior and disturbing the peace is the chief complaint. In the case of these and other groups, however, there is the fear that the young people will cross (or may have already crossed) the line between behavior that is legal, albeit disruptive, and behavior that is criminal.

Increasingly, this line is being crossed by groups of youth which have their counterparts in the West—gangs. Street gangs are not new in the Soviet Union. They have been around for at least 40 years (Konovalov, 1988). Most of the phenomena associated with these gangs are familiar: defense of "turf," hierarchical organization, street fighting, the use of weapons, a requirement for absolute loyalty, intimidation, demands for "tribute," and murder. Of increasing concern to authorities are recent indications of links between youth gangs and the adult criminal world (*Literaturnaia Gazeta,* October 12, 1989, p. 13). This includes evidence that gang leaders are part of organized crime, which, authorities think, is using the gang problem to divert attention and resources from its own activities.

Juvenile Delinquency

What to do with delinquent and wayward youth has long been a problem in the Soviet Union. In fact, A. Makarenko—sometimes rather inaccurately referred to as "the Soviet Dr. Spock"—made his reputation in the years after

---

[20]Youth from other suburbs of Moscow subsequently adopted the same name, clothing, and behaviors (*CDSP, 39,* no. 10, 1987, p. 4).

the Bolshevik Revolution by doing innovative rehabilitative work with homeless and delinquent young people. Historically, much of the problem has been a result of the creation of large numbers of orphaned children by such upheavals as the 1917 Revolution, the subsequent civil war, and World War II.

The absence of such major crises, however, has not meant the absence of problem youth. It has meant that the problem of delinquency has assumed more manageable proportions because of the effective functioning of most families, as well as of the numerous agencies of socialization and control. There were reports (*Izvestiia,* December 22, 1988, p. 6) that the amount of juvenile crime may have peaked in about 1985 and dropped until 1988. Then reports of a rise began to surface (*Radio Liberty Research,* no. 99/88, March 4, 1988, p. 10; *CDSP, 41,* no. 6, 1989, p. 15). In any case, the numbers are still substantial.

The overwhelming majority of juvenile offenders whose cases are processed by the regular courts are 16 or 17 years old and have committed relatively serious offenses, such as homicide or theft. Juveniles who have committed less serious offenses, such as truancy, or who are under the age of 14 (regardless of offense) end up under the jurisdiction of one of the Commissions for Minors' Affairs (Pronina and Stolbov, 1988). These are composed of representatives of the community, as well as of the police and the legal profession.

Commissions for Minors' Affairs have jurisdiction over the parents of juvenile delinquents as well as over the youths themselves. These commissions have the power to censure or fine parents, as well as to refer them to a comrades' court. In deciding what to do with the juveniles themselves, the commissions consider such factors as the social danger of the offense, the reasons why it was committed, and the background of the juvenile. The last factor includes age, health, education, attitude toward work and school, prior behavior, and home environment. Frequently, the decision is made to issue a warning and then pardon the offenses of those youths who seem to realize the implications of what they did and who are likely to avoid such behavior in the future. Local Commissions for Minors' Affairs also function as probation offices. They supervise juvenile delinquents who are serving their time in the community. Also, they function as parole supervisors, keeping an eye on youths who have been discharged from correctional institutions. This supervision includes making sure that the young person either has a job or is attending school.

What sort of people become juvenile delinquents in the Soviet Union? The overwhelming majority are male and live in urban areas. The home environment of these youths is frequently troubled, with absent fathers or alcoholic parents being major factors. Many of these young people have poor records of educational achievement or are dropouts. The nonworker and nonstudent, the idle youth, is most likely to become delinquent. Finally, both alcohol and drug abuse play a role. In summary, Soviet juvenile delinquents, not unlike juvenile delinquents in other countries, tend to be youths who are male, urban, less educated, from problem families, and prone to substance abuse. To list their characteristics, however, does not really answer the why of juvenile delinquency.

It is possible to distinguish two principal approaches that Soviet criminologists use in analyzing the causes of juvenile delinquency. The first, and currently most prevalent in official pronouncements, is the assertion that delinquency stems from a breakdown in the functioning of some of the basic socializing institutions in Soviet society: family, school, youth organizations, and places of employment. The second, which enjoys increasing popularity among Soviet criminologists, focuses on the personality of the adolescent as it dynamically interacts with the environment. In both cases, juvenile delinquency is seen as a basically social, not a psychological or biological, problem, and individuals are held to be responsible for their acts (Zeldes, 1981, pp. 90–94).

How do Soviet socializing institutions break down or malfunction? In the case of the home, the problem may be that both parents work (which is usually the case) and the child does not get proper supervision. Or, as was suggested previously, the alcohol problems of family members may interfere with the proper parenting of the child and subsequently become the problem of the child as well. The tendency for juvenile delinquents to be underachievers or school dropouts is taken by Soviet authorities as an indication that the schools have failed in their responsibilities toward these young people. Malfunctioning of social institutions at the workplace may involve many things, ranging from an unwillingness to hire young people to a tradition of periodic drunkenness in the workers' collective.

Usually the problem is seen as resulting from a complex of antecedents. Most analyses of the problem proceed on the assumption that societal institutions are basically sound and that the problem is to get them functioning properly. For example, there is little effort to create a situation which will do away with the necessity for two working parents in every family. Rather, the labor of both parents is assumed, and the issue is seen as the provision of adequate facilities for the care and supervision of the child while the parents are at work.

What kinds of crimes are most typical of Soviet juvenile delinquents? This is a difficult question to answer, since complete and reliable statistics are still scarce. From the existing evidence, however, it would seem that juveniles in the Soviet Union, like juveniles throughout the developed world, seem to commit the entire spectrum of crimes from murder to rape to petty theft. There is also evidence that for many committing property crimes and muggings, the motivation is to obtain money or other desirable material goods.

As was noted previously, there is a strong emphasis on the prevention of juvenile delinquency. Recently, calls for change have centered on the improvement of the standard of living, the cultural level of the general population, and the functioning of the family. Once a person has shown a proclivity for delinquent behavior, the preventive measures become more specifically directed at what are perceived as the problem areas: (1) aid to children who live in troubled homes or who do not have permanent homes; (2) measures to prevent recidivism in cases where minor offenses have been committed; and (3) corrective and educational efforts directed at youths involved in serious crimes.

When prevention efforts fail, the correctional system takes over. Until recently, there have been four basic types of juvenile educational-labor colonies: (1) special schools for disruptive 11-to-14-year-old children; (2) special vocational-technical schools for difficult and convicted adolescents over 14; (3) medical-educational institutions for minors involved in substance abuse; and (4) educational-labor colonies for convicted criminals. Only the last two have been supervised by the MVD and, strictly speaking, can be regarded as correctional institutions. The fourth type has been divided into those with a general regime and those with an intensified regime. All female prisoners and male first offenders serve their time in a general regime camp. Male recidivists are generally sent to an intensified regime camp.

There is a law which allows conditional early release when a juvenile has served a third of his or her sentence. This depends on good behavior. Also, both the time youths spend in jail during their pretrial investigation and the time they spend waiting to be sent to the juvenile colony are credited to their sentence. Finally, youths have usually been transferred to an adult correctional institution to complete their sentences if they become 18 years old while in a juvenile correctional institution and show little promise of improvement. Those for whom the incarceration seems to be having a beneficial effect but are not ready for conditional early release have been allowed to stay in the juvenile institution until they are 20.

What are these institutions like? Usually there is strong peripheral security in the form of fences, armed guards, and watchtowers. Conditions inside are more relaxed, minimizing such jaillike attributes as barred windows, although the way in which the juveniles are treated can be harsh. There are limits on the number of visits and packages an inmate may receive, and letters are subject to censorship. All inmates are required to work, usually in metalworking, woodworking, or construction. They are paid on a piecework basis with a deduction for the colony's operating expenses. Thirty-three percent is put in the inmate's personal account. Recently there have been accusations that the work system has been abusive in some camps and that this has interfered with rehabilitation (Konovalov, 1987c, p. 5).

Both general- and vocational-education programs are offered. Because of the relatively short period of time a youth usually spends in the colony and because the entry of most youths into the colony does not coincide with the beginning of a school term, however, there is the perennial problem of giving the youths enough education to have meaning in the outside world. Also, there is the constant problem of finding personnel who are willing to work with inmate populations and who possess the necessary training and aptitudes to function in this rather difficult type of situation. The Soviet press has recently raised questions about the competence of some correctional personnel, citing instances of drunkenness, falsification of records, and exploitation of the juvenile inmates (Konovalov, 1987c, pp. 5–6).

Finally, Soviet juvenile correctional institutions, like similar institutions elsewhere in the world, have constant problems coping with inmate subcultures. These include the curbing of exploitation and bullying of some inmates by other inmates. And, of course, the familiar prison problem of sexual attack seems to exist to some extent, although it is not mentioned frequently in Soviet writing on the subject. Correctional authorities try to organize the inmates into collectives, but this tactic has not been overwhelmingly successful, often for reasons which are beyond the control of the colony's staff, such as the brutalizing experiences inmates may have experienced from fellow prisoners while awaiting transfer to the colony. Also, the inmate-to-staff ratio, although better than those in many other countries, is far from ideal.

At present the part of this system that is under the supervision of the MVD is undergoing a process of reform (*Izvestiia,* December 22, 1988, p. 6). This involves the combining of the general- and intensified-regime facilities. It also includes plans for more inmate rights and self-government. Increased contact with parents is to be encouraged, and interaction with adult criminals is to be minimized by isolating juvenile offenders from the rest of the prison population during pretrial investigation. Finally, a new institution is being created to serve as a sort of halfway house for juveniles who show evidence of having reformed. For many juveniles, this would substitute for automatic transfer to an adult facility at the age of 18; the others would continue to serve their terms in the juvenile facility. Widespread introduction of these reforms is planned for the 1990s.

Military Service

At age 18 every Soviet man becomes eligible for draft into the Soviet military. The normal term of service is two years. After this duty has been fulfilled, a Soviet male stays part of the national reserve until he has reached 50. For those Soviet men attending institutions of higher education, this interruption of their education can be a problem. Before 1980 all full-time students were exempt from military duty until their education was complete. At this point, however, a decision was made to limit these deferrals to a special list of higher educational institutions. This decision may have been prompted by the need for additional troops because of the war in Afghanistan.

Gradually, over the next few years the list became shorter and shorter until less than ten institutions remained. Beginning in 1987, the problems caused by this interruption in the educational process of virtually all men began to be widely discussed. Many felt that this policy of allowing virtually no deferrals was harmful, since many of those drafted failed to complete their studies at a time when scientists and engineers were needed as much as soldiers.

The supporters of the draft replied that exempting students was unfair to other groups of young men and could serve as a loophole allowing some people to avoid military service.

In 1989, the issue was resolved in favor of the students. In one of its first assertions of real power, the new Supreme Soviet granted deferrals to all university students. It also reduced the term of service required upon graduation from 18 months to 1 year. Students taking officer training were virtually exempted from active duty and go straight into the reserve officer corps upon graduation. Several factors have made this policy change both possible and attractive. First, the Soviet withdrawal from Afghanistan and Gorbachev's peace initiatives are reducing the need for the military to have such large standing forces. Second, there is a desperate need for many highly educated specialists in relatively new and innovative fields crucial to the success of perestroika. Presumably, this new deferral policy will permit the authorities to increase the pool of such specialists as rapidly as possible. The new draft policy, then, seems to be a compromise between the need to keep the armed forces adequately manned and the need for fresh young minds to fuel the reform process.

REFERENCES

ALEXANDROVA, E. (1984). Why Soviet women want to get married. In T. Mamonova, ed., *Women and Russia*. Boston: Beacon.

ARUTYUNYAN, L. (1988). Job or family: Freedom to choose. *Soviet Life*, 3, 21.

AZAROVA, E.G. (1989). *Problemy ravnopraviia zhenshchiny i muzhchiny b cotzeal'-nom obecpechenii b SSSR*. Moscow: "Nauka".

BINYON, M. (1983). *Life in Russia*. New York: Pantheon.

BOGUSLAVSKAYA, Z. (1988). What are we women? *Soviet Life*, 3, 16, 22.

BOHR, A. (1988). Illegitimate births on the rise in the USSR. *Radio Liberty Research*, no. 402/88.

BOHR, A. (1989). Resolving the question of equality for Soviet women—again. *Report on the USSR, 1*, 14, 10–16.

BROWNING, G. (1985). Soviet politics—where are the women? In B. Holland, ed., *Soviet sisterhood*. Bloomington, IN: Indiana University Press.

DROHOBYCKY, M. (1988). The Lion Society: Profile of a Ukranian patriotic "informal" group. *Radio Liberty Research*, no. 325/88.

GORBACHEV, M. (1987). *Perestroika: New thinking for our country and the world*. New York: Harper & Row.

GRIGORYEVA, G. and SONOVA, S. (1984). Interview with a career woman. In T. Mamonova, ed., *Women and Russia*. Boston: Beacon.

HOLT, A. (1985). The first Soviet feminists. In B. Holland, ed., *Soviet sisterhood*. Bloomington: Indiana University Press.

IAKOVLEV, V. (1987). Kontora "Liuberov." *Ogonek*, no. 5, 20–21.

KHAKHALIN, L. (1989). Emergency aid in Central Asia. *Soviet Life*, 10, 61.

KONOVALOV, V. (1986). Does prostitution exist in the Soviet Union? *Radio Liberty Research*, no. 374/86.

KONOVALOV, V. (1987a). Prostitution made an administrative offense. *Radio Liberty Research,* no. 311/87.

KONOVALOV, V. (1987b). Transmission of AIDS is made a criminal offense. *Radio Liberty Research,* no. 378/87.

KONOVALOV, V. (1987c). Educational-labor colonies and the problems of reeducating juvenile delinquents. *Radio Liberty Research,* no. 460/87.

KONOVALOV, V. (1988). Kazan teenagers: "Street wars." *Radio Liberty Research,* no. 380/88.

KOVAL, V. (1989). Working women: Common problems. *Soviet Life,* 3, 24–25.

LAPIDUS, G.W. (1978). *Women in Soviet society: Equality, development, and social change.* Berkeley: University of California Press.

LAPIDUS, G.W. (1982). Women, work, and family: New Soviet perspectives. In G.W. Lapidus, ed., *Women. work, and family in the Soviet Union,* pp. ix-xlvi. Armonk, NY: M.E. Sharpe.

LIKHANOV, A. (1987). *We are all responsible for our children.* Moscow: Novosti Press Agency Publishing House.

LIKHANOV, A. (1988). Helping children. *Soviet Life,* no. 4, 31.

LUKIN, N.N. (1986). *Zabota o zhenshchine-truzhenitze i materi.* Kishinev: Kartia Moldoveniaske.

MAMONOVA, T., ed. (1984). *Women and Russia: Feminist writings from the Soviet Union.* Boston: Beacon.

MIHALISKO, K. (1988). A profile of informal patriotic youth groups in Belorussia. *Radio Liberty Research,* no. 318/88.

MIHALISKO, K. (1989). Women workers and *perestroika* in Ukraine and Belorussia— A problematic relationship unfolds. *Report on the USSR, 1,* no. 15, 30–33.

MOFFETT, J. (1985a). Contraception in the Soviet Union. *Radio Liberty Research,* no. 229/85.

MOFFETT, J. (1985b). The high abortion rate in the USSR. *Radio Liberty Research,* no. 274/85.

NAHAYLO, B. (1987a). Political demonstration in Minsk attests to Belorussian national assertiveness. *Radio Liberty Research,* no. 481/87.

NAHAYLO, B. (1987b). Soviet newspaper reveals existence of clandestine nationalist youth groups in western Ukraine. *Radio Liberty Research,* no. 495/87.

PETERSON, D.J. (1990). Understanding Soviet infant mortality statistics. *Report on the USSR, 2,* 14, 4–6.

PRONINA, V.S., and STOLBOV, B.A. (1988). *Polozheniia o komissiiakh po delam nesovershennoletnikh.* Moscow: "Iuridicheskaia literatura."

PUKHOVA, Z. (1987). Ravnye prava, ravnoe uchastie. *Kommunist,* no. 10, 98–107.

SHEEHY, A. (1987). Antinatal policy for Tajikistan. *Radio Liberty Research,* no. 56/87.

SHEEHY, A. (1988). Slavs and Balts still failing to reproduce themselves. *Radio Liberty Research,* no. 240/88.

SOLCHANYK, R. (1987). Ukrainian youth to be "internationalized." *Radio Liberty Research,* no. 62/87.

TOLTS, M. (1988). Family situation: Not so bad. *Soviet Life,* 3, 22.

TOLZ, V. (1987). "Informal groups" in the USSR. *Radio Liberty Research,* no. 220/87.

TREHUB, A. (1987). New figures on infant mortality in the USSR. *Radio Liberty Research,* no. 438/87.

TREHUB, A. (1988). Students in the Soviet Union: Political mood and activism. *Radio Liberty Research,* no. 193/88.

VOZNESENSKAYA, Y. (1984). Housework—Soviet Women's Second Shift. *Radio Liberty Research,* no. 448/84.

ZAKHAROVA, N., POSADSKAIA, A., and RIMASHEVSKAIA, N.(1989). Kak my reshaem zhenskii vopros. *Kommunist,* no. 4, 56–65.

ZELDES, I. (1981). *The problems of crime in the USSR.* Springfield, IL: Charles C. Thomas.

FIFTEEN
THE DIFFICULT PATH
TOWARD "NORMALIZATION"

For now we depend too much on a single man, and we have to trust him. We are just lucky it is Gorbachev. But in the future we don't want to have to depend on luck. We want to be sure of our democracy, even with a mediocre man as president. And that will mean that we are finally a normal country.

Sergei Kovalyov (The Washington Post, March 11, 1990, p. A33)

In past editions of this book the final chapter was devoted to what can broadly be called "the information problem": the paucity of data about political, economic, and social matters in the USSR; questions about the usefulness and reliability of the information which was available; and the means used by Western analysts and scholars to try to understand a political system in which information is systematically rationed.

With glasnost, the situation has undergone a radical change. Data deficit has turned into information overload—a condition which has some Western scholars jokingly calling for a temporary reimposition of censorship and other controls so that there will be time for them to absorb and to analyze the information they already have (Balzer, 1989, p. 1). Nor is it only Western observers who feel overwhelmed. Soviet writers and other intellectuals also have trouble keeping up with the rush of information and societal change. Moreover, if they become actively involved in the reform process, their own work suffers. As the poet Andrei Voznesensky lamented in 1989:

> Every night on television, in the papers, there is something new. It is impossible to keep up with everything that's happening. So artists aren't spending time writing—they're reading and talking. People want us to help them, to speak for them—they have to call on poets to do it, because we have no politicians in our country. But if you spend all your time this way, you don't have time to write a good novel. And if you stop fighting, to go off and write a novel, maybe you'll find the freedom has been cut off. (Whitney, 1989, p. 26)

None of this means that there are no limits on the information being released. There are, but they are unclear and seem to be constantly shifting. Both the Soviet leadership and those whose profession it is to generate or dispense information seem to be involved in an elaborate ongoing negotiation about what is officially permissible. In addition, many are concerned about how critical commentaries should be presented, seeing the flood of negative information which has inundated the press as harmful. They argue for more balance in the form of either "good news" or constructive suggestions for change. Nor have all doubts been removed about the reliability of some of the information that is being made available; there is still selectivity and manipulation. Among the achievements of glasnost, however, is the fact that Soviet commentators now feel free to acknowledge and criticize the way in which information is being handled in their society. Previously, this was possible only for outside observers.

The significance of current limits on information cannot be fully discussed here, but it is worth mentioning two of the more politically important ones. First, personal and background information on Soviet leaders is still only sparingly released. As a reader's letter to a Soviet newspaper put it in 1988: "It is really amazing when one learns from our press a lot about Reagan, Thatcher, Mitterand, and almost nothing about our officials" (*Izvestiia,* August 6, 1988, p. 3). Although to those of us familiar with the Western media's obsession with "personalities," this kind of information may seem frivolous, the past of a political leader can often help us understand what they are doing and furnish useful clues to future behavior (Hermann, 1986).

The Soviet Union is in a period of transition. In the past, leaders were much more important than institutions and laws. The current leadership is trying to move the political system toward a situation in which institutions and laws are less susceptible to manipulation by powerful individuals. But who these reformers are will have a profound effect on the extent to which they will succeed and on the new political system that they shape. Moreover, even when everyone plays by the rules of the game, the players matter.

Second, although economic and social statistics (including crime statistics) are more available than in the past, they are still incomplete and often confusing. This means that they are not as useful as they might be. For example, data on the Soviet national budget has long been shrouded in secrecy, and so it was viewed as a welcome move toward openness when the Finance Minister acknowledged in 1988 that the budget deficit projected for the next year was about 35 billion rubles. But suspicions that the deficit was understated were confirmed when it was revealed that this figure did not include funds the government borrowed from state banks. As the well-known Soviet economist, Leonid Abalkin, observed in 1989: "In the whole world bank borrowings are considered a means of covering deficits . . . strictly, scientifically speaking, our deficit is 100 billion rubles" (*The New York Times,* January 26, 1989, p. A3).

So there is much more information available, but problems remain as the Soviet system proceeds on its way toward—toward what? This question can be asked both narrowly and broadly. In the narrower sense, we can ask how the reform leadership will solve the multitude of problems associated with glasnost, perestroika, and democratization. This problem-oriented approach was the original perspective that Gorbachev and his fellow reformers brought to their job. In the broader sense, however, the way in which these problems are resolved will heavily influence the shape of the new political *system* which is being created in the Soviet Union. This system-oriented approach seems to be the perspective that has gradually been forced on the reformers as the consequences of their efforts have emerged over time. Early in the process, the reform began to take on a life of its own and moved in ways not intended or even envisioned by its originators.

As the reform process has proceeded, glasnost, perestroika, and democratization have become increasingly intertwined. Writing in a Soviet newspaper to which he had been invited to contribute, the American sovietologist Abraham Brumberg noted in 1989 that "glasnost is and has been the prerequisite for perestroika: without the freedom to criticize, condemn or censure the misdeeds of the past and the present, no attempt to undo them, and no search for alternative solutions could possibly be undertaken. Conversely, the process of structural changes—perestroika—further encourages the spirit of criticism and inquiry" (Brumberg, 1989a, p. 6). Democratization, in turn, has forced Soviet officials to pay more attention to these criticisms and inquiries. If they want to stay in power or gain power, they must think about voter reactions, that is, be responsible to the people. They need to be attuned to the practical impact on their constituents of the policies being made in the name of reform.

The USSR has reached levels of openness and official tolerance of different views which would quite recently have been inconceivable.[1] The same applies to the level of political participation that has been achieved by persons formerly outside the decision-making elite. The stock phrase "who could have imagined five years ago that this could happen" applies to countless areas of

---

[1]The dark side of this, of course, is that this same process has unleashed forces of ethnic intolerance which have threatened the reform with escalating civil disorder.

Soviet life. An oft-repeated aspiration of the legal reform movement is to achieve the point in Soviet law where "everything that is not prohibited is permitted." Even if this goal is not yet reality, it is significant because it is seen as a reachable objective. The atmosphere created by the reform *does* appear to be having some effect on the political culture of a large segment of the populace, nurturing a belief in their own ability to participate in politics. Though their individual and group goals may vary tremendously, most of them want to maintain and enhance their newly won ability to advance those goals. But what beyond that?

This is where the broader question is raised: What kind of *system* does this politically involved segment of the population want to achieve? Many Soviet commentators and political activists seem to be advocating a "normal" society, an idea attractive for both its simplicity and its comprehensiveness. According to the journalist Robert Kaiser, "What is clearly most important to many Russians [is] the creation of a 'normal' Soviet Union. The adjective normal, used to describe both what is beginning to happen and what is most sought after, is often heard in Moscow conversations today" (Kaiser, 1988, p. 110).

A normal country, in this view, would have at least three significant characteristics. First, citizens would be able to engage in activities of interest to them (both vocationally and avocationally), with the ability to come and go (including abroad) as they please. Second, they could express themselves frankly and honestly on matters of public importance without fear of retribution by political authorities. Third, and perhaps most important, they would have reasonable confidence that these newly won freedoms will not be taken away in a return to the type of system existing prior to Gorbachev. The last is usually discussed in terms of reversibility.

When will the point of irreversibility be reached? Although many commentators have expressed their opinions on this matter, there is no general agreement about what the point of irreversibility might be. This stems from the fact that the concept of reversal is essentially meaningless, in the sense that the present and future are never *exactly* like the past. What analysts seem to be talking about when they discuss irreversibility has more to do with whether the reform process will yield a Soviet Union that is somehow better or worse. And they vary in their definitions of good and bad, usually seeing them in terms of similarity to, or difference from, selected aspects of the Soviet past. Therefore, it is not surprising that there are many differences of opinion.

The well-known Soviet sociologist Tatiana Zaslavskaia wrote in 1988 about the positive and negative results of democratization. On the positive side, she listed achievements like the broadening of freedom of speech and other individual rights. On the negative side, she noted the rise of "chauvinistic, nationalistic, anti-socialist and even fascist groups." "The development of such phenomena," she said, "is like letting a dangerous genie out of a bottle" (*Izvestiia*, December 24, 1988, p. 3). Similarly, Robert Kaiser believes that the significant ethnic disturbances that began in the late 1980s fall into this category: "For decades scholars in the West speculated on what would happen when the ethnic genie got out of its bottle. Now it is out" (Kaiser, 1988, p. 111). Developments of this kind are of landmark importance, to be sure. But they are also destabilizing—signs of weakness rather than strength. Ethnic strife invites a reactionary backlash, imperiling the reform's achievements.

A crucial milestone on the way to normalization might be a dramatic change in attitudes toward the place of Lenin in Soviet political culture. As was indicated in Chapter 1, the myth of Lenin remains, even though the movement toward a more honest treatment of Soviet history is eroding his status. To do away with the mythical aura surrounding the founding father of the Soviet state could either help or hurt the reform leadership. The problem is the tie between the establishment of the Soviet system after the 1917 Revolution and the fact that the CPSU has taken sole responsibility for that and subsequent events. On the one hand, to the extent that Lenin can be disassociated from the current dire straits in which the Soviet Union finds itself, he could remain a valuable legitimizing symbol as leader of the 1917 Revolution against the evils of tsarism. On the other hand, to the extent that his imagery is associated with the failure of one-party rule under the the CPSU, of which he is also the founding father, he could easily become discredited.

The key is the extent to which Stalin and others can be made the major scapegoats for the current problems of the USSR. Lenin could then be regarded as a figure of unrealized potential: He died before he could build a stable set of institutions that would have made the Soviet Union a very different and better country than it became under his successors. This would permit Lenin to remain a heroic, or at least semiheroic, figure. Then the Lenin myth could continue to give legitimacy to the reform efforts of the present leadership and provide ideological justification for reform initiatives which might otherwise be criticized as "unsocialist." In other words, to what extent will the Lenin of the New Economic Policy prevail over the Lenin of War Communism?

A mythical aura surrounds the founders and heroic figures of many political systems. It seems to fill a basic need in political cultures—a need for people to associate their national identity with some idealized person or group. For example, considerable mythology is connected with the memories of George Washington and the other founding fathers of the United States, and these myths are regularly invoked by current politicians to add legitimacy to their policy preferences (Nimmo and Combs, 1980). But until recently, the Soviet leadership has gone much further—casting Lenin as a cult figure, a quasi deity. This, in turn, has prevented any objective examination of Lenin as a political thinker and actor. Current steps in the direction of challenging Lenin's infallibility, as well as changes in the status of the CPSU (Brumberg, 1989b, pp. 38–39; Tolz, 1988), may affect the deification of Lenin. This will not, however, necessarily destroy his usefulness as a legitimizing figure for most of the Soviet citizenry, who are not particularly interested in the subtleties of historical analysis.

Thus, a normalization of the image of Lenin that does not completely destroy the mythology surrounding him could be a significant development in the USSR's political evolution. But the deified status of Lenin has long been closely associated with the sanctity of the Party within a one-party system. Now the Communist Party is no longer sacred, and a multiparty system is moving into place. This will make it easier for historians to examine Lenin in a reasonably clear-eyed, unsentimental matter, with mistakes and shortcomings—as well as accomplishments—acknowledged. But to retain his status as a national symbol, Lenin must be disassociated from the CPSU and made primarily the founding father of the country—a founding father who did not have the opportunity to translate his vision into a stable set of political institutions.

Any such development would be tied to the movement toward pluralism in the Soviet Union which has been under way for some time. Even before Gorbachev, the opinion groups described in Chapter 11 were active in attempting to influence policy-making. With the upsurge in informal groups and the new life which glasnost gave to many established official groups, this process has gathered momentum. The Soviet leadership, who now face either contested elections or the need to have their appointments approved by elected officials, are learning the political meaning of group pressures. The logical outcome (at least from a Western point of view) was some type of multiparty system. And rather early in the reform period, many groups and individuals within the Soviet Union began calling for the introduction of a multiparty system.

At first, Gorbachev took a firm stand in favor of maintaining the exclusive position of the Communist Party. After all, his career was built within the Komsomol and CPSU structure. In this sense, he is the quintessential Party man. But as his problems multiplied, it became harder and harder for him to dismiss calls for a multiparty system. Numerous organizations, such as popular fronts, began functioning more or less as *de facto* political parties. Then some of the republics legally instituted multiparty systems for purposes of republic-level elections. This gave impetus to the formation of even more partylike organizations. Gradually, the Communist Party leadership realized that they had an uncomfortable choice: Either crush these movements or compete with them. A turning point came with the decision by the Lithuanian Communist Party to declare itself independent of the Communist Party of the Soviet Union.

This decision arose out of a bind in which the Lithuanian Communists were caught. They were faced with republic-level contested elections in the near future and the virtual certainty that they would be badly beaten by the Lithuanian popular front organization, Sajudis. The Lithuanian Communist Party decided to try to save itself by playing the game according to pluralistic rules—embracing the desire of the Lithuanian people for a free Lithuanian nation with multiparty democracy. This meant that it had to cut its tie to the CPSU, which symbolized the Lithuanians' perception that they were an involuntary political subdivision within an alien country.

In response, the Soviet leadership made a crucial decision: to use persuasion rather than force. Gorbachev went to Lithuania and behaved much like any American politician campaigning for his party, trying to persuade the voters of its superiority over the opposition. Although he failed to convince the Lithuanian Communists to return to the fold, this trip was a valuable learning experience for Gorbachev and the leadership of the CPSU. The Lithuanians, in effect, forced the CPSU to accept the inevitability of a multiparty system in the Soviet Union. Like it or not, a *de facto* multiparty system was beginning to emerge, and neither Article 6 of the Soviet Constitution nor the use of any acceptable level of force was going to change that fact.

Shortly thereafter, Gorbachev presented his plan for meeting this challenge to a plenum of the Central Committee of the CPSU. What Gorbachev told the CC and, ultimately, the Party apparatus and rank-and-file was that the CPSU needed to reorganize itself and its policies in order to compete effectively in an emerging pluralistic system. There was really no other choice. The leadership, with the help of the military and the security forces, could have crushed the embryonic party organizations springing up all over the country. But they would have also crushed any chance of wide popular support in addressing the deep problems facing the country and may, in addition, have faced a much more serious revolt from below, from the people themselves.

Moreover, it was clear that the Party itself was no longer capable of continuing to operate a rigid one-party system in which the Party was responsible for everything; too much was going wrong. Organized factions were developing within the Party itself, challenging each other on policy matters. In most of the Soviet Union, Party officials were perceived as not responding effectively to the need for reform. In fact, there was a growing conviction that the Party bureaucracy was the chief obstacle to an effective reform process. All of this was seen by Gorbachev and his reformist coalition as demanding a rapid and dramatic reorganization of the Party and its apparatus.

The establishment of a multiparty system—and its acceptance by the CPSU—would seem to be a true watershed event, definitively precluding a return to the Stalinist past. Full acceptance would of course imply the willingness of the Party to turn the reins of power over to others if election returns warranted it—something which it found itself doing in several localities after the republic–level elections in 1990. Pluralism in a country like the Soviet Union, however, may well be a mixed blessing. As Gorbachev said in 1989: "If you have three or four parties, you can still have so much tyranny that nobody can open his mouth or speak freely. . . . First, one or two parties on the basis of class . . . then 120 on the basis of nationality." (Yasmann, 1989, pp. 19–20). This quotation raises two basic issues associated with a multiparty system in the USSR. First, what preparation do the Soviet people have for understanding and accepting the turbulent kind of political competition that tends to emerge in multiparty systems? Second, on what basis might various groups of Soviet citizens coalesce into political parties and how might they handle the necessity for coalition building which characterizes multiparty systems?

To date, the Soviet political system has had extremely limited citizen participation under an oligarchic and paternalistic leadership. This is in line with the historical Russian experience of a single strong leader, the Tsar, backed by an oligarchic elite (Keenan, 1986). During the Soviet period, this single-strong-leader role was played by the leader of the Party, who—particularly in the formative days of Stalin—was held to represent the epitome of wisdom regarding the proper direction in which the government should move. The Party elite was the oligarchy behind the leader, claiming to know what was best for the "masses." This pattern permeated all aspects of the political system, with those in power at all levels taking a paternalistic approach to those whom they governed. All of this tended to give the appearance of a political system which was very neat and orderly, even though it could also be quite repressive.

Most of the Soviet nationalities have few political traditions that might prepare them for the rough-and-tumble nature of representative democracy—the Baltic republics being the most obvious exception. To the Russians in particular, the ambiguity and built-in discord which characterize true democratic systems could be frightening—raising the specter of anarchy and evoking a profound fear of political and social chaos that has deep roots in Russian history. This, in turn, could lead to a nostalgia for a "strong hand" at the controls which might or might not be assuaged by the new strong presidency or the person occupying that office. This is at the base of the present support among many Soviet citizens for a return to Stalinism or something like it. Particularly if the violence in the south continues or spreads to other parts of the country, there may be a conservative reaction, both within the leadership and among the people. Any such development could lead to a return to strong, oligarchic leadership and reactionary policies.

This leads to the second question regarding the kinds of goals which might draw significant segments of the Soviet people into political parties. At this point in time, what seems to be uniting many of the groups who have made an early claim to political-party status is their ethnic identity and discontent with the way in which their part of the USSR is being governed. There are some political groups which rise above ethnic identity and regional concerns, like the Interregional Group in the Supreme Soviet. Greater impact, however, is being made by the nationalistic, militant popular front with a strong base in one of the union republics and little following beyond its borders.

And what sorts of goals do these nascent political parties have? For the most part, they have two major goals. One is an assertion of their national identity, which frequently centers on partial or total independence from Moscow. The other is animosity toward the Russians,[2] and possibly one or more other ethnic groups. This is not the stuff of which a stable, well-functioning multiparty democracy is made. True pluralism demands a focus on cross-cutting issues, a commitment to peaceful competition, and a basic respect for, and acceptance of, all legitimate parties to the contest for power. This basis for a multiparty system does not now exist in the Soviet Union and is not likely to emerge rapidly. In fact, disintegration into civil disorder is a distinct possibility, not just in isolated pockets of the country but on a more wide-spread basis. And so is the breakup of the USSR as a political entity.

It would seem that the current leadership and their rivals are facing a host of choices, all of which are perilous. In our view, the *real* normalization of the Soviet political system will come when there is a stable pluralistic system with peaceful political competition via the ballot box. In other words, the turning point would be a process, not an event. That process would be the establishment *and* stabilization of a new institutional framework for politics in the USSR. Any multiparty system must be built on a minimum of basic consensus and have a government predicated on the rule of law. The need for basic consensus would require the various nationalities to be willing to remain a part of the Soviet Union and to maintain a tolerant and cooperative stance toward those of other ethnic heritages. A situation which would combine these factors still seems to be distant.

History makes it clear that democracy does not guarantee domestic tranquillity or prosperity, especially in countries just embarking upon that path. The USSR faces a multitude of economic, social, ethnic, and other problems, with a populace that is only now moving hesitantly toward experimentation with the day-to-day realities of democratic mechanisms. Genuine political choice places great burdens on both politicians and citizens. Political stability, economic well-being, and ethnic harmony are not easily won. But a large portion of the Soviet populace seems to be saying that they have tried another way and have found it wanting. It is time for change—albeit change fraught with turmoil, uncertainty, risk, and pain.

REFERENCES

BALZER, H. (1989). Can we survive glasnost? *Newsletter, American Association for the Advancement of Slavic Studies, 29,* 1, 1–2.
BRUMBERG, A. (1989a). Conventional wisdom and unfinished agendas. *Moscow News,* 16, 6.
BRUMBERG, A. (1989b). Moscow: The struggle for reform. *The New York Review,* March 30, 1989, 37–42.

[2]Russian nationalists have also organized and are expressing animosity toward other ethnic groups.

HERMANN, M.G., ed. (1986). *Political psychology.* San Francisco: Jossey-Bass.

KAISER, R. (1988). The USSR in decline. *Foreign Affairs, 67,* 2, 97–113.

KEENAN, E.L. (1986). Muscovite political folkways. *The Russian Review, 45,* 115–181.

NIMMO, D. and COMBS, J.E. (1980). *Subliminal politics: Myths and mythmakers in America.* Englewood Cliffs, NJ: Prentice-Hall.

TOLZ, V. (1988). Controversy over Leninist roots of Stalinism. *Radio Liberty Research,* no. 446/88.

WHITNEY, C. (1989). Glasnost writing: So where's the golden age? *The New York Times Book Review,* March 19, 1989, 1.

YASMANN, V. (1989). Gorbachev's formula for second state of *perestroika:* Full ahead but keep right. *Radio Liberty Report on the USSR, 1,* 10, 19–22.

APPENDIX A
CONSTITUTION (FUNDAMENTAL LAW) OF THE UNION OF SOVIET SOCIALIST REPUBLICS*

The Great October Socialist Revolution, fought by the workers and peasants of Russia under the leadership of the Communist Party headed by Lenin, overthrew capitalist and landowner rule, broke the fetters of oppression, established the dictatorship of the proletariat, and created the Soviet state, a new type of state, the basic instrument for defending the gains of the revolution and for building socialism and communism. Humanity thereby began the epoch-making turn from capitalism to socialism.

After achieving victory in the Civil War and repulsing imperialist intervention, the Soviet government carried through far-reaching social and economic transformations and put an end once and for all to exploitation of man by man, antagonisms between classes, and strife between nationalities. The unification of the Soviet Republics in the Union of Soviet Socialist Republics multiplied the forces and opportunities of the peoples of the country in the building of socialism. Social ownership of the means of production and genuine democracy for the working masses were established. For the first time in the history of humanity a socialist society was created.

The strength of socialism was vividly demonstrated by the immortal feat

*Adopted at the Seventh (Special) Session of the Supreme Soviet of the USSR, Ninth Convocation, on Oct. 7, 1977. As amended December 1, 1988, December 20 and 23, 1989, and March 14, 1990.

of the Soviet people and their Armed Forces in achieving their historic victory in the Great Patriotic War. This victory consolidated the influence and international standing of the Soviet Union and created new opportunities for growth of the forces of socialism, national liberation, democracy, and peace throughout the world.

Continuing their creative endeavors, the working people of the Soviet Union have ensured rapid, all-round development of the country and steady improvement of the socialist system. They have consolidated the alliance of the working class, collective-farm peasantry, and people's intelligentsia and the friendship between the nations and nationalities of the USSR. The socio-political and ideological unity of Soviet society, in which the working class is the leading force, has been achieved. The aims of the dictatorship of the proletariat having been fulfilled, the Soviet state has become a state of the whole people.

In the USSR a developed socialist society has been built. At this stage, when socialism is developing on its own foundations, the creative forces of the new system and the advantages of the socialist way of life are becoming increasingly evident, and the working people are more and more widely enjoying the fruits of their great revolutionary gains.

It is a society in which powerful productive forces and a progressive science and culture have been created, in which the well-being of the people is constantly rising, and more and more favorable conditions are being provided for the all-round development of the individual.

It is a society of mature socialist social relations, in which, on the basis of the drawing together of all classes and social strata and the juridical and factual equality of all its nations and nationalities and thier fraternal cooperation, a new historical community of people has been formed—the Soviet people.

It is a society of high organizational capacity, ideological commitment, and consciousness of the working people, who are patriots and internationalists.

It is a society in which the law of life is the concern of all for the good of each and concern of each for the good of all.

It is a society of true democracy, the political system of which ensures effective management of all public affairs, ever more active participation of the working people in running the state, and the combining of citizens' real rights and freedoms with their obligation and responsibility to society.

Developed socialist society is a necessary stage on the road to communism.

The supreme goal of the Soviet state is the building of a classless communist society in which there will be public, communist self-government. The main aims of the people's socialist state are: to lay the material and technical foundation of communism, to perfect socialist social relations and transform them in communist relations, to mold the citizen of communist society, to raise the people's living and cultural standards, to safeguard the country's security, and to further the consolidation of peace and development of international cooperation.

The Soviet people,

guided by the ideas of scientific communism and true to their revolutionary traditions,

relying on the great social, economic, and political gains of socialism,

striving for the further development of social democracy,

taking into account the international position of the USSR as part of the world system of socialism, and conscious of their internationalist responsibility,

preserving continuity of the ideas and principles of the first Soviet Constitution of 1918, the 1924 Constitution of the USSR and the 1936 Constitution of the USSR,

hereby affirm the principles of the social structure and policy of the USSR, and define the rights, freedoms, and obligations of citizens, and the principles of the organization of the socialist state of the whole people, and its aims, and proclaim these in this Constitution.

I. PRINCIPLES OF THE SOCIAL STRUCTURE AND POLICY OF THE USSER

Chapter 1   The Political System

ARTICLE 1. The Union of Sovet Socialist Republics is a socialist all-people's state expressing the will and interests of the workers, peasants, and intelligentsia, the working people of all the nations and nationalities of the country.

ARTICLE 2. All power in the USSR belongs to the people.

The people exercise state power through Soviets of People's Deputies, which constitute the political foundation of the USSR.

All other state bodies are under the control of, and accountable to, the Soviets of People's Deputies.

ARTICLE 3. The Soviet state is organized and functions on the principle of democratic centralism, namely the election of all bodies of state authority from the lowest to the highest, their accountability to the people, and the obligation of lower bodies to observe the decisions of higher ones. Democratic centralism combines central leadership with local initiative and creative activity and with the responsibility of each state body and official for the work entrusted to them.

ARTICLE 4. The Soviet state and all its bodies function on the basis of socialist legality, ensure the maintenance of law and order, and safeguard the interests of society and the rights and freedoms of citizens.

State organizations, social organizations and officials shall observe the Constitution of the USSR and Soviet laws.

ARTICLE 5. Major matters of state shall be submitted to nationwide discussion and put to a popular vote (referendum).

ARTICLE 6. The Communist Party of the Soviet Union and other political parties, as well as trade union, youth, and other social organizations and mass movements, participate in the formulation of the policy of the Soviet state and in the administration of state and social affairs through their representatives elected to the soviets of people's deputies and in other ways.

ARTICLE 7. All political parties, social organizations, and mass movements, in the exercise of the functions stipulated in their programs and statutes, operate within the framework of the Constitution and Soviet laws.

The formation and operation of parties, organizations, and movements having the aim of forcibly changing the Soviet constitutional system and the integrity of the socialist state, undermining its security, or kindling social, national, or religious strife are not permitted.

ARTICLE 8. Labor collectives take part in discussing and deciding state and public affairs, in planning production and social development, in training and placing personnel, and in discussing the deciding matters pertaining to the management of enterprises and institutions, the improvement of working and living conditions, and the use of funds allocated for developing production and for social and cultural purposes and financial incentives.

Labor collectives promote socialist competition, the spread of progressive methods of work, and the strengthening of discipline, educate their members in the spirit of communist morality and strive to enhance their political consciousness and raise their cultural level and skills and qualifications.

ARTICLE 9. The principal direction of the developing of the political system of Soviet society is the extension of socialist democracy, namely ever broader participation of citizens in managing the affairs of society and the state, continuous improvement of the machinery of state, heightening of the activity of public organizations, strengthening of the system of people's control, consolidation of the legal foundations of the functioning of the state and of public life, greater openness and publicity, and constant responsiveness to public opinion.

Chapter 2   The Economic System

ARTICLE 10. The economic system of the USSR develops on the basis of ownership by Soviet citizens and collective and state ownership.

The state creates the conditions necessary for the development of diverse forms of ownership and ensures equal protection for them.

The land, its mineral resources, water resources, and the plant and animal world in their natural state are the inalienable property of the peoples inhabiting a given territory, are under the jurisdiction of the soviets of people's deputies, and are granted to citizens, enterprises, institutions, and organizations for their utilization.

ARTICLE 11. A USSR citizen's property is his personal property and is used to meet material and spiritual needs and carry out autonomous economic activity and other activity that is not banned by law.

Any property for consumption and production purposes acquired out of earned income and on other lawful grounds may be under the ownership of a citizen, with the exception of those forms of property whose acquisition by citizens for their own ownership is not permitted.

In order to pursue peasant and personal subsidiary farming and for other purposes stipulated by law, citizens are entitled to hold land plots in heritable life tenure, and also in use [polzovaniye].

The right of inheritance of a citizen's property is acknowledged and protected by law.

ARTICLE 12. Collective property is the property of leaseholding enterprises, collective enterprises, cooperatives, joint-stock companies, economic organizations, and other associations. Collective property is created through the transformation, by methods stipulated by law, of state property and through the voluntary amalgamation of the property of citizens and organizations.

ARTICLE 13. State property is unionwide property, the property of union republics, and the property of autonomous republics, autonomous oblasts, autonomous okrugs, krays, and other administrative-territorial units (communal property).

ARTICLE 14. The source of the growth of social wealth and of the well-being of the people, and of each individual, is the labor, free from exploitation, of Soviet people.

The state exercises control over the measure of labor and of consumption in accordance with the principle of socialism: "From each according to his ability, to each according to his work." It fixes the rate of taxation on taxable income.

Socially useful work and its results determine the person's status in society. By combining material and moral incentives and encouraging innovation and a creative attitude to work, the state helps transform labor into the prime vital need of every Soviet citizen.

ARTICLE 15. The supreme goal of social production under socialism is the fullest possible satisfaction of the people's growing material and cultural and intellectual requirements.

Relying on the creative initiative of the working people, socialist emulation, and scientific and technological progress, and by improving the forms and methods of economic management, the state ensures the growth of the productivity of labor, raising of the efficiency of production and of the quality of work, and dynamic, planned, proportionate development of the economy.

ARTICLE 16. The economy of the USSR is an integral economic complex comprising all the elements of social production, distribution, and exchange on its territory.

The economy is managed on the basis of state plans for economic and social development, with due account of the sectoral and territorial principles, and by combining centralized direction with the managerial independence and initiative of enterprises, associations, and other organizations for which active use is made of economic accountability, profit cost, and other economic levers and incentives.

ARTICLE 17. In the USSR, the law permits individual labor in handicrafts, farming, the provision of services for the public, and other forms of activity based exclusively on the personal work of individual citizens and members of their families. The state makes regulations for such work to ensure that it serves the interests of society.

ARTICLE 18. In the interests of the present and future generations, the necessary steps are taken in the USSR to protect and make scientific, rational use of the land and its mineral and water resources and the plants and animals, to preserve the purity of air and water, ensure reproduction of natural wealth, and improve the human environment.

Chapter 3   Social Development and Culture

ARTICLE 19. The social basis of the USSR is the unbreakable alliance of the workers, peasants, and intelligentsia.

The state helps enhance the social homogeneity of society, namely the elimination of class differences and of the essential distinctions between town and country and between mental and physical labor and the all-round development and drawing together of all the nations and nationalities of the USSR.

ARTICLE 20. In accordance with the communist ideal—"The free development of each is the condition of the free development of all"—the state pursues the aim of giving citizens more and more real opportunities to apply their creative energies, abilities, and talents and to develop their personalities in every way.

ARTICLE 21. The state concerns itself with improving working conditions, safety and labor protection, and the scientific organization of work, and with reducing and ultimately eliminating all arduous physical labor through comprehensive mechanization and automation of production processes in all branches of the economy.

ARTICLE 22. A program is being consistently implemented in the USSR to convert agricultural work into a variety of industrial work, to extend the network of educational, cultural, and medical institutions, and of trade, public catering, service, and public utility facilities in rural localities, and transform hamlets and villages into well-planned and well-appointed settlements.

ARTICLE 23. The state pursues a steady policy of raising people's pay levels and real incomes through increase in productivity.

In order to satisfy the needs of the Soviet people more fully, social consumption funds are created. The state, with the broad participation of public organizations and work collectives, ensures the growth and just distribution of these funds.

ARTICLE 24. In the USSR, state systems of health protection, social security, trade and public catering, communal services and amenities, and public utilities operate and are being extended.

The state encourages cooperatives and other public organizations to provide all types of services for the population. It encourages the development of mass physical culture and sport.

ARTICLE 25. In the USSR there is a uniform system of public education, which is being constantly improved, that provides general education and vocational training for citizens, serves the communist education and intellectual and physical development of the youth, and trains them for work and social activity.

ARTICLE 26. In accordance with society's needs the state provides for the planned development of science and the training of scientific personnel and organizes introduction of the results of research into the economy and other spheres of life.

ARTICLE 27. The state concerns itself with protecting, augmenting, and making extensive use of society's cultural wealth for the moral and aesthetic education of the Soviet people, for raising their cultural level.

In the USSR, development of the professional, amateur, and folk arts is encouraged in every way.

Chapter 4   Foreign Policy

ARTICLE 28. The USSR steadfastly pursues a Leninist policy of peace and stands for the strengthening of the security of nations and broad international cooperation.

The foreign policy of the USSR is aimed at ensuring international conditions favorable for building communism in the USSR, safeguarding the state interests of the Soviet Union, consolidating the positions of world socialism, supporting the struggle of peoples for national liberation and social progress, preventing wars of aggression, achieving universal and complete disarmament, and consistently implementing the principle of the peaceful coexistence of states with different social systems.

In the USSR, war propaganda is banned.

ARTICLE 29. The USSR's relations with other states are based on observance of the following principles: sovereign equality; mutual renunciation of the use or threat of force; inviolability of frontiers; territorial integrity of states; peaceful settlement of disputes; noninterference in internal affairs; respect for human rights and fundamental freedoms; the equal rights of peoples and their right to decide their own destiny; cooperation among states; and fulfillment in good faith of obligations arising from the generally recognized principles and rules of international law and from the international treaties signed by the USSR.

ARTICLE 30. The USSR, as part of the world system of socialism and of the socialist community, promotes and strengthens friendship, cooperation, and comradely mutual assistance with other socialist countries on the basis of the principle of socialist internationalism and takes an active part in socialist economic integration and the socialist international division of labor.

Chapter 5   Defense of the Socialist Motherland

ARTICLE 31. Defense of the Socialist Motherland is one of the most important functions of the state and is the concern of the whole people.

In order to defend the gains of socialism, the peaceful labor of the Soviet people, and the sovereignty and territorial integrity of the state, the USSR maintains armed forces and has instituted universal military service.

The duty of the Armed Forces of the USSR to the people is to provide reliable defense of the Socialist Motherland and to be in constant combat readiness, guaranteeing that any aggressor is instantly repulsed.

ARTICLE 32. The state ensures the security and defense capability of the country, and supplies the Armed Forces of the USSR with everything necessary for that purpose.

The duties of state bodies, public organizations, officials, and citizens in regard to safeguarding the country's security and strengthening its defense capacity are defined by the legislation of the USSR.

II.   THE STATE AND THE INDIVIDUAL

Chapter 6   Citizenship of the USSR Equality of Citizens' Rights

ARTICLE 33. Uniform federal citizenship is established for the USSR. Every citizen of a Union Republic is a citizen of the USSR.

The grounds and procedures for acquiring or forfeiting Soviet citizenship are defined by the Law on Citizenship of the USSR.

When abroad, citizens of the USSR enjoy the protection and assistance of the Soviet state.

ARTICLE 34. Citizens of the USSR are equal before the law, without distinction of origin, social or property status, race or nationality, sex, education, language, attitude to religion, type and nature of occupation, domicile, or other circumstances.

The equal rights of citizens of the USSR are guaranteed in all fields of economic, political, social, and cultural life.

ARTICLE 35. Women and men have equal rights in the USSR.

Exercise of these rights is ensured by according women equal access with men to education and vocational and professional training, equal opportunities in employment, remuneration, and promotion, and in social and political and cultural activity, and by special labor and health protection measures for women; by providing conditions enabling mothers to work; by legal protection and material and moral support for mothers and children, including paid leaves and other benefits for expectant mothers and mothers, and the gradual reduction of working time for mothers with small children.

ARTICLE 36. Citizens of the USSR of different races and nationalities have equal rights.

Exercise of these rights is ensured by a policy of all-round development and drawing together of all the nations and nationalities of the USSR, by educating citizens in the spirit of Soviet patriotism and socialist internationalism, and by the possibility to use their native language and the languages of other peoples of the USSR.

And direct or indirect limitation of the rights of citizens or establishment of direct or indirect privileges on grounds of race or nationality and any advocacy of racial or national exclusiveness, hostility, or contempt are punishable by law.

ARTICLE 37. Citizens of other countries and stateless persons in the USSR are guaranteed the rights and freedoms provided by law, including the right to apply to a court and other state bodies for the protection of their personal, property, family, and other rights.

Citizens of other countries and stateless persons, when in the USSR, are obliged to respect the Constitution of the USSR and observe Soviet laws.

ARTICLE 38. The USSR grants the right of asylum to foreigners persecuted for defending the interests of the working people and the cause of peace, or for participation in the revolutionary and national-liberation movement, or for progressive social and political, scientific, or other creative activity.

Chapter 7   The Basic Rights, Freedoms, and Duties of Citizens of the USSR

ARTICLE 39. Citizens of the USSR enjoy in full the social, economic, political and personal rights and freedoms proclaimed and guaranteed by the Constitution of the USSR and by Soviet laws. The socialist system ensures enlargement of the rights and freedoms of citizens and continuous improvement of their living standards as social, economic, and cultural development programs are fulfilled.

Enjoyment by citizens of their rights and freedoms must not be to the detriment of the interests of society or the state or infringe the rights of other citizens.

ARTICLE 40. Citizens of the USSR have the right to work (that is, to guaranteed employment and pay in accordance with the quantity and quality of their work and not below the state-established minimum), including the right to choose their trade or profession, type of job, and work in accordance with their inclinations, abilities, training, and education, taking into account the needs of society.

This right is ensured by the socialist economic system, steady growth of the productive forces, free vocational and professional training, improvement of skills, training in new trades or professions, and development of the systems of vocational guidance and job placement.

ARTICLE 41. Citizens of the USSR have the right to rest and leisure.

This right is ensured by the establishment of a working week not exceeding forty-one hours for workers and other employees, a shorter working day in a number of trades and industries, and shorter hours for night work; by the provision of paid annual holidays, weekly days of rest, extension of the network of cultural, educational, and health-building institutions, and the development of a mass scale of sport, physical culture, camping, and tourism; by the provision of neighborhood recreational facilities and of other opportunities for rational use of free time.

The length of collective-farmers' working and leisure time is established by their collective farms.

ARTICLE 42. Citizens of the USSR have the right to health protection.

This right is ensured by free, qualified medical care provided by state health institutions; by extension of the network of therapeutic and health-building institutions; by the development and improvement of safety and hygiene in industry; by carrying out broad prophylactic measures; by measures to improve the environment; by special care for the health of youth, including prohibition of child labor, excluding the work done by children as part of the school curriculum; and by developing research to prevent and reduce the incidence of disease and ensure citizens a long and active life.

ARTICLE 43. Citizens of the USSR have the right to maintenance in old age, in sickness, and in the event of complete or partial disability or loss of the breadwinner.

This right is guaranteed by social insurance of workers and other employees and collective farmers; by allowances for temporary disability; by the provision by the state or by collective farms of retirement pensions, disability pensions, and pensions for loss of the breadwinner; by providing employment for the partially disabled; by care for the elderly and the disabled; and by other forms of social security.

ARTICLE 44. Citizens of the USSR have the right to housing.

This right is ensured by the development and upkeep of state and socially owned housing; by assistance for cooperative and individual house building; by fair distribution, under public control, of the housing that becomes available through fulfillment of the program of building well-appointed dwellings; and by low rents and low charges for utility services. Citizens of the USSR shall take good care of the housing allocated to them.

ARTICLE 45. Citizens of the USSR have the right to education.

This right is ensured by the free provision of all forms of education, by the institution of universal, compulsory secondary education, and the broad development of vocational, specialized secondary, and higher education, in which instruction is oriented toward practical activity and production; by the development of extramural, correspondence, and evening courses; by the provision of state scholarships and grants and privileges for students; by the free issue of school textbooks; by the opportunity to attend a school where teaching is in the native language; and by the provision of facilities for self-education.

ARTICLE 46. Citizens of the USSR have the right to enjoy cultural benefits.

This right is ensured by broad access to the cultural treasures of their own land and of the world, which are preserved in state and other public collections; by the development and fair distribution of cultural and educational institutions throughout the country; by the development of television and radio broadcasting and the publishing of books, newspapers, and periodicals, and by the extension of the free library service; and by the expansion of cultural exchanges with other countries.

ARTICLE 47. Citizens of the USSR, in accordance with the aims of building communism, are guaranteed freedom of scientific, technical, and artistic work. This freedom is ensured by broadening scientific research, encouraging invention and innovation, and developing literature and the arts. The state provides the necessary material conditions for this and support for voluntary societies and unions of workers in the arts, organizes introduction of inventions and innovations in production and other spheres of activity.

The rights of authors, inventors, and innovators are protected by the state.

ARTICLE 48. Citizens of the USSR have the right to take part in the management and administration of state and public affairs and in the discussion and adoption of laws and measures of All-Union and local significance.

This right is ensured by the opportunity to vote and to be elected to Soviets of People's Deputies and other elective state bodies and to take part in nationwide discussions and referendums, in people's control, in the work of state bodies, public organizations, and local community groups, and in meetings at places of work or residence.

ARTICLE 49. Every citizen of the USSR has the right to submit proposals to state bodies and public organizations for improving their activity and to criticize shortcomings in their work.

Officials are obliged, within established time limits, to examine citizens' proposals and requests, to reply to them, and to take appropriate action.

Persecution for criticism is prohibited. Persons guilty of such persecution shall be called to account.

ARTICLE 50. In accordance with the interests of the people and in order to strengthen and develop the socialist system, citizens of the USSR are guaranteed freedom of speech, of the press, and of assembly, meetings, street processions, and demonstrations.

Exercise of these political freedoms is ensured by putting public buildings, streets, and squares at the disposal of the working people and their organizations, broad dissemination of information; and by the opportunity to use the press, television, and radio.

ARTICLE 51. USSR citizens have the right to form political parties and social organizations and to participate in mass movements that promote the development of political activeness and independent activity and the satisfaction of their diverse interests.

Social organizations are guaranteed the conditions for the successful fulfillment of their statutory tasks.

ARTICLE 52. Citizens of the USSR are guaranteed freedom of conscience, that is, the right to profess or not to profess any religion and to conduct religious worship or atheistic propaganda. Incitement of hostility or hatred on religious grounds is prohibited.

In the USSR, the church is separated from the state and the school from the church.

ARTICLE 53. The family enjoys the protection of the state.

Marriage is based on the free consent of the woman and the man; the spouses are completely equal in their family relations.

The state helps the family by providing and developing a broad system of child-care institutions, by organizing and improving communal services and public catering, by paying grants on the birth of a child, by providing children's allowances and benefits for large families, and other forms of family allowances and assistance.

ARTICLE 54. Citizens of the USSR are guaranteed inviolability of the person. No one may be arrested except by a court decision or on the warrant of a procurator.

ARTICLE 55. Citizens of the USSR are guaranteed inviolability of the home. No one may, without lawful grounds, enter a home against the will of those residing in it.

ARTICLE 56. The privacy of citizens, and of their correspondence, telephone conversations, and telegraphic communications, is protected by law.

ARTICLE 57. Respect for the individual and protection of the rights and freedoms of citizens are the duty of all state bodies, public organizations, and officials.

Citizens of the USSR have the right to protection by the courts against encroachments on their honor and reputation, life and health, and personal freedom and property.

ARTICLE 58. Citizens of the USSR have the right to lodge a complaint against the actions of officials, state bodies, and public bodies. Complaints shall be examined according to the procedure and within the time limit established by law.

Actions by officials that contravene the law or exceed their powers and infringe the rights of citizens may be appealed against in a court in the manner prescribed by law.

Citizens of the USSR have the right to compensation for damage resulting from unlawful actions by state organizations and public organizations or by officials in the performance of their duties.

ARTICLE 59. The exercise of rights and freedoms is inseparable from the performance by the citizens of their duties.

Citizens of the USSR are obliged to observe the Constitution of the USSR and Soviet laws, comply with the rules of socialist community life, and uphold the honor and dignity of Soviet citizenship.

ARTICLE 60. It is the duty of, and a matter of honor for, every able-bodied citizen of the USSR to work conscientiously in his chosen, socially useful occupation and strictly to observe labor discipline. Evasion of socially useful work is incompatible with the principles of socialist society.

ARTICLE 61. Citizens of the USSR are obliged to preserve and protect socialist property. It is the duty of a citizen of the USSR to combat misappropriation and squandering of state and socially owned property and to make thrifty use of the people's wealth.

Persons encroaching in any way on socialist property shall be punished according to the law.

ARTICLE 62. Citizens of the USSR are obliged to safeguard the interests of the Soviet state and to enhance its power and prestige.

Defense of the Socialist Motherland is the sacred duty of every citizen of the USSR.

Betrayal of the Motherland is the gravest of crimes against the people.

ARTICLE 63. Military service in the ranks of the Armed Forces of the USSR is an honorable duty of Soviet citizens.

ARTICLE 64. It is the duty of every citizen of the USSR to respect the national dignity of other citizens and to strengthen friendship of the nations and nationalities of the multinational Soviet state.

ARTICLE 65. A citizen of the USSR is obliged to respect the rights and lawful interests of other persons, to be uncompromising toward antisocial behavior, and to help maintain public order.

ARTICLE 66. Citizens of the USSR are obliged to concern themselves with the upbringing of children, to train them for socially useful work, and to raise them as worthy members of socialist society. Children are obliged to care for their parents and help them.

ARTICLE 67. Citizens of the USSR are obliged to protect nature and conserve its riches.

ARTICLE 68. Concern for the preservation of historical monuments and other cultural values is a duty and obligation of citizens of the USSR.

ARTICLE 69. It is the internationalist duty of citizens of the USSR to promote friendship and cooperation with peoples and other lands and help maintain and strengthen world peace.

III. THE NATIONAL-STATE STRUCTURE OF THE USSR

Chapter 8 The USSR—A Federal State

ARTICLE 70. The Union of Soviet Socialist Republics is a unitary, federal, multinational state formed on the principle of socialist federalism as a result of the free self-determination of nations and the voluntary association of equal Soviet Socialist Republics.

The USSR embodies the state unity of the Soviet people and draws all its nations and nationalities together for the purpose of jointly building communism.

ARTICLE 71. The Union of Soviet Socialist Republics unites:

the Russian Soviet Federative Socialist Republic,
the Ukrainian Soviet Socialist Republic,
the Byelorussian Soviet Socialist Republic,
the Uzbek Soviet Socialist Republic,
the Kazakh Soviet Socialist Republic,
the Georgian Soviet Socialist Republic,
the Azerbaidzhan Soviet Socialist Republic,
the Lithuanian Soviet Socialist Republic,
the Moldavian Soviet Socialist Republic,
the Latvian Soviet Socialist Republic,
the Kirghiz Soviet Socialist Republic,
the Tajik Soviet Socialist Republic,
the Armenian Soviet Socialist Republic,
the Turkmen Soviet Socialist Republic,
the Estonian Soviet Socialist Republic.

ARTICLE 72. Each Union Republic shall retain the right freely to secede from the USSR.

ARTICLE 73. The jurisdiction of the Union of Soviet Socialist Republics, as represented by its highest bodies of state authority and administration, shall cover:

1. the admission of new republics to the USSR; endorsement of the formation of new autonomous republics and autonomous regions within Union Republics;
2. determination of the state boundaries of the USSR and approval of changes in the boundaries between Union Republics;
3. establishment of the general principles for the organization and functioning of republican and local bodies of state authority and administration;
4. the ensurance of uniformity of legislative norms throughout the USSR and establishment of the fundamentals of the legislation of the Union of Soviet Socialist Republics and Union Republics;
5. pursuance of a uniform social and economic policy; direction of the country's

economy; determination of the main lines of scientific and technological progress and the general measures for rational exploitation and conservation of natural resources; the drafting and approval of state plans for the economic and social development of the USSR, and endorsement of reports on their fulfillment;

6. the drafting and approval of the consolidated Budget of the USSR and endorsement of the report on its execution; management of a single monetary and credit system; determination of the taxes and revenues forming the Budget of the USSR; and the formulation of prices and wages policy;

7. direction of the sectors of the economy and of enterprises and amalgamations under Union jurisdiction, and general direction of industries under Union-Republican jurisdiction;

8. issues of war and peace, defense of the sovereignty of the USSR and safeguarding of its frontiers and territory, and organization of defense, direction of the Armed Forces of the USSR;

9. state security;

10. representation of the USSR in international relations; the USSR's relations with other states and with international organizations; establishment of the general procedure for, and coordination of, the relations of Union Republics with other states and with international organizations; foreign trade and other forms of external economic activity on the basis of state monopoly;

11. control over observance of the Constitution of the USSR, and insurance of conformity of the Constitutions of Union Republics to the Constitution of the USSR;

12. and settlement of other matters of All-Union importance.

ARTICLE 74. The laws of te USSR shall have the same force in all Union Republics. In the event of a discrepancy between a Union-Republic law and an All-Union law, the law of the USSR shall prevail.

ARTICLE 75. The territory of the Union of Soviet Socialist Republics is a single entity and comprises the territories of the Union Republics.

The sovereignty of the USSR extends throughout its territory.

Chapter 9   The Union Soviet Socialist Republic

ARTICLE 76. A Union Republic is a sovereign Soviet socialist state that has united with other Soviet Republics in the Union of Sobiet Socialist Republics.

Outside the spheres listed in Article 73 of the Constitution of the USSR, a Union Republic exercises independent authority on its territory.

A Union Republic shall have its own Constitution conforming to the Constitution of the USSR with the specific features of the Republic being taken into account.

ARTICLE 77. A union republic participates in the resolution of questions coming under the jurisdiction of the USSR at the Congress of USSR People's Deputies, the USSR Supreme Soviet, the USSR Supreme Soviet Presidium, the Council of the Federation, the USSR Government, and other organs of the USSR.

A Union Republic shall ensure comprehensive economic and social development on its territory, facilitate exercise of the powers of the USSR on its territory, and implement the decisions of the highest bodies of state authority and administration of the USSR.

In matters that come within its jurisdiction, a Union Republic shall coordinate and control the activity of enterprises, institutions, and organizations subordinate to the Union.

ARTICLE 78. The territory of a Union Republic may not be altered without its consent. The boundaries between Union Republics may be altered by mutual agreement of the Republics concerned, subject to ratification by the Union of Soviet Socialist Republics.

ARTICLE 79. A Union Republic shall determine its division into territories, regions, areas, and districts and decide other matters relating to its administrative and territorial structure.

ARTICLE 80. A Union Republic has the right to enter into relations with other states, conclude treaties with them, exchange diplomatic and consular representatives, and take part in the work of international organizations.

ARTICLE 81. The sovereign rights of Union Republics shall be safeguarded by the USSR.

Chapter 10   The Autonomous Soviet Socialist Republic

ARTICLE 82. An Autonomous Republic is a constituent part of a Union Republic.

In spheres not within the jurisdiction of the Union of Soviet Socialist Republics and the Union Republic, an Autonomous Republic shall deal independently with matters within its jurisdiction.

An Autonomous Republic shall have its own Constitution conforming to the Constitutions of the USSR and the Union Republic with the specific features of the Autonomous Republic being taken into account.

ARTICLE 83. An Autonomous Republic takes part in decision making through the highest bodies of state authority and administration of the USSR and of the Union Republic, respectively, in matters that come within the jurisdiction of the USSR and the Union Republic.

An Autonomous Republic shall ensure comprehensive economic and social development on its territory, facilitate exercise of the powers of the USSR and the Union Republic on its territory, and implement decisions of the highest bodies of state authority and administration of the USSR and the Union Republic.

In matters within its jurisdiction, an Autonomous Republic shall coordinate and control the activity of enterprises, institutions, and organizations subordinate to the Union or the Union Republic.

ARTICLE 84. The territory of an Autonomous Republic may not be altered without its consent.

ARTICLE 85. The Russian Soviet Federative Socialist Republic includes the Bashkir, Buryat, Daghestan, Kabardin-Balkar, Kalmyk, Karelian, Komi, Mari, Mordovian, North Ossetian, Tatar, Tuva, Udmurt, Chechen-Ingush, Chuvash, and Yakut Autonomous Soviet Socialist Republics.

The Uzbek Soviet Socialist Republic includes the Kara-Kalpak Autonomous Soviet Socialist Republic.

The Georgian Soviet Socialist Republic includes the Abkhasian and Adzhar Autonomous Soviet Socialist Republics.

The Azerbaidzhan Soviet Socialist Republic includes the Nakhichevan Autonomous Soviet Socialist Republic.

Chapter 11   The Autonomous Region and Autonomous Area

ARTICLE 86. An Autonomous Region is a consistuent part of a Union Republic or Territory. The Law on an Autonomous Region, upon submission by the Soviet of People's Deputies of the Autonomous Region concerned, shall be adopted by the Supreme Soviet of the Union Republic.

ARTICLE 87. The Russian Soviet Federative Socialist Republic includes the Adygei, Gorno-Altai, Jewish, Karachai-Circassian, and Khakass Autonomous Regions.

The Georgian Soviet Socialist Republic includes the South Ossetian Autonomous Region.

The Azerbaidzhan Soviet Socialist Republic includes the Nagorno-Karabakh Autonomous Region.

The Tajik Soviet Socialist Republic includes the Gorno-Badakhshan Autonomous Region.

ARTICLE 88. An Autonomous Area is a constituent part of a Territory or Region. The Law on an Autonomous Area shall be adopted by the Supreme Soviet of the Union Republic concerned.

IV.   SOVIETS OF PEOPLE'S DEPUTIES AND ELECTORAL PROCEDURE

Chapter 12   System and Principles of Activity of the Soviets of People's Deputies

ARTICLE 89. The Soviets of People's Deputies—Congress of USSR People's Deputies and USSR Supreme Soviet, Congresses of People's Deputies and Supreme Soviets of union and autonomous republics, and Soviets of People's Deputies of autonomous oblasts and of krays, oblasts, and other administrative-territorial units—shall constitute a single system of bodies of state authority.

ARTICLE 90. The term of office of soviets of people's deputies is 5 years.

Elections of people's deputies are to be set no later than 4 months prior to the expiry of the term of office of the corresponding organs of state power.

Elections of USSR people's deputies shall be called not later than 4 months before the expiry of the term of the Congress of USSR People's Deputies.

The timing and procedure for calling elections of people's deputies of union and autonomous republics and to local Soviets of People's Deputies shall be determined by the laws of union and autonomous republics.

ARTICLE 91. The most important questions of unionwide, republican, and local significance are resolved at sessions of the congresses of people's deputies and sessions of supreme soviets and local soviets of people's deputies or are put to referendums by them.

Supreme Soviets of union and autonomous republics shall be elected directly by voters, and in republics where it is envisaged to create Congresses—by the Congresses of People's Deputies. Presidiums of Supreme Soviets and local Soviets of People's Deputies shall be constituted, and Soviet chairmen shall be elected, in conformity with the USSR Constitution and the constitutions of union and autonomous republics.

Soviets of People's Deputies shall form committees and permanent commissions and shall create executive and administrative organs and other organs accountable to them.

Officials elected or appointed by Soviets of People's Deputies, with the exception of judges, cannot hold office for more than two consecutive terms.

Any official can be released from his post early if he fails to perform his official duties properly.

ARTICLE 92. The soviets of people's deputies form organs of people's control, combining state control with social control by working people at enterprises, institutions, and organizations.

The organs of people's control verify the fulfillment of the requirements of legislation and state programs and targets; combat violations of state discipline, manifestations of parochialism and a departmental approach to the task, thriftlessness and extravagance, red tape, and bureaucracy; coordinate the work of other control organs; and promote the improvement of the structure and work of the state apparatus.

ARTICLE 93. The soviets of people's deputies, directly and through the organs they set up, lead all sections of state, economic, and sociocultural building, adopt decisions, ensure their execution, and exercise control over the implementation of decisions.

ARTICLE 94. The activity of the soviets of people's deputies is based on collective, free, and businesslike discussion and resolution of questions, glasnost, regular accountability and executive and management organs and other organs created by the soviets to them and to the population, and the wide involvement of citizens in participation in their work.

The soviets of people's deputies and the organs set up by them take account of public opinion, submit the most important questions of statewide and local significance for discussion by citizens, and systematically inform citizens about their work and the decisions adopted.

Chapter 13   The Electoral System

ARTICLE 95. Elections of people's deputies shall be held in single-seat or multiseat electoral okrugs on the basis of universal, equal, and direct suffrage by secret ballot.

Some people's deputies of union and autonomous republics, if so provided by the republics' constitutions, can be elected by public organizations,

ARTICLE 96. Elections of people's deputies from electoral okrugs shall be universal—USSR citizens who have reached the age of 18 shall have the right to vote.

USSR citizens who have reached the age of 21 can be elected USSR people's deputies.

A citizen of the USSR may not be a deputy of more than two soviets of people's deputies simultaneously.

Persons belonging to the USSR Council of Ministers, the Councils of Ministers of union and autonomous republics, and local soviet ispolkoms, with the exception of the chairmen of these organs, leaders of departments [vedomstva], departments [otdely], and administrations of local soviet ispolkoms, judges, and state arbiters, may not be deputies of the soviet to which they are appointed or elected.

Mentally ill citizens who have been adjudged incompetent by the courts and persons kept in places for deprivation of freedom following a court sentence, do not participate in elections. Persons who are remanded in custody according to procedures laid down by the Code of Criminal Proceedings, do not participate in elections.

Any direct or indirect restriction whatsoever of the electoral rights of USSR citizens is impermissible and punishable under the law.

ARTICLE 97. Elections of people's deputies from electoral okrugs are equal: A voter for each electoral okrug has one vote; voters participate in elections on an equal basis.

ARTICLE 98. Elections of people's deputies from electoral okrugs are direct [pryamoy]: People's deputies are elected by citizens directly [neposredstvenno].

ARTICLE 99. Voting at elections of people's deputies is secret: Monitoring [kontrol] of the voters' exercise of franchise [voleizyavleniye] is not permitted.

ARTICLE 100. The right to nominate candidate people's deputies in electoral okrugs shall be vested with labor collectives, public organizations, collectives of secondary specialized and higher education establishments, voters' meetings at places of residence, and servicemen's meetings in military units.

Organs and organizations with the right to nominate candidate people's deputies from public organizations shall be determined by the laws of the USSR and of union and autonomous republics respectively.

The number of candidate people's deputies is unlimited. Every participant in an election campaign meeting can propose anyone's nomination, including his own, for discussion.

Any number of candidates can be included in the ballot papers.

Candidate people's deputies participate in the election campaign on an equal footing.

With a view to ensuring equal conditions for every candidate people's deputy, the expenditure associated with the preparation and holding of elections of people's deputies shall be met by the corresponding electoral commission from a single fund created at the state's expense and from voluntary contributions by enterprises, public organizations, and citizens.

ARTICLE 101. Preparations for elections of people's deputies are carried out openly and in an atmosphere of glasnost [glasno].

The holding of elections shall be conducted by electoral commissions consisting of representatives elected by meetings (conferences) of labor collectives, public organizations, collectives of secondary specialized and higher education establishments, voters' meetings at places of residence, and servicemen's meetings in military units.

USSR citizens, labor collectives, public organizations, collectives of secondary specialized and higher education establishments, and servicemen in military units shall be guaranteed an opportunity for free and comprehensive discussion of the political, business, and personal qualities of candidate people's deputies, as well as the right to campaign for or against a candidate at meetings, in the press, and on television and radio.

The procedure for holding elections of people's deputies is defined by laws of the USSR and of union and autonomous republics.

ARTICLE 102. Voters and social organizations give mandates to their deputies.

The appropriate soviets of people's deputies examine the mandates, take them into account when formulating economic and social development plans and drawing up the budget, and also in preparing decisions on other questions, organize the fulfillment of mandates, and inform citizens about their implementation.

Chapter 14   People's Deputies

ARTICLE 103. Deputies are the plenipotentiary representatives of the people in the Soviets of People's Deputies.

In the Soviets, Deputies deal with matters relating to state, economic, and social and cultural development, organize implementation of the decisions of the Soviets, and exercise control over the work of state bodies, enterprises, institutions, and organizations.

In their activity deputies are guided by statewide interests, take into account the requests of the electoral okrug's population and the expressed interests of the social organization which has elected them, and strive to implement the mandates of the voters and the social organization.

ARTICLE 104. Deputies exercise their powers without, as a rule, interrupting their production or official activity.

During sittings of congresses of people's deputies and sessions of supreme soviets or local soviets of people's deputies, and also for the exercise of deputy powers in other instances envisaged by the law, deputies are released from carrying out their production or official duties and are reimbursed for expenses occasioned by their activities as deputies via funds from the relevant state or local budget.

ARTICLE 105. Deputies have the right of inquiry of the appropriate state organs and officials, which are obligated to respond to the inquiry at a Congress of People's Deputies or a session of the supreme soviet or local soviet of people's deputies.

Deputies have the right to approach any state or public body, enterprise, institution, or organization on matters arising from their work as Deputies and to take part in considering the questions raised by them. The heads of the state or public bodies, enterprises, institutions, or organizations concerned are obliged to receive Deputies without delay and to consider their proposals within the time limit established by law.

ARTICLE 106. Deputies shall be ensured conditions for the unhampered and effective exercise of their rights and duties.

The immunity of Deputies, and other guarantees of their activity as Deputies, are defined in the Law on the Status of Deputies and other legislative acts of the USSR and of Union and Autonomous Republics.

ARTICLE 107. Deputies are obligated to report on their own work and the work of a Congress of People's Deputies or a supreme soviet or local soviet of people's deputies to the voters, the collectives and social organizations which nominated them to be candidate deputies, or to the social organization which elected them.

Deputies who fail to justify the trust of voters or the social organization may be recalled at any time in the legally established manner by a decision of the majority of voters or the social organization which elected them.

V. HIGHER BODIES OF STATE AUTHORITY AND ADMINISTRATION OF THE USSR

Chapter 15

The USSR Congress of People's Deputies and the USSR Supreme Soviet.

ARTICLE 108. The supreme organ of USSR state power is the USSR Congress of People's Deputies.

The USSR Congress of People's Deputies is empowered to adopt for its examination and decide any question within the jurisdiction of the USSR.

The following are within the exclusive jurisdiction of the USSR Congress of People's Deputies:

1. the adoption and amendment of the USSR Constitution;
2. the adoption of decisions on questions of the national-state structure within the jurisdiction of the USSR;
3. the definition of the USSR state border; the ratification of changes in the borders between union republics;
4. the definition of the basic guidelines of USSR domestic and foreign policy;
5. the ratification of long-term state plans and highly important all-union programs for the economic and social development of the USSR;
6. the election of the USSR Supreme Soviet and the chairman of the USSR Supreme Soviet;
7. the ratification of the chairman of the USSR Council of Ministers;
8. the ratification of the chairman of the USSR People's Control Committee, the chairman of the USSR Supreme Court, the USSR prosecutor general, and the USSR chief state arbiter;
9. the election of the USSR Constitutional Oversight Committee on the submission at the chairman of the USSR Supreme Soviet;
10. the repeal of acts adopted by the USSR Supreme Soviet;
11. the adoption of decisions on holding nation-wide polls (referendums).

The Congress of USSR People's Deputies adopts USSR laws and resolutions, upon a vote, by a majority of the total number of USSR people's deputies.

ARTICLE 109. The USSR Congress of People's Deputies consists of 2,250 deputies who are elected as follows:

750 deputies from territorial electoral okrugs with an equal number of voters;

750 deputies from national-territorial electoral okrugs in accordance with the following norms: 32 deputies from each union republic, 11 deputies from each autonomous republic, 5 deputies from each autonomous oblast, and 1 deputy from each autonomous okrug;

750 deputies from all-union social organizations in accordance with the norms laid down by the USSR Law on Elections of People's Deputies.

ARTICLE 110. The USSR Congress of People's Deputies is convened for its first session no later than 2 months following the elections.

On the representation of the credentials commission electable by it, the USSR Congress of People's Deputies adopts a decision to recognize the powers of the deputies, and—in the event of a violation of election legislation—to recognize the invalidity of individual deputies' election.

The USSR Congress of People's Deputies is convened by the USSR Supreme Soviet.

Regular sittings of the Congress of USSR People's Deputies are held at least once a year. Extraordinary sittings are convened on the initiative of the USSR Supreme Soviet on the proposal of one of its chambers, the president of the USSR, or at least one-fifth of the USSR people's deputies, or on the initiative of a union republic in the persons of its highest organ of state power.

The first sitting of the Congress of USSR People's Deputies following elections is conducted by the chairman of the Central Electoral Commission for Elections of USSR People's Deputies, and thereafter by the chairman of the USSR Supreme Soviet.

ARTICLE 111. The USSR Supreme Soviet is the permanently operating legislative and monitoring organ of state power of the USSR.

The USSR Supreme Soviet is elected by secret vote from among the USSR people's deputies by the USSR Congress of People's Deputies and is accountable to the latter.

The USSR Supreme Soviet consists of two chambers: the Soviet of the Union and the Soviet of Nationalities, which are numerically equal. The chambers of the USSR Supreme Soviet possess equal rights.

The chambers are elected at the USSR Congress of People's Deputies by a general vote by the deputies. The Soviet of the Union is elected from among the USSR people's deputies from the territorial electoral okrugs and the USSR people's deputies from social organizations taking into account the number of voters in the union republic or region. The Soviet of Nationalities is elected from among the USSR people's deputies from the national-territorial electoral okrugs and the USSR people's deputies from social organizations in accordance with the following norms: 11 deputies from each union republic, 4 deputies from each autonomous republic, 2 deputies from each autonomous oblast, and 1 deputy from each autonomous okrug.

The Congress of USSR People's Deputies annually renews up to one-fifth of the composition of the Soviet of the Union and Soviet of Nationalities.

Each chamber of the USSR Supreme Soviet elects a chamber chairman and two deputy chairmen. The chairmen of the Soviet of the Union and Soviet of Nationalities chair the sittings of their corresponding chambers and are in charge of their internal proceedings.

Joint sittings of the chambers are chaired by the chairman of the USSR Supreme Soviet or the chairmen of the Soviet of the Union and the Soviet of Nationalities in turn.

ARTICLE 112. The USSR Supreme Soviet is convened annually by the chairman of the USSR Supreme Soviet for regular—spring and fall—sessions lasting, as a rule, three to four months each.

Extraordinary sessions are convened by the chairman of the USSR Supreme Soviet on his own initiative or at the proposal of the president of the USSR, a union republic in the person of its highest organ of state power, or at least one-third of one of the chambers of the USSR Supreme Soviet.

USSR Supreme Soviet sessions take the form of separate and joint sittings of the chambers and of sittings of the chambers' permanent commissions and the USSR Supreme Soviet committees held between sessions. A session is opened and closed at separate or joint sittings of the chambers.

Upon the expiry of the term of powers of the USSR Congress of People's Deputies, the USSR Supreme Soviet retains its powers right until the formation of a new composition of the USSR Supreme Soviet by the newly elected USSR Congress of People's Deputies.

ARTICLE 113. The USSR Supreme Soviet:

1. schedules elections of USSR people's deputies and ratifies the composition of the Central Electoral Commission on Elections of USSR People's Deputies;

2. appoints the chairman of the USSR Council of Ministers on the submission of the president of the USSR;

3. ratifies the composition of the USSR Council of Ministers and alterations to it on the submission of the chairman of the USSR Council of Ministers; forms and disbands USSR ministries and USSR state committees on the proposal of the USSR Council of Ministers;

4. elects the USSR Committee for People's Control and the USSR Supreme Court, appoints the USSR general prosecutor and the USSR chief state arbiter; ratifies the USSR Prosecutor's Office Collegium and the USSR State Board of Arbitration Collegium;

5. regularly hears reports by organs constituted or elected by it and by officials appointed or elected by it;

6. ensures the uniformity of legislative regulations throughout the territory of the USSR and lays the foundations for legislation by the USSR and the union republics;

7. carries out, within the limits of the competence of the USSR, legislative regulation of the procedure for the exercise of citizens' constitutional rights, freedoms, and duties, ownership relations, and organization of management of the national economy and sociocultural building, and budget and financial system, labor remuneration and pricing, taxation, environmental conservation and the utilization of natural resources, and other relations;

8. interprets USSR laws;

9. lays down general principles of the organization and activity of republic and local organs of state power and administration; determines the foundations of the legal status of social organizations;

10. submits for ratification by the USSR Congress of People's Deputies draft long-term state plans and the most important all-union programs for the USSR's economic and social development; ratifies the state plans for the USSR's economic and social development and the USSR state budget; monitors progress in the implementation of the plan and budget; ratifies reports on their performance; introduces amendments to the plan and budget whenever necessary;

11. ratifies and denounces the USSR's international treaties;

12. oversees the granting of state loans and economic and other assistance to foreign states, and also the conclusion of agreements on state loans and credits obtained from foreign sources;

13. determines the main measures in the sphere of defense and the safeguarding of state security; imposes martial law or a state of emergency countrywide; declares

war in the event of the need to fulfill international treaty commitments on mutual defense against aggression;

14. adopts decisions on the utilization of USSR Armed Forces contingents in the event of the need to fulfill international treaty commitments on maintaining peace and security;

15. establishes military ranks, diplomatic ranks, and other special ranks;

16. institutes USSR orders and medals; confers honorary titles of the USSR;

17. promulgates all-union acts of amnesty;

18. has the right to revoke resolutions and orders of the USSR Council of Ministers;

19. repeals resolutions and orders by union republic councils of ministers if they are inconsistent with the USSR Constitution and USSR laws;

20. decides other issues falling within the jurisdiction of the USSR, apart from issues which fall within the exclusive jurisdiction of the USSR Congress of People's deputies.

The USSR Supreme Soviet adopts USSR laws and resolutions.

Laws and resolutions adopted by the USSR Supreme Soviet cannot be contrary to laws and other acts adopted by the USSR Congress of People's deputies.

ARTICLE 114. The right of legislative initiative at the Congress of USSR People's Deputies and the USSR Supreme Soviet belongs to USSR people's deputies, the Soviet of the Union, the Soviet of Nationalities, the chairman of the USSR Supreme Soviet, standing commissions of the chambers and committees of the USSR Supreme Soviet, the president of the USSR, the USSR Council of Ministers, the USSR Constitutional Oversight Committee, union and autonomous republics in the person of their highest organs of state power, autonomous oblasts, autonomous okrugs, the USSR People's Control Committee, the USSR Supreme Court, the USSR general prosecutor, and the USSR chief state arbiter.

The right of legislative initiative also belongs to social organizations in the person of their unionwide organs, and to the USSR Academy of Sciences.

ARTICLE 115. Draft laws submitted for examination by the USSR Supreme Soviet are discussed by its chambers at separate or joint sittings.

A USSR law is deemed adopted if a majority of chamber members votes for it in each chamber of the USSR Supreme Soviet.

Draft laws and other important issues of state life can be submitted for nationwide discussion following a decision by the USSR Supreme Soviet adopted either on its own initiative or on a proposal by a union republic in the shape of its supreme organ of state power.

ARTICLE 116. Each chamber of the USSR Supreme Soviet is empowered to examine any questions falling within the jurisdiction of the USSR Supreme Soviet.

The Soviet of the Union primarily examines questions of socioeconomic development and state building of general importance for the entire country;

of the rights, freedoms, and duties of USSR citizens; of USSR foreign policy; of the USSR's defense and state security.

The Soviet of Nationalities primarily examines questions of ensuring national equality and the interests of nations, nationalities, and ethnic groups in combination with the general interests and needs of the Soviet multinational state; of improvements to USSR legislation regulating interethnic relations.

Each chamber adopts resolutions on questions within its competence.

Any resolution adopted by one of the chambers, if necessary, is referred to the other chamber and, when approved by it, acquires the force of a USSR Supreme Soviet resolution.

ARTICLE 117. In the event of disagreement between the Soviet of the Union and the Soviet of Nationalities, the question is handed over for resolution to a conciliation commission formed by the chambers on a parity basis, after which it is again examined by the Soviet of the Union and the Soviet of Nationalities at a joint sitting.

ARTICLE 118. A USSR Supreme Soviet Presidium headed by the chairman of the USSR Supreme Soviet is set up to organize the work of the USSR Supreme Soviet. The USSR Supreme Soviet Presidium includes: the chairmen of the Soviet of the Union and the Soviet of Nationalities, their deputies, the chairmen of the standing commissions of the chambers and committees of the USSR Supreme Soviet, and other USSR people's deputies—one from each union republic, and also two representatives from autonomous republics and one from autonomous oblasts and autonomous okrugs.

The USSR Supreme Soviet Presidium prepares Congress sittings and USSR Supreme Soviet sessions, coordinates the activity of the standing commissions of the chambers and committees of the USSR Supreme Soviet, and organizes nationwide discussions of USSR draft laws and other most important questions of state life.

The USSR Supreme Soviet Presidium ensures publication, in the languages of the union republics, of the texts of USSR laws and other acts adopted by the Congress of USSR People's Deputies, the USSR Supreme Soviet, its chambers, and the president of the USSR.

ARTICLE 119. The chairman of the USSR Supreme Soviet is elected by the Congress of USSR People's Deputies from among the USSR people's deputies by secret ballot for a term of five years and for not more than two successive terms. He may be recalled by the Congress of USSR People's Deputies at any time by secret ballot.

The chairman of the USSR Supreme Soviet is accountable to the Congress of USSR People's Deputies and the USSR Supreme Soviet.

The chairman of the USSR Supreme Soviet issues resolutions on the convocation of USSR Supreme Soviet sessions and instructions on other matters.

ARTICLE 120. The Soviet of the Union and Soviet of Nationalities elect from among the members of the USSR Supreme Soviet and other people's deputies of the USSR standing commissions of the chambers to carry out the drafting of laws and preliminary examination and preparation of matters falling within the jurisdiction of the USSR Supreme Soviet, and also to promote the implementation of USSR laws and other decisions adopted by the USSR Congress of People's Deputies and the USSR Supreme Soviet and to monitor the activity of state organs and organizations.

For the same purposes, the chambers of the USSR Supreme Soviet may set up USSR Supreme Soviet committees on a basis of parity.

The USSR Supreme Soviet and each of its chambers, when they deem it necessary, set up investigating auditing, or other commissions on any matter.

Up to one-fifth of the composition of the standing commissions of the chambers and the committees of the USSR Supreme Soviet is annually renewed.

ARTICLE 121. Laws and other decisions of the USSR Congress of People's Deputies and the USSR Supreme Soviet and resolutions of its chambers are adopted, as a rule, after preliminary discussion of the drafts by the appropriate standing commissions of the chambers or committees of the USSR Supreme Soviet.

The appointment and election of officials belonging to the USSR Council of Ministers, the USSR People's Control Committee, and the USSR Supreme Court, and also of the collegiums of the USSR Prosecutor's Office and the USSR State Board of Arbitration may take place given the existence of fndings of the relevant standing commissions of the chambers or committees of the USSR Supreme Soviet.

All state and social organs, organizations, and officials must fulfill the requirements of the commissions of the chambers, commissions, and committees of the USSR Supreme Soviet and provide them with the necessary materials and documents.

The recommendations of commissions and committees are subject to compulsory examination by state and social organs, institutions, and organizations. The results of the examination and the measures adopted must be reported to the commissions and committees within the time laid down by them.

ARTICLE 122. A USSR people's deputy has the right to submit a question at sittings of the Congress of USSR People's Deputies and sessions of the USSR Supreme Soviet to the USSR Council of Ministers and leaders of other organs formed or elected by the Congress of USSR People's Deputies and the USSR Supreme Soviet, and to the president of the USSR at sessions of the Congress of USSR People's Deputies. An organ or official to whom a question is submitted is obliged to give an oral or written answer at the Congress sitting in question or the USSR Supreme Soviet session in question within no more than three days.

ARTICLE 123. USSR people's deputies are entitled to be relieved of the performance of their official or production duties for the period necessary to implement their activity as deputies in the Congress of USSR People's Deputies, the USSR Supreme Soviet, its chambers, commissions, and committees, and also among the population.

A USSR people's deputy cannot be subjected to criminal proceedings, be arrested, or incur judicially imposed administrative penalties without the consent of the USSR Supreme Soviet or, in the period between its sessions, without the consent of the USSR Supreme Soviet Presidium.

ARTICLE 124. The USSR Constitutional Oversight Committee is elected by the Congress of USSR People's Deputies from the ranks of specialists in the field of politics and law in the form of a chairman, deputy chairman, and 25 members of the committee, for each union republic included.

The term of the authority of persons elected to the USSR Constitutional Oversight Committee is 10 years.

Persons elected to the USSR Constitutional Oversight Committee may not simultaneously be members of bodies whose instruments are under the supervision of the committee.

Upon performance of their duties persons elected to the USSR Constitutional Oversight Committee are indepedent and subordinate only to the USSR Constitution.

The USSR Constitutional Oversight Committee:

1. at the behest of the Congress of USSR People's Deputies submits to it findings concerning the correspondence to the USSR Constitution of draft laws of the USSR and other instruments submitted for examination by the congress;
2. at the proposals of no less than one-fifth of USSR people's deputies, the president of the USSR, and the supreme organs of state power in the union republics, [the Constitutional Oversight Committee] submits findings to the Congress of USSR People's Deputies regarding the correspondence between USSR laws and other acts adopted by the Congress and the USSR Constitution.
   On the instructions of the Congress of USSR People's Deputies or at the proposal of the USSR Supreme Soviet, submits findings regarding the correspondence between decrees of the president of the USSR and the USSR Constitution and USSR laws;
3. On the instructions of the Congress of USSR People's Deputies or at the proposal of the USSR Supreme Soviet, the president of the USSR, the chairman of the USSR Supreme Soviet, or the supreme organs of state power in the union republics submit findings to the Congress of USSR People's Deputies or the USSR Supreme Soviet regarding the correspondence between union republic constitutions and the USSR Constitution and between union republic laws and USSR laws;
4. On the instructions of the Congress of USSR People's Deputies or at the proposal of no less than one-fifth of the members of the USSR Supreme Soviet, the president of the USSR or the supreme organs of state power in the union republics submit findings to the USSR Supreme Soviet or the president of the USSR regarding the correspondence between acts adopted by the USSR Supreme Soviet and its chambers and draft acts submitted for consideration by these organs and the USSR Constitution and USSR laws adopted by the Congress of USSR People's Deputies, and also the correspondence between resolutions and instruc-

tions adopted by the USSR Council of Ministers and USSR laws adopted by the USSR Supreme Soviet; on the correspondence between USSR and union republic international treaty and other obligations and the USSR Constitution and USSR laws;

5. On the instructions of the Congress of USSR People's Deputies or at the proposal of the USSR Supreme Soviet, its chambers, the president of the USSR, the chairman of the USSR Supreme Soviet, the chambers' standing commissions, USSR Supreme Soviet committees, the USSR Council of Ministers, the supreme organs of state power in the union republics, the USSR People's Control Committee, the USSR Supreme Court, the USSR prosecutor general, the USSR chief state arbiter, all-union organs of public organizations, or the USSR Academy of Sciences submit findings regarding the correspondence between normative legal acts adopted by other state organs and public organizations to which supervision by the prosecutor's office does not apply under the USSR Constitution and the USSR Constitution and USSR laws.

ARTICLE 125. The Congress of USSR People's Deputies and the USSR Supreme Soviet monitor all the state organs accountable to them.

The USSR Supreme Soviet and the president of the USSR direct the activity of the USSR People's Control Committee.

The organization and procedure of work of people's control organs are laid down by the Law on People's Control in the USSR.

ARTICLE 126. The procedure of work of the USSR Congress of People's Deputies, the USSR Supreme Soviet, and their organs is determined by the regulations of the USSR Congress of People's Deputies and the USSR Supreme Soviet and by other USSR laws promulgated on the basis of the USSR Constitution.

Chapter 15(1)   The President of the USSR

ARTICLE 127. The head of the Soviet state—the Union of Soviet Socialist Republics—is the president of the USSR.

ARTICLE 127(1). Any citizen of the USSR no younger than 35 and no older than 65 years can be elected president of the USSR. The same person can be president of the USSR for no more than two terms.

The president of the USSR is elected by USSR citizens on the basis of universal, equal, and direct suffrage by secret ballot for a 5-year term. The number of candidates for the post of president of the USSR is not limited. Elections for the president of the USSR are considered valid if at least 50 percent of voters participated in them.

The candidate who has received over half the votes of voters taking part in the election in the USSR as a whole and in the majority of union republics is deemed to be elected.

The procedure for elections of the president of the USSR is defined by USSR law.

The president of the USSR cannot be a people's deputy.

The person who is president of the USSR can receive wages for that post alone.

ARTICLE 127(2). Upon inauguration the president of the USSR swears an oath at a sitting of the Congress of USSR People's Deputies.

ARTICLE 127(3). The president of the USSR:

1. is the guarantor of observance of Soviet citizens' rights and freedoms and of the USSR Constitution and laws;
2. takes the necessary measures to protect the sovereignty of the USSR and union republics and the country's security and territorial integrity and to implement the principles of the national-state structure of the USSR;
3. represents the Union of Soviet Socialist Republics inside the country and in international relations;
4. ensures coordination among the USSR's supreme organs of state power and management;
5. submits to the Congress of USSR People's Deputies annual reports on the state of the country; briefs the USSR Supreme Soviet on the most important questions of the USSR's domestic and foreign policy;
6. submits to the USSR Supreme Soviet candidates for the posts of chairman of the USSR Council of Ministers, chairman of the USSR People's Control Committee, chairman of the USSR Supreme Court, USSR prosecutor general, and USSR chief state arbiter, and then submits these officials to the Congress of USSR People's Deputies for confirmation; makes representations to the USSR Supreme Soviet and the Congress of USSR People's Deputies regarding releasing the aforementioned officials, with the exception of the chairman of the USSR Supreme Court, from their duties;
7. places before the USSR Supreme Soviet the question of the resignation or of accepting the resignation of the USSR Council of Ministers; in coordination with the chairman of the USSR Council of Ministers releases from their post and appoints members of the USSR Government, subsequently submitting them for confirmation by the USSR Supreme Soviet;
8. signs USSR laws; is entitled within a period of no more than two weeks to refer a law along with his objections back to the USSR Supreme Soviet for repeat discussion and voting. If the USSR Supreme Soviet confirms its earlier decision by a two-thirds majority in each chamber, the president of the USSR signs the law;
9. has the right to suspend the operation of USSR Council of Ministers resolutions and instructions;
10. coordinates the activity of state organs to ensure the defense of the country; is the supreme commander in chief of the USSR Armed Forces, appoints and replaces the supreme command of the USSR Armed Forces, and confers the highest military ranks; appoints the judges of military tribunals;
11. holds talks and signs the USSR's international treaties; accepts the credentials and letters of recall of diplomatic representatives of foreign states accredited to it; appoints and recalls the USSR's diplomatic representatives in foreign states and in international organizations; confers the highest diplomatic ranks and other special titles;
12. awards USSR orders and medals and confers USSR honorary titles;

13. decides questions of admittance to USSR citizenship, withdrawal from it, and the deprivation of Soviet citizenship and the granting of asylum; grants pardons;

14. declares general or partial mobilization; declares a state of war in the event of a military attack on the USSR and immediately refers this question for examination to the USSR Supreme Soviet; declares martial law in particular localities in the interests of the defense of the USSR and the security of its citizens. The procedure for introducing martial law and the regime thereof are determined by the law;

15. in the interests of safeguarding the security of citizens of the USSR, gives warning of the declaration of a state of emergency in particular localities and, if necessary, introduces it at the request or with the consent of the supreme soviet presidium or supreme organ of state power of the corresponding union republic. In the absence of such consent, introduces the state of emergency and submits the adopted decision for ratification by the USSR Supreme Soviet without delay. The USSR Supreme Soviet resolution on this question must be adopted by a majority of at least two-thirds of the total number of its members.

    In the cases indicated in the first part of this point, can introduce temporary presidential rule while observing the sovereignty and territorial integrity of the union republic.

    The regime for a state of emergency, and also for presidential rule is laid down by law;

16. in the event of disagreements between the USSR Supreme Soviet Soviet of the Union and Soviet of Nationalities that cannot be eliminated via the procedure envisaged by Article 117 of the USSR Constitution, the president of the USSR examines the contentious issue with a view to formulating an acceptable solution. If it is not possible to reach consensus and there is a real threat of disruption to the normal activity of the USSR's supreme organs of state power and management, the president can submit to the Congress of USSR People's Deputies a proposal regarding the election of a new USSR Supreme Soviet.

ARTICLE 127(4). The president of the USSR heads the Council of the Federation, which comprises the supreme state officials of the union republics. The supreme state officials of autonomous republics, autonomous oblasts, and autonomous okrugs are entitled to participate in sessions of the Council of the Federation.

The Council of the Federation: examines questions of compliance with the union treaty; elaborates measures to implement the Soviet state's nationalities policy; submits to the USSR Supreme Soviet Soviet of Nationalities recommendations on resolving disputes and settling conflicts in interethnic relations; and coordinates the union republics' activity and ensures their participation in resolving questions of unionwide significance within the competence of the president of the USSR.

Questions affecting the interests of peoples who do not have their own national state formation are examined in the Council of the Federation with the participation of representatives of these peoples.

The chairman of the USSR Supreme Soviet and the chairmen of the chambers are entitled to take part in sittings of the Council of the Federation.

ARTICLE 127(5). A USSR Presidential Council operates under the president of the USSR, its task being to elaborate measures to implement the main directions of the USSR's domestic and foreign policy and ensure the country's security.

Members of the Presidential Council are appointed by the president of the USSR. The chairman of the USSR Council of Ministers is a member of the USSR Presidential Council ex officio.

The chairman of the USSR Supreme Soviet has the right to participate in sittings of the USSR Presidential Council.

ARTICLE 127 (6). The president of the USSR holds joint sittings of the Council of the Federation and the USSR Presidential Council.

ARTICLE 127 (7). The president of the USSR, on the basis of and in execution of the USSR Constitution and USSR laws, issues decrees that are binding throughout the territory of the country.

ARTICLE 127 (8). The president of the USSR has the right of inviolability and may only be replaced by the Congress of USSR People's Deputies in the event of his violating the USSR Constitution or USSR laws. This decision is made by the Congress of USSR People's Deputies on the initiative of the Congress itself or of the USSR Supreme Soviet by a majority of at least two-thirds of the total number of deputies, taking into account the findings of the USSR Constitutional Oversight Committee.

ARTICLE 127 (9). The president of the USSR may entrust the execution of his duties under Points 11 and 12 of Article 127 (3) to the chairman of the USSR Supreme Soviet and the chairman of the USSR Council of Ministers, and the duties under Point 13 of Article 127 (3) to the chairman of the USSR Supreme Soviet.

ARTICLE 127 (10). If the president of the USSR is for any reason unable to continue to execute his duties, until the election of a new president his powers are transferred to the chairman of the USSR Supreme Soviet, or if that is not possible, to the chairman of the USSR Council of Ministers. In this case the election of a new president of the USSR must take place within three months.

Chapter 16   The Council of Ministers of the USSR

ARTICLE 128. The Council of Ministers of the USSR, that is, the Government of the USSR, is the highest executives and administrative body of state authority of the USSR.

ARTICLE 129. The Council of Ministers of the USSR shall be formed by the Supreme Soviet of the USSR at a joint sitting of the Soviet of the Union and the Soviet of Nationalities and shall consist of the Chairman of the Council of Ministers of the USSR, First Vice-Chairmen and Vice-Chairmen, Ministers of the USSR, and Chairmen of the State Committees of the USSR.

The Chairmen of the Council of Ministers of Union Republics shall be *ex officio* members of the Council of Ministers of the USSR.

The Supreme Soviet of the USSR, on the recommendation of the Chairman of the Council of Ministers of the USSR, may include in the Government of the USSR the heads of other bodies and organizations of the USSR.

The Council of Ministers of the USSR shall tender its resignation to a newly elected Supreme Soviet of the USSR at its first session.

ARTICLE 130. The USSR Council of Ministers is responsible and answerable to the USSR Congress of People's Deputies and the USSR Supreme Soviet.

The newly formed USSR Council of Ministers submits for examination by the USSR Supreme Soviet a program of forthcoming activity for its term of office.

The USSR Council of Ministers reports on its work no less than once a year to the USSR Supreme Soviet and regularly briefs the president of the USSR on its activity.

The USSR Supreme Soviet can on its own initiative or at the proposal of the president of the USSR express no-confidence in the USSR Government, which entails the latter's resignation. A resolution on this question is adopted by a majority of no less than two-thirds of the total number of members of the USSR Supreme Soviet.

ARTICLE 131. The USSR Council of Ministers is empowered to resolve all questions of state management under the jurisdiction of the USSR insofar as, under the USSR Constitution, they do not come within the competence of the Congress of USSR People's Deputies, the USSR Supreme Soviet, and the president of the USSR;

Within its powers the Council of Ministers of the USSR shall:

1. ensure direction of economic, social, and cultural developments; draft and implement measures to promote the well-being and cultural development of the people, to develop science and engineering, to ensure rational exploitation and conservation of natural resources, to consolidate the monetary and credit system, to pursue a uniform prices, wages, and social security policy, and to organize state insurance and a uniform system of accounting and statistics; and organize the management of industrial, constructional, and agricultural enterprises and amalgamations, transport and communications undertakings, banks, and other organizations and institutions of All-Union subordination;

2. draft current and long-term state plans for the economic and social development of the USSR and the Budget of the USSR and submit them to the Supreme Soviet of the USSR; take measures to execute the state plans and Budget; and to report to the Supreme Soviet of the USSR on the implementation of the plans and Budget;

3. takes steps to ensure citizens' rights and freedoms, defend the interests of the country, and safeguard property and public order;

4. takes measures to ensure the country's defense and state security;

5. takes general measures in the sphere of relations with foreign states, foreign trade, and Soviet economic, scientific and technical, and cultural cooperation with foreign countries; takes measures to ensure the fulfillment of the USSR's

international treaties; ratifies and denounces intergovernmental and international treaties;

6. forms committees, main administrations, and other departments under the USSR Council of Ministers if necessary.

ARTICLE 132. A Presidium of the Council of Ministers of the USSR, consisting of the Chairman, the First Vice-Chairmen, and Vice-Charimen of the Council of Ministers of the USSR, shall function as a standing body of the Council of Ministers of the USSR to deal with questions relating to guidance of the economy and with other matters of state administration. Upon a decision of the Council of Ministers of the USSR, other members of the Government of the USSR may also be included in the Presidium of the Council of Ministers of the USSR.

ARTICLE 133. On the basis and in execution of USSR laws, other decisions of the Congress of USSR People's Deputies and the USSR Supreme Soviet, and decrees by the president of the USSR, the USSR Council of Ministers issues resolutions and instructions and verifies their implementation. Resolutions and instructions issued by the USSR Council of Ministers have binding force throughout the territory of the USSR.

ARTICLE 134. The Council of Ministers of the USSR has the right, in matters within the jurisdiction of the Union of Soviet Socialist Republics, to suspend execution of decisions and resolutions of the Councils of Ministers of the USSR and of other bodies subordinate to it.

ARTICLE 135. The Council of Ministers of the USSR shall coordinate and direct the work of All-Union and Union-Republican ministries, state committees of the USSR, and other bodies subordinate to it.

All-Union ministries and state committees of the USSR shall direct the work of the branches of administration entrusted to them, or exercise inter-branch administration, throughout the territory of the USSR directly or through bodies set up by them.

Union-Republican ministries and state committees of the USSR direct the work of the branches of administration entrusted to them, or exercise inter-branch administration, as a rule, through the corresponding ministries and state committees and other bodies of Union Republics, and directly administer individual enterprises and amalgamations of Union subordination.

USSR ministries and state committees bear responsibility for the condition and development of the spheres of management entrusted to them; within the limits of their competence, issue acts on the basis and in execution of USSR laws, other decisions of the Congress of USSR People's Deputies and the USSR Supreme Soviet, decrees of the president of the USSR, and USSR Council of Ministers resolutions and instructions; and organize and verify their implementation.

ARTICLE 136. The competence of the Council of Ministers of the USSR and its Presidium, the procedure for their work, relationships between the Council of Ministers and other state bodies, and the list of All-Union and Union-Republican ministries and state committees of the USSR are defined, on the basis of the Constitution, in the Law on the Council of Ministers of the USSR.

VI. BASIC PRINCIPLES OF THE STRUCTURE OF THE BODIES OF STATE AUTHORITY AND ADMINISTRATION IN UNION REPUBLICS

Chapter 17   Higher Bodies of State Authority and Administration of a Union Republic

ARTICLE 137. The highest bodies of state authority in union republics shall be the union republic Supreme Soviets, and in union republics where it is envisaged to create congresses—the Congresses of People's Deputies;

ARTICLE 138. The powers, composition, and standing orders of the highest organs of state authority in union republics shall be determined by the constitutions and laws of the union republics;

ARTICLE 139. The Supreme Soviet of a Union Republic shall form a Council of Ministers of the Union Republic, that is, the Government of that Republic, which shall be the highest executive and administrative body of state authority in the Republic.

ARTICLE 140. The Council of Ministers of a Union Republic issues decisions and ordinances on the basis of, and in pursuance of, the legislative acts of the USSR and of the Union Republic, and of decisions and resolutions of the Council of Ministers of the USSR, and shall organize and verify their execution.

ARTICLE 141. The Council of Ministers of a Union Republic has the right to suspend the execution of decisions and resolutions of the Councils of Ministers of Autonomous Republics, to rescind the decisions and orders of the Executive Committees of Soviets of People's Deputies of Territories, Regions, and cities (that is, cities under Republic jurisdiction), and of Autonomous Regions, and in Union Republics not divided into regions, of the Executive Committees of district and corresponding city Soviets of People's Deputies.

ARTICLE 142. The Council of Ministers of a Union Republic shall coordinate and direct the work of the Union-Republican and Republican ministries and of state committees of the Union Republic and other bodies under its jurisdiction.

The Union-Republican ministries and state committees of a Union Republic shall direct the branches of administration entrusted to them, or exercise interbranch control, and shall be subordinate to both the Council of Ministers of the Union Republic and the corresponding Union-Republican ministry or state committee of the USSR.

Republican ministries and state committees shall direct the branches of administration entrusted to them, or exercise interbranch control, and shall be subordinate to the Council of Ministers of the Union Republic.

Chapter 18   Higher Bodies of State Authority and Administration of an Autonomous Republic

ARTICLE 143. The highest bodies of state authority in autonomous republics shall be the autonomous republic Supreme Soviets, and in autonomous republics where it is envisaged to create congresses—the Congresses of People's Deputies.

ARTICLE 144. The Supreme Soviet of an autonomous republic shall form a Council of Ministers of the autonomous republic—the autonomous republic's government—as the highest executive and administrative organ of state authority in the autonomous republic.''

Chapter 19   Local Bodies of State Authority and Administration

ARTICLE 145. The bodies of state authority in autonomous oblasts, autonomous okrugs, krays, oblasts, rayons, cities, urban rayons, settlements, rural population centers, and other administrative-territorial units, constituted in conformity with the laws of union and autonomous republics, shall be the corresponding Soviets of People's Deputies.

ARTICLE 146. Local Soviets of People's Deputies shall deal with all matters of local significance in accordance with the interests of the whole state and of the citizens residing in the area under their jurisdiction, implement decisions of higher bodies of state authority, guide the work of lower Soviets of People's Deputies, take part in the discussion of matters of Republican and All-Union significance, and submit their proposals concerning them.

Local Soviets of People's Deputies shall direct state, economic, social and cultural development within their territory; endorse plans for economic and social development and the local budget; exercise general guidance over state bodies, enterprises, institutions, and organizations subordinate to them; ensure observance of the laws, maintenance of law and order, and protection of citizens' rights; and help strengthen the country's defense capacity.

ARTICLE 147. Within their powers, local Soviets of People's Deputies shall ensure the comprehensive, all-round economic and social development of their areas; exercise control over the observance of legislation by enterprises, institutions, and organizations subordinate to higher authorities and located in their area; and coordinate and supervise their activity as regards land use, nature conservation, building, employment of manpower, production of consumer goods, and social, cultural, communal, and other services and amenities for the public.

ARTICLE 148. Local Soviets of People's Deputies shall decide matters within the powers accorded them by the legislation of the USSR and of the appropriate Union Republic and Autonomous Republic. Their decisions shall be binding on all enterprises, institutions, and organizations located in their areas and on officials and citizens.

ARTICLE 149. The work of kray, oblast, autonomous oblast, autonomous okrug, rayon, city, and city rayon soviets of people's deputies is organized by their presidiums, headed by the chairmen of the soviets, and in city (cities under rayon subordination) settlement, and village soviets by the chairmen of those soviets.

ARTICLE 150. The executive and administrative organs of local soviets of people's deputies are the executive committees elected by them.

Executive committees report at least once a year to the soviets that elected them, and also to meetings of labor collectives and at citizens' places of residence.

Executive committees of local soviets are directly accountable both to the soviet that elected them and to the higher executive and administrative organ.

VII. JUSTICE, ARBITRATION, AND PROCURATOR'S SUPERVISION

Chapter 20   Courts and Arbitration

ARTICLE 151. In the USSR justice is administered only by the courts.

In the USSR there are the following courts: the Supreme Court of the USSR; the Supreme Courts of Union Republics; the Supreme Courts of Autonomous Republics; Territorial, Regional, and city courts; courts of Autonomous Regions; courts of Autonomous Areas; district (city) people's courts; and military tribunals in the Armed Forces.

ARTICLE 152. All courts in the USSR are formed on the basis of the principle of the election of judges and people's assessors, with the exception of the judges of military tribunals.

People's judges of rayon (city) people's courts and the judges of kray, oblast, and city courts are elected by the relevant superior soviet's of people's deputies.

Judges of the USSR Supreme Court, the supreme courts of the union and autonomous republics, and the courts of autonomous oblasts and autonomous okrugs are elected by, respective, the USSR Supreme Soviet, the supreme soviets of the union and autonomous republics, and the soviets of people's deputies of autonomous oblasts and autonomous okrugs.

The lay assessors of rayon (city) people's courts are elected at citizens' meetings at their place of residence or work by open ballot, and the people's assessors of superior courts are elected by the relevant soviets of people's deputies.

The judges of military tribunals are appointed by the president of the USSR, while people's assessors are elected in an open ballot by servicemen's meetings.

Judges of all courts are elected for a term of 10 years. Lay assessors of all courts are elected for a term of 5 years.

Judges and lay assessors are accountable to the organs or voters which have elected them, report back to them, and can be recalled in accordance with the legally established procedure.

ARTICLE 153. The USSR Supreme Court is the supreme judicial organ in the USSR and oversees the judicial activity of USSR courts and of union republic courts within the parameters laid down by the law.

The USSR Supreme Court consists of a chairman, his deputies, members, and lay assessors. Chairmen of union republic supreme courts are ex officio members of the USSR Supreme Court.

The organization and procedure of work of the USSR Supreme Court are determined by the Law on the USSR Supreme Court.

ARTICLE 154. The hearings of civil and criminal cases in all courts is collegial; in courts of first instance, cases are heard with the participation of people's assessors. In the administration of justice, people's assessors have all the rights of a judge.

ARTICLE 155. Judges and people's assessors are independent and subject only to the law.

Conditions are provided for judges and lay assessors to effectively exercise their rights and duties without hindrance. Any interference in the activity of judges and lay assessors in the administration of justice is impermissible and entails legal liability.

The immunity of judges and lay assessors and other [inoy] guarantees of their independence are laid down by the Law on the Status of Judges in the USSR and other USSR and union republic legislative acts.

ARTICLE 156. Justice is administered in the USSR on the principle of the equality of citizens before the law and the court.

ARTICLE 157. Proceedings in all courts shall be open to the public. Hearings *in camera* are only allowed in cases provided for by law, with observance of all the rules of judicial procedure.

ARTICLE 158. A defendant in a criminal action is guaranteed the right to defense.

ARTICLE 159. Judicial proceedings shall be conducted in the language of the Union Republic, Autonomous Republic, Autonomous Region, or Autonomous Area, or in the language spoken by the majority of the people in the locality. Persons participating in court proceedings who do not know the language in which they are being conducted shall be ensured the right to become fully acquainted with the materials in the case, the services of an interpreter during the proceedings, and the right to address the court in their own language.

ARTICLE 160. No one may be adjuged guilty of a crime and subjected to punishment as a criminal except by the sentence of a court and in conformity with the law.

ARTICLE 161. Colleges of advocates are available to give legal assistance to citizens and organizations. In cases provided for by legislation, citizens shall be given legal assistance free of charge.

The organization and procedure of the bar are determined by legislation of the USSR and Union Republics.

ARTICLE 162. Representatives of public organizations and of work collectives may take part in civil and criminal proceedings.

ARTICLE 163. Economic disputes between enterprises, institutions, and organizations are settled by state arbitration bodies within the limits of their jurisdiction.

The organization and manner of functioning of state arbitration bodies are defined in the Law on State Arbitration in the USSR.

Chapter 21   The Procurator's Office

ARTICLE 164. Supreme power of supervision over the strict and uniform observance of laws by all ministries state committees and departments, enterprises, institutions and organizations, executive-administrative bodies of local Soviets of People's Deputies, collective farms, cooperatives and other public organizations, officials and citizens is vested in the Procurator-General of the USSR and procurators subordinate to him.

ARTICLE 165. The USSR prosecutor general is responsible to the USSR Congress of People's Deputies and the USSR Supreme Soviet and is accountable to them.

ARTICLE 166. The procurators of Union Republics, Autonomous Republics, Territories, Regions and Autonomous Regions are appointed by the Procurator-General of the USSR. The procurators of Autonomous Areas and district and city procurators are appointed by the Procurators of Union Republics, subject to confirmation by the Procurator-General of the USSR.

ARTICLE 167. The term of office of the Procurator-General of the USSR and all lower-ranking procurators shall be five years.

ARTICLE 168. The agencies of the Procurator's Office exercise their powers independently of any local bodies whatsoever and are subordinate solely to the Procurator-General of the USSR.

The organization and procedure of the agencies of the Procurator's Office are defined in the Law on the Procurator's Office of the USSR.

VIII.   THE EMBLEM, FLAG, ANTHEM, AND CAPITAL OF THE USSR

ARTICLE 169. The State Emblem of the Union of Soviet Socialist Republics is a hammer and sickle on a globe depicted in the rays of the sun and framed by ears of wheat, with the inscription "Workers of All Countries, Unite!" in the languages of the Union Republics. At the top of the Emblem is a five-pointed star.

ARTICLE 170. The State Flag of the Union of Soviet Socialist Republics is a rectangle of red cloth with a hammer and sickle depicted in gold in the upper corner next to the staff and with a five-pointed red star edged in gold above them. The ratio of the width of the flag to its length is 1 to 2.

ARTICLE 171. The USSR national anthem is approved by the USSR Supreme Soviet.

ARTICLE 172. The Capital of the Union of Soviet Socialist Republics is the city of Moscow.

IX.   THE LEGAL FORCE OF THE CONSTITUTION OF THE USSR AND PROCEDURE FOR AMENDING THE CONSTITUTION

ARTICLE 173. The Constitution of the USSR shall have supreme legal force. All laws and other acts of state bodies shall be promulgated on the basis of and in conformity with it.

ARTICLE 174. The amendment of the USSR Constitution takes place by a decision of the USSR Congress of People's Deputies adopted by a majority of at least two-thirds of the total number of people's deputies of the USSR.

APPENDIX B
RULES OF THE COMMUNIST PARTY OF THE SOVIET UNION[1]

The Communist Party of the Soviet Union is a self-managing sociopolitical organization, a voluntary association of like-minded communists. Built on the creative development of the ideas of Marx, Engels, and Lenin and operating on the basis of a communist perspective, it sets as its goal the creation of a humane, democratic socialism in the country and the establishment of internationalism and panhuman values. The CPSU rests on the socialist choice of the working class and all working people, expresses and defends the people's interests, and seeks to consolidate the multinational Soviet society on its political platform.

I. MEMBERSHIP OF THE CPSU

1. Any citizen of the USSR who has reached the age of 18, who acknowledges the party Program and Statutes, who works in one of its organizations, and who pays membership dues may be a member of the CPSU.

[1]As described in Chapter 7, the position of the Communist Party in the Soviet system has experienced significant recent change. As a result, Party leaders have considered revamping the rules of internal operation of the Party. The old Rules, most recently revised in 1986, are to be replaced by a new document, to be adopted at the 28th Party Congress in July 1990. To facilitate public discussion, a draft version of the new Rules was published in the Soviet press on March 28, 1990. That version is published here.

2. All party members are equal. They are entitled: to put forward and freely discuss questions of the party's domestic and foreign policy and intra-party life, to participate in the formulation of decisions, to elect and be elected to party organs at all levels and to monitor their work, to criticize any party organ and any communist regardless of the position he holds, to submit applications and proposals to any party body and receive a reply on the substance of the appeal, and to participate in the work of a party organ when the question of their activity or behavior is under discussion.

Membership of the CPSU does not give a communist privileges and does not restrict his civil rights and freedoms. He is entitled to participate in the work of social organizations and movements whose activity is based on the USSR Constitution and is not in conflict with the socialist idea. A CPSU member may not belong to other political parties.

3. A CPSU member has a duty to struggle to safeguard the party's vanguard positions in society, consistently to pursue its political line in labor collectives and among the population and in state, cooperative, and social organizations, to fulfill party decisions, to uphold and propagandize communist ideas, and to set an example of strict compliance with the rule of law and the norms of public morality.

4. Admission to membership of the CPSU takes place on an individual basis, democratically, and with glasnost. The decision on admission to CPSU membership is made by the primary party organization at an open meeting. The meeting's decision is final. A single party card is valid in the CPSU, and the procedure for registering party members is laid down by the CPSU Central Committee.

A CPSU member of at least 40 years' standing in the party, in view of his long, active work in the party, is, by a decision of the primary party organization ratified by the party raykom [rayon committee] and gorkom [city committee], awarded the honorary title "CPSU Veteran."

5. Membership of the CPSU is terminated by a decision of the primary party organization or higher party organ as a consequence of the expulsion of a party member from the CPSU for conduct that brings the party into disrepute or is incompatible with the requirements of its Statutes. A party member found guilty by a court of committing a crime is subject to expulsion from the CPSU when the verdict legally enters into force.

Party membership may be terminated on the basis of a party member's application for voluntary withdrawal from the CPSU; the said application is examined by the primary party organization.

A decision on admission to membership of the CPSU and on expulsion from the party is considered valid if at least two-thirds of those present at the meeting, but more than half of those registered with the organization in question, have voted for it.

The question of the expulsion from the party of a CPSU member who is on an elected party organ is examined at the primary party organization where he is registered or at the organization that recommended him for the said organ. Taking into account the opinion of the primary organization and with the participation of its representative, the question is decided at a plenum of the elected organ by a majority of two-thirds of the votes of those present at the session, making up more than half of the organ's members.

A person expelled from the party retains the right within one year, or at any time in the event of a change in circumstances, to appeal to party control and auditing organs. An appeal is examined within not more than two months of its receipt.

For violations of party discipline and ethics, measures of party education and influence may be applied to party members in the form of comradely criticism or a declaration of censure or a reprimand.

II. INTRAPARTY DEMOCRACY

6. The CPSU lives and operates on the basis of ideological community and party comradeship, on the principles of self-management, combining the power of the party masses and the all-around democratism of intraparty relations with conscious discipline and organization on the part of communists.

Freedom of expression of opinion, the comparison of different views and platforms, and open criticism and self-criticism are guaranteed in the party. Within individual organizations and in the CPSU as a whole, debates and referendums may be held on topical questions of the life of the party and country, and corresponding decisions adopted on the basis of the results.

7. Party organizations are autonomous as to the structure of their internal life and activity. Their decisions, provided they are not in conflict with the program aims and norms of the CPSU Statutes, may not be countermanded by higher organs, with the exception of decisions on personal cases.

8. The work of party organizations and committees is carried out by democratic methods and is built on the principles of collectiveness, ruling out subjectivism and autocracy. Collegiality in the formulation and adoption of decisions is combined with the personal responsibility of communists for their fulfillment.

Party organs form standing commissions on the main areas of work, and also set up ad hoc commissions and working groups and use other ways of involving communists and other citizens in their activity on a nonpermanent basis.

9. Party organizations, leadership organs, and their apparatus operate with glasnost, ensuring—in line with party decisions—the openness of party meetings, conferences, congresses, and sessions of committees and bureaus and the participation of the party press in them, and systematically inform communists and nonparty people about their activity through the mass media and through other channels. A communist is entitled to attend sessions of the

bureau or party committee of his primary party organizations. Members of an elected party organ have free access to sessions of organs that are accountable to them, including party committee bureaus, and also have the right to make use of documents available to the party committee and its apparatus.

10. All leading organs in the party are elected. They are elected on the basis of a wide-ranging discussion of candidates and maximum consideration of communists' views, mainly on a multiple-choice basis, by secret ballot.

At election time party members have the unrestricted right to nominate any candidate, including themselves. A vote is taken on each individual candidate. Candidates are elected when they have obtained more votes than the other candidates and more than half of the votes of the CPSU members participating in the meeting, conference or congress delegates, or members of the party committee or other elected organs.

When nominating and electing delegates, communists propose candidacies for membership of superior party organs, that are then considered by the conference or congress that forms these organs.

Delegates to rayon, city, and okrug (without rayons) party conferences are elected in primary organizations. Elections of delegates to city and okrug (with rayons), oblast, and kray conferences, congresses of union republic communist parties, and the CPSU congress involve the compulsory nomination of candidates by primary party organizations, as a rule by a direct vote by communists. The election procedure is laid down by the relevant party committee on the basis of proposals supported by at least half of the communists in the given territory. A referendum or poll can be conducted to that end.

11. All elected people in the party, in raykom and above, are elected to the same post for no more than two consecutive terms. Members of elected party organs can be individually changed or they can all be replaced [pereizbratsya] before their term expires if one-third of the organization's members demands it or if individuals or all the members of the elected organs voluntarily resign.

First secretaries of party raykoms, gorkoms, okrug committees [okruzhkoms], and kraykoms, and the CPSU chairman and his deputies are elected at the relevant conferences and congresses. The ballot paper can include any number of candidates. During this process the procedure for the early replacement of these officials in the future is also established.

12. Party committees are accountable to their party organizations and superior organs. Party committee bureaus annually report to plenums and party committees and party bureaus report to meetings of primary and shop party organizations. Every member of an elected party organ reports on his work to the party organizations that elected or recommended him.

13. When making decisions, party organizations and committees are obliged to consider all viewpoints. The minority has the right to support its own position, record a minority view in the official record, and demand a repeat examination of disputes in their organization or place them before supe-

rior organs. At the same time, a decision made by the majority is binding on everyone.

In the executive organs of party committees (presidium, bureau), in the event of any disagreement a draft decision is resubmitted for repeat examination and adopted by a majority of at least two-thirds.

Party organs' decisions are binding on subordinate organizations. The latter are entitled to dispute them, by appealing to superior party authorities, without suspending the action of these decisions.

14. The party's leading elected organs establish their working apparatus that is subordinated to them and provides mainly analytical, sociological forecasting, and consultative backup for their activity. The party apparatus is established by the elected organ on the basis of primary party organizations' recommendations which they discuss at their meetings. Party apparatus personnel are covered by labor legislation.

15. In implementing the party's cadre policy, primary party organizations and party committees recommend communists and nonparty people for specific sectors of state, economic, and public activity. Employing political methods, they seek their election or appointment to the posts in question, provide them with support, listen to communists' accounts of their work, and publicize ensuing conclusions and recommendations.

16. Party organizations are authorized to publish newspapers, journals, bulletins, and propaganda, reference, and information material in accordance with state laws out of their own funds or in cooperation with other organizations, and to establish editorial offices and radio and television studios for this purpose. The party mass media operate under the leadership of party committees, which confirm their leaders. The chief editor of PRAVDA is confirmed at a plenum of the CPSU Central Committee.

III. ORGANIZATIONAL STRUCTURE OF THE PARTY

17. The CPSU is built on the basis of the principle of democratic centralism along workplace and territorial lines and has the following structure: primary, rayon, city, okrug, oblast, and kray party organizations, and union republic communist parties. A party organization uniting communists of a given territorial entity is superior to its component organizations.

When necessary, councils of party organization secretaries, party clubs, theoretical seminars, discussion centers, and other forms of party work uniting communists on the basis of common interests or problems can be organized and operate. Proceeding from the CPSU program directives, they discuss various questions to define their positions, and submit proposals and drafts for consideration by party committees at any level.

The creation of factions with their own internal organization, discipline, and ideological principles incompatible with the party's program objectives is not permitted within the CPSU.

Primary Party Organizations

18. Primary organizations are the basis of the party. They may be created if there are at least three CPSU members at their place of work or residence.

A primary party organization may create party groups and shop organizations within itself. Depending on their size and with the permission of the party raykom or gorkom, they are granted the rights of primary organizations on questions connected with CPSU membership.

In light of the specific tasks and conditions of their activity, primary party organizations autonomously resolve questions of admission to the party and termination of membership of the CPSU, the definition of their structure, directions and methods of work, regularity of and procedure for holding meetings, political actions, and financial activity, and form mutual relations with soviet and social organizations.

Primary party organizations propagandize and implement the party's ideas and decisions, defend the principle of social justice, conduct political and organizational work in labor activities and local neighborhoods, and through the democratic mechanism of self-management exert their influence on the activity of cadres and the resolution of economic and social tasks.

Primary party organizations have the right to express their attitude on the decision of any party organ, which is obliged to give a substantive answer to it.

19. The supreme organ of the primary party organization is the general meeting (conference), which is considered competent so long as more than half of CPSU members (delegates) are present, or in the case of reports and elections, at least two-thirds.

For day to day work, the meeting (conference) elects an executive organ—the party bureau (committee) and its secretary—for 2-3 years. In party organizations with fewer than 15 communists, the party organization secretary and his deputy—and in party groups, the party group organizer—are elected for a period and in a manner prescribed by the meeting.

The primary party organization secretary represents it in relations with the administration, self-management organs, and social organizations in the labor collective and outside it. The question of the secretary's dismissal from the collective is subject to examination at a party meeting (conference).

20. Up to 50 percent of members' subscriptions is entitled to be used to finance the activity of primary party organizations, including the maintenance of fulltime workers.

Rayon, City, Okrug, Oblast, and Kray Party Organizations

21. Rayon and city party organizations directly uniting primary party organizations are the pivotal structural link of the party. Rayon organizations in big cities may unite to form city party organizations.

The supreme organ of the rayon or city party organization is the conference. The conference elects the rayon or city party committee for five years and also the control and auditing commission. An extraordinary party conference may be convened by decision of the party committee or at the demand of primary organizations uniting at least one-third of communists.

In the light of primary party organizations' opinions, the rayon or city party committee elects the bureau and secretaries of the raykom or gorkom and creates their apparatus and material and financial base. The raykom or gorkom registers primary party organizations, gives them necessary assistance, and keeps a record of communists.

Party raykoms and gorkoms coordinate and direct the activity of primary party organizations, help to strengthen their ties with the masses, join with them in explaining party policy and decisions, organize work in their implementation in labor collectives and citizens' local neighborhoods, present specific socioeconomic, cultural, and other questions for public scrutiny, and help to implement them.

22. Kray, oblast, and okrug party organizations take part in elaborating party policy and conducting work to implement it within the kray, oblast, or okrug, and organize the execution of superior party organs' resolutions.

The party conference is the supreme organ of kray, oblast, and okrug party organizations. Kray, oblast, and okrug party committees and control and auditing commissions are elected for five-year terms by the conference. Extraordinary conferences are convened by decision of the corresponding committees or at the demand of one-third of the total number of the organization's members.

Conferences, and also party committee plenums, that are convened as and when necessary, but at least twice a year, elaborate and propose to organs of state power and the population programs for solving political, ethnic, social, economic, ecological, and cultural-moral problems in the region. They examine questions of intraparty life, cadre work, the party organization's budget, and publishing activity.

Kraykoms and obkoms autonomously decide questions concerning the structure of their organization, including the formation of raykoms and gorkoms, and allow the largest primary party organizations to exercise the rights of party raykoms on questions of CPSU members' records.

Corresponding plenums elect the bureaus and secretaries of party kraykoms, obkoms, and okruzhkoms.

23. The control and auditing commissions of rayon, city, okrug, oblast,

and kray party organizations elect bureaus and commission chairmen from among party members of at least five years' standing. The control and auditing commissions decide questions associated with the strengthening of party discipline and the observance of the norms of party ethics by communists, hear appeals by party members, and monitor the implementation of the party budget. Control and auditing commissions operate in conformity with regulations ratified by the rayon, city, okrug, oblast, or kray party organization.

Union Republic Communist Parties

24. Union republic communist parties are autonomous within the framework of the CPSU Program and the CPSU Statutes. They elaborate their own programs and normative documents, in accordance with which they decide their own organizational, cadre, publishing, and financial-economic questions, pursue their political line in the sphere of state building and the republics' socioeconomic and cultural development, promote the political consolidation of citizens and the combination of national and international interests, and shape internationalist awareness. Union republic communist parties maintain ties with other parties and social movements, including those abroad.

Fundamental decisions by the CPSU Central Committee Presidium and commissions affecting union republic communist parties are examined with the participation of their plenipotentiary representatives. In the event of disagreement with a decision that has been made, a union republic communist party central committee has the right to demand that a CPSU Central Committee plenum be convened to discuss any disputed questions.

25. A union republic communist party's supreme organ is its congress. Regular congresses are convened at least once every five years. They determine the political line, discuss reports by the central committee and the control and auditing commission, and recommend candidates from the union republic communist party for membership of the CPSU's supreme organs. Republic party conferences can be convened in the period between congresses.

CPSU Organizations within the USSR Armed Forces

26. The activity of party organizations within the USSR Armed Forces is built on the basis of the CPSU Statutes and of documents ratified by the CPSU Central Committee.

Leadership of party work within the USSR Armed Forces is effected through party organs and primary party organizations. Party committees and primary party organizations resolve tasks in close collaboration with military councils, commanding officers, and political organs. They exercise their influence on the life and activity of military collectives through Army communists.

The supreme party organ of the USSR Armed Forces enjoys the rights of a CPSU Central Committee commission.

Communists in the Armed Forces can elect and be elected to leadership organs of territorial party organizations. Delegates to rayon, city, okrug, oblast, and kray party conferences or union republic communist party congresses are elected at party conferences in military units and combined units according to the norms of representation laid down by the corresponding party committees.

The election of delegates from Army and Navy party organizations to CPSU congresses and all-union party conferences takes place at party conferences in military districts, groups of forces, fleets, combined units, and branches of the Armed Forces.

Note: Party work in KGB Troops, Internal Troops, and Railroad Troops is built along lines analogous to those in the Armed Forces.

IV. SUPREME ORGANS OF THE CPSU

27. The congress is the supreme organ of the CPSU. Regular congresses are convened by the CPSU Central Committee at least once every five years. The Central Committee's decision to convene a congress, the agenda, and the representation norms are published no later than three months before the congress. The Central Committee publishes theses on the basic questions to be submitted to the congress.

Extraordinary CPSU congresses are convened by the Central Committee on its own initiative or at the demand of party organizations uniting at least one-third of the total number of communits. Congresses are convened within two months and are considered legally convened if at least half of all party members are represented at them.

In the event of the Central Committee failing to convene an extraordinary congress, the organizations demanding that it be held can form an organizational committee exercising the rights of the party Central Committee as regards convening an extraordinary congress.

28. The CPSU congress:

—hears reports by the Central Committee and the Central Control and Auditing Commission and adopts resolutions on them;

—adopts, revises, and amends the party program and statutes;

—lays down the party line in the sphere of party building, ideological activity, and the CPSU's domestic and foreign policy;

—elects the CPSU chairman and his deputies, simultaneously electing them members of the CPSU Central Committee;

—elects the CPSU Central Committee and Central Control and Auditing Commission.

29. In the period between congresses the CPSU Central Committee convenes, as and when necessary, all-union CPSU conferences to discuss pressing questions of the party's policy and practical activity.

A conference has the right to hear reports by the CPSU Central Committee and the Central Control and Auditing Commission concerning their work, to partially renew their composition (up to one-third in the period between congresses), to adopt other mandatory decisions for the party in the form of CPSU program documents, and to introduce amendments to the party statutes.

Elections of delegates to all-Union party conferences follow the same procedure as that applying to CPSU congresses.

30. In the period between congresses the party's activity is led by the CPSU Central Committee.

The CPSU Central Committee:

—organizes the practical implementation of CPSU congress and conference decisions;
—elaborates and submits to Congresses of USSR People's Deputies and the USSR Supreme Soviet proposals on the content of domestic and foreign policy;
—implements CPSU cadre policy;
—creates party institutions and enterprises and monitors their activity;
—represents the CPSU in relations with other parties.

31. In order to decide political and organizational matters in the period between plenums the Central Committee elects a CPSU Central Committee Presidium drawn from among its membrs. The presidium's members are ratified by the CPSU congress. The Central Committee Presidium also includes on an ex officio basis the chairman of the CPSU and his deputies and the leaders of union republic communist parties.

The CPSU Central Committee Presidium sends decisions to be carried out by party organizations on its behalf. The presidium submits decisions on the most important political issues for ratification by a CPSU Central Committee plenum.

The Central Committee Presidium annually submits a report on its activity to a CPSU Central Committee plenum.

Standing commissions are set up within the CPSU Central Committee on the main avenues of its activity. They are formed at a CPSU Central Committee plenum from among Central Committee members and other communists ratified as advisers. The commissions are headed by CPSU Central Committee secretaries elected by a CPSU Central Committee plenum, and are entitled to make decisions within their purview. Communists working on the CPSU Central Committee and its commissions on a permanent basis receive a salary paid out of party funds.

The CPSU Central Committee Secretariat is formed from the leaders of the commissions. It coordinates the activity of Central Committee commissions, organizes the execution in the party of decisions made by the Central Committee, its Presidium, and its commissions, and directs the work of the Central Committee apparatus.

During the period between Central Committee plenums, leadership of its organs' work is exercised by the chairman and deputy chairmen of the CPSU.

32. The CPSU Central Control and Auditing Commission elects at its plenum its bureau and cochairmen, who must have not less than 10 years' party experience.

The Central Control and Auditing Commission, guided by provisions ratified by a CPSU congress, monitors the fulfillment in the party of program documents, the CPSU Statutes, and decisions made by party congresses and conferences; monitors the state of party discipline and observance of the norms of intraparty life and party ethics; audits the implementation of the CPSU budget and the financial and economic activity of the CPSU Central Committee and its institutions, enterprises, and publishing houses; and examines appeals against expulsion from the party.

33. The CPSU Central Committee and the CPSU Central Control and Auditing Commission hold at least two plenary sessions a year and, if necessary, joint sessions.

CPSU Central Committee members can participate in the work of CPSU Central Control and Auditing Commission plenums and members of the Central Control and Auditing Commission can participate in the work of CPSU Central Committee plenums on a nonvoting basis [s pravom soveshchatelnogo golosa].

Communists elected to the CPSU Central Control and Auditing Commission cannot join other central elected organs of the party.

V. COMMUNISTS IN SOVIETS, PUBLIC ORGANIZATIONS, AND MOVEMENTS

34. The CPSU and all its organizations operate within the framework of the USSR Constitution and Soviet laws. Party organizations and committees do not permit mixing of functions with state and economic organs, and pursue the party's policy line through the communists working in them. The party cooperates with all social forces advocating positions of democracy and social justice and opposes antisocialist, nationalist, and anti-Soviet forces. It bases it relations with trade union, youth, and other sociopolitical organizations and

mass movements on the principles of political collaboration and partnership and respect for different viewpoints.

35. The CPSU, like other sociopolitical organs, struggles for political leadership in society through free elections and other forms whereby Soviet citizens express their will. Party organizations elaborate and publish their election platforms, recommend communists for nomination as candidate people's deputies, and help them to organize their election campaigns.

Party organizations can enter into election agreements with other social organizations and formations operating on the basis of and in accordance with the Constitution and can support candidate deputies nominated by them who are not CPSU members.

At congresses and sessions of Soviets of People's Deputies and congresses and conferences convened by social and cooperative organizations where communists are members, communists unite in party groups to coordinate their activity and increase party influence. Party groups are guided by Soviet laws and the decisions of the relevant party committees.

36. In their work with young people party organs and primary party organizations rely on the Komsomol [All-Union Leninist Communist Youth League] and other youth organizations that support socialist choice; give all possible assistance to their activities in educating young people; and involve them in elaborating and implementing the CPSU's youth policy. The relationship between party and Komsomol organizations is founded on ideological commonality, recognition of the Komsomol's organizational independence, mutual respect, and comradely trust. The party sees the Komsomol as the immediate reserve for replenishing its ranks.

VI. THE PARTY'S PROPERTY AND MONETARY FUNDS

37. The activity of the CPSU and its organizations is carried out using financial, material, and technical resources provided by party income.

The party's property and monetary funds are partywide assets. Facilities owned by the CPSU include buildings, installations, party publishing houses and the property of the periodicals and printing houses under their jurisdiction, enterprises, and other property, as well as monetary funds composed of membership dues, income from party enterprises, and other revenue.

The party budget, the normatives for payments by local party organizations, and the procedure for the redistribution of funds are ratified by a CPSU Central Committee plenum and published in the press.

Monthly membership dues for party members are as follows:

Incomes of up to R70—10 kopeks
R71–100—20 kopeks
R101–150—30 kopeks

R151–200—1 percent of salary
R201–250—1.5 percent of salary
R251–300—2 percent of salary
R301–350—2.5 percent of salary
over R350—3 percent of salary

Working communist pensioners pay their party membership dues separately on their pension and on their salary.

38. Union republic communist parties and kray and oblast party organizations have independent control over their budgets in an attempt to boost income so as to secure the transition to self-financing, and they resolve structural, staff, and financial matters. Profitable economic and commercial activities by party enterprises and institutions that do not run counter to the interests of political work and Soviet legislation are encouraged.

Local party and control and auditing organs systematically inform communists about the state of the party budget and the expenditure of funds.

APPENDIX C
SELECTED PERIODICALS

New writing on Soviet politics and government is published constantly. The following periodicals are devoted largely or exclusively to material on the Soviet Union.

TRANSLATIONS OF SOVIET WRITINGS
OR SOVIET PUBLICATIONS IN ENGLISH

Current Digest of the Soviet Press
International Affairs
Moscow News
News Times
Problems of Economics
Soviet and East European Foreign Trade
Soviet Anthropology and Archeology
Soviet Education
Soviet Law and Government
Soviet Life

Soviet Literature
Soviet Military Review
Soviet Psychology
The Soviet Review
Soviet Sociology
Soviet Statutes and Decisions
Soviet Studies in History
Soviet Studies in Literature
Soviet Studies in Philosophy
Sputnik

WESTERN PERIODICALS

Canadian-American Slavic Studies
Canadian Slavonic Papers
Journal of Soviet Nationalities
Problems of Communism
Radio Liberty Report on the USSR
Review of Socialist Law
Russian Review
Slavic Review
Slavonic and East European Review

Soviet Analyst
Soviet and East European Drama, Theater and Film
Soviet Economy
Soviet Nationality Survey
Soviet Studies
Soviet Union
Studies in Soviet Thought
Survey

In addition to these publications, a valuable source of translations into English of Soviet media releases (printed materials, radio, and television) is the Foreign Broadcast Information Service *Daily Report* on the Soviet Union. This is a U.S. government publication.

INDEX